SAVVY™

S0-AFF-087

FLASH® 8

FLASH® 8

ETHAN WATRALL | NORBERT HERBER

WITH SHAM BHANGAL

WILEY PUBLISHING, INC.

Acquisitions and Development Editor: Mariann Barsolo
Technical Editors: David Powers, Sham Bhangal
Production Editors: Daria Meoli, Martine Dardignac
Copy Editor: Kim Wimpsett
Production Manager: Tim Tate
Vice President and Executive Group Publisher: Richard Swadley
Vice President and Executive Publisher: Joseph B. Wikert
Vice President and Publisher: Dan Brodnitz
Media Development Specialist: Angie Denny
Book Designer: Caryl Gorska
Compositor: Kate Kaminski, Happenstance Type-O-Rama
Proofreader: Ian Golder
Indexer: Ted Laux
Cover Designer: Caryl Gorska, Gorska Design
Cover Image: Getty Images

Dear Reader,

Thank you for choosing *Flash 8 Savvy*. This book is part of a family of premium quality Sybex graphics books, all written by outstanding authors who combine practical experience with a gift for teaching.

Sybex was founded in 1976. Thirty years later, we're still committed to producing consistently exceptional books. With each of our graphics titles we're working hard to set a new standard for the industry. From the paper we print on, to the writers and artists we work with, our goal is to bring you the best graphics books available.

I hope you see all that reflected in these pages. I'd be very interested to hear your comments and get your feedback on how we're doing. To let us know what you think about this or any other Sybex book, please send me an email at: sybex_publisher@wiley.com. Please also visit us at www.sybex.com to learn more about the rest of our growing graphics line.

Best regards,

Dan Brodnitz
Vice President and Publisher
Sybex, an Imprint of Wiley

To my loving wife, Jennifer, who is constantly understanding and patient with my frequent bouts of literary lunacy.

—*Ethan Watrall*

This book is dedicated to Jenny, my wife, who once again endured the unpleasantness of living with an author on a deadline.

—*Norbert Herber*

About the Authors

Ethan Watrall was born in Regina, Saskatchewan (a true Canuck), and went on to do his Ph.D. work in the Department of Anthropology at Indiana University–Bloomington. His research as an archaeologist has allowed him to work in Canada, the United States, and Egypt, where he spent many years working on the Predynastic site of Hierakonpolis. It was his time as a more traditional archaeologist that led Ethan to develop an interest in the convergence of archaeology and digital/interactive media.

Currently, Ethan's work focuses on the effect that video games have on the public's perception of archaeology, archaeologists, and the human past. He is also interested in the art and science of world building for multiplatform and transmedia stories.

Ethan is a faculty member in the Department of Telecommunication, Information Studies, and Media at Michigan State University, where he teaches interactive design and game design, development, and history. He is also a Principle Investigator in the Games for Entertainment and Learning Lab and a Principle Investigator in the Communication Technologies Lab. He has authored (and coauthored) several books about digital design with Flash, Dreamweaver, and Fireworks.

Ethan's digital alter ego lives at www.captainprimate.com.

Norbert Herber is from the twin cities of Minneapolis and St. Paul, Minnesota. At 16, he began his musical career as a jazz saxophonist, trading sets with the swing-tenor legend Irv Williams. His love of jazz and improvised music led him to arranging and composition, where he developed an interest in creating music for interactive applications.

His work focuses on the use of sound in interactive environments, nonlinear and experimental composition, and emergent music—a genre rooted in artificial life systems.

His works have been performed/exhibited in the Vox Novus 60 × 60 concert series, ICMC 2004, the Red Gate Gallery in Beijing, China. You can hear some of his works at www.x-tet.com, www.vonflashenstein.com, and www.mollyz.net.

Norbert is a lecturer in the Department of Telecommunications at Indiana University–Bloomington. He is coauthor of *Flash MX 2004 Savvy* (Sybex, 2003) and the critically acclaimed *Flash MX Savvy* (Sybex, 2002).

Sham Bhangal has written on new media subjects since the turn of the century. In that time, he has been involved in the writing, production, and specification of about 20 books. He also works full time as a Flash developer, currently creating applications for the e-learning industry. He spends time as a freelance web designer, specializing in Flash based sites. Contact: boy@futuremedia.org.uk or browse to weblog.motion-graphics.org.

Acknowledgments

First and foremost, I want to offer thanks to my family—wife, Jennifer; daughter, Taylor; and son, Sam. My dog, Oscar, deserves special thanks (and a treat) for being…well…such a good dog. As always, a big (nay, huge) thanks to my partner in crime, Norb Herber. I talked him into this project, and it's a miracle we both made it out alive. Cheers, dude. Thanks to my colleagues in the Games for Entertainment & Learning Lab at Michigan State University (most notably Carrie Heeter, Brian Magerko, and Brian Winn), who were always interested in the trials and tribulations of this book. Thanks to my parents, Claire and Charles, who are total nut jobs in their own right but always loving and supportive. Finally, thanks to anyone I've forgotten to mention.

Ethan Watrall

Most important, I'd like to thank Ethan Watrall and Mariann Barsolo. Their patience and understanding were essential to the success of this project. Sham Bhangal is also to be commended for his excellent suggestions as a technical editor. His comments pushed me to really think about our readers and the kind of information that would help them most. I'd also like to thank Rory Starks, who generously allowed us to print an image from his interpretation of the game Lucky Wander Boy, based on the novel by D. B. Weiss. Finally, to Jenny, my wife, thank you for helping me get through the final steps of this project.

Norbert Herber

This book was rockier than any other in which we've been involved. Somehow we managed to complete it in spite of a burglary, two natural disasters, and an intensive collaborative process. As such, lots of people deserve thanks. First and foremost (more than ever before), thanks to our acquisitions and development editor, Mariann Barsolo. Every time we hit a roadblock (and there were many), Mariann never wavered from her complete and utter support of the book. Without her, the book might have imploded before we jotted down the first sentence. David Fugate was instrumental, as always, in getting all the contractual matters in place. We'd also like to thank Matt Collins for his help early in the writing process. Next, thanks to Sham Bhangal, who stepped up when we needed him most. Without him, we never would have been able to finish the book (literally). David Powers went above and beyond his duties as a tech editor. His comments were insightful and extremely helpful, ultimately resulting in a far better book. Production editors Daria Meoli and Martine Dardignac were both great, as was Willem Knibbe, who helped with some organizational details early in the project. Copy editor Kim Wimpsett, with whom we've worked before, was great in helping us get our point across using half as many words. Thanks, Kim, for your excellent editing! Finally, thanks to Dan Brodnitz, who probably wanted to throw himself out of the nearest window every time he heard the book was being delayed.

Ethan Watrall and Norbert Herber

CONTENTS AT A GLANCE

Contents

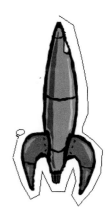

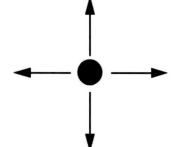

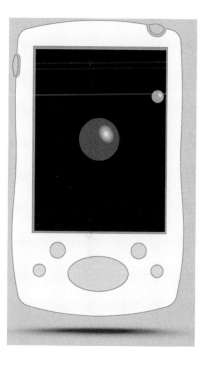

Introduction

Flash-based content has become synonymous with graceful movement, engaging sound, dynamic interactivity, and short download times.

Flash isn't just an animation tool; it's a rich media application development powerhouse. Flash 8 is just as powerful as any previous version of Flash and just as deserving of the Flash name.

Once more, users can choose between two versions of the application: Flash 8 Basic and Flash 8 Professional. This isn't a particularly new development, as the previous release of Flash included two versions as well—Flash MX 2004 and Flash MX 2004 Professional. So, what's with the two versions of Flash 8?

Each version is designed in ways that serve the interests of an incredibly diverse user base. Flash 8 represents the next step for Flash as an authoring tool and offers enhanced features to streamline many of the most important tasks performed in the application. Flash 8 *Professional* is the new release on steroids. It includes all the enhancements of the regular version plus additional features that support project-based Flash development, server communication technologies, enhanced streaming-media support, improved video compression, powerful graphic effects, expanded tools for mobile application development, and PowerPoint-style authoring (among other things)—all in an environment that is conducive to online application development.

In addition, the Professional version provides more tools for big-picture development and offers a few advantages over the regular version. You'll be able to do the same kinds of work with one that you do with the other. The main difference is that with the Professional version, some tasks are easier or more efficient. It offers tools that will be welcome to developers of large-scale Flash projects and applications. If your work requires exchanging data between Flash and a server or you need to code an application from the ground up, the Professional version is for you. If you're interested in interface enhancements and functionality improvements, you'll probably feel more comfortable with the regular version.

With both versions of Flash 8, you can create not only unbelievably cool-looking animations but also incredibly complex interactive experiences that feature rich media and the integration of dynamic, database-driven applications.

Not only are today's web-based Flash creations a quantum leap beyond anything that could have been conceived previously for online media, but they are also pushing the boundaries of interactive digital media. Although Flash was originally intended for the Web, its sheer popularity (and phenomenal power) has taken it far beyond the online domain. These days, you can see the integration of Flash as an authoring tool in mobile devices, broadcast media, and console games.

To really understand the penetration of Flash in the world of interactive digital media, you need look only at the number of people who have downloaded the Flash Player over the years: about half a billion! Need we say more?

About This Book

This book was written while imagining that you, the reader, were sitting beside us. We are teachers, and when it comes to a project like this, we tend to think of the book as a class. The writing process was really just slow-motion teaching with stories, examples, and plenty of hands-on lessons. And as anyone would expect to find in a good class, our book offers an opportunity for learning. Our hope is that it's the kind of learning that sticks with you so you're able to understand concepts and processes rather than what buttons to push and when. We put a lot of thought and planning into the writing process. Our objective was to create the most intuitive, learning-focused Flash reference possible.

This book was written not only to explain *how* to work with Flash but *why*. Knowing why you do things is a crucial step in the learning process because it gives you the means to creatively apply your newfound skills to original ideas of your own. The techniques outlined in this book will give you the skills to create an enormous variety of projects in Flash.

Although you can read this book from front to back, we designed each of the chapters to be stand-alone units. In many cases, you'll see both introductory and advanced topics covered in the same chapter. For example, Chapter 3 covers key basic type-related topics, such as creating type with the Text tool, as well as more advanced type-related topics, such as formatting text with Cascading Style Sheets. The idea is that each chapter, to the extent that it can, serves as your one-step shopping spot for that particular topic. This doesn't mean you won't get similar topics covered in different ways in different chapters—quite the contrary. However, we've done our best to corral similar topics into the same chapter.

This book is best treated as a reference. Although you'll find a certain progression in difficulty across chapters, the book doesn't contain an intentional curriculum. As such, you should feel free to start wherever your interests lead or projects demand.

We've been careful to point out which features are new in Flash 8; this will be useful if you've used Flash MX 2004 or are completely new to both the regular and Professional versions of Flash 8. Be on the lookout for the handy "new to version 8" icon shown in the margin.

Some topics covered in the book pertain only to features available in Flash 8 Professional. You can quickly identify them with the "Pro only" icon shown in the margin.

Who Needs This Book?

We did our best to write a book that is geared toward the intermediate user. We carefully selected the topics and crafted the way we discussed them so that many types of people with varying levels of expertise and with different goals could pick up this book and find it useful.

The people who will get the most from this book are those who've already had some experience with Flash and are looking to go to the "next level." It will also be useful to beginners who aspire to do more in Flash, though we don't walk you through a lot of the basic how-tos in a step-by-step fashion. We assume readers are comfortable with the fundamentals and ready for more intermediate- and advanced-level topics.

This book also covers topics that even some advanced users might not have mastered yet, with chapters on using ActionScript and dynamic data, working with audio, and developing mobile applications.

With this book, focusing on core topics is particularly important because Flash is two different programs with different features. The topics we had to exclude are all pretty high end, and we're sure that nearly all readers will find everything they might want to do with Flash covered. Still, we don't want anyone looking for one of these high-end topics to buy the book and be disappointed.

So, here is an abbreviated list of major topics we didn't cover:

- Creating form-based applications with screens (a Flash 8 Professional feature)
- Using Unicode and the Strings panel to publish in multiple languages
- Data binding and web services

Having said this, anyone eager to take part in the Flash revolution and become a dyed-in-the-wool "Flasher" should read this book! This includes students who have completed a "Flash 101" course and are looking to new horizons, professionals who are ready to make the leap into more advanced ActionScript, designers who find their clients have moved their corporate communications to platforms beyond the Web, educators who need fun and useful projects to present in class, and so on. If you're one of these folks, this book is for you!

How to Use This Book

You can use this book in two ways. You can read this book from cover to cover, confident that when you're finished, you'll have a solid foundation in many intermediate and some advanced Flash development techniques. The book doesn't follow a particular learning curve, but if you want to master the program, page 1 is a fine place to start. As a reader steeped in the basics, you should have no trouble following the nonlinear structure.

This book is best used, however, as a reference. To find specific topics, use the table of contents to search chapter by chapter. The titles should provide a great deal of clarity in terms of what you can expect to find. You'll also discover that the index is extremely useful. Many features and techniques are mentioned in several chapters. It may take several attempts for you to find the specific example you seek.

The bottom line is that whatever way you decide to use this book, you'll learn the skills necessary to continue your journey in the wonderful world of Flash 8 Basic and Flash 8 Professional.

Keyboard Shortcuts

You'll find keyboard shortcuts presented throughout the book with the Windows shortcut followed by the Mac shortcut, as shown here: Ctrl+Shift+A / Cmd+Shift+A.

About the CD

As with many computer books, *Flash 8 Savvy* comes with a handy-dandy companion CD, which is compatible with both Windows and Macintosh platforms. Although some companion CDs probably make pretty decent Frisbees, we've gone to great lengths to include some really useful stuff on this one. The CD contains all the necessary support and example files used in the chapters. The files have been created to provide a contextual example of all techniques discussed in the book. Some are treated as "starters," and others will show you a completed version of the lessons that interest you.

Anytime we want to point you toward files on the CD, a little CD icon will appear in the margin. Feel free to use these files as starter files for your own unique Flash creations. We recommend you open all Flash 8 documents (FLA files) from within Flash. Simply choose File → Open, and browse to the file you need.

The ActionScript Reference on this book's CD provides you with the correct syntax, contextual examples, and tips for working with many ActionScript terms. This isn't a complete reference; rather, it contains what we consider to be *essential* ActionScript elements. It should prove to be helpful when you're composing scripts from scratch.

Getting in Touch and Staying Connected

As authors, we love hearing from readers. We always get a serious jolt out of hearing from someone who has bought any of our books and goes to the trouble of actually sending us some e-mail. While we love getting praise, we also value constructive criticism. Confused by the way in which we covered a particular topic? Wish we would have covered some additional topics? Send us an e-mail!

You can reach Ethan at `ethan.watrall@captainprimate.com`, and you can reach Norbert at `norbert@x-tet.com`. You can also pop in any time and check out our respective digital homes on the Web. You can find Ethan's site at `www.captainprimate.com`, and you can find Norbert's site at `www.x-tet.com`.

Flash: The Beginning

Before you dig into today's Flash, it's a good idea to get an idea of how this virtual revolution in interactive multimedia began. Besides, it's a cool story.

In 1991, Chicago-based Macromind merged with Paracomp to form Macromind-Paracomp. About the same time, a third company, Minnesota-based Authorware, moved west and joined Macromind-Paracomp in Redwood Shores, California, to found the mighty Macromedia—the beginning, so to speak.

A few years later, Jonathan Gay and Charlie Jackson founded FutureWave, a small software company whose first product was an application called Go. FutureWave's angle was to produce software that would dominate the pen computer market. Unfortunately, the early pen computers failed to catch on (and there was some corporate interference by AT&T), so Go became an application without a market.

FutureWave found itself in serious trouble. It was a small software company with no income and had spent a year developing an application that would never be released. Its salvation came in the form of a small drawing program called SmartSketch that it had developed as a sideline product to Go. FutureWave began marketing SmartSketch as a computer-based drawing solution for both Windows and Macintosh platforms. It wasn't long before people were asking why FutureWave didn't turn SmartSketch into a 2D animation program. FutureWave decided to roll the dice, hoping that the Internet—

something that everyone was beginning to talk about—would be a great medium for delivering 2D animation.

FutureWave shipped its FutureSplash Animator in the summer of 1996. FutureSplash Animator was a relatively simple application for creating linear, vector-based animations. After its release, the application gained some attention when it was used in the design of both Microsoft's web version of MSN and Disney's subscription-based Disney Daily Blast. In November 1996, Macromedia (now Adobe) approached FutureWave about the possibility of the two firms working together. For FutureWave, which was still a tiny company with only six employees, this was an astonishing opportunity. So, in December 1996, FutureWave sold the technology to Macromedia, which released the first Flash version in early 1997. The rest, as they say, is history.

The Many Faces of Flash

As you probably know by now, Flash isn't just an animation tool. So, what *is* it, then? Rather than try to define Flash, it's better to exemplify what it can do. Its presence and its application around the world speak volumes.

Broadcast Media

Even though Flash is probably most "at home" on the Web, it has also made its way to broadcast media in recent years. This transition shouldn't come as a surprise. After all, Flash has proven to be a powerful animation tool and can be exported to a variety of file formats.

Flash has been used for several broadcast applications, both in Europe and in the United States. In the United Kingdom, the web design firm Kerb developed one of the first broadcast cartoon series created entirely in Flash. You can check out the series, *Hellz Kitchen,* which is an irreverent and hilarious look at a group of slightly deranged talking vegetables, by visiting Kerb's website at `www.kerb.co.uk`.

You used to be able to see Flash in the United States in the intro animation of *The Rosie O'Donnell Show* (though it has since gone off the air). Another great example of Flash in broadcast media is the Spike TV (formerly TNN) show *Gary the Rat*. Created entirely in Flash, *Gary the Rat* chronicles the escapades of an attorney (voiced by Kelsey Grammer) so unscrupulous that he actually turned into a rat. To explore the show's website, visit `www.spiketv.com/shows/animation/gary_the_rat/index.jhtml`.

For more information about this and other uses of Flash as a "convergent media," see `www.macromedia.com/macromedia/proom/pr/2000/converge.html`.

Mobile Computing/Communications

As computers continue to become both smaller and more communicative, Flash will be part of the revolution. The Flash Player is poised to deliver content to a wide variety of web-ready gadgets and mobile devices. This includes business applications, news services, games, educational applications, maps and geographical aids, event guides, entertainment, wireless applications, and so much more—the works!

 One of the first mobile platforms to support Flash was Microsoft's Pocket PC. You can read more about Flash for the Pocket PC platform at www.macromedia.com/mobile/. For those who use handheld mobile devices that feature Palm OS, don't despair! While the Flash Player is almost always associated with the Pocket PC operating system, the most recent models of Sony's popular CLIÉ handheld (which runs Palm OS) include the Flash Player.

 The new Flash Lite Player has extended Flash's reach to mobile phones and other portable devices. For more information about Flash Lite, see www.macromedia.com/software/flashlite/.

Game Consoles

Arguably one of the most unexpected applications of Flash has been in the interactive entertainment industry—console games, to be precise.

The most noteworthy example was the use of Flash to create the user interface for LucasArts' popular Star Wars: Starfighter game for PlayStation 2 and Xbox. Although LucasArts had designed the in-game/heads-up display (HUD) interface for Starfighter, the company encountered a serious problem near the end of its development cycle when it realized it was lacking a functional out-of-game user interface. Enter Macromedia Flash. LucasArts partnered with two companies, Secret Level (www.secretlevel.com) and Orange Design (www.orangedesign.com), to design the out-of-game interface using Flash. Released in February 2001, first for PlayStation 2 and then for Xbox, the game served as a milestone in Flash history.

 For more information about how Flash was used in Star Wars: Starfighter, see the Gamasutra article at www.gamasutra.com/features/20010801/corry_01.htm (requires free registration).

Excited by the possibilities of using Flash content in console and PC games, Secret Level began developing a software development kit (SDK) called Strobe. Designed to provide hardware-accelerated Flash content rendering for games, Strobe's core engineering supported 60 frames per second (fps) playback on both PlayStation 2 and Xbox. Unfortunately, in June 2001, Strobe's development was put on hold pending the finalization of licensing terms with Macromedia.

Interestingly, in May 2001, Macromedia and Sony announced a partnership geared toward bringing the Flash Player to Sony PlayStation 2. Facilitating in-game visual design like that featured in Star Wars: Starfighter was high on the partnership's list of goals. Offering a complete range of Flash-facilitated connected entertainment experiences in the emerging broadband era was also an important focus for the new partners. Unfortunately, since the announcement, both companies have been silent about any kind of successful completion of the collective goals that emerged from the partnership.

However, this series of rather disheartening events did not spell the end of Flash content on game consoles. Pleased with the process of Flash content integration in Star Wars: Starfighter, LucasArts once again teamed up with Orange Design to develop a Flash-based out-of-game interface for Star Wars: Starfighter's sequel, Star Wars: Jedi Starfighter. Released in March 2002 for PlayStation 2 and in May 2002 for Xbox, Star Wars: Jedi Starfighter showed that console games were an excellent place for Flash content.

Recently, Flash has been regaining popularity in the game design and development industry as a great tool for interface design (both out-of-game and in-game interfaces). One notable example is Electronic Arts' game The Godfather, which uses Flash for the out-of-game interface.

Future Flash/game console collaborations should open new avenues for Flash and Flash developers alike.

Edutainment

As the Web becomes more complex, more easily accessed, and more plentiful in rich media, it is increasingly a destination for those wanting to be educated and entertained at the same time. *Edutainment* is a subset of media (online or offline, interactive or not) that presents science, history, or culture in a compelling and entertaining manner. This is where Flash-based edutainment enters the picture. Flash allows for the creation of nonlinear, self-motivated, educational, exploratory experiences that feature gripping sound, video, imagery, and interactivity. While a select group of outstanding examples of Flash-based edutainment exists, the über example is *Becoming Human* (www.becominghuman.org).

Developed jointly by NeonSky Creative Media (www.neonsky.com) and Terra Incognita (www.terraincognita.com) for the Arizona State Institute for Human Origins, *Becoming*

Human is an original interactive Flash documentary that explores human evolution from our earliest ancestors to the emergence of Homo sapiens. *Becoming Human* features a host of innovative and interactive tools (such as interactive exhibits) that allow you to go beyond the Flash documentary and pursue your personal exploration in the fascinating world of human evolution.

Becoming Human is partitioned into several sections that allow you to explore questions about culture, hominid anatomy, archaeological evidence, and lineage. Each section features not only a spectacular linear Flash documentary narrated by the prestigious paleoanthropologist Dr. Donald Johanson but also topical discussions by many other prominent scholars in the field of human evolution. The combination of the linear documentary and the interactive exploratory tools (both of which are created totally in Flash) makes *Becoming Human* one of the most interesting, innovative, and cutting-edge Flash creations available.

If you're interested in other great examples, check out the following:

- Yin Yu Tang: A Chinese House (`www.pem.org/yinyutang`)
- Theban Mapping Project (`www.kv5.com`)
- The Genographic Project (`www5.nationalgeographic.com/genographic`)

Flash isn't just for edutainment; it's also used in educational settings. You can use a number of third-party applications to create educational Flash-based applications. Easily one of the most interesting (and innovative) applications is from Articulate (`www.articulate.com`). Based in New York, Articulate makes Articulate Presenter, an incredibly cool piece of software that allows you to convert PowerPoint presentations into low-bandwidth Flash movies.

Web Games and Cartoons

Flash is great for creating multimedia and interactive navigation, but it is *superb* for creating fun stuff! Why do we try to pass Flash off as such a "serious" application when a large portion of its development community is dedicated to doing work that is meant to be anything but serious? Games and cartoons are another important part of the Flash oeuvre.

Some great Flash toon/game sites include the following:

- Newgrounds (`www.newgrounds.com`)
- Homestar Runner (`www.homestarrunner.com`)
- Mondo Mini Shows (`www.mondominishows.com`)

FLASH TOON TOOLS

As Flash webtoons and animated shorts have become more and more popular, a spate of tools has cropped up to facilitate their creation. As with all things digital, some tools are better than others. Arguably one of the most mature, usable, and feature-rich tools is Toon Boom Studio (www.toonboomstudio.com). Developed by the Montreal-based company Toon Boom (www.toonboom.com), Toon Boom Studio is a 2D animation application that facilitates the creation of compelling animation targeted to the Web, digital video, wireless devices, and beyond. Among many other things, the program features powerful and intuitive 3D scene planning, advanced camera manipulation, lip-sync tools, and project management. The great thing about Toon Boom Studio, beyond its robust features, is that it's one of the best-priced 2D animation solutions for short-form or "flash"-style productions. All in all, Toon Boom Studio is a great product for Flashers who are looking for a great way to bring their animated aspirations to life.

Kiosk Development

A *kiosk* is a piece of custom computer hardware that delivers a fixed body of information, usually through a user-friendly interactive interface. Kiosks are most commonly used in situations where an organization wants to let the user control access to information (usually through a touch screen or a mouse-driven interface) that would traditionally be delivered by a receptionist or other such individual. Because Flash can create powerful interactive experiences that are both complex and beautiful, it naturally lends itself well to creating kiosks.

While commercial kiosk applications are a great place for Flash to spread its wings, kiosks are equally common in museum exhibits and galleries. One of the most eloquent experts in cultural kiosk Flash design is Second Story Interactive (www.secondstory.com). Based in Portland, Oregon, Second Story Interactive has created a string of Flash-based kiosks that range from the educational and entertaining to the highly compelling.

PART I

Art

With Flash 8 *you can create an incredible array of exciting interactive projects. Whether they are traditional websites, webtoons, kiosks, or other more adventurous Flash applications (online or offline), the common thread is that the majority are visually based. This is no great surprise because one of the most important characteristics of Flash 8 is that it's vector based, allowing you to create some truly stunning visual imagery.*

Ultimately, this means you'll be spending a fair amount of your creative energy crafting the visual aspects of your beautiful Flash creation. To that end, Flash includes an extremely wide variety of tools designed to create, manage, and manipulate all the art in your Flash movie.

CHAPTER 1

Illustrating with Flash

With every new release, Flash has become a more powerful tool for creating visual content. Gone are the days when Flash designers and developers needed to rely on a second application for the bulk of their illustration needs—Flash can now do it all. In this chapter, you'll learn how to harness the powers of Flash's painting and drawing tools and discover the tools that let you manage and manipulate your illustrations.

This chapter gives you a quick sampling of the primary tools and techniques to illustrate with Flash. You'll need to already have some basic knowledge of web design and the way Flash works.

- **Customizing the Stage**
- **Adding depth with layers**
- **Illustrating with the free-form drawing tools**
- **Drawing shapes**
- **Setting and manipulating stroke and fill**
- **Working with digital color**
- **Importing external bitmaps**
- **Erasing content**
- **Using graphic filters**

Using the Stage to the Fullest

The Stage is where it all happens in Flash. This is where you craft your eye candy, where all your animations do their thing, and where all your creations come to life. Ultimately, what happens on the Stage is what your audience sees after you've exported your movie.

Introducing the Pasteboard

The gray area around the Stage is the Pasteboard. You can think of the Pasteboard as the backstage, if you want to continue the theatrical metaphor.

> In previous versions of Flash, the Pasteboard was simply referred to as the *work area*. In fact, the Pasteboard has been greatly expanded (compared to previous versions of Flash), thereby allowing you to store more elements there than ever before.

You can place elements on the Pasteboard as you would place them on the Stage; the difference is they won't be visible in the Flash movie when you export or test it. The benefit is that all the elements placed in the Pasteboard behave in the same way as if they were on the Stage. As a result, you could create an animation where a small sphere, for example, begins its journey in the Pasteboard and ends its journey on the Stage. You can also use the Pasteboard to store elements of your movie that aren't visual in nature—such as data components.

> You can toggle the visibility of the Pasteboard by choosing View → Work Area. Alternatively, you can use the shortcut Ctrl+Shift+W / Cmd+Shift+W.

Customizing the Stage

The Stage starts as a blank slate upon which you create and choreograph your glorious Flash creation. As you might expect, you can mold it to look exactly as you want. Flash wouldn't be exciting if everyone's movie had to be the same size or color.

> The default size of the Stage is 550×400 pixels.

You have two ways to change the size of your Stage (and thereby the size of your published movie):

- Select Modify → Document (or use the shortcut Ctrl+J / Cmd+J) to open the Document Properties dialog box (see Figure 1.1). From there, simply input new values for the width and height.
- With nothing on the Stage selected, open the Property Inspector (select Window → Properties, or press Ctrl+F3 / Cmd+F3), and click the Size button 550 x 400 pixels

(which dynamically displays your Stage's current dimensions). This opens the Document Properties dialog box (see Figure 1.1), where you'll be able to enter new width and height values.

If you want the changes you've made to be the default for all the Flash movies you create, click the Make Default button in the Document Properties dialog box.

When it comes to changing the background color of your Stage (and thereby your movie), the process is almost the same:

- Select Modify → Document (or use the shortcut Ctrl+J / Cmd+J) to open the Document Properties dialog box (refer to Figure 1.1). Click the Background Color swatch, and choose a color.

- With nothing on the Stage selected, open the Property Inspector, click the Background Color swatch , and select the color you want.

Figure 1.1

You can change the dimensions of your Stage (and thereby your movie), as well as its color, in the Document Properties dialog box.

> Unfortunately, you can't have a different Stage color for each scene in your movie. The simplest solution to this conundrum is to create a "background" layer in which you place a rectangle larger than the dimensions of the Stage. The rectangle could be any color you want and can change color from scene to scene. A slightly more complex option would be to create a movie in which all the content comes from externally loaded SWFs. Each SWF, because it is its own movie, could have its own Stage color.

Using Layers to Add Depth to Your Design

Each layer in a Flash movie acts like a transparent sheet upon which any number of individual objects can reside. Ultimately, your final Flash movie will consist of a stack of layers. Although individual layers aren't really recognizable on the Stage, they appear horizontally across (and accessible from) the Timeline.

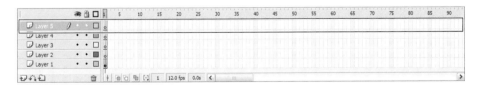

The way each layer appears in relation to other layers in the Timeline is important. Because the layers are stacked vertically (along the Z axis), the contents of topmost layers appear in the foreground of the movie, and the contents of the lowest ones appear in the background.

Layers are extremely (and sometimes deceptively) powerful. It's good practice to use one layer for each discrete object or symbol for a couple of reasons. First, as your movie becomes more complex, you'll want to keep elements organized, and if you have one discrete element (object, symbol, and so on) occupying its own layer (and that layer is named accordingly), you'll always know where everything is.

Second, although layers play an integral part in the creation of static content, they become even more important when you start animating with the Timelines (a topic that will be covered in Chapter 6). Conflicts can arise when you're trying to separately animate two objects that occupy a single layer, so it's particularly important for animation to have a layer for each discrete object (and for you to name that layer appropriately).

> The number of layers you can create is limited only by the amount of available memory on your computer.

Flash offers different kinds of layers—each with its own purpose. Normal layers are the default layer type. They are the "everyday" type of layer you'll use in most situations. Guide layers and mask layers (both of which will be discussed later in this chapter) have their own unique functionality.

> Mask Layers will be covered in more detail in Chapter 6—especially in regard to how you create animated mask layers.

Creating a New Layer

Every new Flash movie has one layer by default. When you create a new Flash document, one layer automatically appears in the Timeline.

> Because Flash "flattens" all the layers upon export, you don't have to worry about multiple layers increasing a file's size.

To create a new layer, do one of the following:

- Click the Insert Layer button 🗒 in the bottom-left corner of the Timeline.
- Choose Insert → Timeline → Layer.
- Right-click / Ctrl+click any layer in the Timeline and choose Insert Layer from the pop-up context menu.

> If you have more than one layer, Flash inserts the new layer above the currently selected one.

Locking

Visibility | Outline

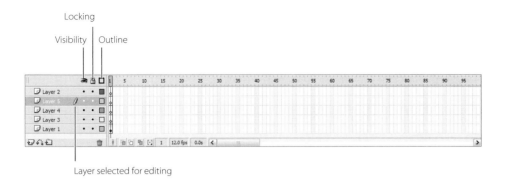

Layer selected for editing

Figure 1.2

The icons of the layer properties appear to the right of the layer's name in the Timeline.

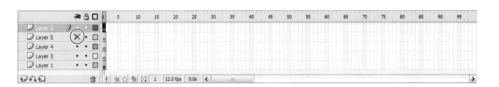

Figure 1.3

When a layer is hidden, a red *X* appears to the right of its name.

Working with Layer Properties

Each layer has a series of properties represented and accessible through the icons to the right of the layer's name (see Figure 1.2).

Turning Layer Visibility On/Off

You can make the content of any given layer in Flash invisible in order to unclutter the Stage and thus focus better on the objects on a particular layer. When you're ready, you simply turn on the layer's visibility.

To change a layer's visibility, do one of the following:

- Click the small dot in the layer's eye column. A red *X* automatically appears, denoting the layer's hidden state (see Figure 1.3). To turn the layer visibility on, click the red *X*.

- To hide all the layers at the same time, click the eye icon. To reverse this process, click the eye icon again. Alternatively, right-click / Ctrl+click a layer, and choose Show All from the context menu.

- To hide all the layers except one, Alt+click / Option+click the small dot in the layer's eye column that you want to stay visible. Alternatively, you can right-click / Ctrl+click, and choose Hide Others from the pop-up context menu.

Viewing Layer Objects as Outlines

Viewing layer objects as outlines allows you to alter all the layer's objects so they appear as colored outlines (see Figure 1.4).

This is particularly useful if you want to speed up the display of your movie when editing or testing animations.

To view layer objects as outlines, do one of the following:

- Click the layer's outline icon (represented in Flash by a colored box). A hollow box means the layer's objects appear only as outlines, and a filled box means the objects appear normally.

- To display the content in all layers as outlines, click the Timeline's box icon (located above the layers themselves). To reverse the process, click the icon again.

- To view all layer objects as outlines except one, just Alt+click / Option+click the outline icon for the layer whose objects you want to remain "solid."

Figure 1.4

On the top, you're seeing the scene normally. On the bottom, you're viewing the scene's objects as outlines.

If you want, you can also easily change the color of the layer's outlines by opening the Layer Properties dialog box for that layer, clicking the Outline Color swatch, and choosing the color you want.

Locking/Unlocking Layers

When you first create a layer in Flash, it's automatically unlocked; otherwise, you wouldn't be able to add to or edit the layer. The tricky thing about layers is that you don't need to have them selected to manipulate their contents. As a result, you might inadvertently modify one layer while working on another. To avoid this, Flash lets you lock layers.

To lock a layer, do one of the following:

- Click the small dot in the layer's lock column (represented by a padlock icon). A little padlock icon automatically appears, denoting the layer's locked state. To unlock the layer, click the padlock icon.

- To lock all the layers at the same time, click the Timeline's padlock icon. To reverse this process, click the padlock icon again.

- To lock all the layers except one, just Option+click the small dot in the layer's padlock column that you want to remain visible. Alternatively, you can right-click / Ctrl+click, and choose Lock Others from the context menu.

Distributing Objects to Layers

You may sometimes find yourself with multiple objects or symbols on a single layer. For example, when you import many types of vector files (such as those from Adobe Illustrator or Macromedia FreeHand), the image will comprise many different ungrouped objects.

To handle this situation, Flash 8 has a helpful option that allows you to select multiple objects and distribute them so each occupies its own discrete layer.

Flash gives all the newly created layers a unique name. If a layer contains a named object (such as a symbol, bitmap, or video clip), Flash gives it the same name as the object. If a layer contains a symbol instance, Flash gives it the same name as the instance. If a layer contains a simple shape, Flash gives it a default name of layer 1, increasing sequentially (layer 2, layer 3, and so on).

To distribute objects to layers:

1. On the Stage, select the objects you want to distribute to layers.

2. Choose Modify → Timeline → Distribute to Layers. Alternatively, right-click / Ctrl+click, and choose Distribute to Layers from the context menu.

Creating and Editing Layer Folders

A great feature of Flash layers is the ability to create *layer folders*. Essentially, these are folders in the Timeline into which you can place multiple layers, thereby organizing your Timeline (see Figure 1.5).

For instance, say you have an animation with a series of cartoon characters. If you've planned your movie correctly, each discrete part of each character (arm, head, leg, floppy ears, and so on) occupies an individual layer. To cut down on the confusion in your Time-line, you could organize the body parts for each character into a layer folder—a Green Lantern folder, a Professor Frink folder, a Bender folder, and so on.

To create a layer folder, do one of the following:

• Click the Insert Layer Folder button ⊞ in the bottom-left corner of the Timeline.

• Choose Insert → Timeline → Layer Folder.

• Right-click / Ctrl+click any layer in the Timeline, and choose Insert Folder from the context menu.

> You can also convert a selected layer to a layer folder by changing its type from Normal to Folder in the Layer Properties dialog box (accessible by selecting the layer and then choosing Modify → Timeline → Layer Properties). The problem with this technique is that if you do it on a layer with content, you'll delete all the content on the layer.

Now you'll want to add layers to the layer folders you've created. Simply click and drag the desired layer to the layer folder's icon (if you're working in Windows, the folder icon will be highlighted when your cursor is directly over it). The layer will move so that it's just below the layer folder. It will also be indented slightly, indicating its position within the layer folder (as illustrated in Figure 1.5).

Figure 1.5

You can organize your Timeline by using a layer folder to hold layers.

One of the cool features of layer folders is that you can expand and collapse them, thereby hiding all the associated layers in the Timeline without affecting what is visible on the Stage. To either collapse or expand a layer folder, just click the small arrow to the left of the layer folder's name.

Creating Guide Layers

Guide layers contain elements (shapes, symbols, bitmaps, and so on) that you can use to align elements on other layers. Guide layers are handy if you have a complex layout and want a standard layout reference for your entire movie.

The good feature of guide layers is that, although they can be used to guide and lay out your movie, they will not be rendered in your final Flash movie when you publish it.

Figure 1.6

Use the Layer Properties dialog box to create a guide layer.

To create a guide layer, do one of the following:

- Double-click the layer icon of the layer you want to convert to a guide layer. When the Layer Properties dialog box appears (see Figure 1.6), select the Guide Layer radio button.

- Right-click / Ctrl+click the layer you want to convert into a guide layer, and select Guide from the context menu.

When converted, the layer's icon will change accordingly.

From there, you can add anything you want to the guide layer (just as if you were adding to a regular layer).

Illustrating with Free-Form Tools

Flash has a host of great tools that will help you both illustrate and manage your illustrations.

When you're working with illustration tools, shapes are composed of stroke and fill. *Stroke* is the character of the line formed when you draw an object. *Fill* is the color or pattern inside a shape.

Drawing Straight Lines with the Line Tool

To use the Line tool ✏, select it from the Toolbox, click where you want the line to begin, drag until it's the desired length, and release your mouse button. You can set the thickness and style of the Line tool using the Property Inspector. To learn more about manipulating an object's stroke, see the section "Setting and Manipulating Stroke and Fill" later in this chapter.

Holding the Shift key down while you're using the Line tool will constrain the line to angles in multiples of 45 degrees.

Using the Pencil Tool

The Pencil tool creates single lines. Unlike the Line tool, however, the Pencil is a freehand tool. Using the Pencil tool is almost as simple as using an actual pencil. All you need to do is select the Pencil tool from the Toolbox, click the area of the Stage where you want

EXERTING GREATER CONTROL OVER THE ILLUSTRATION PROCESS WITH DRAWING MODELS

Easily one of the handiest new features in Flash 8 is the new Object Drawing Model option. In previous versions of Flash, when you drew one shape over another, the two shapes automatically merged. If you then selected a shape that had been merged with another and moved it, the shape below would be permanently altered. For example, if you drew a square, overlaid it with an oval, and then selected the oval and moved it, you would be removing the portion of the square that was overlaid by the circle (as illustrated here).

In Flash 8, this behavior is now the Merge Drawing Model option. The cool feature is that Flash 8 has a second drawing model, the Object Drawing Model. When you're working in this model, separate objects don't automatically merge when overlaid (as illustrated here).

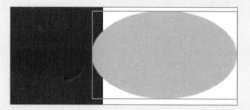

To toggle between Merge Drawing Model and Object Drawing Model, select the drawing tool you want to use (Oval tool, Brush tool, and so on), and click the Object Drawing button located in the Toolbox's Options section.

your line to begin, hold down the mouse button, and draw the shape you want. When you're finished, release the mouse button.

Pencil mode, which is the Pencil tool's only option, contains three properties: Straighten, Smooth, or Ink (all of which are accessible in the Pencil Mode drop-down menu in the Toolbox's Options section when the Pencil is selected). The specific Pencil mode you choose is applied to the line you draw *as you draw it.* However, you can straighten or smooth an already drawn line by selecting the target line and then choosing Modify → Shape → Smooth or Modify → Shape → Straighten. Alternatively, you can also click either the Smooth button or the Straighten button after having selected the already drawn line.

Straighten Straightens all curves in the lines you draw. This creates a line angular in nature.

Smooth Smoothes any angularities in the lines you draw. Unfortunately, you have no real control over the degree to which Flash smoothes your lines.

Ink Ensures that your line is displayed exactly how you've drawn it—no smoothing and no straightening.

Using the Brush Tool

The Brush tool , much like the Pencil tool, creates single free-form lines. Unlike the Pencil tool, however, the shapes created with the Brush tool are all fill.

> The cool feature of the Brush tool is that, as with the Pencil tool, you can smooth or straighten a stroke you create. To do this, select the already created stroke with the Arrow tool, and hit the Straighten or Smooth button. Alternatively, you can choose Modify → Shape → Smooth or Modify → Shape → Straighten.

Using the Brush tool is as easy as using the Pencil tool. Just select the Brush tool from the Toolbox, click the area of the Stage where you want your line to begin, hold down the mouse button, and draw the shape you want. When you're finished, just release the mouse button.

Using a Graphics Tablet with the Brush Tool

If you're using a graphics tablet, such as one produced by Wacom (www.wacom.com), you can dynamically vary the weight of the Brush tool's stroke. Two options for the Brush tool are available when your system detects a graphics tablet: Pressure and Tilt.

The Pressure modifier, which you access by clicking the Use Pressure button when the Brush tool is selected, varies the width of brush strokes as you vary the pressure on the stylus (see Figure 1.7). The Tilt modifier, which you access by clicking the Use Tilt button , varies the angle of brush strokes when you vary the angle of the stylus on the

Figure 1.7

This is a brush stroke drawn with a Wacom graphics tablet.

tablet. The Tilt modifier measures the angle between the top (eraser) end of the stylus and the top (north) edge of the tablet. For example, if you hold the pen vertically against the tablet, the Tilt is 90°.

Setting Brush Size, Shape, and Stroke Interaction

Brushes ranging from tiny to huge are accessible through the Brush Size drop-down menu ● ✓ when the Brush tool is selected. To change the brush size, just make your choice from the drop-down menu *before* you draw your line. You can't dynamically change a line's size by choosing a different brush size after you've drawn it.

Flash also allows you to set your brush's shape. As with setting brush size, you need to make your choice from the Brush Shape drop-down menu ● ✓ *before* you draw your line.

Brush mode ⚬, which is accessed through a drop-down menu in the Toolbox's Options section, is perhaps one of the most interesting aspects of the Brush tool.

Essentially, Brush mode lets you specify exactly how your brush stroke affects an existing drawn or painted element. Figure 1.8 illustrates the effects of the different Brush modes.

Flash 8 has five Brush mode options:

Paint Normal Applies a stroke from the Brush tool on top of existing elements—just as if you took a can of spray paint to the *Mona Lisa* (yikes!).

Paint Fills Applies your brush stroke only to areas made up of fills while leaving the strokes of shapes unaltered.

Paint Behind Applies the strokes from your Brush tool behind any existing element.

Paint Selection Applies your brush stroke only to areas of fill that have been previously selected.

Paint Inside Applies brush strokes only in the same area they were initiated. Paint Inside mode will not paint over existing elements other than the one in which you started the stroke.

Illustrating with the Pen Tool

The Pen tool ✒ is the primary tool for creating free-form vector art within Flash. Granted, the vast majority of the drawing tools in Flash (such as the Line tool or the Pencil tool) create vector graphics. However, the Pen tool is by far the most powerful.

Figure 1.8

Each Brush mode has a different effect on how your brush stroke interacts with other shapes on the Stage.

Paint Normal Paint Fill Paint Behind Paint Selection Paint Inside

The Pen tool works closely with the Subselection tool, which is covered later in this section of the chapter.

If you're familiar with vector illustration programs such as FreeHand or Illustrator, you'll recognize the Pen tool. Designed to build precision paths, the Pen tool works by creating points that are connected by paths to form a segment. The points act as anchors that can be moved around to alter the characteristics of any of the line segments (see Figure 1.9).

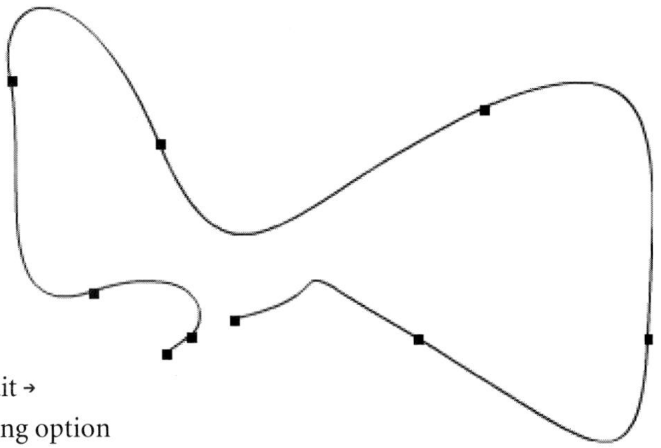

Setting Pen Tool Preferences

The Pen tool's preferences are accessible by choosing Edit → Preferences / Flash → Preferences and clicking the Drawing option on the left side of the Preferences dialog box. From here, you have three choices:

Show Pen Preview Lets you preview line segments as you draw. A preview of the line segment appears as you move the pointer around the Stage.

Show Solid Points Specifies that unselected anchor points appear as solid dots and selected anchor points appear as hollow dots.

Show Precise Cursors Specifies that the Pen tool pointer appears as crosshairs, rather than the default Pen tool icon.

Drawing a Straight Line with the Pen Tool

All you need to do to draw a straight line with the Pen tool is select it from the Toolbox, click a place on the Stage where you want to begin the line (which creates a point), and then move your mouse and click again to define the end point of the line. Figure 1.10 shows a simple one-segment line drawn with the Pen tool.

Drawing a Curved Line with the Pen Tool

The strength of the Pen tool resides in its ability to draw complex shapes. To draw complex shapes, you need curved lines.

When you draw a curve with the Pen tool, you create curve points. When you draw a straight-line segment, you create corner points.

Figure 1.9

Any complex line (which is more than one segment long) is composed of paths linked by a series of points.

Figure 1.10

A simple, one-segment line drawn with the Pen tool; notice that it ends and begins with a point.

Figure 1.11

You create a curve as you move the selected tangent handle away from the original end point. Note that the tangent handle stretches out the farther you drag it away.

To create a curved line with the Pen tool:

1. When the Pen tool is selected, click anywhere on the Stage where you want your curve to begin.

2. Move the cursor to the location where you want the curve to end.

3. Click to add the end point in the segment. However, instead of releasing your mouse button, keep it pressed down and move the mouse a little bit in any direction. You'll notice that as you move your mouse away (with the button still held down), two things happen:

   - First, your cursor is actually dragging one of two tangent handles that is linked to the final point in the segment.

   - Second, the farther away you drag one of the tangent handles from the original point, the more extreme your curve gets (see Figure 1.11).

4. To adjust the curve, simply move the selected tangent handle. When you have the curve as you want it, release the mouse button.

5. To create a line with two (or more) curved segments, simply repeat steps 2–4.

If you want, you can make your first point a curve point. To do so, use the Pen tool to add the first point in the segment. Instead of releasing your mouse button, keep it pressed down and move the mouse a little bit in any direction. The tangent handles will appear, and you can release your mouse button. Then you can create additional points in the path or create a shape (which you can then fill if you want). When you have a curve point on either end of a segment, you'll have a different level of control than if you had one corner point and one curve point.

Adding a Point to a Line

The points in a path determine the way in which the line or shape looks. Given this, it's pretty obvious that the Pen tool wouldn't be very useful unless you could add more points along the path *after* you've drawn it. More points along a path mean more locations along the shape that can be directly manipulated, thereby giving you far more control over the shape of the object.

> You can't actually add a point to a segment that resides between two corner points; you can add only to a segment that exists between two curve points (or a corner point and a curve point).

To add points to a path:

1. Make sure a curved path already exists on the Stage (and make sure it's deselected).

2. Move the Pen tool over the area of the path you want to add the point. Notice that the cursor changes from a pen with a small *x* to its right (which is the default cursor when you're pointing anywhere on the Stage) to a pen with a small plus (+) sign to its right (see Figure 1.12).

3. Click to add the point.

Figure 1.12

When you move the cursor over a curved path, the icon changes to a pen with a plus (+) sign next to it. This indicates you can add a point.

Removing a Point from a Curved Path

You change pen-drawn shapes by adding and manipulating points. Conversely, you can change the shape of an object by removing points. Because points partially determine the shape of an object, removing one will alter the shape of your object.

To remove a path from a curved path:

1. Move the Pen tool over the point you want to remove. The cursor changes from a pen with a small *x* to its right to a pen with a small caret (^) to its right (see Figure 1.13).

2. Click once. This converts the curve point to a corner point. Once you do this, your cursor changes to a pen with a small minus (–) sign to its right (see Figure 1.14).

> If the points on either side of the point you are removing are corner points, the path between the two points will turn into a straight line. However, once you remove the point, if the two remaining points are curve points, the path will regain its curve.

3. Click the point once again to remove it entirely.

> If you place the cursor over a corner point, it will display the minus (–) sign immediately, and you can click once to remove the point.

Figure 1.13

When you move the cursor over a path, the icon changes to a pen with a small caret (^) next to it.

Changing the Position of a Point with the Subselection Tool

Because the points in a path act as a sort of skeleton, moving any of the given points alters the structure of the path.

To move a point with the Subselection tool:

1. With the Subselection tool ⌃ , select the path with the point you want to move (notice that the path changes color when selected).

Figure 1.14

Once you convert the curve point to a corner point, your cursor changes to a pen with a small minus (–) sign to its right.

2. Move your cursor over the point you want to move. The cursor turns from an arrow with a small black box to its right to an arrow with a small empty box to its right, which indicates you're over an editable point.

3. Click and drag the point to the desired location.

If the point you've selected is a curve point, the tangent handles appear when you select it with the Subselection tool.

Changing the Curve of a Segment with the Subselection Tool

You can use the Subselection tool to alter the character of a segment's curve:

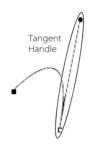

Tangent Handle

1. With the Subselection tool ![cursor], click the path with the point you want to manipulate.

2. Click the curve point on either side of the segment whose curve you want to change. Depending on whether the curve point is at the end or in the middle of the path, either one or two tangent handles will appear (see Figure 1.15).

3. Click the point at the end of the tangent handle, and drag it to adjust the curve's shape.

Figure 1.15

After clicking the desired curve point with the Subselection tool, either one or two tangent handles will appear, depending on whether the point is at the end or in the middle of the path.

Converting a Corner Point to a Curve Point

Corner points are great for drawing angular paths with the Pen tool, but they can't be manipulated to produce (or adjust) a curve. To do that, you need to convert a corner point to a curve point:

1. With the Subselection tool ![cursor], select the corner point you want to convert. When it's selected, the corner point will turn from a hollow square to a filled square.

2. Once it has been selected, hold down the Alt / Option key.

3. Click the corner point you want to convert, and then drag it slightly. Notice that two tangent handles immediately appear. If the point with which you're working is at the end of a path, only one tangent handle will appear.

4. You can then drag either tangent handler to adjust the shape of the curve.

Drawing Shapes

Flash 8 provides you with three tools for drawing basic shapes: Oval, Rectangle, and Polygon. Although they are fairly similar, each has particular characteristics you should explore.

Drawing a Rectangle

Located in the Toolbox's Tools section, the Rectangle tool ![icon] lets you draw rectangles and squares. Much as with the shape tools, you can create a rectangle by selecting the Rectangle tool from the Toolbox, clicking on the Stage where you want the shape to start, dragging until you have created the desired shape and size, and then releasing your mouse button.

> Holding down the Shift key while drawing your rectangle creates a perfect square.

The Rectangle tool has one available option: Round Rectangle Radius ⌀ . When you click the Round Rectangle Radius button in the Toolbox's Options section, the Rectangle Settings dialog box opens, and you can enter a value (from 0 to 100) in the Corner Radius field. The higher the value, the more rounded the corners of your rectangle become.

> You can't change the corner radius of a rectangle that has already been drawn. You can effectively set a rectangle's radius only before you draw the shape.

Using the Oval Tool

Located in the Toolbox's Tools section, the Oval tool ○ helps you draw ellipses and circles. To use the Oval tool, click your mouse where you want the shape to start and then drag until you've created the desired shape and size. When you're finished, release your mouse button.

> Holding down the Shift key while drawing your oval creates perfectly round circles.

Using the PolyStar Tool

Flash 8 offers a third tool for drawing shapes: the PolyStar tool. The PolyStar tool, as its name suggests, allows you to draw both polygons and stars.

By default, the PolyStar tool ⬠ is grouped under the Rectangle tool in the Toolbox. As with other shape tools, to use the PolyStar tool, click your mouse where you want the polygon or star to start, drag until you've created the desired shape and size, and then release your mouse button.

> To group your shape's stroke and fill, make sure you activate Object Drawing Model mode.

By default, the PolyStar tool draws a five-sided polygon. To set the properties of the polygon (before you draw it) or change the shape to a star (and set the star's properties):

1. Select the PolyStar tool ⬠ , and draw a polygon.
2. Select Windows → Properties, and click the Options button `Options...` to open the Tools Settings dialog box.
3. If you want to draw a star, select Star from the Style drop-down menu.

4. Set the properties of the shape you're drawing—including the number of sides (which applies to both polygons and stars) as well as the star's point size (which essentially sets the length of the star's points). A star's point size must be from 0 to 1. A value closer to 0 results in sharp, narrow points, and a value closer to 1 results in fatter, shorter points.

5. From here, you can draw the shape on the Stage.

Working with Digital Color

Flash 8 has a host of tools for creating, using, and manipulating color. Chief among them are the Color Swatches panel and the Color Mixer panel—though others certainly exist.

Sampling Color with the Eyedropper Tool

The Eyedropper tool 🖊 lets you sample the fill or stroke from one object and then apply it to another.

To sample and apply an object's stroke or fill:

1. Move the Eyedropper tool over the stroke of a shape or its fill. You'll notice that the cursor changes from a simple eyedropper to an eyedropper with a small pencil to its right for a stroke and to a paint bucket for a fill (see Figure 1.16).

2. Click your mouse button once. Notice that the Eyedropper tool changes to the Ink Bottle tool for a stroke or the Paint Bucket tool for a fill. This means you're ready to apply the sampled color to another object.

3. Move the Ink Bottle cursor over another stroke or fill, and click. The stroke or fill of the second object changes to that of the first.

> If you select an object's stroke or fill (and keep it selected) and then use the Eyedropper tool to sample the stroke or fill of a second object, the second object's characteristic will be automatically applied to the selected stroke of the first.

Figure 1.16

You can sample a shape's stroke (left) and fill (right).

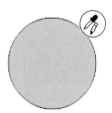

If you hold down the Shift key when you click an object with the Eyedropper tool, the color sampled is applied to both the fill and the stroke color. From there, you can use the Paint Bucket or Eyedropper tool to apply the color to either an object's stroke or an object's fill.

Creating and Saving Custom Colors and Palettes with the Color Swatches Panel

Each Flash movie contains its own color palette, stored in the architecture of the file itself. Flash displays a file's palette as swatches (small squares of color) in the Color Swatches panel.

Although the Color Swatches panel (Window → Color Swatches) displays the web-safe palette by default, you can add, delete, edit, and duplicate colors as you need. You can also import and export custom-created palettes. You perform all these operations through the Color Swatches panel's Options pop-up menu, which you access by clicking the icon in the panel's top-right corner.

These are the most important tasks you can perform:

Importing color palettes Use the Add Colors option to import color palettes that have been saved in the CLR (Flash Color Set) or ACT (Color Table) file format. After choosing this option, just navigate to the file on your hard drive, and select it.

Replacing the color palette Choose Replace Colors to replace the current palette with an imported palette. After choosing this option, navigate to the CLR file, and select it.

Exporting the color palette To export a color palette, choose Save Colors from the drop-down menu. When the Export Color Swatch dialog box opens, navigate to the location where you want to save the palette, choose a desired file type from the Save as Type/Format menu, enter a desired name, and click Save. Generally speaking, the .act file format is more universal, allowing you to transfer a color palette to other applications such as Adobe Photoshop, Illustrator, or Macromedia Fireworks.

Saving the current palette as the default The Save as Default option designates the current palette as the default palette to be loaded when you use the Load Default Colors option in the drop-down menu. To revert to the original web-safe palette, select the Web 216 option.

Mixing Solid Colors

You can use the Color Mixer panel (Window → Color Mixer) to create solid RGB (Red, Green, Blue), HSB (Hue, Saturation, Brightness), or hexadecimal notation colors using a series of different methods. Once you've created colors, you can add them to the current palette and have them appear in the Color Swatches panel.

One of the great features of using the Color Mixer panel is that you can dynamically apply fill. This means you can change and manipulate an object's fill either before or after you create it. If you want to change the fill of an existing object, make sure to select it (with the Arrow tool), and then make the desired changes in the Color Mixer panel.

To mix an RGB color:

Figure 1.17

By selecting Solid from the Type drop-down menu, you can then begin to mix solid colors.

1. Select Solid from the Type drop-down menu in the Color Mixer panel (Window → Color Mixer) (see Figure 1.17).

2. If it isn't already, make sure RGB is selected in the Color Mixer panel's Options menu.

3. From here, simply enter numerical values in the R (red), G (green), and B (blue) fields. Alternatively, you can use the sliders to the right of the individual color channel fields.

   You can also choose a color by clicking anywhere in the color box. The appropriate RGB code automatically appears in the color channel fields.

4. If you want to manipulate the color's transparency, enter a value in the Alpha field (or adjust the slider) to specify the degree of transparency—from 0 for complete transparency to 100 for complete opacity.

To automatically add a color to the Color Swatches panel, use the Add Swatch command from the Color Mixer panel's Options menu. This will also add the color to the standard pop-up Color Picker that appears throughout the program.

Figure 1.18

You can mix colors using the Hex Color field and the color box.

The process for mixing an HSB color works the same as mixing an RGB color. Choose HSB from the Color Mixer panel's Options menu. From there, enter values (in degrees from 0 to 360) in the H, S, and B fields. You can also choose a color by clicking anywhere in the color box. You can also enter a value in the Alpha field (or adjust the slider).

The hex value of any color you create using RGB or HSB automatically appears in the Hex field. You can also mix a color by entering the appropriate hex values in the Hex field (see Figure 1.18).

You can also choose a color by clicking anywhere in the color box with your cursor.

When you choose None from the Fill Style drop-down menu, any object you draw (oval, rectangle, and so on) will have no fill. Unlike the other choices in the Fill Style drop-down menu, you can't dynamically change an object's fill to None after you've drawn it. If you don't want an object to have a fill, select None from the Style drop-down menu before drawing it.

Creating and Manipulating Gradients

A *gradient* is an area of a graphic where one color transitions into another color. In Flash 8, you can create two types of gradients: linear and radial (see Figure 1.19). A radial gradient changes from one color to another in an outward direction starting from a focal point. Linear gradients change from one color to another along a single axis (vertical or horizontal).

Figure 1.19

The image on the left is a radial gradient, and the image on the right is a linear gradient.

Creating a Linear Gradient

To create a linear gradient:

1. With the Color Mixer panel open and an object selected, choose Linear from the Type drop-down menu.

> Alternatively, you can choose Linear from the Fill Style drop-down menu *before* you draw the object. By doing this, your object, when it's drawn, will be filled with the linear gradient you selected and edited beforehand.

2. To change a color in the selected gradient, first click one of the pointers below the gradient definition bar. As a gradient slowly changes from one color to another, the pointer you choose determines the starting or ending color (see Figure 1.20).

3. Double-click the desired pointer. When the Color Picker appears, select a color. Alternatively, you can click the pointer, and then enter an RGB color or a hex color. Additionally, you can set the alpha of the selected pointer—which controls the transparency of the gradient controlled by that pointer.

4. To change the character of the gradient, click and drag either pointer. The farther apart the pointers are, the more gradual the gradient will appear. Conversely, the closer together the pointers are, the more abrupt the gradient will be.

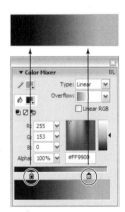

Figure 1.20

The gradient definition bar pointers determine the starting and ending colors of the gradient.

> As you move the pointers around or change the gradient colors, your changes will automatically appear in both the gradient definition bar and the gradient preview box.

5. You can increase the complexity of the gradient by adding colors. To do this, click just below the gradient's color definition bar to add a pointer. Once you've added it, you can change the pointer's color by following the process outlined in step 4.

> To transform a gradient fill of any kind (either linear or radial), you can use the Fill Transform tool described in the section "Transforming Fill" later in this chapter.

6. Select an overflow option for the gradient from the Overflow drop-down menu:

    Extend [ ] Applies the specified color past the edges of the object to which you applied the gradient.

    Reflect [ ] Causes the gradient colors to fill the shape using a reflective mirror effect.

    Repeat [ ] Repeats the gradient from its beginning to its end until the object to which you applied the gradient is filled.

    Overflow modes are supported in Flash 8 Player only.

7. Select the Linear RGB option you want in order to make your gradient Scalable Vector Graphics (SVG) compliant.

Creating a Radial Gradient

A radial gradient is similar to a linear gradient. However, instead of the fill changing from one color to another in a linear pattern, it changes in a circular pattern.

Beyond that detail, creating and editing a radial gradient is the same as if you were working with a linear gradient.

Setting and Manipulating Stroke and Fill

Shapes are composed of stroke and fill—fill being the character of the inside of a shape and stroke being the character of the edge of the shape. Flash 8 offers several tools you can use to manipulate a shape's stroke and fill.

Altering a Shape's Fill with the Property Inspector

You have already seen how to set fill color using the Color Mixer panel, but you can also use the Property Inspector. However, the Property Inspector gives you control only over color. With the Color Mixer panel, you also have access to gradient and bitmap fills.

To set an object's fill using the Property Inspector:

1. Select Window → Properties, and select the object whose fill you want to manipulate.

    If the selected object has both stroke and fill that are ungrouped, simply select the actual fill. If the shape was drawn using the Object Drawing Model, you can still select the object and have access to its fill (something you can't do if the stroke and fill of the object have been grouped).

2. Click the Fill Color swatch. When the color palette opens, select the color you want to use for the object's fill (see Figure 1.21).

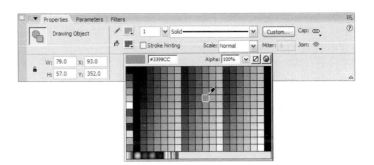

Figure 1.21

You can change the fill's color using the Property Inspector.

You can also set the transparency of the fill by entering a value in the Color Picker's Alpha field (or adjusting the slider to the right of the field).

> Using the Fill Color well in the Toolbox works the same way as if you were to use the Color Mixer panel or the Property Inspector; you just access it from a different location. All you need to do is toggle the Fill Color button, click the color swatch, and then choose the color you want.

Using the Property Inspector to Set Stroke

Stroke is the character of the line formed when you draw an object. Whether you want to change the character of a line drawn with the Pencil tool or the border of a rounded rectangle, you'll need to use the Property Inspector:

1. Select Window → Properties, and select the object whose stroke you want to manipulate.

> If you want to change the stroke of an ungrouped object, make sure you don't just select its fill. The easiest way to avoid this is to select the Arrow tool and then click and drag so the selection box encompasses the entire object.

2. From here, you can set the following attributes:

    Stroke color Click the Fill Color swatch. When the color palette opens, select the color you want to use for the object's stroke. You can also set the transparency of the fill by entering a value in the Color Picker's Alpha field (or adjusting the slider to the right of the field).

> You can also set an object's stroke color through the Stroke Color well in the Toolbox's Colors section—represented by the color swatch just to the right of the Pencil icon. Click the color swatch, and then choose the color you want from the Color Picker that opens.

Stroke height Set the stroke's height (thickness) either by adjusting the slider (accessed by clicking the down arrow to the right of the Stroke Height field) or by simply typing in a numerical value in the Stroke Height field. The minimum stroke height is 0.1, and the maximum is 200.

Stroke style Set the stroke's style by choosing one of the options from the Stroke Style drop-down menu.

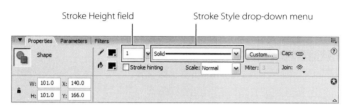

Custom stroke style If you aren't happy with the preset stroke styles, you can create your own by clicking the Custom button Custom... to the right of the Stroke Style drop-down menu. The Stroke Style dialog box that opens initially lets you set the type and thickness of the custom stroke (see Figure 1.22).

Figure 1.22

You can set your stroke's style by using the Stroke Style dialog box.

Your choices automatically appear in the preview window on the left of the dialog box. To get a good feel for how this dialog box works, experiment with the various options, and see what kinds of results you get. Depending on the stroke type you've chosen, you'll have access to a wide range of unique strokes.

Segment joins The join options, which are accessible from the Join drop-down menu Join: , determine how two path segments meet. You have three possible options: Miter, Round, and Bevel.

Miter   Round   Bevel

Miter Enables the Miter Limit field. Use this to enter a value that determines whether the joint remains pointed or is squared off. The value (in points) you enter is compared to the actual length of the point that is created when two segments join. If the length of the point exceeds the value you entered into the Miter Limit field, the join is squared off.

Stroke cap Sets the style for the end of a stroke. You have three possible options (all accessible in the Cap drop-down menu Cap: ⊖).

None aligns the end of the stroke flush with the end of the path.

Round rounds off the end of the stroke slightly.

Square extends the stroke past the end of the path one half the width of the stroke.

Stroke hinting When you have the Stroke Hinting option turned on, the points that are part of any curve are placed in full coordinates (in other words, X=230 instead of X=230.3).

Using the Ink Bottle and Paint Bucket Tools with the Property Inspector

You've seen how to use the Ink Bottle and Paint Bucket tools to apply stroke or fill colors sampled with the Eyedropper tool. You can also use these tools with the Property Inspector. Compared to just selecting the individual stroke or fill and then using the Property Inspector, this makes it easier to change the attributes of multiple objects simultaneously.

> The Ink Bottle and Paint Bucket tools work only on objects whose stroke and fill have not been grouped or objects that have been created with the Object Drawing Model turned on.

To use the Ink Bottle:

1. *Without* anything selected on the Stage, select the Ink Bottle tool ⟨⟩ .

2. Select Window → Properties. The Property Inspector displays the Ink Bottle options (see Figure 1.23).

Figure 1.23

**You can use the
Property Inspector
to set the Ink Bottle
tool's properties.**

3. Choose a stroke color, stroke height, stroke style, and so on.

4. Move your cursor over any object whose stroke you want to change, and click once. The target stroke automatically changes to reflect the options you chose in the Property Inspector.

> Once you've set the properties of the Ink Bottle tool, it remains "filled." This means you could continue clicking other strokes on the Stage, and they would all change to reflect the options you set in the Property Inspector.

While the Ink Bottle tool changes the character of an object's stroke, the Paint Bucket tool 🪣 fills an area with color. It can both fill empty areas and change the color of already filled areas. You can paint with solid colors, gradient fills, and bitmap fills. The Paint Bucket tool can even fill areas that aren't entirely closed.

To use the Paint Bucket:

1. Without anything selected on the Stage, select the Paint Bucket tool 🪣.

2. Select Window → Properties to display the (limited) Paint Bucket options.

3. Click the color swatch, and choose a solid fill color, an alpha value, or a preset gradient.

> Remember, you can add custom mixed colors and gradients to the pop-up Color Picker with the Color Mixer panel and the Add Swatches command (located in the Color Mixer's Options menu).

4. Now move your cursor over the inside of an empty shape or an existing fill, and click once. The target area automatically "fills up" with the new color you set using the Property Inspector.

> If you've "filled" the Paint Bucket tool with a gradient, you have a little added control over how the shape is filled. When you're filling with a radial gradient, if you click and hold the Paint Bucket tool, you'll see a small circle appear—which indicates the center of the gradient. You can drag that center point to where you want and then release your mouse button. When you're filling with a linear gradient, if you click, hold, and drag your mouse, you'll see a small circle with a line appear. The direction in which you drag the line controls the orientation of the linear gradient. The longer the line you drag, the longer the transition between colors in the gradient.

Setting the Paint Bucket Gap Size Option

The Paint Bucket tool can actually fill objects that aren't entirely closed. The Gap Size option ◔ , which you access through the Toolbox's Options section, lets you set the gap size at which the Paint Bucket tool will still fill an open shape.

To set the gap size, just choose from one of these options in the drop-down menu: Don't Close Gaps, Close Small Gaps, Close Medium Gaps, or Close Large Gaps.

Locking Fill

The Paint Bucket's Lock Fill option 🔒 comes into play when you're using gradients or bitmaps as fill. Located in the Toolbox's Options section when you have the Paint Bucket selected, this creates the illusion that the entire Stage is filled with a gradient, and those objects that have the locked fill applied to them are masks that reveal the underlying gradient or bitmap.

To use the Lock Fill option:

1. Select or create a gradient fill using the Color Mixer panel.

2. Select the Paint Bucket tool 🪣 .

3. Select the Lock Fill option 🔒 .

4. Move your cursor over the inside of an empty shape or an existing fill, and click once. The target area automatically "fills up" with the gradient you mixed.

5. Repeat step 4 to fill additional areas until you achieve the illusion that the filled areas reveal the gradient that takes up the entire Stage.

Creating Bitmap Fill

Although fill is normally thought of in terms of either solid color or gradients, Flash 8 allows you to use the Color Mixer panel to create a fill that is a bitmap image:

1. With the Color Mixer panel open and an object selected, choose Bitmap from the Fill Style drop-down menu.

   > Alternatively, you can choose Bitmap from the Fill Style drop-down menu *before* you draw the object. By doing this, your object, when it's drawn, will be filled with the bitmap you selected and edited beforehand.

2. If you haven't already imported another bitmap into your movie, the Import to Library dialog box opens. Navigate to where the bitmap you want to use as fill is located, select it, and then click Open.

3. If you've already imported a bitmap (or bitmaps), it appears in the Bitmap Fill dialog box (see Figure 1.24).

4. Select the bitmap you want to use as fill from the thumbnails displayed in the Bitmap Fill dialog box.

Figure 1.24

Imported bitmaps appear in the Color Mixer's Bitmap Fill dialog box at the bottom.

If you've already imported a bitmap and you want to import more, all you have to do is click the Import button to open the Import to Library dialog box.

To manipulate the way in which the bitmap fill appears, use the Fill Transform tool, discussed in the next section.

Flash handles tiling differently than you might expect The bitmap is rendered at its normal size only if you select an object first or select a fill before creating the object. Applying a bitmap fill to an existing object without first selecting it results in the bitmap fill being rendered the same size as the thumbnail in the Color Mixer panel and in it being tiled.

Transforming Fill

The Fill Transform tool 🔳 lets you adjust the visual properties of a gradient or bitmap fill:

1. Select the Fill Transform tool 🔳 .

2. Click an area filled with a gradient or bitmap fill. Notice that when you select a fill for editing, a bounding box with editing handles appears. Depending on whether you're working with a linear gradient, a radial gradient, or a bitmap fill, you'll get slightly different handles.

If the bitmap you've used is smaller than the space it's filling—and is therefore tiling—a bounding box will appear around each instance of the bitmap. Any change made to one of the smaller images will be mirrored in all the others that fill the object.

- In the case of a linear gradient fill, the bounding box that appears is rectangular with three handles (see Figure 1.25).

- If you're working with a bitmap fill, the bounding box appears with seven handles (see Figure 1.26).

- If you're working with a radial gradient fill, the bounding box is oval, with five handles (see Figure 1.27).

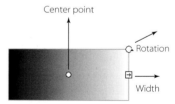

Figure 1.25

A bounding box appears for a linear gradient when you're working with the Fill Transform tool.

When your pointer is over any of these handles, it changes to indicate the handle's specific function.

3. From here, you can perform several distinct actions:

- To reposition the center point of a gradient or bitmap fill, simply click and drag the center point to a desired location within the bounding box.

- To change the width of the linear gradient, radial gradient, or bitmap fill, click and drag the square handle (with the horizontal arrow) on the side of the bounding box.

Changing the width of the gradient or bitmap fill resizes only the fill and not the object itself.

- To change the height of a bitmap fill, click and drag the square handle (with the vertical arrow) at the bottom of the bounding box.

As with adjusting the width, when you adjust the height of a gradient or bitmap fill, you're not adjusting the height of the actual filled object. You can also change the height and width simultaneously, a technique that has its advantages when you're trying to maintain the fill's proportions.

- To rotate the gradient or bitmap fill, drag the circular rotation handle with the small up arrow when you're working with a gradient or bitmap fill.

- To skew or slant a bitmap fill, drag one of the parallelogram handles on the top or right side of the bounding box.

- To change the focal (center) point of a radial gradient, drag the hollow inverted triangle along the axis that runs through the bounding box.

- To change the size of a radial gradient, drag the circle handle with the down arrow that is pointing to the right.

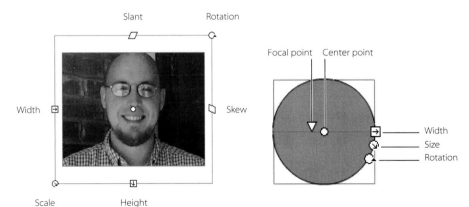

Figure 1.26

A bounding box appears for a bitmap fill when you're working with the Fill Transform tool.

Figure 1.27

A bounding box appears for a radial gradient when you're working with the Fill Transform tool.

Working with External Bitmaps

Bitmap/raster images are larger and more memory intensive than vectors, so it's in your best interest to use vector-based art as much as possible when orchestrating your Flash creation. However, sometimes bitmaps have a distinct advantage over vectors, which are generally unable to efficiently display complex photorealistic images or images with continuous color tones.

Flash is vector based and can't create bitmaps, but it can easily import many types of bitmap files. Once you import a bitmap file, you can manipulate it to minimize the amount of memory it consumes in your Flash creation.

Importing External Bitmaps

You can import bitmaps into Flash in two ways: by using the Import command or by simply pasting an image on the Stage.

> Flash 8 can import the following raster/bitmap files: Windows Bitmaps (BMP/DIB), GIF (GIF), JPEG (JPG/JPEG), PNG (PNG), and PICT (PCT/PIC). Flash can import the following bitmap/raster files *only* if you have QuickTime 4 or later installed: MacPaint (PNTG), QuickTime Image (QTIF), Photoshop (PSD), Silicon Graphics Images (SGI), TGA (TGA), and TIFF (TIF).

 This book's CD contains a copy of QuickTime 7.

To import a bitmap:

1. Choose File → Import → Import to Stage.

> Alternatively, you can select File → Import → Import to Library if you want the bitmap to be placed in your movie's Library; see Chapter 4 to learn more about the Library.

2. When the Import dialog box opens, navigate to the file you want to import, select it, and click the Open button. In Windows, use the Files of Type drop-down menu at the bottom of the Import dialog box to display only files of the type you're trying to import. On a Mac, use the Enable drop-down menu at the top of the dialog box.

3. When the bitmap is imported into Flash, it's automatically placed both on the Stage and in the Library.

Importing a TIFF file requires QuickTime. If you have QuickTime on your system and you're trying to import a file called image.tiff, for example, you might get a rather odd prompt: "Flash doesn't recognize the file format of image.tiff. Would you like to try importing via QuickTime?" The prompt isn't much to worry about. If you select Yes, your imported image won't be adversely affected. On the other hand, if you don't have QuickTime on your system, you'll get this message: "One or more files were not imported because there were problems reading them."

Figure 1.28

When you trace a bitmap, you don't get a perfect vector copy of the original bitmap. The image on the left is the original bitmap, and the image on the right is the traced version of the bitmap.

Although Flash will import a PNG created in any program, if you're importing a Fireworks PNG, you get the Fireworks PNG Import Settings dialog box. From here, you can set a series of options, including whether you want the various layers in your image to be flattened into a single layer.

To copy a bitmap from another application:

1. Copy the intended bitmap from the other application by choosing Edit → Copy.
2. Return to Flash, and paste the bitmap on the Stage by choosing Edit → Paste.

Tracing an Imported Bitmap

The Trace Bitmap option lets you take a bitmap and convert it to a native Flash vector file format with discrete areas of color. This is a definite advantage if you want to manipulate the bitmap image as you would a vector image. Most of the time, when you trace a bitmap and convert it to a vector image, you reduce its file size. However, in cases where the traced bitmap has complex colors and a complex shape, you'll almost always increase its file size (sometimes drastically).

When you trace a bitmap, you sever the link between the image and the symbol in the Library. If you want to place the traced bitmap back into the Library, simply convert it to a symbol. You'll learn about symbols in Chapter 4.

When you trace a bitmap, the results aren't necessarily what you would expect. It's nearly impossible to convert an image into a vector so that it looks the same as it did when it was a bitmap. Figure 1.28 illustrates the difference between the original bitmap and its traced version.

To trace an image:

1. Select a bitmap image on the Stage.
2. Choose Modify → Bitmap → Trace Bitmap to open the Trace Bitmap dialog box (see Figure 1.29).

Figure 1.29

You can use the Trace Bitmap dialog box to trace an image.

From here, you can set the various Trace Bitmap properties:

Color Threshold Specifies (as a number from 1 to 500) how much difference there must be between the RGB color values of adjacent pixels in the bitmap for Flash to treat them as separate colors in the traced image.

Minimum Area Sets the minimum amount of area a block of color in the bitmap must cover (in pixels) to be traced as its own shape by Flash. With a large value, the resulting vector image will be composed of larger, more solid blocks because Flash will ignore small patches of color. By entering a small value such as 10, Flash will draw these smaller areas in the resulting vector image. Tracing large, complex bitmaps at low Minimum Area settings can be a strenuous task for your computer, so work your way down the range from 1,000 until you achieve the desired effect.

Curve Fit Determines how closely to the edges of the pixels in your bitmap the outlines of the traced bitmap are drawn. Options include Pixels, Very Tight, Tight, Normal, Smooth, and Very Smooth. By selecting Pixels, you're telling Flash to draw its lines sharply along the edges of the pixels. The resulting image will have a very boxy, pixelated look to it. If your image has many curves that you want to maintain while avoiding pixelation, select Tight or Very Tight. If you aren't worried about preserving the exact shapes in your image, select Smooth or Very Smooth from the Curve Fit drop-down menu.

Corner Threshold Determines how many corners and points the tracing process uses when drawing vector shapes from portions of your bitmap image. Choosing Many Corners from the drop-down menu preserves complex, twisting shapes in the image; choosing Few Corners smoothes them by telling Flash to draw them in shapes with as few corners as possible.

> To create a traced bitmap that looks as close as possible to its original bitmap form (given the constraints of the tracing process), set Color Threshold to 10, Minimum Area to 1 pixel, Curve Fit to Pixels, and Corner Threshold to Many Corners.

Setting the Properties of an Imported Bitmap

Each bitmap you import into Flash 8 has a series of properties you can manipulate:

1. Open the Library, and select the bitmap whose properties you want to manipulate.

2. Open the Bitmap Properties dialog box by doing one of the following:

    • Click the Properties icon ⓘ .

    • Right-click / Ctrl+click, and choose Properties from the context menu.

    • Choose Properties from the Library's Options drop-down menu.

3. When open, the Bitmap Properties dialog box (see Figure 1.30) has several options:

Preview window Gives you a preview of the selected bitmap. If the bitmap itself is larger than the preview window, a hand icon (which appears when you move your cursor over the preview window) lets you pan the image.

Name field Displays the name of the bitmap and lets you change it if you want. When you change the name of the bitmap in the Bitmap Properties dialog box, you aren't actually changing the filename, just the name given to the bitmap in the Library.

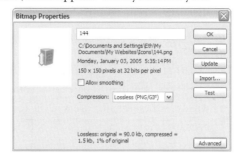

Figure 1.30

Use the Bitmap Properties dialog box to manipulate bitmap settings.

Path, Date, and Dimensions areas Display the bitmap's path, date of creation, and dimensions.

Allow Smoothing option Instructs Flash to *antialias* (or smooth) the image when checked.

Compression drop-down menu Gives you two choices:

- By choosing Photo (JPEG), you compress the image in JPEG format. To use the image's default compression quality, click the Use Imported JPEG Data check box. To choose a new quality compression setting, deselect Use Imported JPEG Data, and enter a value from 1 to 100 in the Quality field. A higher value preserves greater image quality but results in a larger file size.

- By choosing Lossless (GIF/PNG), you maintain the image "as is" by not discarding any of its data. Although lossless compression maintains image quality, it results in a far larger image size.

Use Document Default Quality setting Ensures that the image maintains its original quality. This option is unavailable if you've selected Photo (JPEG) from the Compression drop-down menu.

Test button Allows you to check the file's compression. The results, which include the file sizes of the original and the compressed images, appear at the bottom of the Bitmap Properties dialog box.

Update button Checks to see whether any changes have been made to the original file. If there have been changes, the imported file will update to reflect the changes to its parent.

Allow Smoothing option Antialiases the edges of the bitmap.

Editing an Imported Bitmap

Flash 8 gives you the ability to launch an external image-editing program, such as Fireworks or Photoshop. From here, you can make any changes you want to a given bitmap and then have Flash reflect the changes.

If you're editing a Fireworks PNG file that has been imported as a flattened image (by choosing the Flatten Image option from the Fireworks PNG Import Settings dialog box), you can choose to edit the PNG source file for the bitmap. If you've imported a PNG as an editable object, you won't be able to edit it with an alternate image-editing program.

To edit a PNG with Macromedia Fireworks 3 or later:

1. Open the Library, right-click / Ctrl+click, and choose Edit with Fireworks from the context menu.

2. When the Edit Image dialog box opens, specify whether the PNG source file or the bitmap file is to be opened.

3. When Fireworks opens, make the desired changes to the file.

4. When you're finished, choose Select → Update, and Fireworks automatically updates the file. If you're using Fireworks 4 or later, simply click the Done [Done] button in the upper-left corner of the Document window, and the file will automatically be updated in Flash.

To edit a bitmap with an image-editing program other than Fireworks:

1. Open the Library, right-click / Ctrl+click, and choose Edit With.

2. When the Select External Editor dialog box opens, navigate to the external editor you want to use, and select it.

3. After the external editor opens, make the desired changes to the image, and save it.

4. To update the image in Flash, do one of the following:

   - Select the bitmap in the Library, and choose Update from the Library's Options menu.

   - Right-click / Ctrl+click the bitmap in the Library, and select Update from the context menu.

5. From here, an Update Library Items dialog box opens, giving you a list of all the items you can update. Click the check box next to those items you want to update, and then click the Update button.

Using the Eraser Tool

To use the Eraser tool ⬚, which is a heck of a lot easier than using a real eraser (no little rubber shavings), select it from the Toolbox, move it to the location on the Stage you want to erase, and click and drag until you've erased to your heart's content. Yep, it's that easy.

> One slight catch with the Eraser tool is that it doesn't work on grouped objects (except for objects created with the Object Drawing Model).

Selecting Eraser Mode

The Eraser tool has several modes, all of which are accessible by clicking the Eraser Mode button ⬚ in the Toolbox's Options section when you have the Eraser tool selected. These modes let you specify exactly how your Eraser tool affects an existing drawn or painted element:

Erase Normal ⬚ Erases any fills or strokes over which you drag the Eraser tool.

Erase Fills ⬚ Constrains the Eraser tool so it erases only fills and empty areas without erasing any strokes over which it passes.

Erase Lines ⬚ Erases only strokes and lines. Any fills your cursor passes over will not be affected.

Erase Inside ⬚ Erases within the constraints of a shape. When this mode is selected and you start your stroke in a filled area, only the section inside that area is erased.

Erase Selected Fills ⬚ Affects only fills that are selected at the time when you begin erasing.

Working with the Faucet Option

The Faucet option ⬚, which is located in the Toolbox's Options section when you have the Eraser tool selected, automatically deletes any fill or stroke you click. Just select the Faucet option, and point and click to remove the offending fill or stroke.

Selecting the Eraser Shape

As with the Brush Size mode, you can specify the size and shape of your eraser. The available Eraser tool shapes and sizes range from small to large and are accessible through a drop-down menu in the Toolbox's Options section when the Eraser tool is selected.

To change the eraser shape and size, make your choice from the drop-down menu *before* you use the eraser.

Using Graphic Filters

Effects such as drop shadows, blurs, and glows have become staples in the web and graphic design worlds. Until now, Flash developers have had to create solutions in other programs such as Fireworks or Photoshop. In Flash 8 Professional, many of these effects come with the program in the form of *filters*.

> Filters get their name because they pass the image data of the object through an algorithm that filters the data in a specific way.

In total, Flash 8 Professional has seven filters (Drop Shadow, Blur, Glow, Bevel, Gradient Glow, Gradient Bevel, and Adjust Color), all of which can be applied only to text, Button symbols, and Movie Clip symbols.

> Flash Professional 8 provides support for Fireworks filters. When you import a Fireworks PNG file, you can keep many of the filters you had applied to objects within Fireworks and then continue to modify those filters and blends using Flash Professional 8.

When you import art from another program (to create the glow on an object, for instance), it may take some time to render. The Flash Player, by contrast, renders filters in real time. This means you might not get the kind of slowdown you might get if you were using an imported raster image to simulate an effect. Another advantage to filters is that you can animate them just like anything else in Flash. You can easily tween a drop shadow or a glow—something that might allow you to add that special professional polish to your movie.

> The more filters applied to an object, the more calculations Flash has to make to render the object. As a result, you'll find that a filter-heavy movie will probably move a little slower than one that doesn't have filters—even with the improved performance of the Flash 8 Player. As with all work in Flash, you must balance your needs (as a designer and a developer) with the needs of your audience (to have an immersive experience that isn't clunky, choppy, or unnecessarily slow or taxing on their Internet connection or computer).

To apply a filter to an object:

1. Select the object to which you'd like to apply the filter.
2. Open the Property Inspector, and click the Filters tab.
3. Click the Add Filter button ⊞ , and select one of the filters from the menu.

From here, the options that appear in the Property Inspector depend on the specific filter you choose.

The following options are common to most filters:

- Blur X and Blur Y control the width and height of the effect. The values are in pixels and can be set by either entering a value or dragging the slider to the right of their fields. If you'd like, you can also link/unlink the two values by clicking the padlock icon next to their fields.

- Quality, as its name suggests, controls the visual quality of the effect. Although a higher quality will look better, it also means playback performance won't be maximized.

Many filters also offer a Strength option, which controls the intensity of the effect (via a slider or a percentage value), and a Knockout option, which removes the original object and displays only the effect. Figure 1.31 shows the Knockout effect with a drop shadow. Many filters also offer a color swatch you can click to select a color for the effect.

Figure 1.31

The image on the left is the object with the regular drop shadow, and the image on the right shows the image knocked out.

Drop Shadow As its name suggests, the Drop Shadow filter allows you to create a drop shadow effect on text, a button, or a Movie Clip. Figure 1.32 shows the options; the following are unique to drop shadows:

- Angle, which can be adjusted by entering a value or dragging the angle dial, sets the angle at which the shadow is cast off the object.

- Distance lets you control the distance between the object and the shadow. You can enter the value manually (in pixels) or adjust it using the slider.

- The Inner Shadow option moves the shadow from the outside of the object to the inside.

- The Hide Object option removes the object entirely, leaving only the shadow behind.

Blur The Blur filter softens the edges of text, buttons, or Movie Clips. You can use it to simulate depth of field or use it in an animation to simulate a motion blur. The options, which appear in the Property Inspector once you've selected Blur from the Add Filter menu, are Blur X/Blur Y and Quality.

Glow The Glow filter lets you add color around the edges of an object (see Figure 1.33). As with all of the other filters, it can be animated to create some very interesting effects.

- Strength controls the sharpness of the glow. The higher the value (up to 1000 percent), which can be entered manually or set using the slider, the darker the shadow.

- The Inner Blur option moves the blur from the outside of the object to the inside.

Figure 1.32

Set the Drop Shadow filter's options in the Property Inspector.

Bevel The Bevel filter allows you to apply highlights and shadows to the inside of an object so it appears to be three-dimensional:

- By clicking the Shadow swatch, you can select the color of your bevel's shadow. If you think about your beveled object as three-dimensional, the area that is shadowed is the area that is blocked by the raised portion of the bevel and therefore shadowed.

- By clicking the Highlight swatch, you can select the color of your bevel's highlight. As with the bevel's shadow, when you think about the beveled object as three-dimensional, the highlighted area is the first portion of the object that is lit by whatever source is casting the light.

- Angle, which can be adjusted by entering a value or by dragging the angle dial, sets the angle (that is, location) of the light source that creates the highlight and the shadow area of the bevel.

- Distance, which can be set by manually entering a value (either negative or positive) or by dragging the slider, defines the thickness of the bevel (that is, the highlight area and the shadow area).

- The Type drop-down menu lets you set the kind of bevel. Inner places the highlight and shadow areas within the confines of the beveled object. Outer places the highlight and shadow areas outside the object, and Full combines both the Inner and Outer types.

The Gradient Glow filter requires you to choose one color at the beginning of the gradient with an alpha value of 0, which can't be moved.

Gradient Glow The difference between a Gradient Glow and a regular Glow is that the Gradient Glow filter isn't one color but a gradient. Figure 1.34 shows the options, of which the following are unique to Gradient Glow.

- Distance, which can be set by entering a value manually or dragging the slider, changes the position of the glow along the axis defined by the Angle value.

> By changing the distance of the Gradient Glow filter slightly so that it isn't centered directly on the object, you can create a gradient drop shadow.

- The Type drop-down menu lets you set the kind of gradient glow. Inner places the gradient within the confines of the beveled object. Outer places the gradient outside the object, and Full combines both the Inner and Outer types.

- The Gradient Definition Bar lets you control and change exactly how the Gradient Glow filter looks. To change the colors in the gradient, click one of the pointers, and select a color when the Color Picker appears. To add more colors to the gradient, just click below the Gradient Definition Bar to add more pointers. You can then change the color of the new pointer as you see fit. To change the transition between the colors, click and drag the pointers closer together (for a sharper transition between colors) or farther apart (for a more gradual transition).

Gradient Bevel A Gradient Bevel filter is almost the same as a regular bevel. The only real difference is that the shadow and the highlight areas can be gradients instead of just solid colors. The following are specific to the Gradient Bevel filter:

- Angle, which can be adjusted by entering a value or by dragging the angle dial, sets the angle (that is, location) of the light source that creates the highlight and the shadow area of the bevel.

- Distance, which can be set by manually entering a value (either negative or positive) or by dragging the slider, defines the thickness of the bevel (that is, the highlight area and the shadow area).

- The Type drop-down menu lets you set the kind of bevel. Inner places the highlight and shadow areas within the confines of the beveled object. Outer places the highlight and shadow areas outside the object, and Full combines both the Inner and Outer type.

- The Gradient Definition Bar lets you control the gradients of both the highlight area and the shadow area (which, in a normal bevel, can be only solid colors). The Bevel Gradient filter requires one color in the middle of the gradient with an alpha value of 0. You can't move the position of this color, but you can change the color. The gradient on the left side of the Gradient Definition Bar represents the highlight portion of the bevel, and the gradient on the right side represents the shadow portion. To change the colors in the gradient, click one of the pointers, and select a color when the Color Picker appears. To add more colors to the gradient, just click below the Gradient Definition Bar to add more pointers. You can then change the color of the new pointer as you see fit. To change the transition between the colors, click and drag the pointers closer together (for a sharper transition between colors) or farther apart (for a more gradual transition).

Adjust Color The Adjust Color filter lets you adjust the brightness, contrast, hue, and saturation of the selected Movie Clip, button, or text object. The options appear in the Property Inspector once you've selected Adjust Color from the Add Filter menu (see Figure 1.35).

If you want to apply the Brightness control only to an object, use the color controls located on the Properties tab of the Property inspector. Using the Brightness option in the Properties tab provides improved performance over applying a filter.

- Contrast adjusts the highlights, shadows, and midtones of an image. Values range from −100 to 100, and can be entered manually or adjusted with the slider.

- Brightness adjusts the brightness of an image. Values range from −100 to 100 and can be entered manually or adjusted with the slider.

- Saturation adjusts the intensity of a color. Values range from −100 to 100 and can be entered manually or adjusted with the slider.

- Hue adjusts the shade of a color. Values range from −180 to 180 and can be entered manually or adjusted with the slider.

- The Reset button Reset lets you convert the object to its original state.

Figure 1.35

You can set the Adjust Color options in the Property Inspector.

Removing a Filter

To remove a filter:

1. Select the text, button, or Movie Clip from which you want to remove the filter.

2. Select the Filter tab in the Property Inspector.

3. Select the filter you want to remove in the list of applied filters.

4. Click the Remove Filter button ▭ to remove the filter.

> To disable a filter temporarily (but not remove it entirely), just click the check mark next to the filter's name. When you want to enable it, just click the red X.

Saving a Filter as a Preset

If you find yourself working repeatedly with the same filter, you'll want to save your property settings for it. Luckily, you can save a filter as a preset—essentially allowing you to save a custom filter that you can use whenever you want:

1. Select a specific filter, and customize it to your needs.

2. Click the Add Filter button ⊕ , and select Presets → Save As.

3. When the Save Preset As dialog box appears, enter a name, and click OK.

Your preset filter will now appear under the Preset submenu when you click the Add Filter button ⊕ . You'll be able to apply it like any other filter.

CHAPTER 2

Modifying Visual Assets

The success of your Flash creation depends, at least partly, on your ability to exert complete control over the look of your movie elements. To this end, Flash 8 offers a host of tools with which to manipulate and modify objects (shapes, text, symbols, and so on). Whether you want to modify their shape, move them around the Stage, or group them with other objects, this chapter explores all the ways you can exert control over the look of the objects in your Flash creation.

- Selecting items for manipulation

- Grouping and ungrouping objects

- Moving objects

- Aligning, distributing, and spacing objects

- Arranging objects

- Transforming objects

Selecting Items for Manipulation

Flash 8 has an extensive set of tools that you can use to select lines, shapes, text, groups, symbols, buttons, and a multitude of other items to place on the Stage. In the following sections, you'll quickly explore each of the various selection tools available, including the Arrow tool, the Subselection tool, and the Lasso tool. Because the Pen tool and the Subselection tool are intrinsically connected, it is difficult to separate them in a discussion such as this. Chapter 1 provides a more in-depth discussion of the Subselection tool's functionality in conjunction with the Pen tool.

Using the Arrow Tool

The Arrow tool ![arrow] lets you select and move single or multiple items around the Stage. The Arrow tool also allows you to change the shape of an unselected line, stroke, or object.

Selecting Content

Selecting an object with the Arrow tool is quite simple: just point and click. However, a few tips and tricks will help you take better advantage of its functionality. For instance, when you select an ungrouped object, a checkered pattern appears over it to indicate that it is currently selected.

On the other hand, a grouped object or an object drawn with the Object Drawing Model that has been selected has a thin rectangular box around it (see Figure 2.1).

> Objects that aren't drawn using the Object Drawing Model usually have both a fill and a stroke. Therefore, if you want to select the entire object, you'll need to select both the fill and the stroke separately. You can also double-click an object's fill to select both the fill and the stroke.

To deselect an item that you've selected with the Arrow tool, click anywhere else on the Stage, choose Edit → Deselect All, hit your Esc key, or use the keyboard shortcut Ctrl+Shift+A / ⌘+Shift+A.

Figure 2.1

The three objects on the left are ungrouped (and individually selected), while the three on the right are grouped (and the group is selected).

Changing the Shape of an Object

Although you can alter the shapes of objects more easily with other Flash tools, the Arrow tool is a quick way to fiddle with the form of an unselected line, stroke, or shape.

> This process doesn't work if the object was drawn using the Object Drawing Model.

To change the shape of an object:

1. Select the Arrow tool from the Toolbox. Make sure you have an ungrouped and unselected object on the Stage.

2. Move the Arrow tool close to the edge of the ungrouped and unselected object— notice that the cursor changes slightly (see Figure 2.2).

3. When the cursor changes, click and drag the edge of the object to where you want it. Notice that you get a ghostlike preview of the line's position (see Figure 2.3). When the line, edge, or shape is altered as you want, release your mouse button— the changes will be automatically applied.

Figure 2.2

The Arrow tool changes when you move it close to the unselected line, stroke, or shape.

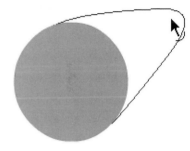

Figure 2.3

You get a preview of the new position of the line, stroke, or shape.

Snapping to Objects

When you toggle Snap to Objects 🧲 , which is located in the Toolbox's Options section when the Arrow tool is selected, you cause the selected objects to snap to other objects on the Stage. You can snap selected objects to just about anything: lines, free-form paths, shapes, and so on. In addition, you can even snap objects to the Stage's grid. Using the Snap to Objects option is useful when you want to make sure the objects on the Stage line up or when you want to arrange them in a consistent manner.

> To view the grid, select View → Grid → Show Grid. To snap objects to the grid, choose View → Snaping → Snap to Grid. Finally, if you want to edit the grid properties, select View → Grid → Edit Grid.

When you have the Snap to Objects option toggled, you'll notice that a small circle appears in the center of the selected object when you move it with the Arrow tool. This small circle is called the *transformation point* in Flash (see Figure 2.4).

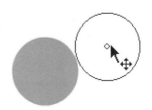

Figure 2.4

A small circle appears in the center of the selected object when you move it with the Arrow tool.

Sometimes the Transformation Point is referred to as a Registration point.

The transformation point, and not the object itself, is doing the snapping; however, this is pretty much moot because the transformation point and the object are the same. When you move the transformation point of one object (and therefore the object itself) over another object (a straight line drawn with the Line tool, for instance), the transformation point enlarges to about twice its size and snaps to the object.

Snapping to Pixels

In addition to employing the Snap to Objects option, you can also use the Snap to Pixels option. Although it's not accessible in the Toolbox's Options section when the Arrow tool is selected, the Snap to Pixels option is best explored at this stage of the discussion.

Essentially, when the Snap to Pixels option is turned on (View → Snapping → Snap to Pixels), a pixel grid (visible only if the Stage is magnified to at least 400 percent) appears to which all objects will snap.

To temporarily make the pixel grid invisible, press X. When you hold down the X key, the grid will disappear, reappearing when you release the button.

Straightening and Smoothing

The Arrow tool's Smooth option ⤳, which is located in the Toolbox's Options section when you have the Arrow tool selected, reduces the number of bumps in a selected curve. The result is a smoother curve than you had previously.

To use the Smooth option, select a curve with the Arrow tool, and click the Smooth option. Alternatively, you can select the curve with the Arrow tool, and choose Modify → Shape → Smooth.

The Smooth option does not work with grouped objects, though it works with objects drawn with the Object Drawing Model.

The Arrow tool's Straighten option ⤳, located in the Toolbox's Options portion next to the Smooth option, takes the curve out of relatively straight lines, making them perfectly straight.

It's worth mentioning that you can both smooth and straighten repeatedly.

To use the Straighten option, select a line with the Arrow tool, and click the Straighten option. Alternatively, you can select the curve with the Arrow tool and choose Modify → Shape → Straighten.

The Straighten option doesn't work with grouped objects, though it does work with objects drawn with the Object Drawing Model.

Manipulating a Shape's Points with the Subselection Tool

Any shape you draw in Flash (be it a free-form shape with the Pen tool or with one of the shape tools) consists of points and paths/segments. In Chapter 1, we discussed how you illustrate using the Pen tool and then manipulate the points created with the Pen tool using the Subselection tool. However, you can also use the Subselection tool to manipulate the points that are naturally part of anything drawn with one of the shape tools (Oval, Rectangle, or Polystar):

1. Make sure you've drawn a shape with the Rectangle tool, the Oval tool, or the Polystar tool. Select the Subselection tool ⬚ .

2. Move your cursor close to the edge of the shape—the cursor will change to an arrow with a small, black square in its lower-right corner.

If you move the cursor over one of the shape's points (opposed to one of the paths/ segments between the points), the cursor will change to an arrow with a small, white square in its lower-right corner.

Selecting with the Lasso Tool

While the Arrow tool selects individual objects, the Lasso tool ⬚ selects all the objects (or parts of objects) in a specific area.

You can select portions of individual ungrouped objects (say, the corner of a large square) with the Lasso tool. That area will be selected independently from the rest of the object and can therefore be moved with the Arrow tool, creating the illusion that you took a pair of scissors, cut off the corner, and then moved it away from the square. This, however, doesn't work with an object drawn using the Object Drawing Model—the Lasso tool will simply select the entire object.

The Lasso tool contains three options in the Toolbox's Options section: Polygon mode ⬚ , Magic Wand ⬚ , and Magic Wand Settings ⬚ . Much like the Arrow tool, the Lasso tool is amazingly easy to use. All you need to do is click and drag the tool to draw a line around the area you want to select.

For selection purposes, the Lasso tool automatically closes an area that you don't close yourself.

Selecting with the Lasso Tool's Polygon Mode

Polygon mode 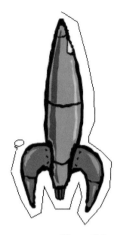 lets you assert a great deal more control over selection than you'd get if you were simply using the Lasso tool.

Essentially, Polygon mode lets you select an area by drawing multiple, connected, straight edges (see Figure 2.5). In Polygon mode, the Lasso tool draws a straight line. Every time you hit your mouse button, you create a selection point. You can then draw another straight line (which is attached to the selection point you just created). The process is repeated until you encircle the entire selection area. When you double-click, you'll select the area.

> Just as with the Lasso tool when it isn't in Polygon mode, an unclosed area automatically closes when you finish your making your selection. If you want to finish the selection in Polygon Mode, you need to double-click.

Figure 2.5

Polygon mode lets you select an area by drawing straight lines that are connected.

Working with the Magic Wand Tool

The Lasso tool's Magic Wand option 🪄 selects similar colors in a bitmap image that has been separated.

> When you break apart a bitmap (which isn't the same as tracing a bitmap), you are simply telling Flash to regard the image as a collection of individual color areas.

After you have broken apart the bitmap image (by selecting the image and then choosing Modify → Break Apart), you can then click individual colors with the Magic Wand option to select them.

> A checkerboard pattern denotes a color area that is selected with the Magic Wand option.

Setting the Properties of the Magic Wand Tool

The Magic Wand Settings option 🪄 is located in the Toolbox's Options section when you have the Lasso tool selected. When you click the Magic Wand Settings option, the Magic Wand Settings dialog box opens, and you can make the appropriate adjustments to the Magic Wand option (see Figure 2.6).

The options are as follows:

Figure 2.6

Use the Magic Wand Settings dialog box to modify the Magic Wand tool.

Threshold Defines the degree to which the Magic Wand tool will select similar (but not identical) colors. Choices range from 0 to 200. For example, if you use a threshold setting of 0, you will select only identical colors. As you increase the threshold setting, the amount of similar colors that are selected will increase.

Smoothing Determines how edges of a selection should be smoothed. The choices are Normal, Pixels, Rough, and Smooth.

Grouping and Ungrouping Objects

When you combine multiple objects (shapes, text, symbols, and so on) into one unit, it's called *grouping*. The process is useful for a number of reasons. Say you want to create a flower to use in your Flash movie. You can get a lot more visual detail and control over the way the flower looks if you draw the individual parts separately. So, you could draw the petals, the stem, and the leaves and then arrange them on the Stage exactly how you want. However, what happens when you want to move the *whole* flower? Well, you could select each of the elements and then move them with the Arrow tool. However, what if you accidentally forgot to include a vital part of the flower (say, the stem) in the selection? When you moved the flower, the stem would stay behind, putting your beautiful creation out of whack.

Don't laugh; this kind of thing happens all the time to even the most accomplished Flash developers. How could you avoid this potentially calamitous situation? This is where grouping comes in. When you group a series of objects, you can treat them as one unit. So, in the silly flower example, if you had grouped all the elements, you'd be able to select and move them all as one unit, leaving no part behind.

To group objects:

1. With the Arrow tool, select any objects on the Stage you want to include in the group.

To select multiple objects, hold down the Shift key, and click any items you want included in the selection.

2. With the various objects selected, choose Modify → Group or use the shortcut Ctrl+G / ⌘+G. Figure 2.7 illustrates a series of grouped objects.

The Property Inspector will identify an object (or objects) as being grouped.

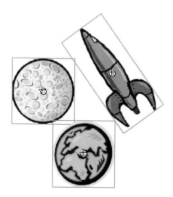

Figure 2.7

At the left is a series of individual objects. At the right, the same objects have been grouped. Notice the line that surrounds the entire group as if its parts were all one object.

Ungrouping objects is just as easy as grouping them:

1. Select the grouped objects with the Arrow tool.

2. Choose Modify → Ungroup, or use the shortcut Ctrl+Shift+G / ⌘+Shift+G.

One of the great things about the way Flash deals with grouped objects is that you can edit individual elements (for instance, the petals in the flower example) without having to ungroup them. This is quite helpful if you've created a particularly detailed image with which you don't want to go through the entire grouping process again. To edit individual elements:

1. Select a group with the Arrow tool.

2. Choose Edit → Edit Selected.

   Alternatively, you can also simply double-click an object in an already selected group. The Edit bar, which is located along the top of the Stage, indicates that you are currently editing the group (usually represented by the default name of Group).

3. From here, make any changes you want to any of the objects within the group.

4. When finished, simply choose Edit → Edit All, double-click anywhere outside the group with the Arrow tool, or click the scene name in the Edit bar.

Moving Objects

When it comes to working with objects, you'll often need to move them around the Stage. You can move objects in four ways: with the Arrow tool, with the arrow keys, through the Property Inspector, or with the Info panel.

To move an object with the Arrow tool:

1. Select an object. To select a series of objects, hold down the Shift key and click.

2. With the Arrow tool, click and drag the object (or series of objects) to the desired position on the Stage. If you want to constrain its movement vertically or horizontally, hold down the Shift key while moving the object(s).

If you hold down the Alt/Option key while dragging, Flash creates a copy of the object and moves the copy instead of the original.

To move an object with the arrow keys on your keyboard:

1. Select an object or group of objects you want to move.

2. Use the arrow keys on your keyboard to move the selected object 1 pixel at a time in any direction. If you want to move the selected object 10 pixels at a time, hold down your Shift key while using the arrow keys.

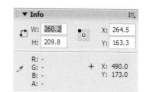

Figure 2.8

Both the Property Inspector and the Info panel have X and Y fields, which represent the vertical (Y) and horizontal (X) positions of the selected object on the Stage.

To move an object or a group of objects with the Property Inspector or the Info panel:

1. Open the Property Inspector by choosing Window → Properties → Properties, or open the Info panel by choosing Window → Info.

2. Select the object or objects you want to move. Enter a value into the X and Y fields in either the Property Inspector or the Info Panel (see Figure 2.8).

The X/Y coordinate system is relative to the upper-left corner of the Stage—the location of which is 0/0.

The units of measure used in the Info panel's X/Y coordinate system are determined by what you specified in the Ruler Units option in the Document Properties dialog box. To change them, choose Modify → Document (or use the shortcut Ctrl+J / ⌘+J), and choose an alternate one from the Ruler Units drop-down menu. Additionally, when you change the Ruler Units, the display in the Property Inspector changes as well.

Aligning, Distributing, and Spacing Objects

The Align panel, which is accessible by selecting Window → Align (or by using the shortcut Ctrl+K / ⌘+K), is a handy tool that lets you do all manner of interesting things.

Beyond aligning objects on the Stage, the Align panel also lets you distribute, match the size of, and space objects. In the following sections, you'll look at each of these options separately.

If you want to align objects to the Stage (opposed to other objects), click the Align/Distribute to Stage button in the right portion of the Align panel.

Aligning Objects

The top section of the Align panel contains a series of buttons that lets you align selected objects horizontally or vertically. From left to right, the buttons let you align objects by their left edges ⊟ , by their horizontal center points ⋮ ⋮, and by their right edges ⊒ . The second set of buttons, from left to right, lets you align objects by their top edges ⊤ᵒ, by their vertical center points ⬓ᵒ, and by their bottom edges ⬓ᵒ .

Flash aligns objects according to their bounding boxes, not any feature of the object itself.

To align a series of objects:

1. With the Align panel open (Windows → Align), select the objects you want to align.

2. Select one of the alignment options from the Align panel. Figure 2.9 illustrates the effects that the various alignment options have on images.

When aligning to the left, Flash uses the left edge of the leftmost object in the selection for the alignment's position. The same applies when you are aligning to the top, bottom, or right; Flash uses the edge of the topmost, bottommost, or rightmost object for the alignment.

Distributing Objects

The Align panel gives you the ability to distribute selected objects. This comes in handy if you want to evenly space three or more selected objects. From left to right, the buttons in the Distribute section of the Align panel let you distribute objects evenly by their top edges ☴, their center points vertically ☲, and their bottom edges ☱. The next distribute buttons, from left to right, let you distribute objects evenly by their left edges ▯▮, their center points horizontally ▯▮, and their right edges ▮▯.

Figure 2.9

The first row is an illustration of three unaligned objects. The bottom row illustrates the three same objects aligned horizontally to the top edge.

Figure 2.10

The left row of objects is undistributed. The right row, however, contains the same objects after they've been distributed vertically to their center points.

To distribute a series of objects:

1. Select a series of objects (distributing fewer than three won't have any visible effect, so remember to select three or more).

2. Click one of the distribute buttons in the Align panel. Figure 2.10 provides an example of the Distribute option's effects.

Matching Object Size

When you use the Match Size buttons in the Align panel, you can resize a series of selected objects so that their horizontal or vertical dimensions match those of the largest in the selection. From left to right, the Match Size buttons in the Align panel let you match two objects' width ⊟ , height ⊡ , or both width and height ⊞ .

To match the size of objects:

1. Select two or more objects on the Stage.

2. Click one of the Match Size buttons in the Align panel. Figure 2.11 illustrates the Match Size option's effects.

Spacing Objects

The Space feature in the Align panel allows you to equally space selected objects vertically or horizontally. Although you won't see much difference between two similarly sized objects if they were either spaced or distributed, the difference is obvious when you're working with differently sized objects.

When you use the Space Evenly Horizontally button ⊟ or the Space Evenly Vertically button ⊞ , you are guaranteed that there will be a fixed number of pixels between each object. When you distribute objects of varied sizes, you'll find that the larger the object is, the less space there will be between it and the next one. This is primarily because the Distribute options use a central reference point to arrange the objects. As a result, you might want to use the Space option in the Align panel instead.

To equally space objects:

1. Select two or more objects on the Stage.

2. Click one of the Space buttons in the Align panel. Figure 2.12 illustrates an example of the Space Evenly Horizontally option.

Figure 2.11

The top two objects are unaltered. The bottom two are examples of the same objects after their heights have been matched. Because the one on the left was the larger of the two, it has remained unchanged. The right object, however, has been stretched.

Figure 2.12

The top three objects are unaltered. The bottom three show what happens when you use the Space Evenly Horizontally option in the Align panel.

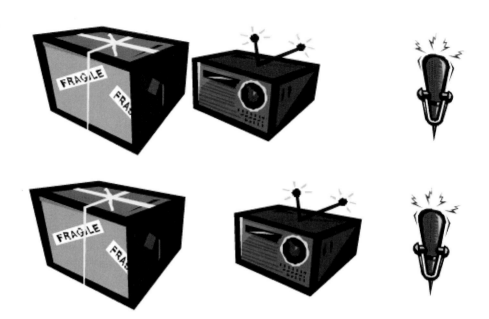

Arranging Objects

Although you can use layers to position objects in your Flash creation vertically, you can also stack them within a single layer using the Arrange option. The result of both methods is that some objects appear to be either behind or in front of other objects.

The difference between layers and the Arrange option is that layers provide you a great deal more control over the Z (depth) organization of your movie. However, in cases where all the elements in your movie exist within a single layer, the Arrange options are your best bet for manipulating the stacking order of your objects.

The Arrange options, which are accessible by selecting Modify → Arrange, allow you to change the position of any selected object in the stack, thereby moving them in front of or behind other objects. The options in the Arrange menu are pretty straightforward:

Bring to Front Moves the selected object to the absolute top/front of the stack in the currently selected layer

Bring Forward Moves the currently selected object one increment forward/up in the stack of the currently selected layer

Send Backward Moves the currently selected object backward/downward one increment in the stack of the currently selected layer

Send to Back Moves the currently selected object to the absolute bottom/back of the stack of the currently selected layer

Lock Locks the position of all the objects in the stack of a given layer

Unlock All Unlocks the stack of the currently selected layer

Transforming Objects

Located in the Toolbox's Tools section, the Free Transform tool ▶ has several *modifiers* that let you transform a selected object. These modifiers are accessible in the Toolbox's Options section when the Free Transform tool is selected.

Although you can specify the action you want to take on an object by selecting a specific transform modifier, the Free Transform tool also lets you manipulate an object without selecting any of the options. All you need to do is select the Free Transform tool, click the object you want to manipulate, and then move your cursor over any of the handles on the object's bounding box. Depending on the transform you can perform on that specific handle, your cursor will change accordingly.

> The following sections show you how to use the Free Transform tool in conjunction with its various modifiers.

Flash also allows you to perform many of the same types of transformations with the Transform panel (which is accessible by choosing Window → Transform).

Scaling an Object

By scaling an object, you change its size (either horizontally, vertically, or uniformly). You can scale an object with either the Free Transform tool or the Transform panel.

To scale an object with the Free Transform tool:

1. Select the desired object with the Arrow tool, and then choose the Free Transform tool ▶ from the Toolbox. Alternatively, click the desired object with the Free Transform tool to select it.

2. From here, a bounding box with handles appears around the selected object (see Figure 2.13).

3. Select the Scale option ⬚ in the Toolbox's Options section (accessible when you've selected the Free Transform tool). Alternatively, you can select Modify → Transform → Scale.

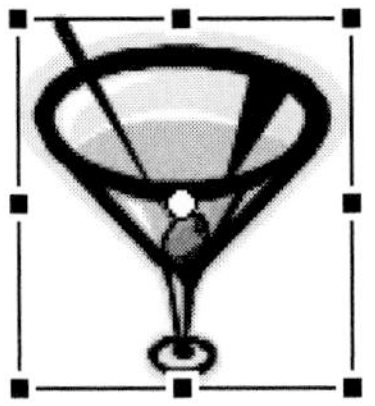

Figure 2.13

When you select an object and then the Free Transform tool, a bounding box appears.

> Remember, because of the nature of the Free Transform tool, you can bypass step 3 if you want and go straight to step 4.

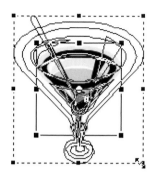

Figure 2.14

The Free Transform tool lets you scale an object horizontally.

Figure 2.15

The Free Transform tool lets you scale an object vertically.

Figure 2.16

The Free Transform tool lets you scale an object horizontally and vertically simultaneously.

4. To scale horizontally, click one of the transform handles on the left or right of the bounding box, and drag until the object reaches the desired size (see Figure 2.14).

5. To scale vertically, click one of the transform handles on the top or the bottom of the bounding box, and drag until the object reaches the desired size (see Figure 2.15).

6. To scale vertically and horizontally at the same time, click one of the corner transform handles, and drag until the object reaches the desired size. By doing this, you'll also maintain the object's proportions (see Figure 2.16).

7. When you've finished, click anywhere off the object to deselect the object.

You can also scale an object with the Transform panel:

1. Select the object you want to scale.

2. Choose Window → Transform to open the Transform panel (see Figure 2.17).

3. To scale the object horizontally, enter a value (in percent) in the Width field and hit Enter/Return.

4. To scale the object vertically, enter a value (in percent) in the Height field.

5. To scale the object both horizontally and vertically, click the Constrain check box, and then enter a value (in percent) in either the Width field or the Height field.

6. When you've finished, click anywhere off the object to hide the transform handles.

Figure 2.17

You can scale an object using the Transform panel.

Rotating an Object

As with many of the transformation operations, you can rotate an object with the Free Transform tool or the Transform panel.

When you rotate an object, it turns around its registration point.

To rotate an object with the Free Transform tool:

1. Select the desired object, and then choose the Free Transform tool 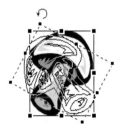 from the Toolbox. Alternatively, click the desired object with the Free Transform tool to select it.

2. Select the Rotate and Skew button 🖅 in the Toolbox's Options section. Alternatively, you can choose Modify → Transform → Rotate and Skew.

> Remember, because of the nature of the Free Transform tool, you can bypass step 2 if you want and go straight to step 3.

3. Move your cursor just off the *corner handles*. If the selected object is not a group, you'll notice that your cursor changes to the circular arrow icon (see Figure 2.18).

4. Click and drag in a circular motion to rotate your object.

To rotate an object with the Transform panel:

1. Select the object you want to rotate.

2. Choose Window → Transform to open the Transform panel.

3. Click the Rotate radio button.

4. Enter a value (in degrees) in the Rotate field.

5. Press Enter/Return to apply the rotation to the selected object.

Figure 2.18

Note how the cursor changes when you move it just off one of the corner handles of an object that has been selected with the Free Transform tool.

> You can also rotate a selected object 90° clockwise or counterclockwise by choosing Modify → Transform → Rotate 90° CW or Rotate 90° CCW.

Flipping an Object

Flash lets you flip a selected object horizontally or vertically without changing its relative position on the Stage.

1. Use the Arrow tool to select the object you want to flip.

2. Select Modify → Transform → Flip Horizontal or Flip Vertical. Figure 2.19 illustrates the effects of the Flip Horizontal and Flip Vertical options.

Figure 2.19

Three copies of the same object. The left one shows the original position. The middle one illustrates the object after it has been flipped horizontally. The right one illustrates the same object after it has been flipped vertically.

Skewing an Object

Skewing slants an object along its vertical or horizontal axis. You can slant an object in two ways.

To slant an object with the Free Transform tool:

1. Select the desired object with the Arrow tool, and then choose the Free Transform tool ⬧ from the Toolbox. Alternatively, click the desired object with the Free Transform tool to select it.

2. Click the Rotate and Skew button ⬧ in the Toolbox's Options section (when you have the Free Transform tool selected).

> Remember, because of the nature of the Free Transform tool, you can bypass step 2 if you want and go straight to step 3.

3. When the handles appear, move your cursor over one of handles in the middle of the sides of the bounding box. Your cursor changes into a pair of arrows pointing in opposite directions, oriented either vertically or horizontally (depending on which handle you moved your cursor over).

4. As shown in Figure 2.20, click and drag horizontally or vertically (depending on which handles you are manipulating).

5. To finish, click anywhere off the object to hide the transform handles.

To skew an object with the Transform panel:

1. Select the object you want to skew.

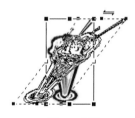

Figure 2.20

Drag horizontally or vertically to skew the selected object.

2. Choose Window → Transform to open the Transform panel.

3. Click the Skew radio button.

4. To skew an object horizontally, enter a value (in degrees) in the Skew Horizontally field.

5. To skew the object vertically, enter a value (in degrees) in the Skew Vertically field.

6. When you are finished, press Enter/Return.

Distorting an Object

When you apply a distort transformation, you can change the position of either the corner or the side handles of an object's bounding box (see Figure 2.21).

This process not only changes the position of the selected handles (and therefore the shape of the object itself) but it also changes its adjoining edges.

> It's worth noting that the Distort transformation won't work on a group, but it works just fine on a group of individually selected objects or an object drawn with the Object Drawing Model.

If you hold down the Shift key while applying a distort transformation, the object will be tapered.

To distort an object:

1. Select the object you want to distort, and select the Free Transform tool ▶ .

2. Click the Distort button ▱ in the Toolbox's Options section (when you have the Free Transform tool selected). Alternatively, you can select Modify → Transform → Distort.

3. When the bounding box appears, move your cursor over any of the handles—your cursor changes to a larger, white pointer.

4. Click and drag the handle. When you've reached the location on the Stage where you would like the handle to be moved, simply release your mouse button. Your object will distort accordingly.

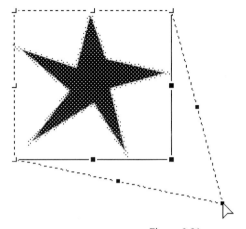

Figure 2.21

Try distorting an object by moving an object's bounding box.

Manipulating an Object's Envelope

An *envelope* is the bounding box that surrounds one or more *ungrouped* objects. With the Edit Envelope transform, you can effectively manipulate this envelope and thereby warp an object with a fair amount of precision.

> The Edit Envelope transformation does not work on grouped objects, symbols, bitmaps, gradients, or text. It does, however, work on an object drawn using the Object Drawing Model. And although the Edit Envelope transformation won't work on a group (Modify → Group), it works just fine on a group of individually selected objects.

To manipulate an object's envelope:

1. Select the object (or objects) whose envelope you want to edit.

2. Select the Free Transform tool ▶ .

3. Click the Envelope button ▨ in the Toolbox's Options section (when you have the Free Transform tool selected). Alternatively, you can select Modify → Transform → Envelope.

4. When the bounding box opens, move your cursor over any of the handles (either square or round)—your cursor changes to a larger, white pointer.

> You'll note two types of handles: square and circular. The square handles can be moved to a new physical position, while the circular ones are used to adjust the curve of the envelope.

5. Click and drag the handle (see Figure 2.22). When you've reached the location on the Stage where you want the handle to be moved, simply release your mouse button. Your object will warp accordingly.

6. When you click and drag one of the envelope handles, tangent handles will appear. Much as in the case of path created with the Pen tool, you can manipulate the tangents (by clicking and dragging the handle at the end of the tangent) to further warp the object's envelope (see Figure 2.23).

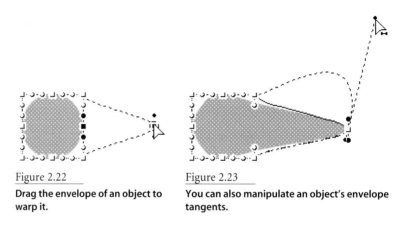

Figure 2.22

Drag the envelope of an object to warp it.

Figure 2.23

You can also manipulate an object's envelope tangents.

Restoring Transformed Objects

As you can see, you can apply a number of transformations to any given object. It is quite easy to go wild and transform an object beyond all hope of returning it to its previous state. You'd be surprised how far away an object can wander from its initial appearance, leaving you totally stumped as to how it originally looked. But you can restore objects to their pre-transformed state easily:

> The is one little wrinkle when it comes to restoring transformed objects. If you transform the object, and then deselect it, you won't be able to restore it. However, if you transform and object and leave it selected, you'll be able to restore it.

1. Make sure the object you want to transform is still selected.

2. Choose Modify → Transform → Remove Transform. Alternatively, you can click the Reset button in the bottom-right corner of the Transform panel.

Working with Transformation Points

A transformation point is a reference that Flash uses when it performs transformations. When you rotate an object, you rotate it around the transformation point. When you align or distribute objects, the registration point acts as a reference for the procedure.

Unfortunately, you can't directly manipulate an object's transformation point. What you can do, however, is temporarily change its position. Ultimately, this allows you to get better control over the result of any given transformation.

When you move an object's transformation point, its new location is merely temporary. As soon as you apply a new transformation, the transformation point will reset to its default location, which is in the center of an object.

Figure 2.24

You can move an object's transformation point.

To move an object's transformation point:

1. Select the object whose transformation point you want to manipulate.

2. Initiate any transform (either using the Free Transform tool or choosing Modify → Transform). This will cause the bounding box to appear around the selected object.

3. Click and drag the transformation point (which appears in the center of the object as a white circle) to the desired location (see Figure 2.24).

4. When the transformation point is in the desired location, perform the transformation.

To reset the transformation point to its default location manually, double-click anywhere within the selected object.

CHAPTER 3

Working with Type and Typography

Type is an extremely powerful tool for giving your digital creation extra life and meaning. Because of Flash's vector animation tools, text—especially if it's properly crafted—can have an incredible impact on your visitors. Taking the time to choose the right type for your textual content can turn a good Flash creation into a great Flash creation.

- Using antialiasing and improving text readability
- Working with Flash's font limitations
- Creating type with the Text tool
- Checking your spelling
- Using ActionScript to dynamically manipulate text
- Formatting text with Cascading Style Sheets

Exploring Antialiasing, Text Readability, and Font Limitations

Flash 8 features a new text-rendering engine called FlashType, which provides wonderfully high-quality text rendering both in the Flash authoring environment and in published SWF files. Although FlashType is available in both Flash 8 Basic and Flash 8 Professional, the new custom antialiasing option (discussed in the "Working with Static Text" section) is available only in Flash 8 Professional.

By default, FlashType is automatically enabled when you export your movie for the Flash 8 Player, and it automatically sets the Anti-Alias for Readability option or Custom Anti-Alias option in the Property Inspector. However, using FlashType might cause a slight delay when loading your SWF files. This delay becomes especially pronounced if you are using several fonts (four or five) within the first frame of your SWF file. In this situation, you'll find that the Flash Player's memory usage will increase—four or five fonts can increase memory usage by as much as 4MB.

Despite the great features of FlashType, working with text in Flash does have some fundamental problems, such as its font limitations.

Flash movies can use Type 1 PostScript fonts, TrueType fonts, and bitmap fonts (on the Macintosh only). To use PostScript fonts, you must have Adobe Type Manager (ATM) installed on your system.

If you're using Windows 2000, you don't need to install ATM to use Type 1 PostScript fonts.

For the most part, when you publish your movie, Flash embeds the necessary information about fonts, thereby allowing your audience's computers to display them properly. However, in rare cases, fonts still appear incorrectly in your Flash movie if someone doesn't have that font installed on their machine.

You can avoid this problem in two ways. First, if you are not picky about the actual font used, employ the _sans, _serif, or _typewriter fonts available in the Font drop-down menu of the Property Inspector. Essentially, when you use these fonts (which are called *device fonts*—the fonts your operating system employs to display its own textual information), you are telling the Flash movie to use the equivalent fonts installed on your audience's computers. This way, you always know that your text will appear correctly.

Second, to keep your fonts from displaying incorrectly when your Flash creation is viewed, you can break apart the given text and turn it into shapes instead of text—a process covered in the "Breaking Apart Blocks of Text" section.

Besides the problem of users not having a certain font installed, you'll probably encounter some other specific font issues. For example, when it comes to Windows machines, PostScript fonts are prone to displaying incorrectly. As a result, it is strongly suggested that Windows users limit themselves to TrueType fonts.

Mac users need to be cautious when employing Adobe PostScript fonts. For the most part, PostScript fonts function properly, but in some situations they cause problems. Sometimes, PostScript fonts will display properly while you are creating your Flash movie but will display incorrectly when the movie is actually published.

Creating Type with the Text Tool

Although the vast majority of your text editing in Flash will be facilitated by the Property Inspector, you always need to start by actually creating some text—a process made possible by the Text tool **A** .

To use the Text tool, select it from the Toolbox, click anywhere on the Stage, and begin typing. Don't worry too much about how the text appears at this early stage of creation; you'll learn how you can get it to look exactly how you want in the next section.

> To edit text, simply click a text block with the Text tool (or double-click it with the Arrow tool), and make the changes you want. When finished, click anywhere outside the text box.

Setting Text Attributes

The Text tool is the primary method for creating text, and the Property Inspector is the primary tool for editing and manipulating it.

In Flash 8, three types of text exist: Static Text, Dynamic Text, and Input Text. Each type, which will be discussed in the following sections, has its own place and function within a Flash creation.

To create and edit each of the three types using the Property Inspector:

1. Open the Robert Frost.fla file on the CD, or insert some text onto the Stage using the Text tool.

2. Make sure your text box is "live" (or, editable), and select the text using your cursor (either all the text or specific portions). If you've deselected the text box, simply reselect it with the Arrow tool. (A light blue box will appear around the selected text block.) Selecting the entire text box applies any changes you make to the entire block of text.

3. Open the Property Inspector (Window → Properties → Properties).

4. Select the specific type of text you want to create from the Text Type drop-down menu (see Figure 3.1).

Figure 3.1

The Text Type drop-down menu in the Property Inspector lets you select the type of text you want to use.

From here, the Property Inspector will change to reflect that text type's specific properties, all of which are described in the following sections.

This step-by-step process describes how you can manipulate already existing text. If you want to create some text with specific properties, just select the Text tool from the Toolbox, open the Property Inspector, set the text properties (all of which are described next), and then insert the text onto the Stage. The inserted text will automatically have all the properties (font, color, size, and so on) that you set with the Property Inspector.

Working with Static Text

Although Static Text is the default type of text in Flash, it isn't always selected by default in the Text Type drop-down menu. Instead, the menu will default to the last text type used. So, if you used Dynamic Text that last time you created some text, that option will be automatically selected in the Text Type drop-down menu.

Beyond its innate ability to convey textual information, Static Text doesn't have any extra functionality—like Dynamic Text or Input Text (which will be discussed in the next sections). This doesn't mean Static Text isn't powerful—quite the contrary. Well-crafted type (both from a typographic perspective and from a content perspective) is extremely powerful and can add a dimension to your Flash movie that you cannot get with any other tool. As a result, you'll find that you'll probably use it the most, so it's good that you become intimately familiar with all the following Static Text options accessible through the Property Inspector (see Figure 3.2).

Font option This menu displays the current font when the Text tool is active. The list shows every font currently installed on your computer. You can choose a font with the Font drop-down menu before you begin typing, or you can select existing text within a text block (or the text block itself) and change its font with the Font drop-down menu.

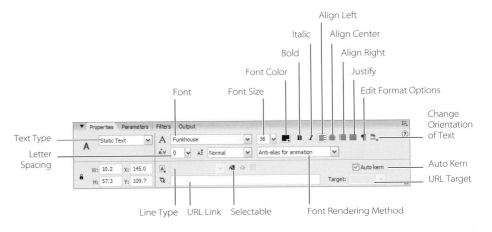

Figure 3.2

You can set Static Text properties in the Property Inspector.

> You can also change the font of selected text by choosing Text → Font and then picking from the list of fonts installed on your machine.

Font Size option This drop-down menu sets a font's size. You can either enter a value (in point size) in the Font Size field or use the Font Size slider (which is accessible by clicking the small down-arrow button to the right of the field).

> You can also change the font size by choosing Text → Size and picking from the sizes available.

Text Style option These options set the text to bold or italic. As with the rest of the options in the Property Inspector, you either select a block of text with the Arrow tool or use the Text tool to select the text when the text block is "live," and then click one of the style buttons. You can also click one of the style buttons before you create a new string of text.

> Unfortunately, the Property Inspector offers a limited array of style options. For more (though not many more) options, select Text → Style, and choose a style from the list, which includes Plain, Bold, Italic, Superscript, and Subscript.

Text Color option This option opens the Text Color palette so you can set your text's color. If you are unhappy with the available color choices, mix your own using the Color Picker (accessible by clicking the small color wheel in the top-right corner of the Text Color palette). You can also set the color's alpha setting by entering a value in the Alpha field.

Letter Spacing option This option represents the distance between characters in a string of text. The higher the Letter Spacing value, the farther apart the characters will be. Figure 3.3 illustrates different letter spacing, also referred to as *tracking*.

The Property Inspector lets you set the letter spacing for any given text block (either before or after it has been created). If the text has already been created, all you need to do is select the text block or the actual text and enter a value in the Letter Spacing field. Alternatively, you can use the Tracking slider, which is accessible by clicking the small down-arrow button just to the right of the Letter Spacing field, to adjust the amount of tracking.

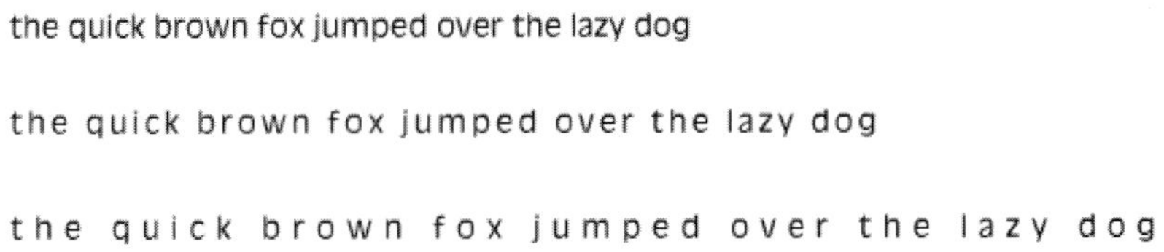

the quick brown fox jumped over the lazy dog

the quick brown fox jumped over the lazy dog

the quick brown fox jumped over the lazy dog

Figure 3.3

The top line of text has a character spacing of 0, the middle line has a character spacing of 2, and the bottom line has a character spacing of 5.

Character Position option Character Position, which is also referred to as *baseline shift* in graphic design, refers to how closely the text sits above or below its natural baseline (the bottom of the letters). By changing a text block's Character Position value, you can create superscript or subscript characters. Unlike most graphic design programs that allow you to set an exact baseline shift value, Flash gives you only three default settings: Normal, Superscript, and Subscript (see Figure 3.4).

this is some normal text

this is some superscript text

this is some subscript text

To set the character position, select a string of already created text, and choose one of the three baseline shift options from the Character Position drop-down menu. As with all the other options in the Property Inspector, you can also set the baseline shift *before* you create text with the Text tool.

> In addition to changing some text's Character Position value, you can also create superscript or subscript by choosing Text → Style → Superscript or by choosing Text → Style → Subscript.

Auto Kern option Checking the Auto Kern box evens out the spacing between individual characters in a string of text. When you select the Auto Kern option, you activate the built-in kerning option of many (but not all) fonts. In typography, *kerning* refers to the process of adjusting letter spacing in a `proportional font`. In a well-kerned font, blank spaces between letters all have similar widths.

> If you want to apply the Auto Kern option, a font must have kerning information built into the file; this is why some fonts will auto kern and others won't.

Change Orientation of Text option This button accesses a drop-down menu with options that change the direction of the selected text. The default Horizontal option makes the text flow from left to right horizontally. The two remaining options—the Vertical, Left to Right option and the Vertical, Right to Left option—make the text flow vertically. The difference between the two is that if you apply the Vertical, Left to Right option to a block of text with more than one line, the first line will remain the leftmost vertical line. However, if you choose the Vertical, Right to Left option, the last line in a text block with more than one line of text will be the leftmost vertical line.

Rotate Text option When you have the orientation of the text set to one of the vertical options, the Rotate Text button 🄳 changes the text's rotation. With rotation turned on, the individual characters will face downward. With rotation turned off, individual characters will face to the right. Figure 3.5 shows the differences between text with the rotation turned on and text with the rotation turned off.

> If you want to rotate text counterclockwise, you have to use the Rotate Text button to rotate the characters and then use the Modify menu to rotate the entire text block.

URL Link option Flash offers several ways in which to link to a URL, but the easiest method uses the URL Link field in the Property Inspector. Simply select the string of text you want to turn into a link, and type a URL in the URL Link field. Any Flash text to which you've attached a URL will appear on the Stage with a dotted underline.

> You can add a URL only to horizontal text.

URL Target option Because it's entirely possible that your Flash movie will be delivered in a framed Hypertext Markup Language (HTML) document, the URL Target drop-down menu lets you set the location in which the URL loads. Flash has four default options:

- Choosing _blank loads the link in a new browser window, maintaining the window in which the hyperlink was located just below the newly opened window.

- If you choose _parent, the document, when loaded, will occupy the entire area of the frameset document in which the link resides.

- Choosing _self (which is the default link target) simply opens the document in the frame where the link resides.

- If you choose _top, the document will be loaded into the uppermost (hierarchically speaking) frameset—wiping out all frames and nested framesets.

You can also manually enter a frame name in the URL Target field if you want to target a specific named frame in the HTML document.

Selectable option Under normal circumstances, Static Text is part of the Flash movie and is therefore not selectable as text would be in an HTML document, for example. However, if you want your audience to be able to select the Static Text in your movie (and therefore copy and paste it), make sure the Selectable button is toggled.

Font Rendering Method option The options in the Font Rendering drop-down menu let you control how Flash renders your text:

- By selecting the Use Device Fonts option, you tell Flash not to embed the font used in a given text block. Instead, Flash will look at the user's computer and employ the most appropriate font on their system to display the text. Ultimately, because the font information is not embedded, the SWF file's size will be slightly smaller.

- The Bitmap Text (No Anti-Alias) option turns off antialiasing—thereby providing no text smoothing. The resulting SWF's file size is increased because the font outlines are embedded in the file. Although bitmap text looks sharp at the exported size, it tends to look bad when it is scaled.

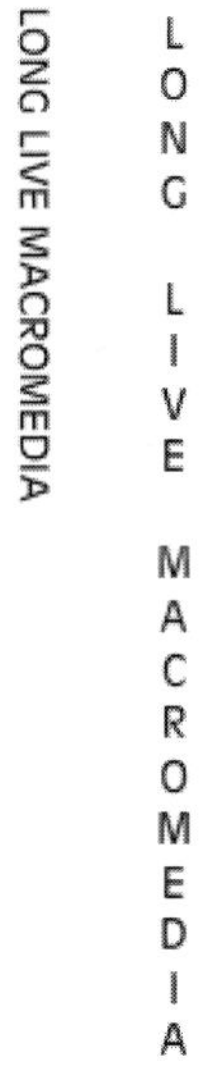

LONG LIVE MACROMEDIA

LONG LIVE MACROMEDIA

Figure 3.5

The text on the left has the rotation turned on, while the text on the right has the rotation turned off.

- When you select the Anti-Alias for Animation option, Flash optimizes your text so that it looks better when animated. When selected, this option results in a larger SWF file size because the font outlines are embedded in the file.

The Anti-Alias for Animation option creates text that is less legible at smaller sizes.

- The Anti-Alias for Readability option, which takes advantage of Flash 8's new text-rendering engine, greatly improves the legibility of fonts—especially at small sizes. Because font outlines are embedded when you use the Anti-Alias for Readability option, the size of your SWF file increases.

To use the Anti-Alias for Readability option, you must publish to Flash Player 8.

- The Custom Anti-Alias option opens the Custom Anti-Alias dialog box where you can modify the font's rendering properties as you see fit (see Figure 3.6). Sharpness determines the smoothness of the transition between the edge of the text and the background. Thickness determines how thick the transition between the text edge and the background is. The higher the value, the more robust the text looks.

The ActionScript parameters displayed at the bottom of the Custom Anti-Alias dialog box provide information about the sharpness of the text edge. If you want, you can override the inside and outside cutoff values by using the setAdvancedAntialiasingTable () method.

Alignment buttons The Property Inspector offers you four alignment options: Align Left, Center, Align Right, and Justify (see Figure 3.7). To align text, select a text block (or a string of text within a text block), and click one of the alignment buttons.

Edit Format Options button By clicking the Edit Format Options button ¶ , you can access a Format Options dialog box (see Figure 3.8); this box contains several options that affect the way in which an entire block of text (opposed to individual characters within the text block) looks.

Figure 3.6

Use the Custom Anti-Alias dialog box to change the font's rendering capabilities.

- The Indent setting changes the distance, in pixels, between the left side of the text box and the first line of text.
- The Line Spacing setting represents the vertical distance, in points, between lines in a text block. To set the line spacing, enter a value numerically in the Line Spacing field, or use the Line Spacing slider.

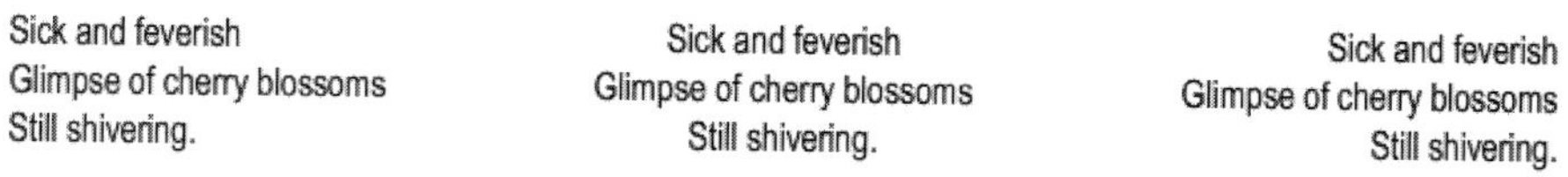
Sick and feverish
Glimpse of cherry blossoms
Still shivering.
Sick and feverish
Glimpse of cherry blossoms
Still shivering.
Sick and feverish
Glimpse of cherry blossoms
Still shivering.

Figure 3.7

This text shows the results of the three alignment options from left to right: Align Left, Center, and Align Right.

- When you set the left margin of a text block, you set the distance, in pixels, between the left side of the text box and the text itself. Enter a value numerically in the Left Margin field, or use the Left Margin slider.
- When you manipulate the right margin, you set the distance, in pixels, between the right side of the text box and the text itself. Enter a numerical value in the Right Margin field, or use the Right Margin slider.

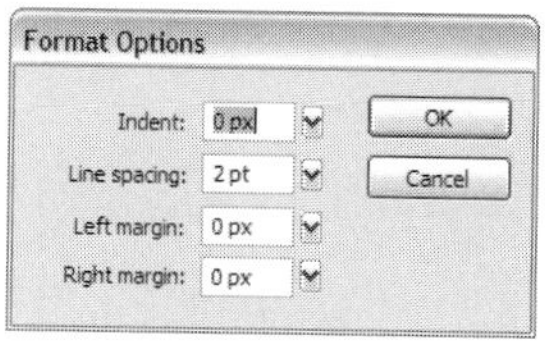
Format Options
Indent: 0 px
Line spacing: 2 pt
Left margin: 0 px
Right margin: 0 px
OK
Cancel

Figure 3.8

Use the Format Options dialog box to set the formatting of a block of text.

Working with Dynamic Text

When you create Dynamic Text, you produce a text box with content dynamically updated from another source, say, a database or text file on your server. So, Dynamic Text is not really fixed or unchanging *per se*, even though it's created in the same way as Static Text. Instead, it's sort of like a text container with contents that can change.

> If you are interested in exploring how you load external content into a Dynamic Text field, refer to Chapter 12.

If you want to create and manipulate Dynamic Text, you have to take an extra step that you wouldn't normally have to do if you were working with Static Text—you'll need to manually select Dynamic Text from the Property Inspector's Text Type drop-down menu.

From there, you'll be able to access other properties in the expanded Property Inspector when Dynamic Text is selected (see Figure 3.9).

Line Type option The Line Type option displays three choices: Single Line, Multiline, and Multiline No Wrap. Single Line displays the text as one line, and both Multiline and Multiline No Wrap display it as more than one line. The difference between the two multiline options is that Multiline No Wrap will break a single line into more than one line only if the last character is a breaking character, such as Enter/Return.

Instance Name field This box contains the name of the text block so that dynamic content intended for that specific text block will know exactly where it needs to go.

Properties
Parameters
Filters
Output
Dynamic Text
<Instance Name>
Arial Narrow
15
0
Normal
Anti-alias for readability
Embed...
W: 156.0
X: 263.9
H: 59.0
Y: 80.0
Single line
Var:
Auto kern
Target:

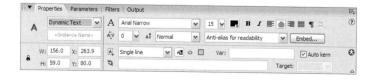

Figure 3.9

You can set many Dynamic Text options using the Property Inspector.

Make sure the name you enter in the Instance Name field is unique.

Var field Introduced in Flash 5, the Var field allows you to enter the name of the Action-Script variable associated with a particular string of Dynamic Text.

For more information on variables, refer to Chapter 9.

Selectable Text option This allows your audience to select the text within the Dynamic Text box, much as in the case of the Static Text option.

Render Text as HTML option This option tells Flash to allow you to use certain HTML tags in the text box for formatting its contents. Unfortunately, only some HTML tags are supported.

Flash supports only the following tags: `<a>`, `<b>`, `<br>`, `<font>`, `<img>`, `<i>`, `<li>`, `<p>`, `<span>`, and `<u>`. In addition, only some HTML entities are supported: `&lt;` (<), `&gt;` (>), `&amp;` (&), `&quot;` ("), and `&apos;` (').

Show Border Around Text option This tells Flash that you want the text box to be surrounded by a visible border.

Figure 3.10

Click the Edit Character Options button to open the Character Embedding dialog box.

Edit Character Options button When you click the Edit Character Options button (shown as the Embed button), the Character Options dialog box opens (see Figure 3.10).

From here, you can determine exactly how many characters of the font are embedded in the file. Embedding a character in the file allows Flash to "remember" how to render it when the movie plays back on a system that does not have the specific font you specified for the text box. The Character Embedding dialog box refers to characters as *glyphs* to remind you that elements of a font are not necessarily characters.

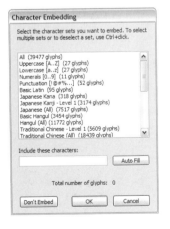

By clicking the Don't Embed button, you are instructing Flash to not store the shapes of any characters. You can include specific characters by typing them in the Include These Characters field. If you click the Auto Fill button, Flash reads all the text inside the text box and places each character appearing in its contents in the Include These Characters field. At the bottom of the Character Embedding dialog box, you will find a running total of the number of glyphs you have instructed Flash to store within the movie. The fewer characters of a font you embed, the smaller the resulting Flash movie.

Working with Input Text

Input Text is similar to Dynamic Text. The real difference is that data is traveling in the other direction—from the user to somewhere else (the movie, a server, and so on). Simply put, an Input Text box refers to the same kind of form field you see when working with HTML. Most of the Input Text options, which are available once you select Input Text from the Text Type drop-down menu in the Property Inspector, are the same as described previously (see Figure 3.11).

However, you'll see two additional options:

Password option Beyond the Single Line, Multiline, and Multiline No Wrap options in the Line Type drop-down menu, you have a fourth option: Password. Use the Password option to disguise the on-screen text to maintain password security.

> Selecting the Password option affects only the display of the text entered by the user. To make the password work, you have to use ActionScript to pass data to a server-side application or database; see Chapter 12.

Maximum Characters field Entering a numerical value in the Maximum Characters field limits the number of characters a user can enter in a given text field.

Creating a Scrollable Text Box

You can create scrollable text in a number of ways. You could create a custom scrollbar or use a UIScrollBar component (both of which are discussed in Chapter 8). If you are working with Dynamic Text, however, you have a far easier (though arguably feature-poor) way of creating scrollable text—by making the text box itself scrollable.

The odyssey.fla file on the CD shows a simple, yet complete, example of a scrollable text box.

> When you use the following technique, an interface element (a scrollbar, for example) is not added to the Dynamic Text. Instead, this allows the user just to scroll though text using their arrow keys if the amount of text exceeds the height of the field.

Figure 3.11

You can set Input Text properties using the Property Inspector just like with the other types of text.

You have three ways to make a text box scrollable:

- Shift+double-click the handle on the Dynamic Text block. The handle will turn from a hollow circle to a filled square.
- Select the Dynamic Text block with the Arrow tool, and select Text → Scrollable.
- Select the Dynamic Text block with the Arrow tool. Right-click / Ctrl+click and select Scrollable from the pop-up menu.

Creating a Font Symbol

If you are planning on creating and using a Shared Library, you would do well to become familiar with *font symbols.* Essentially, a font symbol allows you to stick any font into a Shared Library, which sits on a server somewhere. From there, any number of Flash movies can link to the Shared Library and use the font without it having to be embedded in their files, thereby reducing their overall sizes.

> It's important to note that when you are creating a Shared Library (something that will be discussed in much more detail in Chapter 4), you should make sure the FLA file (and eventually the SWF file) has nothing in it except those symbols that are going to be shared. In other words, don't create a movie that not only has its own content but also has content that will be shared with other movies. Keeping elements separate is considered a "best practice" in terms of Flash development.

To create a font symbol:

1. Open the FLA file you want to house the Shared Library. You can use the font symbols.fla movie on the CD.
2. Open the Library (Window → Library).
3. Choose Library Options → New Font. The Font Symbol Properties dialog box opens (see Figure 3.12).
4. In the Name field, enter the name for the font that will appear in the Library.

> The name you give isn't the official name of the font itself, just an identifier that you assign for your own purposes. The name can include any characters as well as spaces.

5. Select the actual font from the Font drop-down menu.
6. Choose whether you want the font symbol to be bold or italic.
7. If you want to use bitmap rendering, select the Bitmap Text check box.

The Bitmap Text option turns off antialiasing and provides no text smoothing. The text is displayed using sharp edges, and the resulting SWF file size increases because the font outlines are embedded in the SWF file. Bitmap text is sharp at the exported size but scales poorly.

8. If you are using bitmap text, enter a size in the Size field. If the Bitmap Text check box is not selected, any font size you enter in the Size field is ignored.

9. When you are finished, click OK.

Breaking Apart Blocks of Text

When you create text, it's inserted onto the Stage as a block. Whether it's a letter, a word, or an entire Shakespearean soliloquy, you can't independently manipulate (scale, skew, move, and so on) individual portions of the text block.

Although this is especially irksome, you can get around the problem easily. Essentially, you break the text block down into its parts.

Figure 3.12

Use the Font Symbol Properties dialog box to set the properties of a font symbol.

When you break text apart, you should be aware of two issues. First, broken-apart text increases your Flash movie's file size considerably. Second, once text is broken apart, you can no longer edit it with the Text tool.

To break apart the text:

1. Select a text block with the Arrow tool.

2. Choose Modify → Break Apart.

3. The result will be that the text block will be broken into its individual characters, each of which can be edited, moved, and manipulated independently of the others (see Figure 3.13).

Manipulating the Shape of Individual Characters

One of the really neat tricks you can do in Flash is manipulate the shape of the individual characters of a given font. If you don't like how the *G* looks in Arial, you can change it to look how you want. The process involves taking the text and breaking it apart several times.

Figure 3.13

This is the same block of text as it appears normally (left) and after it has been broken apart (right).

When you use the Break Apart command, you will affect only TrueType fonts. Bitmap fonts disappear when you break them apart, and PostScript fonts can be broken apart only on Mac systems running ATM.

To manipulate the shape of individual characters:

1. Make sure the Stage has some already created text.

2. Select the text box with the Arrow tool.

3. Choose Modify → Break Apart. At this point, the text should break down into a group of several selected items, each of which is composed of one character.

4. Without deselecting anything, again choose Modify → Break Apart.

5. Deselect the shape by clicking anywhere else on the Stage or by choosing Edit → Deselect All.

6. By doing this, you convert the text into a shape like any other. From here, you can use the Arrow tool to manipulate the shape of the character(s), as shown in Figure 3.14.

Figure 3.14

Once you've completely broken apart the text, you can manipulate the shape of the individual characters with the Arrow tool.

One of the coolest features of text that has been broken apart is that you can use the Ink Bottle tool to add an outline around the individual characters.

Using the Spell Checker

Just because Flash doesn't produce reams of text doesn't mean the text it does produce can't be misspelled. Hey, even the best spellers among us misspell a word or two now and then and need the occasional help of a spell checker. For those who can't spell our way out of a paper bag (ourselves included), the spell checker is that much more of a blessing.

The process by which you check your document's spelling involves two steps. First, you have to set the properties of the spell checker. Second, you run the spell checker, which includes dealing with any misspelled words that don't appear in your chosen dictionary.

To alter the spell checker's default settings:

1. Choose Text → Spelling Setup. The Spelling Setup dialog box appears (see Figure 3.15).

2. Set the scope of the spell-check by selecting one (or more) of the options from the Document Options section (in the top-left corner of the dialog box).

3. Select the dictionary to be used during the spell-check from the Dictionaries list.

Although you can choose as many dictionaries as you like, you need to choose at least one for the spell checker to work.

4. To use a personal dictionary (a text file composed of words you have designated), click the Browse for Personal Dictionary File button 🗁 next to the Path field. When the Open dialog box displays, navigate to the location of the text file you would like to use as the designated personal dictionary, select it, and click the Open button.

> Creating a personal dictionary is a handy feature if your Flash movie uses specialized words that aren't normally found in the general dictionaries.

5. To add words to your personal dictionary, click the Edit Personal Dictionary button. When your personal dictionary is open in the Edit Personal Dictionary dialog box, you can change the spelling of existing words and add new words (see Figure 3.16). Make sure you've spelled them correctly! When you've finished editing your personal dictionary, click the OK button.

6. To specify how the spell checker checks your document, select any of the choices in the Checking Options section of the Spelling Setup dialog box.

7. When you've finished setting the properties of the spell-check, click OK.

To check your movie's spelling:

1. Select Text → Check Spelling.

2. If you have any misspelled words (based on the search criteria you set in the Spelling Setup dialog box), the Check Spelling dialog box opens (see Figure 3.17).

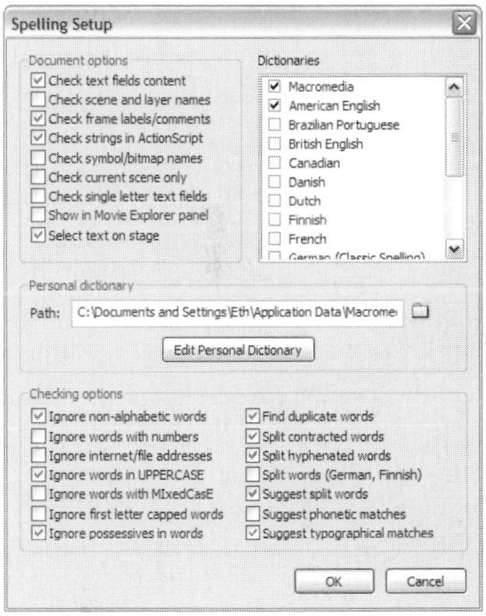

Figure 3.15

Open the Spelling Setup dialog box to set up the spell checker.

Figure 3.16

Use the Edit Personal Dictionary dialog box to create a custom list of correctly spelled words.

Figure 3.17

The Check Spelling dialog box lets you decide how to deal with misspelled words that were found during the spell-check.

3. From here, you have several options as to how you want to deal with misspelled words that were identified.

Click the Setup button in the Check Spelling dialog box if you want to open the Spelling Setup dialog box to change the way in which your document's spelling is checked.

- If the word in question is in fact spelled correctly (but simply doesn't appear in the dictionary or dictionaries you selected in the spell checker's properties), you can click the Add to Personal button.
- Click the Ignore button if you want the spell checker to ignore that single instance of the misspelled word.
- Click the Ignore All button if you want the spell checker to ignore all instances of the misspelled word in the current document.
- To change the spelling of the word, select one of the options from the Suggestions list. If you want, you can manually enter a correction in the Change To field. From there, click the Change button to make the correction. If you want to correct all instances of the misspelled word, click the Change All button instead of Change.
- If you want to remove the misspelled word entirely from the movie, click the Delete button.

4. When the spell-check ends, you'll be presented with a Spelling Check Complete dialog box with a simple OK button.

Controlling Text with ActionScript

Although you are going to be looking at ActionScript in many other chapters in this book, it is worth noting that both Dynamic Text and Input Text fields are instances of the TextField object. As such, once one is given an instance name, you can use Action-Script to set, change, and format the text field and its contents.

If you are unfamiliar with ActionScript, you can review Chapters 9 through 12 for a solid discussion of how the topics covered in the following sections fit into the overall ActionScript landscape.

Dynamically Setting the Properties of a Text Field

When you assign a text field an instance name, you can control the look of that text field using properties of the TextField object.

1. Open the text field manipulation.fla file on the CD, or add some text to the Stage—remember, if you want to manipulate the text field's properties with ActionScript, it has to be either Dynamic Text or Input Text.

2. Select the text field, open the Property Inspector (Window → Properties → Properties), and enter an instance name in the Instance Name field.

> The instance name needs to be unique.

3. From here, select the frame or the object (a button, for example) that will trigger the ActionScript to set or change the properties of the text field.

4. Open the Actions panel (Window → Actions).

5. In the ActionScript Toolbox section of the Actions panel, double-click one of the TextField properties (which are accessible by selecting ActionScript 2.0 Classes → Movie → TextField → Properties).

> If you are attaching the script to something other than a frame (a button, for example), you'll need to add an event handler before you add the script that will alter the text field's properties.

6. From there, alter the script that was added to the Script pane with the instance name of your text field. The following code sets the instance name of the text field to paraText and sets the values of the `textColor`, `border`, and `borderColor` properties:

```
paraText.textColor = 0xFf0000;
paraText.border = true;
paraText.borderColor = 0x00Ff00;
```

> For a complete list of TextField object properties and detailed descriptions of each, see "TextField Class" in the ActionScript 2.0 Language Reference, accessible by selecting Help → Flash Help.

Remember, you can always type the script manually in the Script pane.

Using ActionScript to Dynamically Manipulate Text

In Flash 8, you can control the formatting of either Dynamic Text or Input Text fields with the TextFormat object. Working with the TextFormat object can seem a little strange at first (especially for those who might just be starting out with ActionScript) because it is essentially nothing more than formatting properties (that is, font family, font size, font color, and so on) that are then applied to a text field. The part that people often find confusing is that the TextFormat object, when used, is completely separate from the actual text field to which you want to apply the properties. Frankly, this is the point of an object. You can create your formatting properties once and then apply them to many text fields. This means you keep your formatting in one place—and you can change the look of many text fields by changing one value (namely, that of the TextFormat object) rather than changing the value in every text field.

You'll find a completed version of the following steps in the `text property manipulation.fla` file on the CD.

To create a TextFormat object and set its properties:

1. Select the first keyframe of your main Timeline, open the Actions panel (Window → Actions), and add the following code to the Script pane to create the TextFormat object:

   ```
   var myTextFormat = new TextFormat ();
   ```

   This line of code creates a new TextFormat object and stores it in a variable named `myTextFormat`.

2. Go to the next line (after the one in which you defined the TextFormat object). To do that, enter the name of the TextFormat object (in this case it's `myTextFormat`), then a dot, then the name of the property you want to define, then an equals sign, and then the property's value. The following example code defines three properties (`font`, `size`, and `color`):

   ```
   myTextFormat.font = "Arial";
   myTextFormat.size = 12;
   myTextFormat.color = 0x006699;
   ```

   For a complete list of TextFormat object properties and detailed descriptions of each, see "TextFormat Class" in the ActionScript 2.0 Language Reference, accessible by selecting Help → Flash Help. You can also go online to `http://www.macromedia.com/support/flash/action_scripts/actionscript_dictionary/actionscript_dictionary788.html` to see detailed descriptions of the TextFormat object's properties.

Now that you have a TextFormat object (named `myTextFormat`) with some formatting values, you can apply this TextFormat object to a text field. Every text field has available to it a method called `setTextFormat ()`.

To apply a TextFormat object to a text field:

1. Add some text to the Stage—remember, it has to be either Dynamic Text or Input Text.

2. Select the text field, open the Property Inspector (Window → Properties → Properties), and enter an instance name in the Instance Name field.

   The instance name needs to be unique.

3. From here, select the frame or the object (a button, for example) that will invoke the `setTextFormat ()` method to apply the TextFormat object to the text field.

4. Open the Actions panel (Window → Actions).

> Remember that if you are attaching the script to something other than a frame (a button, for example), you'll need to add an event handler before you add the script outlined in step 5.

5. In the Script pane, type the name of the text field (in this case, `infoTextField` is the instance name), followed by a dot, followed by the name of the method (in this case, `setTextFormat ()`), and finally followed by the name of the TextFormat object you want to apply to the text field, as follows:

```
infoTextField.setTextFormat (myTextFormat);
```

Formatting Text with Cascading Style Sheets

When you are working with Static Text and want to change the properties, all you have to do is select the text and change the options in the Property Inspector. But what happens when you want to change the appearance of text that is loaded into a Dynamic Text field? In the previous two sections, we discussed some solutions to this problem. However, as you saw, the range of properties you can manipulate is limited—at least compared to what you can do in a traditional print document. This is where HTML and Cascading Style Sheets (CSS) come into the picture.

> The supported HTML options are covered in the "Working with Dynamic Text" section earlier in this chapter.

In the previous versions of Flash (Flash MX 2004 and Flash MX 2004 Professional), Macromedia introduced a feature that allowed you to style dynamic text using CSS. However, as opposed to the ActionScript-based methods already discussed), CSS offers you a far wider range of formatting that can be applied to text, thereby allowing you to manipulate your text with a far greater degree of control and precision.

> This section assumes you are already familiar with the process of loading content from an external source, such as an Extensible Markup Language (XML) file, a text file, a database, and so on, into a Dynamic Text box. If you are neither familiar nor comfortable with the process, see Chapter 12. This chapter also assumes you have at least a rudimentary understanding of how CSS works.

You can use CSS to style dynamic text in three ways (each of which are based on the same principles). The first way involves using an external CSS file to style text with HTML markup (and rendered as HTML) that has been manually entered into a dynamic text field. The second way involves using CSS markup directly in the Flash authoring environment. For example, if you were writing some script that specifies a string of text be inserted into a field, you could include CSS markup directly in that text. The third way, which is a variation of the first, is to load an external CSS file directly into Flash, and then use the information within that file to style text that has been dynamically loaded from an external file of some sort (text, etc.) .

> To get a full list of all the supported CSS properties supported in Flash, see "Supported CSS Properties" in the ActionScript 2.0 Language Reference, accessible by selecting Help → Flash Help.

When it comes to working with an external style sheet, you'll need to write a new object called `TextField.stylesheet`—which allows you to dynamically load styles from an external style sheet and then apply those styles to content that is either being loaded into a Dynamic Text field or is already present (manually entered) into a Dynamic Text field.

The files `css_text.fla` and `style.css` on the CD show the complete steps for the following exercise.

To style existing text in a Dynamic Text field with an external CSS file:

1. Add a new text box to your Flash movie. If you haven't already, change its type to Dynamic. Make sure you've set the contents of the text box to render as HTML by selecting the text box and then clicking the Render Text as HTML button ⟨⟩ . You also need to make sure that the text box's Line Type is set to Multiline No Wrap.

> By selecting the Render Text as HTML button I'm ensuring that any HTML tags that are included in either the externally loaded text or the manually entered text are properly displayed.

2. Give the Dynamic Text box an instance name. In the code used in this example, the instance name used is `intro_text`.

3. Select the first keyframe of your main Timeline, and open the Actions panel (Window → Actions)

4. In the Script pane, enter the following script that will create the necessary `TextField.stylesheet` object:

```
var cascadingstyles = new TextField.StyleSheet();
```

This code creates the `TextField.StyleSheet` object, and stores it in a variable called `cascadingstyles`.

5. Then, enter the following code just below the code you entered in the previous steps:

```
var path = "style.css";
```

This code creates a variable, called `path`, which contains the location of the external CSS file. If the CSS file was not located in the same directory as the SWF file, you would need to provide the full path.

6. From there, enter the following code just below the line of code you entered in the previous steps:

```
var text = "<p class='styled_text'>CSS is the best thing to happen
since sliced bread.</p>;
```

This line of code creates a variable called `text` which contains the text, complete with HTML tags and reference to a CSS class (in this case, `styled_text`) which will be displayed in the text box. While this example only has a single line of text, you could have easily added as much as you want.

7. On the next line, enter the following code:

```
format.load(path);
```

This code tells Flash to load the CSS file (the path of which is contained in the `path` variable) to the variable `cascadingstyles` (which contains the `TextField.StyleSheet` object).

8. On the next line, enter the following code:

```
format.onLoad = function(success) {
if (success) {
    output.styleSheet = cascadingstyles;
    output.text = path;
} else {
    output.text = "Error loading CSS file!";
 }
};
```

This function (called `success`) applies the CSS formatting to your text field. Before the CSS file is applied, however, we need to make sure that the CSS file loads before the text is displayed in the text field. Only after the CSS file loads is Flash told to load and format the text into the text field (with, as outlined in step 2, an instance name of `intro_text`).

Of course, there might be times when the CSS might not load. This is where the `else` portion of the above code comes into play. If the CSS file doesn't load properly, the error text will be displayed in the text field.

If you had wanted, you could have attached the code outlined in step 8 to a button—so that instead of the text being loaded and the CSS file being applied automatically when the playhead hits the first keyframe, the code is activated when the user clicks a button. Remember, however, that you need to insert the appropriate event handler.

Now that you've looked at the techniques you'll need to style text in Flash with an external style sheet, the big question is, why would you want to do this? A couple of important reasons exist—beyond that CSS allows you exert a great deal of visual control over your text. First, if you use a CSS file to style externally loaded text, you don't have to go into the SWF file to change how the text looks. All you'd need to do is make changes in the CSS file—which is far easier. If you were working with a client, you might even let them make the modifications themselves. The other cool feature of working with style sheets in Flash is that you could actually create one style sheet and use it both for your XHTML web page and for the externally loaded text in your SWF file—thereby creating a unified identity.

CHAPTER 4

Working with Symbols

Symbols are easily one of the most powerful tools in Flash. They allow you to create reusable elements. Some of these symbols, such as Movie Clip and Button symbols, have built-in properties, such as animation or interactivity, while some are simpler, such as Graphic symbols. Symbols help streamline the creative process and maximize your artistic juices. They are the core of any quality Flash movie. In this chapter, you will look at how to work with Graphic symbols and Movie Clip symbols. (We'll cover Button symbols in Chapter 8 when we talk about interactive controls.)

- ▪ **Getting to know symbols**

- ▪ **Working with Graphic symbols**

- ▪ **Creating Movie Clip symbols**

- ▪ **Using the Library to work with symbols**

- ▪ **Implementing symbol instances**

- ▪ **Tutorial: Creating an Underwater Scene with Movie Clips**

Understanding Symbols

Symbols are reusable elements that reside in the Library. You can use them repeatedly in either the same Flash creation or another one entirely. Whenever you create a symbol, it is automatically placed in the Library, where it is stored for future use. When you drag a symbol from the Library onto the Stage, the symbol itself is not placed on the Stage. Instead, Flash creates a copy, called an *instance,* and places it on the Stage. You can change instances as many times or in as many different ways as you want without altering the original symbol. In other words, you will always find the original symbol in the Library. Each FLA has its own Library, but you can import symbols from other FLAs, too.

> You can create complex animations with symbols only. As a result, it's important that most, if not all, of the graphical elements you create in Flash are either converted to symbols or created as symbols from the start.

Symbols are beneficial for a couple of reasons. First, they allow you to streamline the creative process. All you need to do is create a single symbol and then manipulate its instance on the Stage to create multiple variations without having to re-create the element from scratch every time. Second, symbols are powerful because they help you reduce the overall file size of your Flash creation. Each time you use a symbol, Flash simply refers to the profile of the original in the Library. If you're using multiple instances based on a single symbol, Flash needs to save only the information about their differences, thereby eliminating repetitive information. If you were to use a different symbol for each similar object, each symbol's information would be included in the Flash file, increasing the overall file size.

You'll be working with three primary types of symbols in Flash:

Graphic symbols Graphic symbols are static graphic objects created with the various Flash drawing and painting tools. They work in conjunction with the main movie and are most commonly used as elements in Timeline animations.

Button symbols While the Graphic symbols are static elements, Button symbols are dynamic, altering their appearance when clicked. Buttons are one of the most popular interactive elements you can create in Flash. Although you'll explore Button symbols (and how you make them) in Chapter 8, it's important to know they consist of four static images (referred to as *states*). Each state is visible based on how the user interacts with the button: when the button is "up," i.e., not clicked, (the Up state); when the user's mouse is over the button (the Over state); when the user clicks the button (the Down state). The fourth button state, the Hit state, is not a visible element in the button. Instead, it acts more like a hotspot that determines the active area of the button.

One of the most important features of Button symbols, at least in terms of creating interactivity, is that they can be tightly integrated with ActionScript.

Movie Clip symbols It's no exaggeration to say that Movie Clip symbols  are probably one of the most important aspects of Flash. Movie Clips are small, self-contained movies that you can place within another movie. They are infinitely nestable, so you could have a Movie Clip within a Movie Clip within a Movie Clip, and so on.

Movie Clips, which are in no way limited in their composition, run *independently* of the Timeline. You can also place them within other symbols; for example, you could insert a Movie Clip into a Button symbol state, thereby creating an animated button.

Movie Clips become even *more* powerful when you realize that they can be controlled using ActionScript. As a result, you could have any number of Movie Clips in your movie and send various commands to them (based on either user interaction or some purely non-user-based occurrence in your movie) using ActionScript.

To learn more about ActionScripting for movies with multiple Movie Clips (referred to as *multiple Timelines*), check out Chapter 14.

Creating Graphic Symbols

Graphic symbols are the most basic of the symbols you'll find in Flash. That doesn't mean they aren't useful—quite the contrary. Although they are static (unlike an animated Movie Clip or an interactive Button symbol), they are the workhorses of animations you create in the Timeline—a process that we will cover thoroughly in Chapter 6. In the meantime, the following sections explore how you create Graphic symbols.

Creating Graphic Symbols from Scratch

When it comes to Graphic symbols, it's more than likely you'll create most within Flash with the painting and drawing tools:

1. Choose Insert → New Symbol. The Create New Symbol dialog box opens (see Figure 4.1).

   You can switch to the advanced options in the Create New Symbol dialog box by clicking the Advanced button. The options available in the Advanced section relate to creating a Shared Library, which is discussed in the section "Working with Shared Symbol Libraries" later in this chapter.

Figure 4.1

Open the Create New Symbol dialog box when you want to create a Graphic symbol.

2. In the Create New Symbol dialog box, make sure the Graphic radio button is selected, enter a name for your symbol in the Name field, and click OK.

> If your Flash creation will use a great deal of graphics, it's a good strategy to give each symbol a distinct name so you won't get confused. By default, if you don't name the symbol, Flash will use the name *Symbol X*, where *X* is a sequential number.

3. From here, Flash adds the symbol to the Library and switches you to the Symbol Editor (see Figure 4.2). The name of the symbol appears in the Edit toolbar, just to the right of the name of the scene in which you're currently working. For reference, the symbol's registration point is represented by the crosshairs in the middle of the Symbol Editor.

4. Create the desired symbol with Flash's painting and drawing tools. Alternatively, you can import an object created in another application (such as a vector file created in Adobe Illustrator).

5. When you're finished, you need to exit the Symbol Editor. To do this, either choose Edit → Edit Document, click the scene name in the Edit toolbar, or click the back button ⇦ .

> The Symbol Editor is a little tricky in that it looks almost exactly like the regular Flash environment. Don't get confused, though; you can tell the difference because the symbol's name is displayed in the Edit toolbar just to the right of the actual scene's name, and a small cross, representing the symbol's eventual registration point, appears on the Stage.

Figure 4.2

The Symbol Editor enables you to create your symbol with the same painting and drawing tools you use in the Stage.

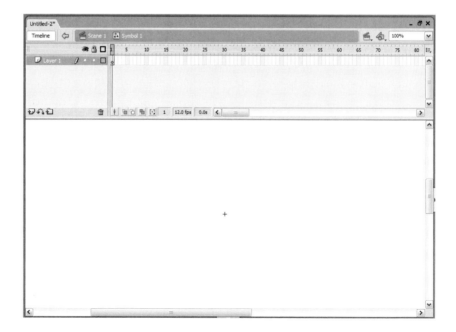

Converting Existing Objects to Symbols

Although you'll probably make many of your Graphic symbols from scratch, you might occasionally need to convert an existing object (something you didn't create in the Symbol Editor) into a symbol:

1. On the Stage, select the object you want to turn into a Graphic symbol.

2. Choose Modify → Convert to Symbol.

3. When the Convert to Symbol dialog box opens, make sure you select the radio button appropriate for the type of symbol you want to create.

4. Enter a name for your symbol in the Name field.

5. From here, you can set the location of your symbol's registration point. To do this, click one of the nine small boxes in the registration point diagram. Each box represents the location of the symbol's registration point within its square bounding box (see Figure 4.3).

> The registration point is "sticky." Flash remembers the last symbol you created, and uses the same registration point.

6. When you're finished, click OK; the symbol is automatically added to the Library. The original object you converted on the Stage is switched into an instance with a parent symbol residing in the Library.

Working with Movie Clip Symbols

It's not an exaggeration to say that Movie Clips are probably one of the most useful elements in Flash. Movie Clips are essentially self-contained movies that you can nest within your primary movie. Because they are self-contained, their Timelines run independently of the main Timeline.

You can use Movie Clips in conjunction with other symbols or alone on the Stage. For instance, you could place a Movie Clip in one of the states of a Button symbol to create an animated button—a process we'll discuss in Chapter 8. One of the great things about Movie Clips is that, unlike regular Timeline animations that use a great deal of frames and keyframes, Movie Clips need only one keyframe in the main Timeline to run.

> If you are unfamiliar with animation, check out Chapter 6 for a far more in-depth discussion.

Because Movie Clips run independently of the main Timeline, they can be quite detached from your main movie. Say, for instance, that you have an animation in which several birds (each of which is a Movie Clip) fly across the sky. Under normal circumstances, the

Figure 4.3

You can use the Convert to Symbol dialog box to convert objects to symbols; note the registration point diagram.

Movie Clips will either loop or play once and stop—both actions are pretty limiting when it comes to intricate animations. This, however, is where ActionScript comes into the picture.

Flash's scripting language, ActionScript, allows you to exert enormous control over how a Movie Clip behaves within the main Timeline. Essentially, you can write simple (or complex) scripts that control the behavior of an individual Movie Clip. For example, returning to the "flock" of birds example, you could write a script that would make sure none of the Movie Clips ever comes in contact with one another. If you were really ambitious, you could write a script that would force the bird Movie Clips to emulate flocking behavior.

Creating a Movie Clip from Scratch

When you create a Movie Clip from scratch, you draw on Timeline animation skills (which we will cover in Chapter 6):

1. Choose Insert → New Symbol.

2. When the Create New Symbol dialog box opens, make sure the Movie Clip radio button is selected, enter a name in the Name field, and click OK.

3. This opens the Symbol Editor. From here, use the Timeline in the Symbol Editor to create an animation. Remember, a Movie Clip is the same as a regular Timeline animation. You can use any of the Timeline animation techniques (tweening, frame by frame, special effects, Timeline Effects, and so on) that are covered in Chapter 6. You also aren't limited to a single animated object in a single layer—you could have multiple layers with multiple animated objects.

> Because Movie Clips can contain complex animations, you will probably need to use Graphic symbols. You can create them directly from within the Movie Clip much as you would from the main Timeline, and they're automatically placed in the main movie's Library for future use.

4. When you're finished crafting the animation in your Movie Clip, return to the main Timeline either by clicking the scene link in the Edit toolbar, by clicking the back button ⇦ in the Edit bar, or by selecting Edit → Edit Document.

5. Once you've returned to the main Timeline, you can view and test your Movie Clip by opening the Library (Window → Library), selecting the Movie Clip, and clicking the Play button ▶ in the preview window's top-right corner.

> You can also test the Movie Clip's animation directly from within the Symbol Editor—just hit the Enter/Return key.

Converting an Existing Animation into a Movie Clip

It's more than likely that the majority of Movie Clips you create will be produced from scratch. However, you might want to occasionally turn an existing animation into a Movie Clip:

1. In the main Timeline, select every frame in every layer that you want to turn into a Movie Clip.

2. Copy the frames you've selected by choosing Edit → Timeline → Copy Frames.

3. Select Insert → New Symbol.

> Make sure nothing on the Stage is selected before you insert a new symbol.

4. When the Create New Symbol dialog box opens, enter a name in the Name field, select the Movie Clip radio button, and click OK.

5. When the Symbol Editor opens, select the first frame in the Timeline, and choose Edit → Timeline → Paste Frames. This pastes all the copied frames into the Movie Clip.

6. To return to the main Timeline, either click the scene link in the Edit bar, click the back button ⇦ , or select Edit → Edit Document.

7. Now that you've returned to the main Timeline, you can remove the animation you copied to create the Movie Clip (if you so desire). Just reselect all the frames that you previously selected and then delete them by choosing Edit → Timeline → Cut Frames.

Using the Library to Work with Symbols

The Library, accessible by choosing Window → Library, is the repository for all symbols in a given Flash movie. Whether you're using Graphic symbols, Button symbols, or Movie Clip symbols, the Library is where they'll be. In the following sections, you'll learn how to use the Library to manage and manipulate the symbols within your movie.

Adding a Symbol to the Stage

The Library is a two-way street: you can place symbols on the Stage just as easily as you can add them to the Library.

> Remember that when you place a symbol onto the Stage, you're creating an *instance*. An instance is a copy of the parent symbol that you can change and manipulate without altering the original symbol.

To add a symbol to the Stage:

1. Open the Library by choosing Window → Library.

2. Click and drag the desired symbol onto the Stage.

Changing a Symbol's Name

When you initially create a symbol, you give it a name. You have a number of quick and easy ways to change the name:

1. Open the Library (Window → Library).

2. Select the symbol that has the name you want to change.

3. Do one of the following:

   • Right-click / Ctrl+click,and choose Rename. When the current name is highlighted in the Library, enter a new name.

   • Choose Options → Rename. When the current name is highlighted, just enter a new one.

   • Choose Options → Properties (or click the Properties button 🔳 in the bottom of the Library) to open the Symbol Properties dialog box. From here, enter a new name in the Name field.

   • Double-click the symbol name (not the symbol icon), and enter a new name.

Duplicating Symbols

Flash allows you to duplicate symbols in the Library with a minimum of trouble. You might find this handy if you've created a complex symbol that you wanted to copy, alter, and then add to the Library. Instead of a complex process, you can easily duplicate the symbol and then edit the copy in whichever way you want. Also, duplicating a symbol allows you to create a new symbol (to which you can make any changes) without actually changing any of that symbol's instances on the Stage. Further, it's a great process if you want to make drastic experimental changes to a symbol without risking the original.

To duplicate a symbol:

1. Open the Library (Window → Library).

2. Select the symbol you want to duplicate.

3. Do one of the following:

   • Right-click / Ctrl+click, and choose Duplicate.

   • Choose Options → Duplicate

4. When the Duplicate Symbol dialog box opens, enter a new name. If you want to retain the original format, make sure to select the appropriate radio button. If you want to turn the duplicate symbol into an alternative format, click the desired radio button.

5. Click OK. The duplicated symbol is automatically placed in the Library.

6. From here, you can edit the duplicate symbol and make any changes you want.

Editing a Symbol

Sometimes you might want to make more significant changes to a symbol that go beyond changing its name:

1. Open the Library (Window → Library).

2. Select the symbol you want to edit.

3. Do one of the following:

    • Double-click the symbol's icon (to the left of the symbol name in the Sort window).

    • Right-click / Cmd+click, and choose Edit.

    • Choose Options → Edit in the Library.

4. When Flash switches to the Symbol Editor, make any changes you want.

5. When you're finished, you need to exit the Symbol Editor. To do this, choose Edit → Edit Document, click the Scene link in the Edit toolbar, or click the back button ⇐ .

When you change a symbol, all its associated instances automatically change as well.

Organizing Your Library

As your experience with Flash develops, you'll find that many of your projects use a large number of symbols. This can certainly lead to some work flow and organizational problems. You can solve this problem in several ways.

The first solution involves creating various folders to organize similar symbols (see Figure 4.4). Just as you can create folders in a website to better organize your files, you can make folders in a Flash Library to categorize your symbols, bitmaps, and sounds.

To create a folder, click the New Folder button 🗊 in the bottom-left corner of the Library. You can also choose Options → New Folder in the Library. From here, simply click and drag the various symbols into their intended folders. Alternatively, you can also select a symbol and choose Options → Move to New Folder in the Library.

The second way to organize your Library, which has decidedly less of an impact on the Library's overall organization (but is nonetheless useful), involves using the Sort window's columns. By clicking the name of either the Date Modified column or the Name column, you reorganize the contents of the Library in descending order.

Figure 4.4

You can organize your Library by categorizing symbols by folder.

Opening External Flash Libraries

One of the great features of Flash is that you're not limited to the Library that is being used in your current Flash project; you can also open another Flash movie's Library by using the Open External Library option.

> An external Library isn't a different kind of file. Essentially, it just contains regular FLA files, the Library contents of which you've taken and put in your Library. Because of this, no special procedure exists for creating an external Library; you just need to create a Flash movie like any other.

To open external Libraries:

1. Open the Library (Window → Library).

2. Choose File → Import → Open External Library.

3. When the Open as Library dialog box opens, navigate to the FLA file that has the Library you want to access, select it, and click Open. The external Library appears as another Library panel in your movie.

> If you've undocked your Library, the new Library window might open directly on top of the old one. Drag the new Library window until you can see both windows.

4. Click and drag any symbol from the newly opened Library to your current movie's Library. This automatically copies the desired symbol from the imported Library into your current movie's Library; you can use the symbol as you would any other.

Working with Shared Symbol Libraries

As Flash development teams become larger and projects become more complex, sharing assets becomes important. With Shared Symbol Libraries, also referred to as *Shared Library Assets* or *Shared Libraries,* you can use graphics, buttons, movies, audio files, and other assets in your movie by linking to the Library of a centrally located SWF file (on a web server, for example). The result is that a Flash movie no longer has to have its own Library.

NAVIGATING BETWEEN MULTIPLE OPEN LIBRARIES

As you know, you can have multiple FLA files open in the Flash authoring environment at any given time. However, to access the Library of one movie from within another, you would have to open that Library in the same way you would access the Library of a FLA file that wasn't even open—by opening it as an external Library. In Flash 8, this has changed. The Library now has a drop-down menu that allows you to toggle between the libraries of any open Flash file—a handy feature if you don't want to have multiple Library panels open at the same time.

The beauty of Shared Symbol Libraries is that teams can share a standard set of symbols across multiple movies. You can make any final modification to a symbol in the Shared Library. After the Shared Library has been published, any other movies that use the Shared Library are updated automatically. In addition, when you draw your symbols from a Shared Symbol Library, your final movie doesn't need any embedded symbols and therefore is smaller.

Although Shared Symbol Libraries are beneficial to large projects, they have, unfortunately, proven to be somewhat unreliable and unpredictable. We strongly suggest that if you need to use Shared Libraries, you limit their use to storage of relatively small elements (in terms of file size).

Before you learn how to create and work with Shared Symbol Libraries, you need to learn about the two models for Shared Libraries: *runtime* and *author-time*.

- In a runtime Shared Symbol Library, assets are loaded into the destination movie from a source movie when the movie actually plays. Although the source movie (the movie you're drawing the symbols from) doesn't have to be accessible when you initially author the movie, it must be posted to a web server and be accessible for the destination movie to draw the symbols at runtime. Using a runtime Shared Symbol Library is really appropriate only when you're distributing your Flash movie on the Web; this way, it will have access to the actual Shared Symbol Library.

- In an author-time Shared Symbol Library, you can replace any symbol in the movie you're currently working on with a symbol from another movie. Although the symbol in the destination movie retains its original name and properties, its contents are replaced. For example, you could use an author-time Shared Symbol Library when you want to integrate symbols into your movie that were created by someone else. The primary difference between an author-time Shared Symbol Library and a runtime Shared Symbol Library is that the source movie must be accessible on your local network (or on your hard drive). Because you integrate symbols from a Shared Symbol Library into your own movie when you're creating it, you can use author-time Shared Symbol Libraries whether you're distributing your movie over the Web or by some other means.

Creating a Runtime Shared Symbol Library

Creating and using a runtime Shared Symbol Library involves two steps. The first step involves creating the source movie (in which the Shared Symbol Library resides) and identifying symbols (through the use of unique names) within the source movie. Assigning unique identifiers for symbols in the Shared Symbol Library is vital so that the destination movie can successfully locate and acquire the symbols it needs to run properly.

If you plan to use a runtime Shared Symbol Library, get into the habit of using the same name for the unique identifier as you did for the symbol's actual name; this might avoid some confusion in the long run.

The second step, which you do when you create the destination movie, involves telling Flash that the symbols being used will be drawn from a source movie at runtime.

To create a runtime Shared Symbol Library:

1. Create or import all the elements you want to include in the final runtime Shared Symbol Library and add them to the currently active movie's Library.

2. If you want to include an entire font in your Shared Symbol Library, choose Options → New Font in the Library. When the Font Symbol Properties dialog box opens, type a name for the font you want to include, locate the font in the Font menu, and select the style you want to include (see Figure 4.5).

Figure 4.5

Use the Font Symbol Properties dialog box to include a font.

3. Delete all objects from your Stage that will be included in the final Shared Symbol Library.

Now that you've included all the symbols that will reside in the final runtime Shared Symbol Library, you need to assign a unique identifier to each so that the destination movie can successfully locate and use them:

1. Select one of the symbols in the Library on which you're working.

2. From here, you have two options:

   - Choose Options → Linkage in the Library.
   - Select Options → Properties in the Library. In the Symbol Properties dialog box that opens, click the Advanced button. The Shared Symbol Library's advanced options appear (see Figure 4.6).

3. Select the Export for Runtime Sharing option.

4. Type a unique name (without any spaces) in the Identifier field.

5. Enter the URL for the place where the source SWF file will be located into the URL field. The cool thing about this step is that because this URL will be the same for every symbol within the shared library, Flash automatically populates the URL field with the same path for every subsequent symbol.

The URL you enter in the URL field must be absolute (for example, `http://someURL.com/movies/mymovie.swf`, not `/movies/mymovie.swf`). If you don't place the source movie in the location you set or you don't enter the correct URL, the destination movie will not be able to locate and draw the necessary symbols.

6. Repeat the process for each symbol that will be included in the final Shared Symbol Library.

> Although the process of tagging each symbol with a unique identifier is tedious (especially if you have a lot of symbols), it is necessary. Any of the symbols that aren't assigned a unique identifier will not work properly in the final Shared Symbol Library.

7. When you're finished identifying all the desired symbols as assets within the runtime Shared Symbol Library, click OK.

Now that you've set up all the properties of the source movie (which will act as the runtime Shared Symbol Library), save and publish:

1. Save the currently open Flash file (which contains the Library on which you've been working). So you don't get confused later, make sure you give the file a distinct name that will identify it specifically as containing a runtime Shared Symbol Library.

2. From here, publish the FLA file as a SWF file (Flash's web format). All you need to do is select File → Publish Settings. Make sure Flash is the only format chosen in the Formats tab. Beyond that, you don't need to set any other option.

3. Once you're finished adjusting the necessary publish settings, click OK. Then choose File → Publish. The SWF file will be saved to the same directory where you saved the original FLA file on which you were working.

4. Take the SWF file (which includes the tagged symbols) and upload it to the server with the URL that corresponds to what you entered in the URL field.

Figure 4.6

You can view the advanced Shared Symbol Library options in the Symbol Properties dialog box.

Linking to a Runtime Shared Symbol Library

Now that you've created a runtime Shared Symbol Library (the source movie), you can use its assets in another Flash movie (the destination movie).

The effect of linking to a runtime Shared Symbol Library is something like opening external Flash Libraries. The most important difference is that when you change a symbol in your runtime Shared Symbol Library (source movie), you change all the linked symbols in the destination movies that use it.

> Unless you have a copy of the symbol you want to draw from the runtime Shared Symbol Library (source movie) in the destination movie's Library, you won't be able to do any linking at all. Although this seems a little counterproductive (what's the point of drawing the symbol from a runtime Shared Symbol Library if it's already in the destination movie?), it's important to realize that the symbol won't actually get exported if it has been linked to a runtime Shared Symbol Library. It really just acts as a placeholder in your movie.

To link to a Library:

1. Create a new Flash movie (or open an existing one) to act as the destination movie.

2. Open the movie's Library (Window → Library).

3. Make sure that copies of the symbol you want to draw from the runtime Shared Symbol Library (source movie) are in the Library of the newly created movie. You can do this by opening both Libraries and then dragging the symbols from the source movie into the target movie.

4. Select the Graphic, Movie Clip, or Button symbol, and open the Symbol Properties dialog box by choosing Options → Properties in the Library. If the Symbol Properties dialog box isn't expanded, click the Advanced button.

5. Select the Import for Runtime Sharing option.

6. Enter the unique identifier for the symbol you're drawing from the runtime Shared Symbol Library (source movie) in the Identifier field.

> If you don't enter the exact identifier in the field, the destination movie will not be able to locate the symbol you want to use.

7. In the URL field, enter the exact location for where the runtime Shared Symbol Library (source movie) is posted.

> If you don't enter the exact URL, the destination movie won't be able to locate the source movie or access the required symbol.

8. When you're finished, click OK.

Severing the Link to a Runtime Shared Symbol Library

Although linking to a runtime Shared Symbol Library is definitely handy, you might want to sever the link between your destination movie and the source movie:

1. Open the destination movie that contains the symbol you want to de-link.

2. Open the Library (Window → Library).

3. Select the Movie Clip, Button, or Graphic symbol you want to de-link.

4. Open the Symbol Properties dialog box by selecting Options → Properties in the Library.

5. De-select the Import for Runtime Sharing option.

6. Click OK.

Linking to an Author-Time Shared Symbol Library

As mentioned, when you employ an author-time Shared Symbol Library, you can replace any symbol in the movie that you're currently working on with a symbol from another movie entirely.

> When you're working with an author-time Shared Symbol Library, the source movie must be directly accessible at the time you publish your movie, either over a local network or on your own computer.

Remember that although the symbol in the destination movie retains its original name and properties, its contents are replaced by those of the symbol you're drawing from the source movie.

> Any asset that the symbol from the source movie uses (such as an audio file in a Movie Clip) is also copied to the destination movie.

To replace a symbol in a destination movie with one drawn from an author-time Shared Symbol Library:

1. Open the movie that contains the symbol you want to replace.

2. Open the Library (Window → Library).

3. Select the symbol you want to replace.

4. Open the Symbol Properties dialog box by selecting Options → Properties in the Library.

5. Click the Browse button located at the bottom of the Symbol Properties dialog box.

6. When the Locate Macromedia Flash Document File dialog box opens, navigate to where the FLA file containing the symbol you want to use as the replacement is located, select it, and click Open.

7. When the Select Source Symbol dialog box opens (which lists all the symbols in the FLA file you picked), select the symbol you want to use as the replacement (see Figure 4.7).

8. Click OK.

9. When you are returned to the Symbol Properties dialog box, click OK again. Note that the contents of the symbol have been replaced.

Figure 4.7

Use the Select Source Symbol dialog box to select a replacement symbol.

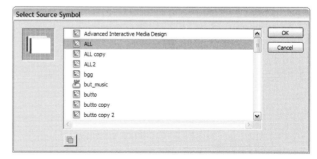

> To replace one symbol for another in the same movie, click the Symbol button in the Source section of the Symbol Properties dialog box to access the Select Source Symbol dialog box.

Working with Symbol Instances

When you drag a symbol from the Library to the Stage, you're not really adding the symbol *per se.* Instead, you're creating a copy (called an *instance*) that you can alter without changing the parent symbol (which remains in the Library). As such, you can change an instance to look quite different from its parent symbol. Although editing the symbol in the Library updates all its instances, editing an instance of a symbol updates only that instance.

In the next sections, you'll investigate how you can manipulate the various visual characteristics of symbol instances, replace one instance with another, and transform an instance on the Stage. You'll also learn how to name an instance.

Modifying the Appearance of Instances with the Property Inspector

Instances have a series of properties that you can manipulate to change the instance's visual character. You'll find that many, if not all, of these instance properties are particularly important when it comes to animation. You can animate each property—including transparency, brightness, and color—to create a change in the instance's visual appearance over time (something that will be covered in Chapter 6). For example, you could animate an instance's transparency so it appears to fade in over time.

> You can also apply a graphic filter to either a Movie Clip or a Button symbol (but not a Graphic symbol) to change its appearance—something covered in Chapter 1. You can also animate the graphic filters, thereby creating interesting effects.

This section of the chapter will make you familiar with the tools to change the overall appearance of any given symbol instance.

When it comes to the visual character of an instance property, you'll rely exclusively on the Color drop-down menu in the Property Inspector to make any changes:

1. Select the symbol instance that has the visual properties you want to manipulate.

2. If the Property Inspector isn't already open, choose Window → Properties → Properties (see Figure 4.8).

3. Select one of the options in the Color drop-down menu (each of which has unique properties).

   None Leaves the symbol instance unaltered. Applying the None effect is a good way to revert a symbol instance to its original form after you've fiddled with its visual properties.

   Brightness Changes the relative brightness of the selected symbol instance when you input a value (in percent) in the Brightness field or use the Brightness slider (see Figure 4.9). The value can range from 100 percent (white) to −100 percent (black).

Figure 4.8

Use the Property Inspector's Color drop-down menu to make appearance changes.

Setting the Brightness to 0 percent retains the original color of the symbol instance.

Figure 4.9

You can set the brightness of a symbol instance.

Tint Offers several ways to alter the color of the selected symbol instance. You can click the Tint swatch (which opens the Color Picker) and choose a color. Alternatively, you can mix your own RGB color by entering a value into the R, G, and B fields (see Figure 4.10).

Remember, you can also use the sliders (accessed by clicking the down arrow just to the right of each field) to adjust the value of the individual RGB channels.

Finally, you can adjust the amount of tint by entering a value (in percent) from 0 to 100 in the Tint field.

Figure 4.10

You can set tint properties by entering RGB values.

Like the R, G, and B fields, you can manipulate the tint by adjusting the slider (accessed by clicking the down arrow just to the right of the field).

Alpha Lets you adjust the transparency of a selected symbol instance. Enter a value in the Alpha field or use the slider (accessed by clicking the down arrow to the right of the field) to adjust the value. The value can range from 0 (totally transparent) to 100 (no transparency) (see Figure 4.11).

Figure 4.11

Set the alpha properties to adjust the transparency.

Figure 4.12

Use the Advanced Effect dialog box to make several changes at once.

Advanced Allows you to change the color and transparency of an object simultaneously. When you select Advanced from the Color drop-down menu and click the Settings button in the Property Inspector, you open the Advanced Effect dialog box (see Figure 4.12).

In the Advanced Effect dialog box, you'll notice two sets of tint and alpha controls. The four controls on the right (R, G, B, and Alpha) change the color and transparency of a selected symbol instance by an absolute value. The four controls on the left change a symbol instance's tint and alpha value by a relative amount (percentage).

Replacing One Instance with Another

You might want to swap one instance for another. This is particularly useful when you have a complex scene where you want to swap one symbol instance with another but want to make sure the new one is placed in the same location as the old one:

1. Select the symbol instance you want to replace.

2. Choose Window → Properties → Properties.

3. Click the Swap button ⌈Swap…⌋.

4. When the Swap Symbol dialog box opens, select the symbol you want to swap, and click OK (see Figure 4.13).

Transforming an Instance on the Stage

Symbol instances are exact copies of their parent symbols in the Library. You can transform them without changing the parent. As such, you're probably going to transform symbol instances on a regular basis:

1. On the Stage, select the symbol instance you'd like to edit.

2. From here, use any of Flash's transformation tools to manipulate the symbol instance.

Figure 4.13

Use the Swap Symbol dialog box to replace one instance with another.

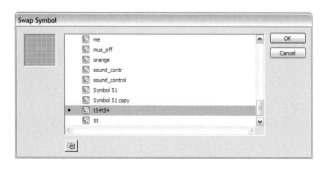

To transform every aspect of the symbol instance, you'll probably have to break it down into its parts—a process accomplished by selecting the symbol instance and then choosing Modify → Break Apart.

If you want to edit the parent symbol of a given instance, you can open the Library, select the symbol, and choose Options → Edit in the Library. Alternatively, you can double-click the symbol, which opens the Symbol Editor, where you can make any changes you want.

Remember, when you change the parent symbol, all its associated symbol instances also change.

Naming a Symbol Instance

A powerful feature of Movie Clips is that they can be manipulated with ActionScript. To do this, however, you need to identify each Movie Clip symbol instance with a unique name so that you can appropriately target the ActionScript. So, although the process by which you name a Movie Clip symbol instance is really quite easy (as you'll find out shortly), it is vital to the creation of any moderately complex Flash creation that fully leverages the phenomenal power of Movie Clips.

As button instances can also be manipulated with ActionScript, they can, and should, be assigned an instance name.

To name a Movie Clip symbol instance:

1. Select the Movie Clip symbol instance.
2. If it isn't already open, open the Property Inspector by choosing Window → Properties → Properties.
3. Enter a unique name in the Instance Name field.

When entering a name in the Instance Name field, avoid using spaces. If you want a two-word name, use a hyphen (-), an underscore (_), or camel cases (camelCase).

Tutorial: Creating an Underwater Scene with Movie Clips

What better way to experiment with the power and versatility of Movie Clips than by using them to create a scene that, under normal circumstances, would prove complex enough to be somewhat overwhelming if it were constructed using the main Timeline alone? In this step-by-step tutorial, you'll create an animated seascape in which a single fish swims by the camera.

The files `seascape.swf` and `seascape.fla` on the CD provide an example of how the final product might look.

> This tutorial assumes you have a decent understanding of Timeline animation—a topic covered in Chapter 6.

Creating the Water

To start, you'll need to create the water in which the marvelous seascape will take place:

1. Create a new document by choosing File → New.

2. When the New Document dialog box opens, select the Flash Document option, and click OK.

3. Choose Modify → Document. When the Document Properties dialog box opens, if it isn't already, change the width to 550 and the height to 400.

4. Choose light blue for the document's background color.

5. Click OK to exit the Document Properties dialog box.

6. Now choose File → Import → Import to Stage.

7. When the Import dialog box opens, locate the `water.swf` file on the CD, and click Open. This imports the premade water (complete with gentle rolling waves) onto the Stage and into your Library.

8. Position the water so that it lines up with the edges of the movie. At this point, the Stage should look like this:

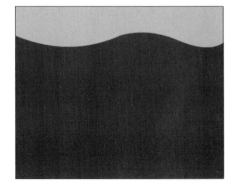

9. Because you are going to have several layers in your scene, it's wise to name each. Double-click your only layer's icon. When the Layer Properties dialog box opens, enter **Water** in the Name field. Click OK.

Adding the Fish

Now that the ocean is occupying a single keyframe of a single layer, it's time to create some fish:

1. Choose Insert → New Symbol.

2. When the Create New Symbol dialog box opens, click the Movie Clip radio button, enter **fish1** in the Name field, and click OK.

3. When the Symbol Editor opens, choose File → Import → Import to Stage, select either `fish1.swf`, `fish2.swf`, or `fish3.swf` on the CD (choose whichever file's fish you like best), and click Open. This imports the image you'll use to create your fish Movie Clip.

> If the image doesn't appear, it's possible that Flash placed it out of view. Scroll down until it's visible, and drag it up. Remember, the crosshairs represent the symbol's registration point.

4. Now it's time to create the animation where the fish "swims" horizontally from the right to the left. Select the fish with the Arrow tool.

> The fish files are composed of a bunch of groups. As a result, you'll need to group all these parts together. To do this, just select all the parts of the fish, and choose Modify → Group.

5. If it isn't already, open the Property Inspector by choosing Window → Properties → Properties.

6. Enter **470** in the X field and **−78.5** in the Y field.

> You might want to zoom out so that you can see the entire area that the fish will traverse.

7. Click frame 90, and choose Insert → Timeline → Keyframe.

8. With the newly created keyframe selected, select the fish with the Arrow tool.

9. Enter **−470** in the X field and **−78.5** in the Y field.

10. Select the first keyframe, and choose Insert → Timeline → Create Motion Tween.

> The whole point of creating an animation that covers this amount of distance is to ensure that you can place the Movie Clip on one side of the Stage in the work area, have it pass through the ocean scene, and then have it pass into the work area on the other side of the Stage before it loops. This gives the illusion that the fish is simply passing by your line of sight.

11. If you want to add a little more life to your scene, you can have the fish follow a wavy path—opposed to the straight one it currently follows. To add a motion guide, follow the steps described in Chapter 6.

12. Now that you've created the Movie Clip of the fish, you can insert it into the water. Return to the main scene by choosing Edit → Document, by clicking the scene link in the Edit bar, or by clicking the back button ⇦ .

13. Create a new layer by choosing Insert → Timeline → Layer or clicking the Insert Layer button in the bottom-left corner of the Timeline.

14. Enter **fish** for the new layer's name.

15. If it isn't already, make sure the fish layer is above the ocean layer in the Timeline— this is important. If you don't do it, the fish actually will be obscured by the water.

16. Select the first keyframe of the fish layer.

17. Open the Library (Window → Library), and click and drag the fish Movie Clip onto the Stage. You should position the Movie Clip in the work area to the right of the Stage. So far, your scene should look like this:

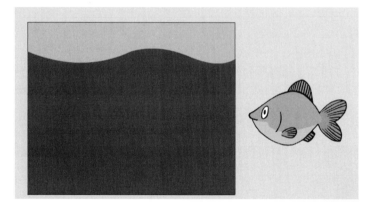

Now that you've created a basic ocean scene, you can test it—choose Control → Test Movie or Control → Test Scene.

Adding Bubbles to the Seascape

You'll finish off this tutorial by adding some floating bubbles to the ocean:

1. Choose Insert → New Symbol.

2. When the Create New Symbol dialog box opens, click the Graphic radio button, enter **bubble template** in the Name field, and click OK.

3. When the Symbol Editor opens, click the first keyframe of the only layer in the Time-line, and draw a small circle with the Oval tool in the lower portion of the screen. Because this will be the template for your floating bubbles, you should choose a sufficiently bubble-like color for the stroke and fill. From there, exit the Symbol Editor.

4. You are going to want to take the bubble template Graphic symbol that you created and use it in a Movie Clip to create an animation of a rising bubble. Choose Insert → New Symbol.

5. When the Create New Symbol dialog box opens, enter **bubble animation** in the Name field, select the Movie Clip radio button, and click OK.

6. When you enter the Symbol Editor, select the first blank keyframe in the only layer, and drag the bubble template Graphic symbol from the Library onto the Stage.

7. With the bubble template still selected, open the Info panel. Enter **–20** for the X value, and enter **70** for the Y value.

8. Click frame 30, and choose Insert → Timeline → Keyframe.

9. With the second keyframe selected, enter **–19** for the bubble template's X value, and enter **–292** for the Y value.

10. Reselect the first keyframe in the layer, and choose Insert → Timeline → Create Motion Tween. This creates the animation of the rising bubble.

11. To add a little character to the rising bubble, click somewhere in the middle of the tween (say, frame 15 or so).

> Even though the entire tween gets selected, don't be fooled into believing that you aren't selecting a specific frame. The playhead indicates the actual frame you've selected.

12. Choose Insert → Timeline → Keyframe. By doing this, you've added another keyframe to the middle of the tween you created.

13. With the newly created middle keyframe selected, use either the Transform panel (Window → Transform) or the Scale tool (located in the Toolbox's Options section when the Free Transform tool is selected) to increase the size of the bubble slightly. By doing this, you've created a tween in which the bubble starts off small, gradually gets bigger, and then returns to its previous size. All of this happens when the bubble is moving.

14. Now you'll add a little more subtlety to your rising bubble by making it disappear as it nears the top of its tween: select the final keyframe in the tween.

15. Select the bubble.

16. If it isn't already open, open the Property Inspector by choosing Window → Properties → Properties.

17. Choose Alpha from the Color drop-down menu, and enter **0** in the Alpha Value field. This makes the bubble appear transparent by the end of the tween.

Adding More Bubbles

Now that you've created the animation of one rising bubble, you can then add several more that rise at staggered intervals:

1. With the bubble Movie Clip still open in the Symbol Editor, add a layer (give it a unique name if you want) by choosing Insert → Timeline → Layer or by clicking the Insert Layer button in the bottom-left corner of the Timeline.

2. Click frame 5, and choose Insert → Timeline → Keyframe. This guarantees that the second bubble won't appear and start rising until the playhead reaches frame 5. As a result, the two bubbles will be staggered.

3. Drag the bubble template Graphic symbol from the Library onto the Stage. With the Info panel, enter **–64** for the new bubble's X value and **104** for its Y value.

4. Click frame 35, and choose Insert → Timeline → Keyframe.

5. Repeat the process described in the previous section—the only difference is that you set the bubble's X value to **–60** and its Y value to **–245** using the Info panel to create the second rising bubble.

Now that you've created two rising bubbles, you can continue adding rising bubbles. The only element you have to vary is the frame at which the specific animation starts. You can also vary the size of each bubble instance to add variety.

Adding the Bubbles to the Main Scene

Now you can add your rising bubble Movie Clip to the main scene:

1. Return to the main scene by choosing Edit → Document, by clicking the Scene button in Edit bar, or by clicking the back button ⇦ .

2. Create a new layer by choosing Insert → Timeline → Layer or by clicking the Insert Layer button in the bottom-left corner of the Timeline.

3. Now, rename the new layer to **bubbles**.

4. Select the first keyframe of the bubbles layer.

5. Open the Library (Window → Library), and click and drag the bubbles Movie Clip onto the Stage. You should position the Movie Clip in the work area just below the Stage. By doing this, you'll get the illusion that the bubbles are passing into view from the bottom of the scene. Your scene should look like this:

6. Now that you've created a basic ocean scene, you can test it. Choose Control → Test Movie, or choose Control → Test Scene.

Congratulations, you're done! Experiment with the scenes by adding more objects. For example, try adding other fish or swaying sea plants.

CHAPTER 5

Managing Your Flash Movie Project

With each version, Flash becomes a more intricate authoring tool. Now, not only is there more you need to master in the Flash authoring environment, you also have to be able to manage the multitude of assets generated during the authoring process. In addition, given the complexity of the tool, you need to come up with ways to streamline the production process so that you don't waste time on pointless or unnecessarily repetitive tasks. Fortunately, Flash engineers recognize that it takes a lot of efficiency and skill to create a great Flash movie. Therefore, they've included hordes of tools that help you address the complex nature of the program and the authoring process.

- Creating and organizing Flash Projects

- Managing and manipulating moviewide assets with the Movie Explorer

- Working with the Find and Replace function

- Automating tasks by creating commands

Working with a Flash Project

A Flash Project enables you to manage and manipulate multiple document types (such as SWF files, FLA files, ActionScript files, and external Flash Video files) that make up a complex movie from a centralized location: the Project panel. A Flash Project, which is little more than a specialized XML file with an .flp extension, simply references all the documents you've defined as being part of the project.

Besides centralized management, creating and working with a Flash Project has many benefits. First, any changes you make to any of the files in the project are automatically updated to the FLP file. You have no need to save the project file because it's automatically always kept current. Second, you can test your project directly from within the Project panel. Under normal circumstances, without the benefit of the Project panel, you'd need to individually export all the files that make up your movie and then test all of them.

Third, you can set the default publishing settings and then publish all the files in your project directly from within the Project panel. This is especially helpful if, for example, you're working with more than just one SWF file. Under normal circumstances, you'd have to set the publish properties for each of the FLA files separately and then export each to SWF separately—a process that could become fairly time-consuming. However, when you're working with a Flash Project, you simply set the default publish settings for all files of a specific type; then, when you're ready, you can publish them all from within the Project panel.

Finally, when working with a Flash Project, multiple authors (who can be in the same place or in different places) can simultaneously work on the same Flash Project. In this kind of situation, you can also establish version control to make sure each author working on a project file is always using the latest version of a file and that multiple authors on a project do not overwrite each other's work.

Creating a New Flash Project

Before you can start grouping files into a project, you need to create a Flash Project. You can do this using the New Document dialog box or the Project panel.

The book's CD includes a sample Flash Project file (called `fish.flp`) and all its associated files for you to use for the how-tos in this chapter.

To create a Flash Project file from the New Document dialog box:

1. Choose File → New.

2. When the New Document dialog box opens, make sure the General tab is active, select Flash Project from the Type list box, and click OK.

3. When the New Project dialog box opens, navigate to the location on your hard drive where you want to save the project file, enter a name for the file in the File Name field, and click Save.

Remember, the Flash Project file, which has an .flp extension, is just a specialized XML file that references all the other physical files in the project.

Besides using the New Document dialog box to create your Flash Project file, you can also use the Project panel:

1. Open the Project panel by choosing Window → Project or using the shortcut Shift+F8.

2. When the Project panel opens, click the New Project link in the main window of the Project panel (see Figure 5.1).

3. When the New Project dialog box opens, navigate to the location on your hard drive where you want to save the project file, enter a name for the file in the File Name field, and click Save.

Figure 5.1

Click the New Project link to create a Flash Project file.

If you've already created a project file and want to create a new one from within the Project panel, the steps are a little different:

1. With the Project panel open (Window → Project), click the Project button 👁. in the panel's upper-left corner.

2. Select New Project from the subsequent drop-down menu.

3. When the New Project dialog box opens, navigate to the location on your hard drive where you want to save the project file, enter a name for the file in the File Name field, and click Save.

When you create a Flash Project file from directly within the Project panel, you'll see the project file displayed within the panel's main work area.

Opening an Existing Flash Project

Opening an existing Flash Project is easy:

1. Choose File → Open.

2. When the Open dialog box opens, navigate to where the Flash Project file (.flp) is located, select it, and click Open.

3. The Flash Project file automatically opens in the Project panel.

You can also open a Flash Project file directly from within the Project panel:

1. Make sure the Project panel is open (Window → Project).

2. If you already have an existing project file open, click the Project button 👁. , and select Open Project from the subsequent drop-down menu.

3. If you don't have an existing project file open in the Project panel, click the Open link in the panel's main window.

4. When the Open dialog box opens, navigate to where the Flash Project file (`.flp`) is located, select it, and click Open.

> You can have only one Flash Project open at a time. If you try to open a second Flash Project, you'll be asked whether you want to close the existing project.

Managing and Manipulating Your Flash Project

As your Flash Project increases in size and complexity, it will include more files. If you don't maintain total control, things can easily spiral out of control, and you'll be left with nothing more than a disorganized mess of files, many of which were originally created for good reason but now only confound you. To prevent this, you need to do everything you can while building the project to maintain order so that you can streamline your work flow and save yourself frustration and wasted time.

Adding Files to a Flash Project

After you've created a Flash Project file, you need to start building the project by adding files:

1. Make sure you've either created a new project file or opened an existing project file and that you have the Project panel open (Window → Project).

2. From here, you have two ways of adding files:

   - Select the project you want to work with, and then click the Add Files to Project button ⊡ in the bottom-right corner of the Project panel.

   > If you don't select the project file first, the buttons at the bottom of the panel will not be available.

   - Ctrl+click / right-click the Flash Project file you've just opened or created, and choose Add File from the context menu.

3. When the Add Files to Project dialog box opens, navigate to the location on your hard drive (or other storage device) where the file is located, select it, and click the Open button. The file appears in the Project panel underneath the project file (see Figure 5.2).

> You can add a given file to a project only once. If you attempt to add the same file a second time, you will get an error message.

Organizing Your Flash Project with Folders

Every computer user knows the value of organizing files in a logical folder structure, and with large, complex Flash Projects, this organization is particularly important. The Project panel allows you to create folders within a project and store files within them. You can also nest folders within folders, increasing your project's organization.

Figure 5.2

When you add a file to a Flash Project, it appears indented just below the project file.

ADDING A FOLDER TO THE PROJECT PANEL

Adding a folder to organize your project is actually a really easy process—and might save you a lot of hardship later:

1. Make sure you've either created a new project file or opened an existing project file and you have the Project panel open (Window → Project).

2. From here, you have two ways of adding a folder:

   - Click the Add Folder to Project button 🗐 in the bottom-right corner of the Project panel.

   - Ctrl+click / right-click the Flash Project file you've just opened or created, and choose Add Folder from the context menu.

3. When the Project Folder dialog box opens, enter a unique name for the folder in the Name field, and click OK (see Figure 5.3). A new folder appears in the Project panel below the project file (see Figure 5.4).

> Folders that occupy the same level of the project's structure *must* each have a unique name. If you try to create a new folder with the same name as an existing folder at that level of the project, you'll get an error message. However, because folder names are case-sensitive, you can have two folders with the same name but at least one letter in a different case.

Project folder

Figure 5.3

Name the folder using the Project Folder dialog box.

Figure 5.4

When you add a top-level folder to a Flash Project, it appears indented just below the project file.

MOVING FOLDERS

Because you can nest folders within folders, it's a good idea to become familiar with how you move folders from one location in the project hierarchy to another.

> When you move a folder from one location to another in the project hierarchy, the contents of the folder move as well.

To move a folder:

1. Select the folder you want to move.

2. Drag the folder to where you want to move it. As you drag it, a small document icon appears next to your cursor and the location you move your mouse over is highlighted.

3. When the cursor/icon/highlight is over the desired location, release your mouse button.

> If you attempt to move a folder to a location in the project's hierarchy that has an existing folder with the same name, the folder you're moving will be deleted and its contents placed in the existing, identically named folder.

ADDING FILES TO FOLDERS

Of course, the purpose of creating folders in a project is to organize related files within them. The important point to remember is that when you organize files in your project, you aren't changing the structure of your computer's physical file system.

To add a new file to an existing folder:

1. Make sure you've created the folder that should include your file.

2. Select the folder in which you want to place the file.

3. From here, you have two ways of adding a file:

    - Click the Add Files to Project button ⬀ in the bottom-right corner of the Project panel.

    - Ctrl+click / right-click the target folder, and choose Add File from the context menu.

4. When the Add Files to Project dialog box opens, navigate to the location on your hard drive (or other storage device) where the file is located, select it, and click the Open button.

Now, what if you wanted to move an existing file from one folder to another within a project?

1. Select the file you want to move.

2. Drag the file over the folder to which you want to move it. As you drag the file, a small document icon appears next to your cursor, and the location you move your mouse over is highlighted (see Figure 5.5).

3. When the cursor/icon/highlight is over the desired folder, release your mouse button.

OPENING AND EDITING PROJECT FILES

Given the fact that, as you've already learned, a Flash Project is simply a group of files referenced by a specialized XML file (with an .flp extension), it's good to learn how to go about opening and editing files directly from within the Project panel.

Figure 5.5

You'll see a document icon while moving a file between folders in the Project panel.

> Although a Flash Project can contain many types of files, you can open and edit only native Flash files (SWF files, FLA files, AS files, FLV files, and so on). When you're working from within the Project panel, non-native file types (such as QuickTime MOV files, PNG files, and GIF files) will automatically open in the application your operating system associates with that specific file type.

1. Make sure a Flash Project is open in the Project panel (Window → Project).

2. Double-click the file you want to edit.

3. When the file opens on the Stage, make any changes you want.

4. Choose File → Save to save the file.

> When you save the file, it doesn't actually close (you have to close it manually), which can be somewhat annoying if you're expecting it to close.

REMOVING FILES FROM A FLASH PROJECT

As you continue to work with a Flash Project, you'll obviously encounter a situation where you'd like to remove a file from the project:

1. Make sure you have a project open in the Project panel (Window → Project).

2. Select the file you want to delete.

3. From here, you have two ways of deleting a file:

   - Click the Remove from Project button 🗑 in the lower-right corner of the Project panel.

   - Ctrl+click / right-click the target folder, and choose Remove from the context menu.

Once you've deleted a file from a project, you cannot undo the process. However, remember that when you delete a file from a project, you're removing the reference to the FLP file, not deleting the file from your system. Therefore, this isn't such a huge deal, because you can easily add it again later if you want.

FINDING LOST FILES

You've already learned that a Flash Project is a specialized XML file that simply references all the other files you've added to your project. The next point you need to know is that, when added, the files aren't actually embedded in the project file. Instead, they stay where they are, and a link is created between them and the project file. The link, much like a uniform resource locator (URL), is severed if an external file (or the project file) is moved (or deleted). When this happens, the external file, while still listed in the Project panel, isn't included when the overall project is tested or exported. If this happens, it's up to you to reinstate the link between the project file and the external file:

1. Make sure the project with the missing file is open in the Project panel (Window → Project).
2. Select the missing file, which is designated with a special icon 📄 .
3. Click the Project button 🔧 , and select Find Missing File from the subsequent pop-up menu.
4. When the Find Missing File window opens, navigate to the location of the missing file, select it, and click Open.

RENAMING A PROJECT OR FOLDER

At some point, you may want to return to a project you've been working on and either change its name or change the name of one of its associated folders:

1. Make sure you have a project open in the Project panel (Window → Project).
2. Depending on what you want to rename, select either the folder or the project name.
3. From here, you have two choices:
   - Click the Project button 🔧 in the top-left corner of the Project panel, and select Rename from the subsequent pop-up menu.
   - Ctrl+click / right-click the target folder, and choose Rename from the context menu.
4. When the Rename Project dialog box or the Rename Project Folder dialog box opens (depending on whether you're renaming a project file or a folder), enter a new name in the Name field (see Figure 5.6).
5. When you've finished, click OK, and the project file or folder is automatically renamed.

Figure 5.6

On the left is the Rename Project dialog box; on the right, the Rename Project Folder dialog box.

Testing Your Flash Project

A Flash Project is more than a simple movie; it's a collection of files that work together to create an overall interactive experience. So, you need to make sure all the parts work together, and you need to do that testing directly from within the Flash authoring environment. The good news is that you can easily test your entire project from within Flash.

Before you can test your project, you have to designate an FLA file as the default file. What's the point of a default file? Well, it's the FLA file that is the "central" movie that launches, controls, or displays all the other files in the project.

To set a file as the default:

1. Make sure you have the project you want to test open in the Project panel (Window → Project).

2. Ctrl+click / right-click the FLA file you want to make the default file of the project, and choose Make Default Document from the context menu. Notice that the file's icon changes from the regular FLA icon to the default file icon ⬇ .

Once you've set one of the FLA files as the project's default file, you can then test the project:

1. Make sure the project you want to test is open in the Project panel (Window → Project).

2. Select the project file you want to test.

3. From here, you have three ways of testing:

   • Click the Test Project button ⌈Test Project⌋ , which is located in the lower-left corner of the Project panel.

   • Click the Project button 🔧 in the top-left corner of the Project panel, and select Test Project from the subsequent pop-up menu.

   • Ctrl+click / right-click the project file, and choose Test from the context menu.

From here, Flash publishes the default document as well as all the other FLA files so you can test your entire project.

If no FLA has been designated as the project's default file, the Default Document Required dialog box appears. Click the Select button, choose the file you want to act as the default from the Select Default Document dialog box, and click OK. Flash will then publish your project using the selected FLA file as the default.

Publishing Your Flash Project

One of the great features of working with a Flash Project is that you can establish a default publish setting for the FLA files in your project and then publish your entire project in one fell swoop.

Before you actually publish, you need to set up a default publishing profile for your project's FLA files.

Why do you need to set a publishing profile only for the FLA files in your project? Well, the FLA files are the only files that can be added to a project that aren't in their final state. All other files in a project, such as SWF files, FLV files (Flash video files), and external digital video files (such as QuickTime MOV files), are already in their final format and therefore don't need any kind of export.

1. Make sure you have a Flash Project file open in the Project panel (Window → Project).

2. Select the Flash Project file.

3. From here, you have two ways to launch the Settings dialog box:
   - Click the Project button 🐾 in the top-left corner of the Project panel, and select Settings from the subsequent pop-up menu.
   - Ctrl+click / right-click the project file, and choose Settings from the context menu.

4. When the Project Settings dialog box opens, select the FLA file whose publish properties you want to set (see Figure 5.7).

5. Choose one of the publish profiles from the Profile drop-down menu. If you haven't set up any publish profiles, the only option available will be Default.

6. If you have additional FLA files in your project whose publishing properties you want to set, you can repeat steps 4 and 5.

For more information on how to create publish profiles, refer to Chapter 19.

Now that you've set the publish profile for the FLA file(s) in your project, you can publish your grand interactive creation:

1. Make sure the project you want to publish is open in the Project panel (Window → Project).

2. Select the project file you want to publish.

3. From here, you have two ways to publish:
   - Click the Project button 🐾 in the top-left corner of the Project panel, and select Publish Project from the subsequent pop-up menu.
   - Ctrl+click / right-click the project file, and choose Publish from the context menu.

Working Collaboratively on a Flash Project

One of the greatest strengths of a Flash Project is that multiple authors can work on the same project at the same time. Further, in this kind of situation, you can establish version control to make sure each author working on a project file is always using the latest version of a file and that multiple authors on a project don't overwrite each other's work. This is how it works: Everybody who is working on the project connects to the remote location where the project file and all of its associated files are stored. When one author wants to work on one of the files in the project, they check it out from the remote site. When they're finished, they check in the file.

Fortunately, when one of the authors checks out a file from the remote location, the file is locked until they check it in; this prevents other authors from overwriting each other's work.

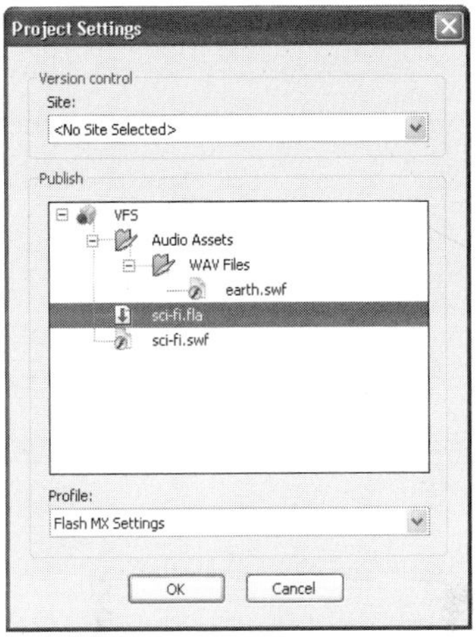

Defining a Site for Your Flash Project

One of the key concepts in collaboratively working on a Flash Project is a *site*. Essentially, a site is a set of rules that defines where the project is located (either on a LAN or a remote server) and how you access it (either locally or through FTP), where your local version of the project sits on your hard drive, and what information is visible regarding the status of a given file in the project. Without a site, it's nearly impossible to collaboratively work on a project. So, the bottom line is that if you want to work on a project with a series of other authors, you must set up a site.

> When you're defining the site for your Flash Project, make sure all its associated files are in the same folder as the one designated as the local root when you define the site.

To set up a site for your Flash Project, first create the project using the procedures outlined earlier in this chapter. Then follow these steps:

1. Open the Edit Sites dialog box in one of two ways:

    • Choose File → Edit Sites.

> If you use Dreamweaver, you'll see that Flash populates the Edit Sites dialog box with all the sites you've defined in Dreamweaver.

    • With the Project panel open (Window → Project), click the Version Control button 🔀 , and select Edit Sites from the subsequent pop-up menu.

2. When the Edit Sites dialog box opens, click the New button (see Figure 5.8).

Figure 5.7

Select the publish properties in the Project Settings dialog box.

3. When the Site Definition dialog box opens, enter a name for your site in the Site Name field (see Figure 5.9).

   The name you give to your site isn't a filename; it's just the name Flash uses to reference the specific site associated with a specific project.

4. From here, you need to tell Flash where the local version of the project resides on your hard drive. Click the Browse for Folder icon to the right of the Local Root field.

5. When the Browse for Folder dialog box opens, navigate to the location on your hard drive where the local copy of your project resides, select the folder, and click OK.

   While it's not completely required, it's advisable that *all* the files in your project are located in the folder on your hard drive that you define as your site root.

6. Enter your e-mail address in the Email field.

7. Enter your name in the Check Out Name field.

   What you enter in the Email and Check Out Name fields is important, because if anyone tries to check out a file that is currently checked out, that information appears in a dialog box indicating who currently is working on the file.

8. You need to tell Flash how you access the remote location where the project is located. Select one of these options from the Connection drop-down menu:

   - If the project file is located on a remote computer (server) that you don't have direct access to, select FTP.

   - If you have direct access to the computer that the project is located on, select Local/Network.

   - If you have access to a server running Microsoft Visual SourceSafe (a version-control system), select Microsoft Visual SourceSafe.

   If only for the sake of organization, it's wise to make sure the project occupies its own folder/directory regardless of whether it's on a remote server or a local machine.

   The options that appear next in the Connection section of the Site Definition dialog box depend on the connection type you chose in step 8. If you selected the Local/Network option, you'll see the options in Figure 5.10.

Figure 5.8

Create a new site by clicking New in the Edit Sites dialog box.

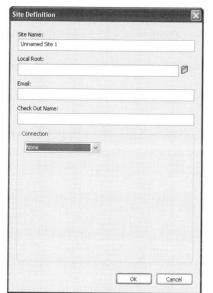

Figure 5.9

Name your site through the Site Definition dialog box.

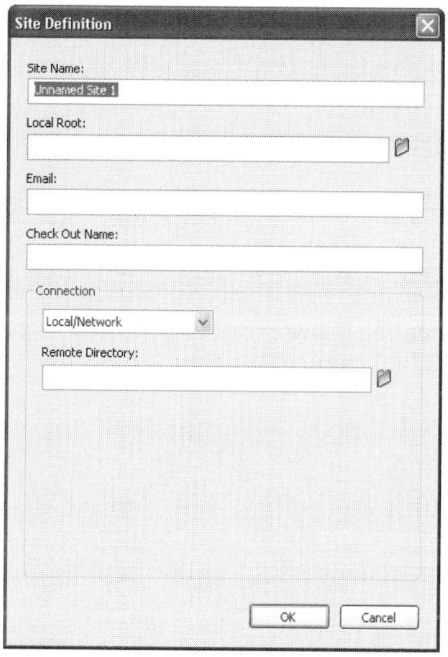

Figure 5.10

The Site Definition dialog box shows the Local/Network connection option selected.

If you selected Local/Network:

1. Click the Browse for Folder icon to the right of the Remote Directory field.

2. When the Browse for Folder dialog box opens, navigate to the location where the remote copy of your project resides, select the folder, and click OK.

If your project resides on a server to which you don't have direct access, and you've selected FTP from the Connection drop-down menu, you need to set some additional properties, all of which are accessible in the Site Definition dialog box (see Figure 5.11).

If you selected FTP:

1. Enter the name of the FTP host in the FTP Host field.

2. If the folder that the project resides in isn't in the root directory of the FTP host, you need to input the exact path to the correct folder in the FTP Directory field.

3. Enter your login name in the Login Name field.

Figure 5.11

The Site Definition dialog box with the FTP connection option selected.

4. Enter the password you use to access the remote server in the Login Password field.

5. If you want the password to be saved, check the Save box. If you leave it unchecked, you'll have to manually enter your password every time you connect to the remote server.

6. If you want to check whether all the information you've entered is correct, you can test the connection by clicking the Test button.

7. When you've finished entering all the necessary information in the Site Definition dialog box, click OK.

8. When you're pushed back to the Edit Sites dialog box, click Done.

Uploading Your Project to the Remote Location

After you've set up a site, you're just about ready to work collaboratively on your project. You must, however, perform one last task. If you're the primary author (in other words, you're the person who originally created the project file), you need to move a copy of the project to the remote location where it will reside. If you don't do this, none of the other authors will be able to access the project files, which pretty much defeats the whole point of the process.

To move a copy of the project to its intended remote location:

1. Make sure you've set up a site for your project following the steps outlined in the previous section.

2. From the Project panel (Window → Project), open the Project Settings dialog box.

3. When the Project Settings dialog box opens, select the site from the Site drop-down menu, and click OK.

4. Now, with the Project panel open, select the project file.

5. From here, you have a couple ways of checking in the project file:

   • Click the Version Control button in the top-left corner of the Project panel, and select Check In from the subsequent pop-up menu.

   • Ctrl+click / right-click the project file, and choose Check In from the context menu.

   Several actions will take place. First, Flash connects with your site's remote location. If you're using FTP, the negotiation that happens between Flash and the remote computer might take some time (depending on the speed of your connection and the speed of the remote server). You'll then get a pop-up message indicating whether the connection was made successfully.

6. Once the project file has been checked in, a padlock icon appears to the left of its name in the Project panel (see Figure 5.12). This means the project file has been checked into the remote location and is locked. It cannot be edited until it has been checked out from the remote location (something we'll talk about next).

7. Once you've checked in the project file, you need to check in all the other files in the project. If you don't do this, the files won't be available to other authors. To do this, first select the additional file(s) you want to check in, and then follow the instructions outlined in step 5.

8. As with the project file, a padlock icon appears next to the name of the other checked-in files. You won't be able to edit them unless you check them out from the site.

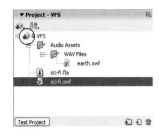

> If all your associated files aren't located in the local root, you won't actually be able to do this. As a result, as mentioned previously, make sure you place all your project files in the same folder that you define as the site's local root.

Figure 5.12

When a project file has been checked into a site, a padlock icon appears to the left of its name in the Project panel.

Editing a File Located on a Site

Once you've established a site and checked all the files within your project into that site (as described in the previous section), you can then check files out and edit them. This process ensures that all the authors working on a project have access to the most recent versions of the files. Remember, when a file is checked out, it's locked until it's checked back in.

To edit a file located on a site:

1. Make sure you have the correct project open in the Project panel (Window → Project), and then open the Project Settings dialog box.

2. When the Project Settings dialog box opens, select the specific site you want to connect to from the Site drop-down menu, and click OK.

> Once you connect with a site, the Project panel displays all the files in that project as well as any new files that were added by other means.

3. Select the file you want to check out from the site.

4. From here, you have two ways of checking out a project file:
   - Click the Version Control button 🔁 in the top-left corner of the Project panel, and select Check Out from the subsequent pop-up menu.
   - Ctrl+click / right-click the file you want to edit, and choose Check Out from the context menu.

5. Once a file is checked out, a green check mark icon appears to the left of its name.

6. Now you can open the file and make any changes you want. Once finished, save the file, close it, and then check it back into the site.

> Remember, if you don't check a file back into the site, other authors won't have access to it.

Opening a File Located on a Site

When multiple authors are working on a project, the check-in/check-out feature is a valuable safeguard for maintaining version control and avoiding files being overwritten.

However, what if you wanted to bypass all the checking-in/checking-out shenanigans and simply open a file that is located in a site? Flash includes a handy little Open from Site option. For obvious reasons, this technique is really only good when you are working alone. You should stick to checking-in/checking-out when you are working in a group:

1. Choose File → Open from Site.

2. When the Open from Site dialog box opens, select the site from which you want to open the file from the Site drop-down menu. Flash will connect with the chosen site and then display its contents (see Figure 5.13).

3. Double-click the file you want to edit, and it will open.

Figure 5.13

The contents of the site appear in the Open From Site dialog box.

Using the Movie Explorer to Manage and Manipulate Moviewide Assets

Essentially, the Movie Explorer, which is accessed by selecting Window → Movie Explorer or using the shortcut Alt+F3 / Opt+F3, displays the contents of your movie hierarchically (see Figure 5.14). The Movie Explorer lets you search your entire movie for any symbol or symbol instance. In addition, you can replace text and fonts with a few easy steps. You can also copy the contents of the Movie Explorer as text to the Clipboard or print the display list in the Movie Explorer.

Understanding the Movie Explorer Options

The Movie Explorer panel offers the following options:

Go to Location Jumps to the selected layer, scene, or frame in the movie.

Go to Symbol Definition Automatically selects all items in the Symbol Definitions section of the Movie Explorer associated with the selected symbol. If the Symbol Definitions section isn't visible in the display list, you can enable it by selecting Show Symbol Definitions from the Options drop-down menu. The Go to Symbol Definition option works only if you have the Show Buttons, Movie Clips, and Graphics button toggled, and it's active only when you're working in the Movie Elements section of the display list.

Select Symbol Instances Automatically jumps to the scene in the Movie Elements section of the display list that contains the selected symbol's instance. This option is accessible only when the Show Buttons, Movie Clips, and Graphics button is toggled. In addition, the feature is active only when you're working in the Symbol Definitions section of the display list.

Find in Library Opens the Library (if it isn't already open) and jumps to the selected symbol.

Rename Lets you rename the currently selected symbol.

Edit in Place Allows you to edit the currently selected symbol on the Stage without entering Symbol Editing mode. The real significance of this option is that you can see all the other items on the Stage when you're editing the symbol.

Edit in New Window Opens a new window in which you can make changes to the selected symbol.

Figure 5.14

The Movie Explorer displays the contents of your movie hierarchically.

Show Movie Elements Automatically displays all elements in the Flash movie, organized by scene.

Show Symbol Definitions Displays all the files associated with the currently selected element (by toggling on and off).

Show All Scenes Displays all the scenes in your movie (by toggling on and off).

Copy All Text to Clipboard Copies selected text to your Clipboard so that you can paste it into another program (a word processor, for example).

Cut Cuts any selected element.

Copy Copies a selected element (but doesn't place it in the Clipboard as the Copy All Text to Clipboard option does).

Paste Allows you to paste an element that has been copied from within Flash or from another application.

Clear Clears the selected element. It's important to remember that when you use the Clear option, you're performing the operation on the on-Stage instance of the test you've selected in the Movie Explorer.

Expand Branch Expands the currently selected branch of the hierarchical tree. You can accomplish the same result by clicking the plus (+) sign to the right of any given section of the hierarchy.

Collapse Branch Collapses the currently selected branch of the hierarchy. You can accomplish the same effect by clicking the minus (−) symbol to the right of any given section of the hierarchy. This is the opposite of the Expand Branch option.

Collapse Others Automatically collapses all sections of the hierarchy except for the one currently selected.

Print Automatically prints all the contents of the Movie Explorer (with all sections of the hierarchy expanded). This is a good way to create a hard-copy version of your Flash movie's structure.

Exploiting the Power of the Movie Explorer

The Movie Explorer is a powerful tool—especially when your movie contains many assets or is layered/nested in a particularly complex fashion. It's in your best interest to become intimately familiar with what it's capable of offering you and your design and production process.

Filtering the Displayed Categories

The Show buttons located at the top of the Movie Explorer allow you to choose the category or categories of items displayed in the Movie Explorer. When you click any of the buttons (or a combination thereof), the Movie Explorer displays only those elements in your file.

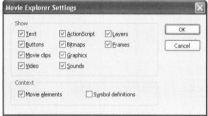

Figure 5.15

The Movie Explorer Settings dialog box lets you set which items are visible.

From left to right, the buttons are Show Text **A** ; Show Buttons, Movie Clips, and Graphics ⬚ ; Show ActionScripts ↗ ; Show Video, Sounds, and Bitmaps ⊙ ; and Show Frames and Layers ⬚ . The final button, Customize Which Items to Show ⬚ , opens the Movie Explorer Settings dialog box, which allows you to set the items you want visible, giving you slightly more control over the display (see Figure 5.15).

Searching for Items

When you're working with a particularly large movie with many discrete elements, it can take a long time to locate a given symbol or instance. In that case, the Movie Explorer provides you with a search tool. All you have to do is enter the name of a symbol, instance, font, block of code, or frame number in the Find field, and the Movie Explorer automatically jumps to the location in the hierarchy where the item is located.

If you can't recall the exact name of the element you're looking for, you can enter any part of the name, and the Movie Explorer will display any items whose names contain the string you specified.

Editing Symbols

You'll occasionally want to alter a given symbol instance from within the Movie Explorer. For instance, if your movie has a large number of symbols and you're looking for a specific one, you might use the Movie Explorer. However, once you find that symbol, you don't want to have to close the Movie Explorer and then locate the symbol in the Library. Instead, you can locate it using the Movie Explorer and then open it directly from within the Movie Explorer:

1. Make sure the Movie Explorer is open (Window → Movie Explorer).

2. Locate the symbol instance you want to edit. You can either navigate to its location in the hierarchy manually or use the Movie Explorer's search tool to find it.

3. Ctrl+click / right-click, and choose Edit in Place or Edit in New Window from the pop-up menu. Alternatively, you can choose either of these options from the Movie Explorer's Options menu (accessible by clicking the right-pointing arrow in the top-right corner of the Movie Explorer).

> You can also double-click the symbol instance in the Movie Explorer to enter Symbol Editing mode.

4. Make any changes you want to the symbol instance, and then return to working on your movie.

Replacing Fonts

The Movie Explorer lets you search for and replace any specific font you've used in your movie. This is particularly useful if you have many instances of a given font that you want to change and don't want to change each by hand:

1. Make sure the Movie Explorer is open (Window → Movie Explorer).

2. Type the name of the font in the Find field.

3. After the Movie Explorer has gone to the location in the hierarchy where the font in question resides, select it. If you've used the same font more than once, it will display all occurrences.

4. Open the Property Inspector (Window → Properties → Properties).

5. Make any changes you want—font, style, color, size, and so on.

6. When you make your changes, your movie is automatically updated.

Using the Find and Replace Function

With Flash's Find and Replace function, you can search the current document or scene for a string of text, a font, a color, a symbol, a sound file, a video file, or an imported bitmap and then replace it with something. It works like a typical Find and Replace feature offered by other software programs. Access it by selecting Edit → Find and Replace.

From here, depending on what you're searching for, you have a bevy of options, each of which will be outlined in the following sections. (These sections assume you know how to open the Find and Replace dialog box and set the scope of your search.)

Finding and Replacing Text

To find and replace text:

1. With the Find and Replace dialog box open, select Text from the For drop-down menu to display the text-specific options (see Figure 5.16).

2. Enter the text you want to search for in the Text box.

3. Enter the text you want to replace it with in the Replace with Text box.

4. From here, you can select any of the following options:

   - Whole Word searches for the text string as a whole word only, bounded on both sides by spaces or punctuation. When Whole Word isn't selected, the text can be part of a larger word. For example, when Whole Word is deselected, you can enter **sin** to find the word *single* and the word *sinister*.

   - Text Fields Contents searches only the contents of your movie's text fields.

   - Match Case searches for text that matches the case (upper or lower) of the specified text.

   - Frames/Layers/Parameters searches only frame labels, layer names, scene names, and component parameters.

   - The Regular Expressions option allows you to use regular expressions to conduct a find-and-replace operation. For example, you can enter **error\d** to locate the words *error1*, *error2*, and *error3* in your movie's ActionScript.

   - Strings in ActionScript searches any strings in your movie's ActionScript.

   - ActionScript searches your movie's ActionScript. When you choose any of the ActionScript options, external ActionScript files (AS files) aren't included in the search.

5. Check the Live Edit box if you want to be able to edit the specific element directly on the Stage.

6. To find text, you have two options:

   - Click the Find Next button [Find Next] to locate the next occurrence of the specified text.

   - Click the Find All button [Find All] to locate all occurrences of the specified text.

7. To replace text, you have two options:

   • Click the Replace button ⟨ Replace ⟩ to replace the currently selected occurrence of the specified text.

   • Click the Replace All button ⟨ Replace All ⟩ to replace all the occurrences of the specified text.

Whether you're just finding text or finding and replacing it, the results appear in the list box at the bottom of the Find and Replace dialog box (as shown here). If you've just searched for text and you've selected the Live Edit option, you can double-click any of the individual results to jump to the specific string of text in your movie, which you can then edit.

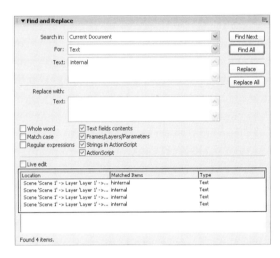

Finding and Replacing Fonts

To find and replace fonts:

1. With the Find and Replace dialog box open, select Font in the For drop-down menu to display font-specific options (see Figure 5.17).

2. If you want to search for a font by name, check the Font Name box. Then, when the Font drop-down menu appears, select the specific font for which you want to search.

3. If you want to search for a specific font style (bold, italic, underline, and so on), check the Font Style box. Then, when the Style drop-down menu appears, select the specific style for which you want to search.

4. If you want to search for a specific font size, check the Font Size box. When the Min and Max fields appear, enter a minimum (Min) and maximum (Max) size range for the font for which you're searching.

Figure 5.17

Use the Find and Replace dialog box's font-specific options to find and replace fonts.

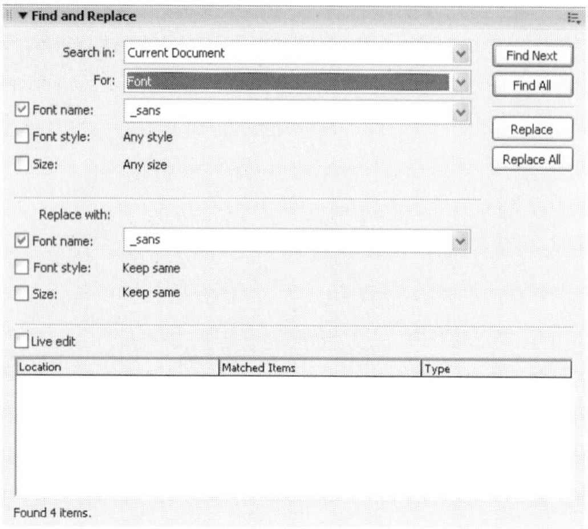

5. To replace the specified font with a different font, check the Font Name box in the Replace With section of the Find and Replace dialog box. When the Font drop-down menu appears, select the font you want to use instead of the font for which you're searching.

> When either the Font Name check box or the Font Style check box in the Replace With section is deselected, the current font name or style remains unchanged.

6. To replace the specified font style with a different font style, check the Font Style box in the Replace With section. When the Font Style drop-down menu appears, select the style you want to use instead of the style for which you're searching.

7. To replace the specified font size with a new font size, check the Font Size box in the Replace With section. When the Size field appears, enter the value of the replacement size.

8. Check the Live Edit box if you want to be able to edit the specific font directly on the Stage.

9. To find a font, click the Find Next button ⬚ Find Next to locate the next occurrence, or click the Find All button ⬚ Find All to find all occurrences of the specified font.

10. To replace a font, click the Replace button ⬚ Replace to replace the currently selected occurrence, or click the Replace All button ⬚ Replace All to replace all occurrences of the specified font.

Whether you're just searching for a font or searching and replacing a font, the results appear in the list box at the bottom of the Find and Replace dialog box. If you've just searched for a font and you've selected the Live Edit option, you can double-click any of the individual results to jump to the specific font in your movie, which you can then edit.

Finding and Replacing Colors

Any Flash movie, large or small, comprises many different colors, all of which were most likely chosen very carefully. So, what happens if you decide that, instead of a color you initially chose, you want to use another? Well, you could go through your entire movie, carefully selecting the unwanted color and then replacing it with a new color. However, this can be a lengthy process. Instead, you can use the Find and Replace function to search for a specific color and then automatically replace it with another.

To find and replace a color:

1. With the Find and Replace dialog box open, select Color in the For drop-down menu to display the color options (see Figure 5.18).

2. To select the specific color you want to search for, click the color swatch, and choose the color from the pop-up color palette.

> If the color you want to search for isn't in the pop-up color palette, you can enter a hexadecimal code in the pop-up color palette's Hex Edit text box, click the Color Picker button, or specify your own custom color using RGB or HSL. Alternatively, if you move your mouse cursor outside the palette, it will change into an eyedropper, allowing you to select any color visible inside the Flash application's window by clicking it.

3. To select a color to replace the color you're searching for, click the color swatch in the Replace With section of the Find and Replace dialog box.

4. Select the Fills, Strokes, or Text option (or any combination of the three) to choose the occurrence of the color for which you're searching and replacing.

5. Check the Live Edit box if you want to be able to edit the color directly on the Stage.

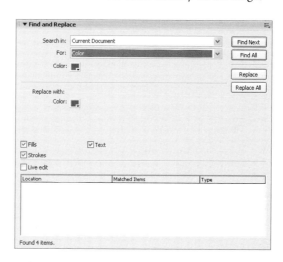

Figure 5.18

Use the Find and Replace dialog box's color-specific options to replace colors.

6. To find a color, you have two options:

   - Click the Find Next button [Find Next] to locate the next occurrence of the specified color.

   - Click the Find All button [Find All] to locate all occurrences of the specified color.

7. To replace a color, you have two options:

   - Click the Replace button [Replace] to replace the currently selected occurrence of the specified color.

   - Click the Replace All button [Replace All] to replace all the occurrences of the specified color.

Whether you're just searching for a color or searching and replacing a color, the results appear in the list box at the bottom of the Find and Replace dialog box. If you've just searched for a color and you've selected the Live Edit option, you can double-click any of the individual results to jump to the specific color in your movie, which you can then edit.

Finding and Replacing Symbols

To find and replace symbol instances:

1. With the Find and Replace dialog box open, select Symbols in the For drop-down menu to display symbol options.

2. Select the symbol instance you want to replace from the Name drop-down menu (see Figure 5.19).

3. Now you need to select the symbol to replace the symbol for which you're searching. Select the symbol instance in the Name drop-down menu located in the Replace With section of the Find and Replace dialog box.

4. Check the Live Edit box if you want to be able to edit the specific symbol instance directly on the Stage.

Figure 5.19

Use the Find and Replace dialog box's symbol-specific options to replace symbols.

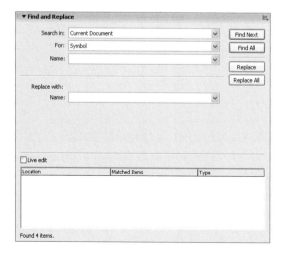

If you use Live Edit when searching for a symbol instance, Flash opens the symbol in Edit in Place mode.

5. To find a symbol instance, you have two options:
   - Click the Find Next button `Find Next` to locate the next occurrence of the specified symbol instance.
   - Click the Find All button `Find All` to locate all occurrences of the specified symbol instance.

6. To replace a symbol instance, you have two options:
   - Click the Replace button `Replace` to replace the currently selected occurrence of the specified symbol instance.
   - Click the Replace All button `Replace All` to replace all the occurrences of the specified symbol instance.

Whether you're just searching for a symbol instance or searching and replacing a symbol instance, the results appear in the list box at the bottom of the Find and Replace dialog box. If you've just searched for a symbol instance and you've selected the Live Edit option, you can double-click any of the individual results to jump to the specific symbol instance in your movie, which you can then edit.

Finding and Replacing Audio Files, Video Files, and Bitmaps

To find and replace audio files, video files, or imported bitmaps:

1. With the Find and Replace dialog box open, select the Sound, Video, or Bitmap option in the For drop-down menu to display the specific options (see Figure 5.20).

2. Depending on the option you selected in the For drop-down menu, select the audio file, video file, or imported bitmap you want to replace from the Name drop-down menu.

3. Now you need to select the file to replace the file for which you're searching. Select the file from the Name drop-down menu located in the Replace With section of the Find and Replace dialog box.

4. To find the audio file, video file, or imported bitmap, you have two options:
   - Click the Find Next button `Find Next` to locate the next occurrence of the specified file.
   - Click the Find All button `Find All` to locate all occurrences of the specified file.

5. To replace the audio file, video file, or imported bitmap, you have two options:
   - Click the Replace button `Replace` to replace the currently selected occurrence of the specified file.
   - Click the Replace All button `Replace All` to replace all the occurrences of the specified file.

Figure 5.20

The Find and Replace dialog box's audio-specific options. The options for video and bitmaps are the same.

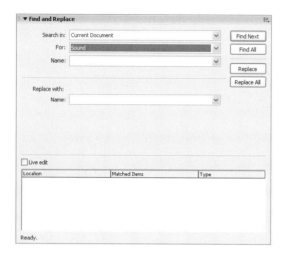

Whether you're searching for an audio file, a video file, or a bitmap or you're finding and replacing it, the results appear in the list box at the bottom of the Find and Replace dialog box.

Automating Tasks with Commands

During the process of creating a Flash movie, however big or small, you'll be performing a lot of tasks over and over again. What if you could record tasks that have many steps and then replay them whenever you wanted? In Flash 8, this isn't just a pipe dream; it's a reality. With the help of the History panel, you can choose any of the steps you've performed since you started a new document and compile them into a command that can be saved and run anytime you please. The commands themselves, which are something like macros, are retained permanently (regardless of whether you're working in the document they were created in) and become accessible through Flash's Commands menu. To actually run a command, all you need to do is select it from this menu.

The History panel lists the steps you've performed in the currently active document since you opened it. The History panel doesn't show steps you've performed in other documents. The slider in the History panel initially points to the last step you performed. Beyond using it to create commands, you can use the History panel to undo or redo individual steps or multiple steps at once. You can apply steps from the History panel to the same object or to a different object in the document. However, you cannot rearrange the order of steps in the History panel.

Creating Commands

To create a command:

1. Manually perform a series of steps that you want to turn into a command.

2. Open the History panel by choosing Window → Other Panels → History or by using the shortcut Ctrl+F10 / Cmd+F10. You'll notice that the steps you've taken in the currently active document are listed in the panel. The earliest steps appear at the top of the panel, and the most recent appear at the bottom (see Figure 5.21).

3. Select the steps you want included in the command. To select multiple steps, hold down the Shift key.

Figure 5.21

The History panel shows the steps you've performed.

> You might have noticed that some of the steps' associated icons have a small red *x* in their lower-right corner. Those steps, because of their nature, can't be saved in a command. If you try to include one of these kinds of steps in a command, you won't be able to save the command.

4. Click the Save As Command button 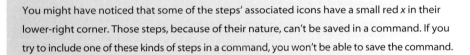 located in the lower-right corner of the History panel.

5. When the Save As Command dialog box opens, enter a name for the command in the Command Name field (see Figure 5.22).

> Give your command a descriptive name. By doing this, you'll be able to distinguish the purpose of each command when you view them in the Commands menu.

6. When you're finished, click OK.

After you've converted a series of steps into a command, the command appears in Flash's Commands menu.

Managing Commands

After you've created a series of commands, you need to be able to manage them. Flash lets you change a command's name as well as delete a command.

Figure 5.22

Name the command in the Save As Command dialog box.

Changing a Command's Name

Although you give a command a name when you initially create it, you might find yourself wanting to change its name during the course of your work:

1. Choose Commands → Manage Saved Commands.

2. When the Manage Saved Commands dialog box opens (see Figure 5.23), select the command whose name you want to change, and click the Rename button [Rename...].

3. When the Rename Command dialog box opens, enter a new name in the Command Name field, and click OK (see Figure 5.24).

Figure 5.23

Access your commands through the Manage Saved Commands dialog box.

Figure 5.24

Rename a command using the Rename Command dialog box.

Deleting a Command

As you work more with Flash, you'll begin to accumulate commands, which will inevitably clog up Flash's Commands menu. So, it's a good idea to remove commands that you no longer use:

1. Choose Commands → Manage Saved Commands.

2. When the Manage Saved Commands dialog box opens, select the command you want to delete, and click the Delete button [Delete].

3. When the pop-up alert appears, depending on whether you want to delete the command, click OK or Cancel.

CHAPTER 6

Creating Animation with the Timeline

When Macromedia acquired FutureWave in 1997, FutureSplash Animator (which would later become Flash) was a simple vector-animation program. Though the most recent version of Flash has about 100 times the bells and whistles that FutureSplash did, it's still, at its core, an animation program. Although you can do much more than animate objects, much of the power of Flash 8 lies in its ability to create movies with content that changes over time.

If you wanted to create only static images, you could easily have turned to Macromedia Fireworks or Adobe Photoshop. But, no—you want to create images that move and spin and bounce! Whether it's a character who walks across the screen and promptly gets hit by a falling anvil or a button that spins around when users move their cursors over it, you want to create *animations*. In this chapter, you'll explore the primary tool you use to construct and manipulate animations in Flash 8.

- Understanding animation
- Creating frame-by-frame and tweened animations
- Animating a mask
- Extending a still image through time
- Tutorial: Creating an animated sci-fi space spectacular
- Creating animated visual effects with filters
- Animating a symbol instance's visual properties with the Property Inspector
- Organizing animated content using scenes

Understanding the Subtle Art of Animation

Every animation, whether it's the latest Hollywood 3D animated blockbuster, Walt Disney's original Fantasia, or your Flash creation, contains frames. Each frame contains one static image that, when displayed in succession with other images in other frames, creates the illusion of movement. In Flash 8, frames appear as small boxes horizontally in the Timeline. Each frame's content appears as the playhead passes through it, thereby creating something of a digital "flipbook."

Introducing Keyframes and Frame Rate

In Flash, any frame populated by content that you've directly manipulated (as opposed to, for example, a frame placed by Flash in a tweened animation) appears in the Timeline as a small, black circle called a *keyframe*. A keyframe represents a point on the Timeline where a change occurs in the animation that the animator has directly created or caused. For now, know that any time you want to change your animation (add content, subtract content, start the motion of an object, and so on), you'll use a keyframe.

Although a keyframe and a frame can have the same content, you can directly manipulate that content only if it resides in a keyframe. If it resides within a frame, you have no way, short of turning the frame into a keyframe (which is a perfectly functional solution), to directly manipulate its content.

Beyond frames and keyframes, you should be aware of a third type of frame. Somewhere between an ordinary frame and a keyframe, an *empty keyframe* is essentially a keyframe that has yet to be "filled" with content. An outline of a small circle represents an empty keyframe.

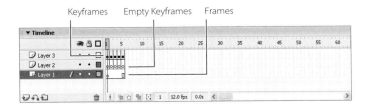

By default, Flash designates the first frame of any animation as an empty keyframe. The remaining frames in any given layer are placeholders for future empty keyframes or keyframes (which you need to create).

Frame rate determines the rate at which an animation plays. Represented in frames per second (fps), an animation's frame rate is related both to the speed the animation plays at and to its overall quality. Think of it this way: if you have a high frame rate, more frames are displayed per second, increasing the animation's quality. Conversely, the lower your frame rate, the fewer frames displayed per second, increasing the animation's choppiness and decreasing its quality.

The most important reason you shouldn't always set a high frame rate concerns memory and bandwidth. When you set a high frame rate, you force the user's computer to display more information per second. A higher frame rate might cause some slower computers or slower Internet connections to "choke" on the higher rate of information, causing the animation to hang, skip, or crash entirely.

To set your animation's frame rate:

1. Choose Modify → Document to open the Document Properties dialog box. Alternatively, you can double-click the frame-rate indicator at the bottom of the Timeline (see Figure 6.1). You can also enter a value into the Property Inspector's Frame Rate field (which is accessible when you don't have anything selected on the Stage).

2. Enter a value in the Frame Rate field.

> Although 12fps is Flash's default frame rate, you can use a higher frame rate if you want. However, unless you're confident your users' systems can cope with more information, it's wise to set a frame rate no higher than 20.

How Flash Represents Animation in the Timeline

The Timeline represents the various kinds of animations (and Timeline elements) differently. As a result, it's in your best interest to become familiar with each so that when you animate with the Timeline, you won't be caught off guard by the way an animation looks.

- A frame-by-frame animation is usually represented by a layer with a series of sequential keyframes.

- A motion tween is denoted by a keyframe at the beginning and end, between which a black arrow (representing the actual tween) runs. In addition, a motion tween has a light-blue background.

Frame-Rate Indicator

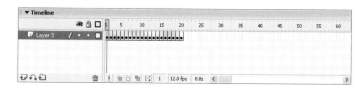

Figure 6.1

Use the Timeline's frame-rate indicator to set your animation's frame rate.

- When a dashed line follows a keyframe, a motion tween is incomplete (usually the result of the final keyframe being removed or not added).

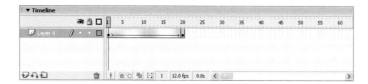

- Like a motion tween, a shape tween is denoted by a keyframe at the beginning and end, between which a black arrow (representing the actual tween) runs. The difference is that the intervening frames are light green instead of light blue.

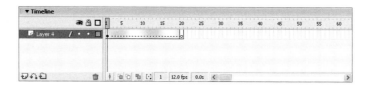

- When a series of gray frames begins with a keyframe and ends with a hollow rectangle, all frames after the keyframe have the same content.

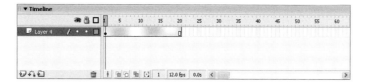

- A frame or keyframe with a lowercase *a* represents a point in the animation where a frame action (*global function*) has been added.

- A frame or keyframe with a red flag indicates the presence of a frame label.

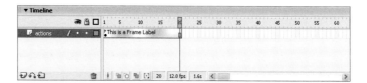

Frame labels are extremely useful for identifying and targeting specific frames when you're using actions. You can also use them in the development process to add comments or notes to specific frames. To insert a frame label, select the frame, open the Property Inspector, and enter the label in the Frame Label field.

Introducing Frame-by-Frame Animations

Way back in the dark ages of animation, animators had to painstakingly create the individual images in each frame, varying each slightly to get the illusion of movement.

In Flash, the most basic form of animation, *frame-by-frame animation*, works the same way. Essentially, frame-by-frame animation works by creating a unique image in each frame. Each frame then becomes a keyframe (because it has content that alters the animation). As the playhead passes through each of the frames, the frame's content displays, creating the illusion of change over time. Frame-by-frame animations are great if you want to exert direct control over the details in your animation.

Creating a frame-by-frame animation has one problem, however. Because you need to populate each frame by content unique from the previous frame, you end up creating a *lot* of static material. Imagine if your movie contained an animation that was 300 frames long. You'd have to create at least 300 static images—a laborious undertaking. Granted, using the Library, symbols, and symbol instances to recycle some of your material could help reduce the workload. However, whichever way you look at it, you'd be spending a great deal of time creating art assets for your animation.

Creating a Frame-by-Frame Animation

You'll now learn how to actually create a frame-by-frame animation. You'll start with something particularly mundane—a simple Graphic symbol (of your design) moving across the Stage:

For a little hands-on experience with animation, check out the "Creating an Animated Sci-Fi Space Spectacular" tutorial later in this chapter.

1. Select the keyframe (or empty keyframe) where you want the frame-by-frame animation to start. Drag the symbol you're going to animate from the Library to the left side of the Stage. Notice that the first frame automatically becomes a keyframe (denoted by the small, black circle).

Remember, Flash automatically designates the first frame of any layer as an empty keyframe. As a result, you don't have to insert a keyframe. However, if you're starting the animation anywhere but the first frame, you'll have to insert each keyframe.

2. Now that you've populated the first keyframe with content, you can create the remainder of the sequence. Click the frame to the right of the keyframe you created), and choose Insert → Timeline → Keyframe (or use the shortcut F6). This inserts a second keyframe. Flash automatically populates the keyframe with the content of the previous keyframe. You could keep adding successive keyframes, and Flash would continue to populate them with the contents of the first one.

If, for some reason, you don't want the same content in the second frame, just insert a blank keyframe (select Insert → Timeline → Blank Keyframe, or use the shortcut F6). To add content to the blank keyframe, select it, and then add something to the Stage. When you do this, the blank keyframe becomes a keyframe.

3. Make sure you've selected the second keyframe. Select the symbol with the Arrow tool, and move it to the right slightly.

4. Select the third frame in the Timeline, and insert a new keyframe (Insert → Timeline → Keyframe).

5. Make sure you've selected the third keyframe. From here, select the symbol, and move it slightly to the right.

6. Continue adding successive keyframes and moving the symbol to the right in each one until it has reached the right side of the Stage. Depending on how much you move the symbol each time (the less you move it, the more keyframes it will take to move it to the right side of the screen), your Timeline should be filled with a number of keyframes (as shown here).

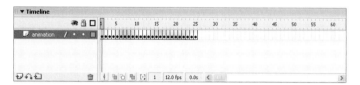

To test it, you can do any of the following:

- Drag the playhead through the Timeline to view the animation.
- Choose Control → Play, or hit Return/Enter.
- Choose Control → Test Scene (Ctrl+Alt+Enter / Opt+Cmd+Return) or Control → Test Movie (Ctrl+Enter / Cmd+Return), which opens a new window where the animation will continue to loop.

Working with the Onion Skinning Option

When you were creating a frame-by-frame animation in the previous section, you moved the sphere in each successive keyframe without having a real reference as to its position in the preceding frame. Without a way to get the symbol exactly in line with the one in the previous frame, the animation will look a little jumpy. Granted, you could simply click the previous frame, check the position of the sphere, and then click back and adjust the position of the next one. However, this process is time-consuming and frustrating. This is where *onion skinning* comes in.

Onion skinning lets you see the contents of the frames preceding and following the currently selected frame. The concept comes from the traditional pen-and-paper animation technique of using tracing paper to view a sequence of animation frames. With onion skinning, you can do away with all the guesswork inherent in flipping back and forth to see the contents of previous frames and smoothly animate a moving object.

You have several options when using onion skinning:

Turning onion skinning on To turn onion skinning on, click the Onion Skin button located at the bottom of the Timeline. By doing this, two things happen. First, the Onion Skin marker is displayed in the Timeline header. The Onion Skin marker displays the range of frames included in the onion skinning. To increase, decrease, or change the number of frames included, click one of the handles on either side of the Onion Skin marker, and drag it accordingly.

Onion Skinning Markers

Second, the frames' content within the Onion Skin marker displays as partially transparent. In addition, the contents of the currently selected frame display normally.

If any layers are locked in your animation, they won't be displayed when you have onion skinning turned on.

Turning onion skinning outlines on By clicking the Onion Skin Outlines button , which is located at the bottom of the Timeline, you can display the content of multiple frames as outlines (instead of as transparent). Note that the currently selected frame appears normally when Onion Skin Outlines is activated.

The particular layer's outline color determines the color of the onion skin outlines.

Editing multiple frames When you have onion skinning turned on, you can't actually edit the contents of a frame unless you've selected it in the Timeline. This can prove a little frustrating, because you'll constantly have to switch to a given frame to edit its content. One of the great features of onion skinning is the Edit Multiple Frames button.

Located to the right of the Onion Skin Outlines button, the Edit Multiple Frames button  lets you edit the contents of all frames without having to move from frame to frame. Unlike with simple onion skinning, the Edit Multiple Frames button displays all the contents without any transparency.

Modifying onion markers The Modify Onion Markers drop-down menu is accessible by clicking the Modify Onion Markers button ⊡, which is located to the right of the Edit Multiple Frames button at the bottom of the Timeline. Each of the options contained in the menu affects the position of the Onion Skin marker and therefore the frames that are displayed:

- Always Show Markers displays the Onion Skin markers in the Timeline header regardless of whether onion skinning is turned on.
- Under normal circumstances, the onion skin range is relative to the current frame pointer and the Onion Skin markers. By selecting Anchor Onion, you lock the Onion Skin markers to their current position in the Timeline header.
- Onion 2 displays two frames on both sides of the currently selected frame.
- Onion 5 displays five frames on both sides of the currently selected frame.
- Onion All displays all the frames on both sides of the currently selected frame.

Creating Tweened Animations

The process of tweening allows you to create animations in a far less laborious manner than when you create frame-by-frame animations. Essentially, *tweening* is the process by which you define a starting point/form and ending point/form for an object and then tell Flash to fill in all the in-be*tween* frames.

Two types of tweening are available depending on what you want your animation to do. *Motion tweening* allows you to create a tweened animation of a moving object. You can also create a motion tween that follows a path—thereby allowing you to create far more complex animations. *Shape tweening* allows you to create an animation in which one shape "morphs" into another.

Creating a Motion-Tweened Animation

Motion tweening is a quantum leap beyond frame-by-frame animation—no more working with frame after frame, painstakingly crafting each image in your animation so it's just right. With motion tweening, you merely create the first and last keyframes in your animation; from there, Flash completes the in-between frames. And because Flash has to save the contents of only the first and last keyframes (along with numerical values concerning how the object changes), tweened animations generally result in smaller file sizes than frame-by-frame animations.

Although you'll use tweening primarily for animating motion, you can also animate size, color, and orientation. In short, any transformation you can apply to an object can be animated with tweening.

You can use motion tweening on text as well as groups of objects.

To illustrate how you create a tweened animation, we'll show you something simple (akin to what you did previously with the frame-by-frame animation)—creating an animation of a symbol moving across the Stage :

1. Select the keyframe (or empty keyframe) where you want the tweened animation to start. Drag the symbol you're going to animate from the Library to the left side of the Stage. Notice that the first frame automatically becomes a keyframe (denoted by the small, black circle).

2. Now that you've created the first keyframe in the animation, you can create the last one. Click the frame where you want the animation to end, and insert a keyframe by choosing Insert → Timeline → Keyframe. At this point, your Timeline should look like this:

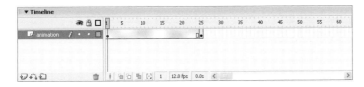

The frames between the two keyframes are just that: frames. They really don't do much except contain the content that is automatically generated by Flash. If you want them to become more, you must insert a keyframe.

Much as in the case of frame-by-frame animation, Flash populated the second keyframe you created with the content of the first. As a result, you'll want to move the symbol in the last keyframe to the location on the Stage where you want it to be at the end of the animation:

1. Select the final keyframe.

2. Using the Arrow tool, click and drag the symbol to the right side of the Stage. By doing this, you tell Flash that in the first keyframe the symbol is at the left side of the Stage and in the last keyframe it's in the right side of the Stage.

3. Now comes the tweening. Select the first keyframe.

4. Choose Insert → Timeline → Create Motion Tween. Alternatively, you can select the first keyframe, open the Property Inspector, and select Motion from the Tween drop-down menu.

5. Flash fills all the in-between frames, thereby creating the animation. You'll also notice that the Timeline itself changes. The change in the frames' colors, as well as an extra arrow, indicates the presence of a tween.

To test it, do one of the following:

•   Drag the playhead through the Timeline to view the animation.

•   Choose Control → Play, or hit Return/Enter.

•   Select Control → Test Scene/Test Movie to open a new window in which the animation will continue to loop.

Even though the motion tween you've just created is quite simple, don't think that motion tweening creates only simple animations. You can create some amazingly complex and varied animations with tweening. As an experiment, take the animation you just created, insert a keyframe in the middle, and alter the symbol's location. When you play the animation, Flash moves the symbol to the new location defined in the keyframe you just added and then to the position you set in the final keyframe.

You also don't have to merely move your symbol across the Stage. Try increasing the object's size in the final keyframe using the Transform panel (Window → Transform) or the Free Transform tool. When played, the symbol slowly grows until it reaches the defined size in the final keyframe.

You can also change the visual properties of a tweened symbol using the Property Inspector or using graphic filters—something you'll learn how to do in the "Creating Animated Visual Effects with Graphic Filters" section.

Creating a Motion-Tweened Animation That Follows a Path

When it comes to motion tweening, you've explored how to move an object along a straight line. Granted, you can vary the course of the object's motion by adding more keyframes to the animation (as discussed earlier), creating a zigzag pattern. However, what if you wanted to make an object move along a circle? *Motion paths* let you move objects along specific paths (see Figure 6.2).

Figure 6.2

The motion path can take any form you desire. This one was drawn with the Pen tool.

In this section, you'll take the concept of motion paths and combine it with motion tweening to craft an animation that has an object traveling along a complex path.

To create an animation that follows a path:

1. Create a simple motion-tweened animation with two keyframes, one at the beginning and one at the end.

2. Select the layer with the tweened animation, and choose Insert → Timeline → Motion Guide. This creates a motion guide layer just above the layer containing the animation.

3. Now, with the first frame (the empty keyframe) in the motion guide layer selected, draw the path you want the object to follow (as shown in Figure 6.2). You can use any of Flash's drawing tools: Pencil, Oval, Rectangle, Brush, Pen, or Line. At this point, your Timeline will look something like this:

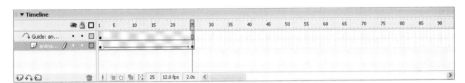

4. Select the first keyframe of your tweened animation, open the Property Inspector, and make sure the Snap box is checked so your object's registration point will snap to the motion path, as shown here:

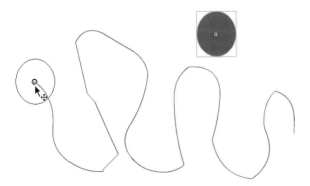

5. Click and drag the object so the registration point snaps onto the beginning of the path you've drawn.

> If the registration point doesn't appear when you click the object, release it, click the central portion of the object (represented by a set of crosshairs), hold your mouse button down for a few seconds, and then drag it to the beginning of the path.

6. Now, click the final keyframe in the animation, and click and drag the object so the registration point snaps onto the end of the path you've drawn.

7. If you want the object to point in the direction of the path that it's moving along, make sure the Orient to Path box is checked in the Property Inspector.

8. From here, test your animation by hitting Return/Enter, choosing Control → Play, or selecting Control → Test Scene/Test Movie.

> You can "unlink" a layer from a motion guide by selecting the layer, next either clicking and dragging the layer above the motion guide layer in the Timeline or choosing Modify → Timeline → Layer Properties, and then clicking the Normal radio button when the Layer Properties dialog box opens.

Editing a Tweened Animation

Although you can create a motion-tweened animation with the Tween dropdown menu in the Property Inspector, you can't do much to edit the animation's characteristics this way. Instead, you use the Property Inspector to manipulate all the tweened animation's characteristics, including those specific to motion tweening.

Some of the options in the Property Inspector apply to other types of tweening, such as shape and motion-path tweening—each of which we'll discuss in the following sections.

Easing a Motion Tween Animation

Under normal circumstances, tweened animations move at a consistent speed. If you want, you can use the Property Inspector to ease the object in or out of the animation. Easing it in means it can start more slowly, gaining speed through the process of the animation. On the other hand, if you ease the object out of the animation, it slows down near the end.

To ease your motion tween:

1. Select the first frame in the motion tween.

2. Open the Property Inspector.

3. Enter a value in the Ease field. A positive number eases the object out of the animation, and a negative eases it in. A higher value (either negative or positive) increases the effect. Alternatively, you can use the Ease slider to adjust the value.

You can enter values from –100 to 100 in the Easing field.

4. If you click the Edit button ⌜ Edit... ⌟ , you can get access to the Custom Ease In/Ease Out dialog box, where you can adjust the easing rate of the animation by manipulating the curve (see Figure 6.3).

Rotating a Motion-Tweened Object

To get an object to rotate through the tweening:

1. Select the first frame in the motion tween.

2. Open the Property Inspector.

3. Choose one of these options from the Rotate drop-down menu:

    None Applies no rotation to the object.

    Auto Rotates the object once in the direction that requires the least amount of movement.

    CW Rotates the object clockwise. You define the number of rotations by entering a value in the Times field (which is to the right of the Rotate drop-down menu).

    CCW Rotates the object counterclockwise. You define the number of rotations by entering a value in the Times field (which is to the right of the Rotate drop-down menu).

Figure 6.3

Manipulate your curve with the Custom Ease In/Ease Out dialog box.

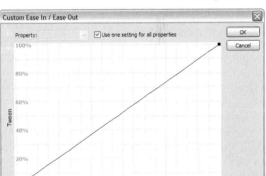

Creating a Shape-Tweened Animation

While motion tweening moves an object from one point of the Stage to another (or changes its characteristics, such as size or orientation), shape tweening morphs an object from one shape to another.

You need to remember that shape tweening works only on shapes drawn on the Stage. You can't shape tween symbol instances, bitmaps, text, or groups of objects. You must break apart these elements (Modify → Break Apart) before you can apply shape tweening to them.

You can create some decidedly interesting effects by using shape tweening.

For a little hands on experience with animation, check out the "Creating an Animated Sci-Fi Space Spectacular" tutorial later in this chapter.

To create a shape tween:

1. Select the keyframe in which you want the shape tween to start. If you haven't created a keyframe, you'll need to create one by selecting the desired frame and selecting Insert → Timeline → Keyframe.

2. Use the drawing tools to create the shape with which you want to start.

3. Click the frame where you want the shape tween to end, and insert a keyframe. As usual, Flash populates the last keyframe with the first keyframe's contents.

4. In the final keyframe, manipulate the object (using one of the various transform tools) so it looks like what you want for the final shape tween. (Alternatively, delete the image, and create a new one.)

If you place the last keyframe's shape in another location, Flash automatically motion tweens the animation as well. Not only will your object "morph," but it will do so as it moves from one location to another on the Stage.

5. Now select the first frame, and open the Property Inspector.

6. Choose Shape from the Tweening drop-down menu.

7. From here, you can set these shape tween's characteristics:

   • Enter a value in the Ease field to ease the tween in or out. Remember, a positive number makes the tween faster at the beginning, and a negative number makes it faster at the end. Alternatively, use the Ease slider to adjust the value.

   • Choose an option from the Blend drop-down menu. Choosing Distributive creates an animation in which the edges of the intermediate shapes are smoother. Alternatively, choosing Angular creates an animation in which straight edges are preserved in the intervening frames.

8. When you're finished, test your animation by moving the playhead, hitting Return/Enter, and selecting Control → Play or Control → Test Scene/Test Movie.

Animating a Mask

Mask layers are used to create a hole through which the contents of the underlying layer are visible. Imagine looking through a keyhole at a complex scene. Because of the shape of the keyhole, you can see only a limited portion of the scene itself. This is essentially how a mask layer works. In Flash, you create the size and shape of the "hole" through which the scene beyond (or, because of the nature of layers, *below*) is visible.

One of the neat things about mask layers is that you can animate the mask so that it moves. Mask layers are useful for creating all sorts of effects such as a scene viewed through a telescope or a landscape revealed by a spotlight—the possibilities are endless.

You cannot mask layers inside Button symbols. Button symbols are covered in Chapter 4, "Working with Symbols."

Here, we'll show you how to create a static mask layer. To do this, you should be familiar with the drawing tools and with importing images, both of which are topics covered in Chapter 2, "Modifying Visual Assets."

First, let's take a look at how you go about creating a mask layer:

1. Make sure you've got two layers—one layer that will act as the mask layer, and one (with content) that will act as masked layer.

A mask layer works *only* on the layer immediately below it.

2. On the mask layer, draw the "hole" through which the other layer will be visible. Although the hole doesn't have to be circular (it can be any shape), it *must* be filled. When the layer is converted into a mask layer, all areas composed of a solid fill will be transparent. On the other hand, all areas not composed of a solid fill will be opaque.

3. Right-click/Ctrl-click the layer's name and choose Mask from the context menu. Alternatively, you can open the Layer Properties dialog box (by double-clicking on the layer's icon) and select the Mask radio button.

4. The layer is automatically turned into a mask layer. Note that both the mask layer's and the masked layer's icons change.

Extending a Still Image Through Time

One additional trick, although straightforward, is incredibly useful. Specifically, you can integrate an image into your Flash movie that occupies a span of time (a series of frames) but doesn't actually move. For instance, you could build a movie that had a static background throughout the course of the movie. That background could be a static Graphic symbol that resides on the lowest layer of a movie that you extend through time.

1. Select the keyframe in which you want the spanned image to start.
2. Place the desired image on the Stage.
3. Click the last keyframe on which you'd like the image to be visible.
4. Choose Insert → Timeline → Frame.
5. Notice that all the intermediate frames are gray, and a small outline of a rectangle appears in the final frame. This means the content from the first keyframe has been carried over to all the frames.

Tutorial: Creating an Animated Sci-Fi Space Spectacular

Ever wanted to travel into space? Well, here's your chance. You aren't really going to travel into space, but with the power of Flash you'll create the next best thing—a sci-fi animated voyage through the cosmos. The project will be broken up into six scenes. The first will be an animation of a rocket taking off from Earth. From there, you'll create four outer space scenes: one with the rocket blasting further away from Earth, one with the rocket traveling through deep space, one with the rocket heading toward a planet, and one where the rocket lands on the mysterious planet. The last scene you create will add a little "Hollywood" to the animation.

 You can find all the images and files used in this tutorial on the book's CD. You'll also find a copy of the finished movie (sci-fi.swf and sci-fi.fla) so you can get an idea of what it looks like. By doing the animation, however, you'll be able to put much of what you learned in this chapter into practice.

Creating the Rocket Ship

Start this tutorial by creating the first scene in the animation—your rocket ship blasting off from Earth:

1. Create a new document. Change its frame rate to 15fps and its background color to black—both of which you can do using the Document Properties dialog box (Modify → Document).
2. Now, double-click the existing layer's name. When it becomes editable, enter **sky**.
3. Select the Rectangle tool ⬜.

4. If it isn't already, open the Property Inspector, and set the stroke color to No Color (by clicking the box with the red line through it just to the left of the color wheel in the Color Picker).

5. Set the fill color to a light blue (suitable for the sky).

6. Once you've set the Rectangle tool's fill and stroke, select the first keyframe of the sky layer, and drag a rectangle that is either the same size as the Stage or slightly larger.

> Why are you creating a blue rectangle? Why don't you just make the background of the movie the necessary light blue? Well, for any given movie, Flash applies the background color across all scenes. So, given that the majority of your scenes are going to take place in space (and therefore require a black background), you'll use the Rectangle tool to create a "false" background with the color you require for the intro scene.

7. Create a new layer by clicking the Add Layer button 🗗 in the lower-left corner of the Timeline or by selecting Insert → Timeline → Layer.

8. Rename this newly created layer **ground**.

9. Once again, select the Rectangle tool 🔲 from the Toolbox.

10. Click the Stroke Color swatch in the Toolbox, and hit the No Color button—which is the box with a red line through it just to the left of the color wheel. This guarantees the shape you draw won't have any stroke.

11. Now, click the Fill Color swatch, and choose a brown or green color. (The rectangle will serve as the ground, so pick an appropriate color.)

12. Select the first keyframe in the ground layer, and draw a rectangle that occupies about a third of the bottom of the Stage. So far, your animation should look something like this:

This tutorial focuses almost no energy on creating a landscape in the first scene. To spruce up your movie, you might want to add elements (buildings and so on)—it's up to you.

13. Now, to keep things tidy, you need to name your scene. Open the Scene panel (Window → Other Panels → Scene), double-click Scene 1 (the only scene in your movie thus far), and type the name **takeoff**.

14. Now, you'll need to import all the graphics you'll use in the scene. Select Insert → New Symbol. When the Create New Symbol dialog box appears, make sure the Movie Clip radio button is selected, type **rocket ship** in the Name field, and click OK.

15. Now, when the Symbol Editor opens, select File → Import → Import to Stage. When the Import dialog box opens, navigate to the `rocketship.swf` file on the CD, and click Open. By doing this, you'll place the rocket ship graphic in the Symbol Editor.

If you don't see the image in the Symbol Editor, scroll down. Sometimes Flash doesn't place the imported graphic in the center of the Symbol Editor. All you need to do is click and drag the rocket ship to the center of the Symbol Editor. Remember, where you put the image in relation to the small crosshairs determines where its registration point is. You can also you the Align panel to place the symbol directly in the center of the Symbol Editor. Just select the symbol, and then align it both horizontally to the center and vertically to the center to the Stage.

16. Now It's time to add some animated flames to the rocket. Name the existing layer **rocket ship**. (Remember, you're still working on the Movie Clip within the Symbol Editor.)

17. Create a new layer, and call it **flames**.

18. Move the flames layer so that it's below the rocket ship layer in the Timeline.

19. Now, select frame 5 in the rocket ship layer, and choose Insert → Timeline → Frame.

20. Now, select the second frame in the flames layer, and choose Insert → Timeline → Keyframe.

The first keyframe will be left blank to simulate the rocket ship without any flames. The reason for this will become far more apparent when you put the scene together.

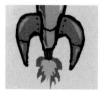

21. With the second keyframe selected (the one you just added), draw some flames coming from the exhaust of the rocket ship with the Pen tool. Use the Paint Bucket tool to fill the outline you've created with a red color. So far, your flames should look something like this:

22. Now, click the third frame in the flames layer, and choose Insert → Timeline → Keyframe.

23. Click the fourth frame in the flames layer, and choose Insert → Timeline → Blank Keyframe.

> If you're having trouble remembering how to use the Pen tool or the Paint Bucket tool, see Chapter 4.

24. With the newly created blank keyframe selected, draw another set of flames coming from the rocket ship's exhaust. Make sure they're similar, but not identical, to the first set of the flames you drew, and fill them with an orange color using the Paint Bucket tool. They should look something like this:

25. Now, click the fifth frame in the flames layer, and choose Insert → Timeline → Keyframe. By doing this, you've created a Movie Clip in which the flames you've drawn will alternate. Because the Movie Clip will loop indefinitely when it's used in the main Timeline, you'll get a simple moving flame effect.

26. Now it's time to insert the rocket ship Movie Clip into the launch scene. If you're still in the Symbol Editor, switch back to the main Timeline by clicking the takeoff link in the Edit bar.

27. Insert a new layer, and call it **rocket ship**.

28. With the first keyframe of the rocket ship layer selected, click and drag the rocket ship Movie Clip from the Library to the Stage. Position it so it's in the middle of the scene. So far, the scene should look something like this:

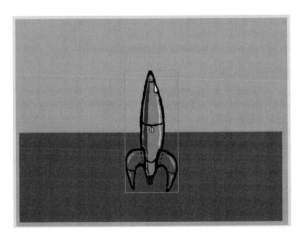

> Remember when you were creating the rocket ship Movie Clip and you left the first keyframe in the flames layer blank? Well, here is where that amazing foresight comes in. If you hadn't left the first keyframe blank, you would have had flames coming from the rocket ship while it was simply sitting there. The blank keyframe gives the illusion of the rocket ship starting up.

29. Select frame 30 in the ground layer, and choose Insert → Timeline → Frame.

30. Select frame 30 in the rocket ship layer, and choose Insert → Timeline → Keyframe.

31. Select frame 30 of the sky layer, and choose Insert → Timeline → Frame.

32. Now, with frame 30 in the rocket ship layer selected, move the rocket ship Movie Clip up until it's outside the Stage.

33. Select the first keyframe in the rocket ship layer, and choose Insert → Timeline → Create Motion Tween. This creates a tweened animation in which the rocket ship flies up into the sky.

34. To add a little more detail, select the first keyframe in the rocket ship tween, open the Property Inspector, and set the Ease to –**100**. This gives the illusion that the rocket ship starts slow but then picks up speed as it rises.

35. Now, save the file by selecting File → Save—name the file **sci-fi**.

You can test your movie by hitting Return/Enter. If you want the rocket ship Movie Clip to play, select Control → Test Movie.

Speeding Away from Earth

Now that you've created the first scene in your animation, you can create the second one. You'll be continuing your space voyage by creating a scene in which the rocket ship speeds into space with Earth receding in the background. Because it will add another dimension to the scene, we'll show how to engineer a little visual trickery to simulate the illusion of depth and distance:

1. Make sure you have the sci-fi file open.

2. Open the Scene panel, if it isn't already open (Window → Other Panels → Scene), and add a second scene by clicking the Add Scene button or by choosing Insert → Scene.

3. Double-click the name of the scene you've just created, and enter **departure** in the field.

4. If it isn't already, select the departure scene.

5. Now, you'll start creating the stars that will be scattered throughout the space portions of your animation. Select Insert → New Symbol. When the Create New Symbol dialog box appears, enter **star** in the Name field, select the Graphic radio button, and click OK.

6. When the Symbol Editor appears, use the Oval tool to draw a small, yellow circle about 4 pixels in diameter. Make sure the circle's stroke is also yellow.

You might be thinking that it would be better to create a star that was star shaped, instead of circular. However, at the size that it is (about 4 pixels wide), a star shaped symbol wouldn't be any more recognizable than a small circle.

7. When you're finished creating your star (which you'll use repeatedly in the space scene), return to the main Timeline by clicking the departure link in the Edit bar.

8. Now, import the graphic you'll be using for Earth. Select Insert → New Symbol. When the Create New Symbol dialog box opens, enter **earth** in the Name field, select the Graphic radio button, and click OK.

9. When the Symbol Editor Opens, select File → Import → Import to Stage. When the Import dialog box opens, navigate to the earth.swf file on the book's CD, and click Open.

10. Now, you're set to start adding assets to your scene. Use the Edit Scene button (in the right portion of the Edit bar) to switch the departure scene.

11. Change the existing layer's name to **stars**.

12. If it isn't already, open the Library (Window → Library), select the first keyframe in the stars layer, and repeatedly drag the star symbol to the Stage. The number of stars you place on the Stage is up to you.

13. Add a layer to the main Timeline, and change its name to **earth**.

14. With the Library open, drag the earth symbol to the Stage. Position it so it's located in the bottom-left corner of the Stage. So far, your scene should look something like this:

15. Create a third layer, and call it **rocket ship**.

16. Select the first keyframe in the rocket ship layer, open the Library, and drag the rocket ship Movie Clip (which you created in the previous section of the tutorial) to the Stage.

17. The rocket ship Movie Clip's current size and orientation isn't appropriate for the current scene (the cockpit is actually facing downwards). As a result, you'll have to fiddle with it a bit. First, select it, and then select Modify → Transform → Flip Horizontal.

18. Select Free Transform tool ⊡ from the Toolbox, click the rocket ship Movie Clip, and select the Rotate and Skew button in the Options section of the Toolbox.

19. Rotate the rocket ship Movie Clip roughly 45° clockwise. This gives your rocket ship a decent trajectory as it speeds away from Earth.

> Alternatively, you can simply use the Transform panel (Window → Transform). Just click the Rotate radio button, and enter **45** in the Rotate Value field.

20. With the first keyframe still selected, use either the Free Transform tool or the Transform panel to shrink the rocket ship symbol so it's small. By doing this, you create the illusion that the rocket ship is far away at the start of the animation. Later, you'll add to the illusion of depth and distance by having the rocket ship fly "toward" the viewer.

21. Select the rocket ship symbol with the Arrow tool, and position it so that it's somewhere over the middle of the earth symbol. So far, your scene should look something like this (note the small rocket ship symbol in the middle of the earth symbol):

22. Now that you've placed all the elements you're going to use in the scene, it's time to do some animating. Select frame 35 in the stars layer, and select Insert → Timeline → Frame.

23. Select frame 35 in the earth layer, and select Insert → Timeline → Frame.

24. Select frame 35 in the rocket ship layer, and select Insert → Timeline → Keyframe.

25. Select the keyframe you just created in the rocket ship layer. Click and drag the rocket ship symbol to a location just outside the top-right corner of the Stage.

26. With the Free Transform tool or the Transform panel, increase the rocket ship symbol to larger than its original size. Once you've scaled the symbol, make sure all of

it is off the Stage. Once animated, this will create the illusion that the rocket ship flies from Earth past your point of view. At this point, frame 35 should look some thing like this:

27. Select the first keyframe in the rocket ship layer, and select Insert → Timeline → Create Motion Tween. This creates a tweened animation of the rocket ship increasing in size as it "flies" past the camera. However, depending on where the rocket ship is in the final keyframe, the animation could look a little bit funny—like the rocket ship is flying without its nose pointed exactly forward. You'll remedy this by adding a straight path along which the rocket ship will move.

28. Select the first keyframe in the rocket ship layer, and click the Add Motion Guide button ⁺ⁱᵢ at the bottom-right corner of the main Timeline.

29. Select the first keyframe in the motion guide layer (which appears directly above the rocket ship layer), and use the Line tool to draw a trajectory from the middle of the earth symbol an inch or so past where your rocket ship ends up in the final keyframe.

> Because the scene's background is black, you'll have some problems with the line (whose default color is also black) getting lost. To avoid this, either change the stroke color before you draw the line (by using the stroke's Color Picker in the Toolbox's Colors section) or change the background color of your movie temporarily by selecting Modify → Document and clicking the Background color swatch.

30. With the first keyframe in the rocket ship layer selected, click and drag the small rocket ship symbol so that it snaps to the start of the linear motion path. Because the rocket ship symbol is small, you might want to use the Zoom tool 🔍 to get a better look at the area with which you're working.

31. Click the last keyframe in the layer, and click and drag the larger rocket ship symbol so that it snaps onto the end of the motion path.

> If you have trouble snapping the rocket ship's registration point to the path, make sure Snap to Objects is turned on (View → Snapping → Snap to Objects). Also, you might have to click the registration point and then hold your mouse down for a second before dragging to make the snapping registration point appear.

32. Select the first keyframe in the layer, and open the Property Inspector.

33. Check the Orient to Path box, and set Easing to **−100**. By doing this, the rocket ship will always point in the direction of the path. By changing the Easing setting, the rocket ship will start slowly and gain speed as it travels along the path, thereby furthering the illusion of depth and distance.

34. It's time to animate Earth receding into the distance. Click frame 35 in the earth layer, and select Insert → Timeline → Keyframe.

35. With the newly created keyframe selected, click and drag the earth symbol into the work area, just outside the bottom-left corner of the Stage. With frame 35 still selected, use the Free Transform tool or the Transform panel to shrink the earth symbol to about 25 percent of its former size. When animated, this creates the impression that Earth is moving off into the distance.

36. With the first keyframe of the earth layer selected, select Insert → Timeline → Create Motion Tween.

You've just finished the second scene in the animation! To test it, simply hit Return/ Enter. If you want the rocket ship Movie Clip to work properly, select Control → Test Scene. If you want to view the entire animation thus far (including scene 1), select Control → Test Movie.

Zipping Through Space

Now that you've created the scene in which the rocket ship zips away from Earth, you can start on the third scene in the animation, the rocket ship careening through space:

1. If it isn't already, open the Scene panel, and add a third scene by clicking the Add Scene button **+** or by selecting Insert → Scene.

2. Double-click the name of the scene you've just created, and enter **travel** in the field.

3. Select the single layer in the Timeline, and change its name to **stars**. Now, with the stars layer still selected, click frame 30, and then select Insert → Timeline → Frame.

4. Select the first blank keyframe in the stars layer, open the Library, and click and drag as many instances of the star symbol as you want to the Stage.

5. From here, you'll need to add some "texture" to the scene by including a planet for the rocket ship to pass by. Select Insert → New Symbol. When the Create New Symbol dialog box opens, enter **planet1** in the Name field, click the Graphic radio button, and click OK.

6. When the Symbol Editor opens, select File → Import → Import to Stage. When the Import dialog box opens, select the `planet1.swf` file on the CD.

7. Remember to click and drag the graphic to the registration point marker in the middle of the Symbol Editor.

8. Return to the main Timeline. From there, create a new layer by clicking the Insert Layer button in the bottom-left corner of the Timeline or by selecting Insert → Timeline → Layer, and then name it **planet**.

9. With the first keyframe of the planet layer selected, click and drag the planet1 symbol from the Library to the right portion of the Stage. At this point, your scene should look something like this:

10. Now, with the planet layer selected, click frame 30, and select Insert → Timeline → Keyframe.

11. Select the final keyframe in the planet layer, and click and drag the planet1 symbol about 1.5 inches (4 centimeters) to the left. Now, select the first keyframe in the planet layer, and select Insert → Timeline → Create Motion Tween. By adding a little motion to the planet, you'll create the illusion that the rocket ship is traveling at high speed.

12. Now for the actual rocket ship. Create a new layer in the main Timeline, and call it **rocket ship**.

13. Select the first keyframe in the rocket ship layer, and drag the rocket ship Movie Clip from the Library into the work area just to the left of the Stage. Use the Free Transform tool or the Transform panel to orient the rocket ship horizontally. So far, your scene should look something like this:

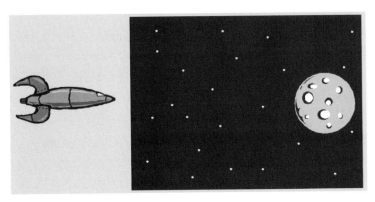

14. Now, with the rocket ship layer selected, click frame 30, and select Insert → Timeline → Keyframe.

15. Click the final keyframe in the rocket ship layer, and click and drag the rocket ship Movie Clip to the other side of the Stage into the work area.

16. Select the first keyframe in the rocket ship layer, and select Insert → Timeline → Create Motion Tween.

You've just completed the animation of the rocket ship hurtling though space. To test it, simply hit Return/Enter. If you want the rocket ship Movie Clip to work properly, you'll have to select Control → Test Scene. If you want to view the entire animation thus far (including scene 1 and 2), select Control → Test Movie.

Approaching Planet X

Now it's time to create the sequence in the animation in which your little rocket ship flies toward its intended destination, the mysterious planet X:

1. Open the Scene panel, if it isn't already open (Window → Other Panels → Scene), and add a fourth scene by clicking the Add Scene button **+** or by selecting Insert → Scene.

2. Double-click the name of the scene you've just created, and enter **descent** in the field.

3. Select the single layer in the Timeline, and change its name to **stars**. Now, with the stars layer still selected, click frame 30, and select Insert → Timeline → Frame.

4. Select the first blank keyframe in the stars layer, open the Library, and click and drag as many instances of the star symbol as you want to the Stage.

5. From here, you'll need to add the planet to the scene. Select Insert → New Symbol. When the Create New Symbol dialog box opens, enter **planet2** in the Name field, click the Graphic radio button, and click OK.

6. When the Symbol Editor opens, select File → Import → Import to Stage. When the Import dialog box opens, select the `planet2.swf` file on the book's CD.

7. Remember to click and drag the graphic to the registration point marker in the middle of the Symbol Editor.

8. Return to the main Timeline. From there, create a new layer by clicking the Insert Layer button in the bottom-left corner of the Timeline or by selecting Insert → Layer, and then name it **planet x**.

9. With the first keyframe of the planet x layer selected, drag the planet2 symbol from the Library to the lower-right portion of the Stage. Because the symbol is fairly large, use the Free Transform tool or the Transform panel to shrink it to about 1 inch (3 centimeters) across—or about 123×123 pixels. So far, your scene should look something like this:

10. Select frame 30 in the stars layer, and select Insert → Timeline → Frame.

11. Now, click frame 30 in the planet x layer, and select Insert → Timeline → Keyframe.

12. With the last keyframe selected in the planet x layer, select the planet2 symbol, and increase its size (either with the Free Transform tool or the Transform panel) to the point where it dominates much of the Stage. At this point, the scene should look something like this:

13. Now, with the first keyframe in the planet x layer selected, select Insert → Timeline → Create Motion Tween.

14. At this point, you can start working on the rocket ship itself. Create a new layer, and call it **rocket ship**.

15. Select the first keyframe in the rocket ship layer, and drag the rocket ship Movie Clip from the Library to the Stage. Position it so that it's in the work area just outside the top-left corner of the Stage.

16. Use either the Rotate tool or the Transform panel to rotate the rocket ship Movie Clip so that it's pointing toward the planet2 symbol. The result should be something like this:

17. Now, with the rocket ship layer still selected, click frame 30, and select Insert → Time-line → Keyframe.

18. Select the keyframe you've just created, and move the rocket ship Movie Clip over the middle of the planet. Then, use the Scale tool or the Transform panel to reduce its size substantially. The result should be something like this (note the small rocket ship symbol in the middle of the planet):

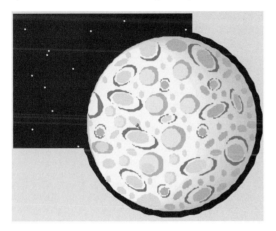

19. Select the first frame in the rocket ship layer, and select Insert → Timeline → Create Motion Tween.

20. Much like in the case when you created the first scene, your rocket ship's movement might look a little off. To correct this, you'll create a straight motion path for it to follow.

21. Select the first keyframe in the rocket ship layer, and click the Add Motion Guide button ![icon] at the bottom-left of the main Timeline.

22. Select the first keyframe in the motion guide layer (which appears directly above the rocket ship layer), and use the Line tool to draw a trajectory from where the rocket ship starts to where it ends in the final keyframe—remember, you could run into problems if the Line tool draws a black line along the black background.

23. With the first keyframe in the rocket ship layer selected, click and drag the large rocket ship symbol so that it snaps to the start of the linear motion path.

24. Now, click the last keyframe in the layer, and click and drag the small rocket ship symbol so that it snaps onto the end of the motion path—you'll probably need to zoom in because the rocket ship is so small.

25. Select the first keyframe in the layer, and open the Property Inspector.

26. Check the Orient to Path box, and set Easing to **100**. By doing this, the rocket ship with always point in the direction of the path. By changing the Easing setting, the rocket ship will start fast and slow down as it travels along the path, thereby further-ing the illusion of depth and distance.

You've just finished the animation in which your rocket ship approaches planet X. To test it, hit Return/Enter. If you want the rocket ship Movie Clip to work properly, you'll have to select Control → Test Scene. If you want to view the entire animation thus far (including the other scenes), select Control → Test Movie.

Landing on Planet X

Now that you've animated your rocket ship approaching the mysterious planet X, you need to animate the scene in which your intrepid explorer actually lands:

1. Open the Scene panel, if it isn't already open (Window → Other Panels → Scene), and add a fourth scene by clicking the Add Scene button **+** (at the bottom of the Scene panel) or by selecting Insert → Scene.

2. Double-click the name of the scene you've just created, and enter **landing** in the field.

3. Rename the existing layer to **alien landscape**.

4. Select the first keyframe of the alien landscape layer, and select File → Import → Import to Stage.

5. When the Import dialog box opens, select the `alien_landscape.swf` file on the CD.

> We've created the imported alien landscape background so you don't have to go through the fuss and muss of creating it yourself. However, if you want to see something else on the surface of the mysterious planet X, feel free to create it yourself.

6. Position the imported background so that it overlays the Stage exactly. At this point, your scene should look something like this:

7. Insert a new layer, and call it **rocket ship**.

8. With the first keyframe of the rocket ship layer selected, click and drag the rocket ship Movie Clip from the Library to the Stage. Position it so that it's in the work area just above the top of the Stage. At this point, the scene should look something like this:

9. Now, it's time to do some animating. Select frame 30 in the rocket ship layer, and select Insert → Timeline → Keyframe.

10. Select frame 30 in the alien landscape layer, and select Insert → Timeline → Frame.

11. Now, with frame 30 in the rocket ship layer selected, move the rocket ship Movie Clip up until it's "sitting" on the ground of the alien landscape.

12. Select the first keyframe in the rocket ship layer, and select Insert → Timeline → Create Motion Tween. This creates a tweened animation in which the rocket ship lands on planet X.

13. To add a little more detail, select the first keyframe in the rocket ship tween, open the Property Inspector, and set the Ease to **100**. This gives the illusion that the rocket ship starts fast but then slows down as it lands.

Adding Some Hollywood Glamour

You're just about there! You've finished the first five scenes in your animation. In the final scene, you'll add a bit of cheesy "Hollywood" to cap it all off:

1. If it isn't already, open the Scene panel, and add a sixth scene by clicking the Add Scene button or by selecting Insert → Scene.

2. Double-click the name of the scene you've just created, and enter **finale** in the field.

3. Select Insert → New Symbol.

4. When the Create New Symbol dialog box opens, type **To Be Continued** in the Name field, click the Graphic radio button, and click OK.

5. Select the Text tool from the Toolbox.

6. *Before* you add any text, open the Property Inspector.

7. When the Property Inspector opens, choose a font from the Font drop-down menu. (To preserve the effect, choose something big and blocky.) Then, enter a size (make it large) in the Size field. Also, make sure that you've selected Static Text from the Text Type dropdown menu.

8. Because the background of your movie is black, choose a light color for the text such as white.

9. Now, click in the center of the Symbol Editor, and type **To Be Continued...**.

10. When you've finished, click your cursor anywhere outside the text box. Click and drag the text to the center of the Symbol Editor (if it isn't already there).

11. Now, to create a "dramatic" fade-out text effect, switch to the main Timeline by clicking the finale link in the Edit bar, and select the first keyframe in the scene's single layer. (If you want, you can name the layer something distinct. However, because it will be the only one in the scene, it's not necessary.)

12. Drag the To Be Continued symbol from the Library to the middle of the Stage.

13. Click frame 15, and select Insert → Timeline → Keyframe.

14. Select the keyframe you just created.

15. In the Property Inspector, choose Alpha from the Color drop-down menu, and enter **0** in the Alpha Value field.

16. Now, click the first keyframe in the layer, and select Insert → Timeline → Create Motion Tween. This creates the fade-in text effect.

Congratulations—you've completed the final scene in the animation! To view the entire animation, select Control → Test Movie.

Animating a Symbol Instance's Visual Properties with the Property Inspector

One of the great features of tweening is that you aren't limited to position, size, and shape. You can also tween more complicated changes to an object's appearance. You can animate a fade-in/fade-out effect or color change by taking what you've learned about tweening thus far and combining it with the tools in the Property Inspector. In Chapter 4, you manipulated a symbol's visual properties with the Property Inspector, so its options should be familiar to you. In the following sections, you'll learn how to animate changes in an object's transparency, brightness, and tint.

> You can perform the following processes only on symbols, not on shapes or groups of shapes created with Flash's painting and drawing tools directly on the Stage.

Animating a Symbol's Transparency

By animating an object's alpha effect (or transparency), you can create the illusion of a fade-in/fade-out:

1. Click the first keyframe in the tweened animation, and select the symbol instance that you want to fade in with the Arrow tool.

2. If it isn't open already, open the Property Inspector.

3. Choose Alpha from the Color drop-down menu.

4. Enter **0** in the Alpha Value field. By doing this, you're making the object in the first keyframe transparent.

5. Click the last keyframe in the animation, and select the object you're working on with the Arrow tool.

6. With the Property Inspector open and Alpha selected from the Color drop-down menu, enter **100** in the Alpha Value field. This makes the object opaque (solid) in the final keyframe.

7. Now, test your animation by hitting Return/Enter and selecting Control → Play or Control → Test Scene/Test Movie. Your object will now fade in.

> To have an item fade out, do the opposite. Set Alpha Value in the first keyframe to 100 and in the last keyframe to 0.

Animating an Object's Brightness

Animating an object's brightness is almost identical to the process of animating an object's transparency:

1. Click the first keyframe in the tweened animation, and select the symbol instance whose brightness you want to change.

2. If it isn't open already, open the Property Inspector.

3. Choose Brightness from the Color drop-down menu.

4. Enter a value in the Brightness Value field (or use the Brightness slider).

5. Click the last keyframe in the animation, and select the object with which you're working.

6. With the Property Inspector open, enter a different value in the Brightness Value field.

7. Now test your animation by hitting Return/Enter and choosing Control → Play or Control → Test Scene/Test Movie.

> Because you can't simulate the same sort of brightness experienced in the real world, altering the brightness of an object actually does more to change the intensity of its color.

Animating a Color Change

Like the previous two procedures, animating a color change is just a matter of using a different area of the Property Inspector:

1. Click the first keyframe in the tweened animation, and select the symbol instance whose color you want to change.

2. If it isn't open already, open the Property Inspector.

3. Choose Tint from the Color drop-down menu.

4. From here, click the Tint color swatch to open the Color Picker. From here, choose one of the colors. Alternatively, you can mix a custom RGB color by inputting values in the R, G, and B fields.

5. Click the last keyframe in the animation, and select the object with which you're working.

6. With the Property Inspector open, choose another color.

7. Now test your animation by hitting Return/Enter and selecting Control → Play or Control → Test Scene/Test Movie. Your object will change from the color set in the first keyframe to the color set in the last keyframe.

> If you want to combine a color change with a fade, you need to use the Advance option (which was discussed in Chapter 4).

Creating Animated Visual Effects with Graphic Filters

Graphic filters are extremely powerful tools for adding extra visual complexity to your movie. In total, Flash 8 has several filters (Bevel, Drop Shadow, Blur, Gradient Glow, Gradient Bevel, and Adjust Color), all of which can be applied to text, Button symbols, and Movie Clip symbols.

Besides that filters open a new horizon of design possibilities, they're important for a couple of reasons. First, unlike with art imported from another program (to create the glow on an object, for instance), filters are rendered in real time by the Flash Player. This means you might not get the kind of slowdown that you might get if you're using an imported raster image to simulate an effect. The second important feature of filters, and certainly the most pertinent to this chapter, is that you can animate them just like you can animate anything else in Flash. For example, you can easily tween a drop shadow or a glow—something that might allow you to add that special professional polish to your movie.

The process by which you animate a graphic filter is similar to animating a symbol instance's visual properties with the Property Inspector. All you need to do is apply a graphic filter of your choice to a symbol, tween that symbol, and then change the filter's properties between the first keyframe in the tween and its properties in the final keyframe. You can also combine an animated graphic filter with a series of other tweened animation techniques. For example, you could create a symbol that tweens along a path while at the same time changing the symbol's size during the tween and animating the glow filter.

Tutorial: Creating Motion Blur

To get more familiar with how you can animate graphic filters, you'll learn how you use the Blur Graphic filter to create an animation with motion blur—in this case, a simple animation of a sphere moving across the Stage:

1. Create a small symbol of a sphere. The color and size aren't really that important, though a smaller sphere would most likely be better.

> Remember, graphic filters work only with text, Button symbols, and Movie Clip symbols. As a result, you need to make sure you aren't using a Graphic symbol.

2. Drag the sphere from the Library to the left side of the Stage.

3. Insert a keyframe (Insert → Timeline → Keyframe) in the fifth or sixth frame.

4. Select the last keyframe, and drag the sphere to the right size of the screen.

5. Select the first keyframe, and select Insert → Timeline → Create Motion Tween.

6. Select Modify → Document. When the Document Properties dialog box appears, change the frame rate to 25. This frame rate, coupled with the short animation, will mean that the sphere will move quickly across the Stage.

7. Click somewhere in the middle of the tween, and insert a keyframe (Insert → Timeline → Keyframe).

8. Select the newly created keyframe, and then select the sphere with the Arrow tool.

9. Open the Properly Inspector, and click the Filters tab.

10. Click the Add Filter button, and select Blur from the drop-down menu.

11. Set the Blur X value to **30**—this will blur the sphere horizontally, thereby creating the illusion of a motion blur.

Clicking the little padlock icon to the right of the Blue X and Blur Y fields will constrain (or de-constrain) the X and Y values to the same value.

12. If it isn't, set the quality of the blur to High.

13. To add a little more detail to the animation, compress the sphere vertically, and elongate it slightly using the Free Transform tool ⊞ . This further reinforces the feeling of rapid movement.

14. Now test your animation by hitting Return/Enter and choosing Control → Play or Control → Test Scene/Test Movie.

A finished version of this tutorial has been provided in the Chapter 6 folder of the book's CD.

Using Scenes to Organize Animated Content

Scenes are wondrous little tools that segment the overall content of your movie into self-contained, manageable chunks. The scenes act as mini-movies that play one after the other. Although they appear to be somewhat separated from one another within the Flash authoring environment, they really aren't. When you play the overall movie (either from within Flash or after it has been published), the scenes string together as if they were one movie and play according to the sequence listed in the Scene panel. You'll never see any perceivable lag or flicker between scenes.

The number of scenes you can have is limited only by the amount of memory in your computer.

The possibilities for scenes are endless. Say, for instance, you're creating an entire Flash site. You could use a scene for each section and subsection of the site. Another possibility is along the lines of traditional film or theater. Web-based Flash animated shorts are becoming increasingly popular these days. You could use scenes to partition an animated short you created into…well, scenes!

For the most part, you access the majority of scene functionality through the Scene panel, which you open by choosing Window → Other Panels → Scene (see Figure 6.4). The Scene panel displays the number and organization of your movie's scenes. In addition, it lets you duplicate, add, move, and delete scenes.

Figure 6.4

Use the Scene panel to duplicate, add, move, and delete scenes.

Although scenes are great for organizing animated content, they tend to create a fairly linear product. Granted, you can't do anything about the linearity of scenes; you certainly can't have two scenes playing at the same time. However, what if you wanted to play your first scene, followed by your third scene, your second scene, and finally your fourth scene? Alternatively, what if you wanted your scenes to play from last to first, instead of from first to last? Under normal circumstances, this defies the natural laws of Flash. However, by using ActionScript (specifically frame actions), you can be your own Einstein, shattering the conventions of the known Flash universe! But seriously, as is the case in many aspects of Flash, ActionScripting greatly extends scene functionality.

The most basic of actions (global functions) can help in this regard:

- `gotoAndPlay()` determines the specific scene and frame that the playhead jumps to when it evokes the action.

- `gotoAndStop()` goes to a specific scene or frame and stops the movie. This is a variation of the `gotoAndPlay()`.

- `play()` restarts a movie that has been previously stopped.

- `stop()` ends the movie from playing any further.

Adding a Scene

As your movie increases in size and complexity, you'll want to add more scenes to keep a firm grip on its organization. By using the Scene panel, you can add as many scenes as you want:

1. Make sure you have a document open.

2. Choose Window → Other Panels → Scene to open the Scene panel.

3. Click the Add Scene button **+** located in the bottom-right corner of the Scene panel. Alternatively, besides using the Scene panel to add a new scene, you can select Insert → Scene.

4. You'll notice that Flash has added a scene to the movie. By default, Flash always adds the new scene below the currently selected one. The default naming convention for a new scene is numerical—for instance, scene 1, scene 2, and so on.

5. Now all you have to do is select the newly added scene in the Scene panel and start creating.

When you create a new scene, Flash automatically switches to the newly created scene.

Deleting a Scene

To delete a scene:

1. Open the Scene panel by choosing Window → Other Panels → Scene.

2. Select the scene you want to delete.

3. Click the Delete Scene button 🗑 located in the bottom-right corner of the Scene panel.

4. When the prompt appears, click OK. As indicated in the prompt, you can't undo a scene deletion.

Duplicating a Scene

Macromedia has integrated a simple duplicate function that lets you create a copy of any given scene with a click of a button:

1. With the Scene panel open (Window → Other Panels → Scene), select the scene you want to duplicate.

2. Click the Duplicate Scene button 🔁 in the bottom-right section of the Scene panel.

3. You'll notice that a duplicate of your selected scene, with the word *copy* tagged onto the original name, appears in the Scene panel.

Renaming a Scene

The default name that Flash assigns to a new or duplicate scene isn't very original. Although logically numbered, the names aren't particularly useful when it comes to identifying the content of individual scenes in a large movie.

To rename a scene:

1. With the Scene panel open, double-click the scene whose name you want to change. By doing this, as shown in Figure 6.5, the scene's name becomes editable.

2. Type a new name, and press Return/Enter (or click anywhere off the Scene panel).

Figure 6.5

The Scene panel shows an editable scene name.

Rearranging Scenes

Scenes play sequentially based on their positions in the Scene panel. But you certainly aren't stuck with the order in which the scenes were created (and therefore the sequence that they play).

To change the arrangement of scenes:

1. Open the Scene panel (Window → Other Panels → Scene).

2. Click and drag the scene to the location you want. You'll notice that as long as you keep your mouse button down, your cursor changes and a blue line appears in the scene's projected location.

3. To move the scene, just release the mouse button.

Moving Between Scenes

Because you'll want to switch back and forth between various scenes as you work on them, Flash has provided several scene navigation tools:

Scene panel To navigate between the various scenes in your movie, all you need to do is click the desired scene in the Scene panel. Your current scene is displayed in the Edit bar.

Edit Scene button Two buttons dominate the right portion of the Edit bar. The leftmost one, when clicked, provides a menu of all the current scenes in your movie. All you need to do is select one, and Flash automatically switches to that scene.

Movie Explorer As discussed in Chapter 9, the Movie Explorer (Window → Movie Explorer) displays the contents of your movie hierarchically, lets you search your entire movie for any symbol or symbol instance, and replaces text and fonts.

Because scenes are part of the overall movie, they're displayed in the Movie Explorer as top-level items in the organizational hierarchy. Simply locate the scene by its name, and click it. Flash automatically switches you to the selected scene.

> Under normal circumstances, the Movie Explorer displays the contents of the currently selected scene only. To display all scenes (and their contents), choose Show All Scenes from the Movie Explorer's drop-down Options menu.

Testing Scenes

When it comes to scenes, if you were to simply hit Return/Enter to play your movie within the Flash authoring environment, you'd be able to preview the currently active scene only. When exported, the movie plays all the scenes sequentially; however, it doesn't do so from within Flash. As a result, you need to do one of the following:

- To test a scene other than the current one, use the Scene panel to select it, and then hit Return/Enter. Alternatively, you can choose Control → Test Scene.

- Now, if you want to test the movie in its entirety, select Control → Test Movie or use the shortcut Ctrl+Enter / Cmd+Return. This opens the movie in the Flash Player and plays all the scenes according to their sequence within the Scene panel.

> You can also play all the scenes in your movie by choosing Control → Play All Scenes.

CHAPTER 7

Animating with ActionScript

ActionScript has come a long way since its early days and is now a fully fledged environment within Flash. ActionScript has many uses, but one of the most common is creating animation. In this chapter, we'll cover the concepts behind animating with ActionScript (a.k.a. scripted animation). We'll also cover the Flash Player and show you how to create movies that use it efficiently.

- **Using the Flash Player efficiently and correctly**
- **Creating and scheduling events**
- **Scripting motion**

Using the Flash Player

The Flash Player is at version 8 as of this writing. Version 8 of the Flash Player has a number of new features:

- Enhanced video, including better codecs and alpha channel support
- Better security, putting the Flash Player security model closer to the security imposed on traditional web documents
- New graphic effects, including per-pixel effects and the potential for faster screen rendering
- An updated text-rendering engine

> The code examples in this chapter use scope via the this keyword, which is covered in detail in Chapter 12. We recommend you read about scope before reading the code-specific sections of this chapter.

The Flash Player is required to play all Flash SWFs. The Flash Player comes in a number of slightly different forms. Ignoring the operating system-specific and device-specific versions of the Flash Player, you may come across the following versions of the Flash Player on a standard desktop computer:

- The Flash Player your browser uses. Depending on which browser you use, this will be either an ActiveX control (Microsoft Internet Explorer) or the Flash plug-in (a number of other non-Microsoft browsers).
- The stand-alone Flash Player is installed along with the Flash authoring environment. You shouldn't assume anyone other than a developer will have this version installed.
- The Flash projector consists of a stand-alone Flash executable containing a SWF file. You can produce an executable projector file by checking the Windows projector or Macintosh Projector check boxes on the Formats tab of the Publish Settings dialog box (File → Publish Settings).

> Flash 8 has some security constraints that may prevent you from testing Flash content (via a SWF file) on a local machine. One quick way around this is to simply create an executable file, because a projector has far fewer security limitations imposed on it. For example, we use this route often when we need in-house testing teams to evaluate Flash content on local computers; in those cases, we distribute projectors (rather than SWFs) to the testers.

- The debug player is a version of the Flash Player that runs within the Flash authoring environment when you select either Test Movie (Control → Test Movie) or Debug Movie (Control → Debug Movie). The debug player allows you to use the Debug panel and the Output panel. Also, one version of the debug player is for use in browser environments. If you have the Flash authoring application installed on your computer, you will usually be able to find the installer for the browser debug player in a folder called Debug.

That's a lot of different versions, and we haven't even covered the mobile and palmtop versions of the Flash Player. When you include them in the mix, you have almost a dozen Flash Player versions with which to work. The following sections will help you keep them all straight.

Using the Flash Player Efficiently

Any long-term Flash designer will tell you that efficient use of the Flash Player involves more than just knowing how to maintain high frame rates in the current version of the Flash Player. Knowing who will view the site, what they will view it on, and what the content will be are also important, as is the level of backward compatibility the client will expect.

Considering Development Techniques

The first topic to consider when you want to use the Flash Player efficiently is making sure you're designing for the right version. For web content, you will design for the browser-based versions. If you're developing web applications, you will almost always need to use the debug version of the browser-based Flash Player. If you're creating CD-based content, you may have to use projectors. It's important that you test your Flash movies early and often against the final version of the Flash Player that you will use. It's common to hear stories of someone who designed for a web audience but forgot to test the site on Firefox (and the client used Firefox) or the designer who created CD content but didn't test it from a CD-based environment until the final week (and unsurprisingly, nothing worked).

Additionally, you should test Flash content destined for the Web on a number of different browsers. It is entirely possible to have the top five browsers installed on the same computer without any issues.

> Most browsers will not change the way the SWF plays, but they can change the placement of the SWF within its HTML slightly. For example, just a 1-pixel difference caused by how two browsers parse your Cascading Style Sheets (CSS) can leave a nasty gap in your design!

You should test any Flash site on Windows and on a Mac. Cross-platform differences between the Windows and Mac flavors of the Flash Player can cause problems. The top two big differences are as follows:

- The two versions can display text that's slightly different in terms of size. You shouldn't count on pixel-accurate text position for flowing text. If you really need pixel accuracy for small amounts of text, you should consider breaking the text into vectors. However, it's better to make sure your design can stand a few pixels difference in text size.

- The two versions can have slightly different frame rates for the same content. The Mac version of the Flash Player was slower than the Windows version in the earlier versions of the Flash Player, although fewer differences exist in the Flash 8 Player.

Occasionally, you will find that the Flash Player slows down on one operating system but will work perfectly in the other. Increasing the frame rate by 1 frame per second (fps) usually fixes the problem. This issue seems to be much more frequent in the Flash 5 and 6 Players and occurs much less frequently in more recent versions of the Flash Player.

Finally, it is a good idea to decide on a minimum computer system on which your site should work well. Many professional web designers have cutting-edge hardware, but the general web population will be at least a year behind the curve. In fact, you could buy an old laptop that's three years behind your development hardware so that you can test your sites on a less powerful system. Having such a computer also allows you to install older versions of browsers and/or older versions of the Flash Player for testing purposes.

Different types of sites imply different minimum hardware requirements of the typical user. Sites for new cars and luxury goods can usually assume higher than average minimum hardware. This may be one reason why car websites tend to feature highly in web design awards—they're able to use cutting-edge effects.

Considering Flash Player Versions

Most clients want some level of backward compatibility, and you should always ask about this up front. Most clients will ask for minimum support that includes the previous version of the Flash Player. As of this writing (with the Flash 8 Player being the latest version), few clients will accept Flash 8-only content unless they specifically want to use Flash 8's new video or per-pixel graphic capabilities. Most clients require Flash 7 Player compatibility, and some still want Flash 6 Player support.

Not asking the client about minimum support and using all the cool-wow features of the latest Flash Player version can be a recipe for disaster. You may have to redevelop a substantial part of the site, and you will have to do it at the last minute, resulting in something that works but may not be the most efficient implementation. *Always ask the client about the target version of the Flash Player.* If they don't know, it's a good idea to assume the last version of the Flash Player unless you have a compelling reason to decide otherwise.

> Even if a client is keen to use the latest version of the Flash Player, experience shows that many clients become less keen when their customer support team starts seeing e-mails from users who had to install the latest Flash Player before they could enter the company site. The cool Flash 8 content you see on the top Flash designers' sites is meant for the consumption of other Flash designers; clients are somewhat more conservative in their use of technology.

Another important tip when showing the performance of a site to a client for the first time is to show them the site on your machine and not theirs (or at least have a stand-alone laptop handy). Many clients have network-connected machines, and the background network traffic can often cause a Flash movie's playback to become glitchy and uneven for short periods, especially on mid-range business machines.

> The following issues are likely to occur only in projects undertaken by Flash developers of large scale projects. Designers who write SWFs that generate a couple hundred variables have nothing to fear.

Certain versions of the Flash Player are particularly bad at some types of applications:

- Flash 5 Player and Flash 6 Player have inefficient support for XML. If you're creating web applications, you should use Flash 7 Player as a minimum.

- Flash 7 Player and previous versions have memory leakage problems under certain conditions. Such problems are likely to occur if you create local instances that can contain a lot of data (such as `Array`, `XML`, `XMLNode`, or `Object` objects) within event handlers, especially anonymous event handlers. Such local data may not be cleared correctly once the event terminates and will therefore contribute to memory leakage. When the leakage gets up to about 40MB, the Flash Player will usually become sluggish or simply lock up. Flash 8 Player has better memory management, and this problem is less likely to occur. If you have to use Flash 7 Player for data-intensive operations, you should consider explicitly clearing all instances containing large amounts of data using the `delete` keyword.

Maintaining High Frame Rates

Assuming you have decided on your audience, have sorted out the minimum version of the Flash Player you will be supporting with your client, and know whether the content will play over the Web or from a CD, the next big step is implementing the movie in a way that keeps the frame rate sufficiently high to maintain fluid animation and responsive interaction.

You can do this in a number of ways, which can be broadly split into animation and code efficiencies.

A common practice when high performance is required is to simply increase the frame rate. This will increase the performance only as long as the Flash Player has performance to give. Increasing the frame rate on an overworked Flash Player has no effect (and may even cause problems of its own, such as choppy sound and slow response to user inputs). The following guidelines highlight ways to reduce the workload of the Flash Player by creating efficient animations and code. This can make even an overworked Flash Player perform better.

As a rule of thumb, a good frame rate is from 18fps to 30fps. Any higher, and your frame rates may become choppy or prone to sudden slowdowns. Any lower, and you may lose smoothness in your animations because the frame rate is simply too slow.

> The default frame rate of 12fps is rarely used. It is largely historic, but Macromedia has never changed the default (mainly because it sees so many different suggestions from users on what the new default frame rate should be).

Guidelines for Creating Efficient Animation

The biggest cause of low frame rates by far is screen redraws. Flash uses vector animation to reduce bandwidth requirements. Vector graphics are often less bandwidth heavy than the corresponding bitmaps because vector graphics are composed of the instructions for drawing the graphics rather than the instructions for the graphics themselves.

If you use complex or large vector graphics, you will notice that they will animate slowly because of the high number of calculations Flash has to perform per frame. This problem has two solutions.

The most sensible solution is to limit the amount of change per frame. You can gain a lot of speed simply by simplifying your animations in ways the user will not even notice:

- Limit the amount of change per frame. If you have an animation of a boat bobbing in a sea, you would naturally make both the sea and the boat bob. But if you created an animation where only the boat or only the sea was bobbing at any one time, Flash would see far less change per frame. And if you switched between the sea and the boat often, the user wouldn't even notice!

- Use small and hollow shapes where possible. A moving hollow circle causes much less change than a filled circle, and a small hollow circle causes far less change than a large filled circle.

- Avoid using large areas of alpha. Semitransparent areas require approximately twice the processing power of fully opaque areas.

- Make the amount of detail in moving objects proportional to their speeds. A fast-moving object will appear as a blur, so you can get away with making it from a few shapes. A stationary object can have a lot of detail in it without affecting the frame rate. A stationary and highly detailed object in a scene can even give the impression that the less-detailed, fast-moving object is equally detailed.

Many graphic artists are used to creating static (and therefore detailed) artwork and may add more detail than required to animated objects just through habit. Remember, moving objects require far less detail. The faster they move, the less detail required.

- Use motion tweening in preference to shape tweening where possible. Motion tweening is faster (and less bandwidth heavy) than shape tweening. Consider changing your animations to use motion tweening more if performance is an issue.

- Create objects that look like they're moving quickly. A slow-moving object that's drawn so it looks like it is moving quickly gives the impression that it actually is moving quickly. For example, consider the two circles in Figure 7.1. The circle on the right has a blur filter applied to it, whereas the one on the left doesn't. If both were made to move in an up-down motion, the blurred one gives more of an impression of speed, simply because it looks like it is moving even when it is stationary.

- Avoid using strokes around fills. If you really must use stroke outlines, consider using hairline strokes, because they're the easiest for Flash to draw quickly.

Figure 7.1

Create graphics that give the impression of motion.

Flash 8 has two features that can significantly speed up your graphics—redraw regions and bitmap caching.

When Flash redraws the Stage per frame, it optimizes the redraw by looking for the smallest rectangular regions of the Stage that contain a change since the last frame, and it updates only the areas of the Stage within the rectangles. These rectangular regions are called *redraw regions*, and Flash 8 allows you to view them.

The redraw regions feature is accessible when you test a movie. Select (right-click / ctrl + click) the running SWF, and select Show Redraw Regions. Each redraw region will display as a red rectangular outline.

Seeing the redraw regions allows you to optimize your animations by trying to make the redraw regions as small and as less frequent as possible. More important, viewing redraw regions allows you to see where Flash is redrawing more than it needs to do so.

A good example of unneeded redraws occurs when one object moves behind another. Flash *doesn't* take into account depth when an animated object is hidden by another. Figure 7.2 shows four frames in a simple animation consisting of a black circle moving behind a gray rectangle. When the circle is hidden from view, you might expect that no redrawing is going on, but if you test this animation with redraw regions shown, you will see a different story. Figure 7.3 shows the redraw regions caused by the circle as it animates. Notice that when the circle is hidden behind the rectangle, *it is still forcing redraws* because you still see a redraw region.

Figure 7.2

Test your animation for redraw regions.

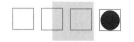

Figure 7.3

These are the redraw regions caused by the animating circle in Figure 7.2.

Thus, one optimization you could make is simply not to draw anything that's hidden. For example, you will not see the legs of a figure walking in tall grass, but unless you split the figure so that you can remove the legs from the Stage when they aren't seen, Flash will still waste power by drawing them.

Another time that the circle will cause redraw regions to be drawn is if you set the circle's alpha to zero. Even though you can't see the circle, it is still causing a redraw! This suggests another optimization—never hide a Movie Clip that's no longer needed by setting its alpha to zero. Instead, you should either remove the Movie Clip or set the Movie Clip's _visible property to false.

Finally, redraw regions become very large for symbols that have few pixels but have large bounding boxes. Figure 7.4 is animating a symbol that consists of a diagonally oriented line. This line creates a large redraw region consisting of the rectangle of which the line forms the diagonal. Flash has a lot of pixels to change in every frame just to make sure the black pixels that make up the diagonal line get moved!

Therefore, when creating your graphics, keep the size of the redraw region they will create in mind; it's an easy way to reduce the amount of redraw Flash will perform.

Even if you're creating content for versions of the Flash Player earlier than Flash 8 Player, you can still use redraw regions to check for efficient redraws.

The other useful feature of Flash 8 that can decrease the amount of work Flash has to do per frame is bitmap caching. Flash 8 can draw all but the simplest of Movie Clips faster as bitmaps. Flash will render anything you apply a filter to as a bitmap automatically. For any other Movie Clip you want to render as a bitmap, select the Movie Clip's instance on the Stage, and select the Use Runtime Bitmap Caching check box on the Properties tab of the Property Inspector.

Flash will then handle bitmap caching behind the scenes, and the graphic will continue to act as if it's a vector (and the sharpness of the vector will not be compromised). Whenever Flash detects a change in the Movie Clip, it will generate a new bitmap.

Figure 7.4

The redraw regions of some objects can be excessively large.

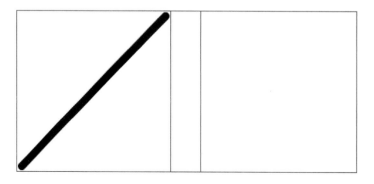

Some Movie Clips will change every frame, and such Movie Clips aren't suitable for bitmap caching because the time taken to cache them as bitmaps in every frame can actually make the SWF slower than no caching. Movie Clips that aren't suitable are those that rotate every frame and those that contain tweening that causes the Movie Clip's pixels to change appearance every frame.

For example, if a Movie Clip consisted of a side view of a car, with a car body and two rotating wheels, then the following points are true:

- The wheel Movie Clips aren't suitable for caching because they rotate.

- The car body is suitable for caching. Although it will move as the car moves, the pixels within the car body will not change.

- The entire car Movie Clip (containing the car body and two wheels) isn't suitable for caching because the rotating wheels are introducing changing pixels every frame.

> Although bitmap caching can significantly increase the speed of a SWF, you can use it only in the Flash 8 Player.

Guidelines for Creating Efficient Scripts

Flash code is executed at the start of every frame, and most scripts finish well before the end of the frame. Unless you're creating code with long loops or code that animates graphics, you usually won't need to optimize code. If you're writing clear, well-structured code, it's probably fairly fast anyway. If your scripts finish well before the end of a frame and you make your scripts twice as fast, Flash itself will not play twice as fast, because the frame rate is the limiting factor. The things most likely to slow Flash scripts down so much that the code is still running by the end of the frame are graphics. Code that controls graphics has to wait for the code to move, and waiting for that to happen will make the code appear sluggish. This can be an illusion—the code is simply waiting for redraws and isn't the limiting factor.

Flash 7 and 8 are optimized for code that uses functions, arguments, and local variables often (or class-based code). Writing such code is desirable for readability reasons in any case, but it might also give you an edge in performance if your code is doing anything intensive or contains long loops.

As mentioned, the biggest potential slowdown is code that's controlling animation. If the code isn't animating efficiently, the code may generate a slowdown because of the extra work it is causing through graphics redraws. The biggest single reason for avoidably slow code is code that redraws the graphics too often. Reasons for this occurring include the following:

Using onEnterFrame events instead of dedicated events In earlier versions of Flash (Flash 4 to 6), you could implement many common tasks only via an onEnterFrame event. For example, if you wanted to check when some external content was loaded, you would have to set up an onEnterFrame that checked the loading progress and updated the load progress graphics every frame. An onEnterFrame that runs at 30fps may see a change in the load progress only every second or so, meaning that for 29 of 30 frames, the code effectively does nothing! Flash 7 and 8 contain many new events that can handle this process much more efficiently via the MovieClipLoader class. A familiarity with the alternatives to onEnterFrame will lead to much more efficient code. You can see examples of the two ways of creating preloaders in Chapter 12, and we'll cover one of the best alternatives to onEnterFrame, setInterval, later in the next section.

Updating text fields at the frame rate   Text contains many vector shapes, and redrawing a single text field at the frame rate (via an onEnterFrame) can soak up as much as a quarter of the total Flash performance! You should instead update text fields only when they actually change.

> In a video game we were creating some years ago, we found that updating a text field containing the player's score at the frame rate was making the game 30 percent slower! Using a setInterval event that ran every two seconds made the game significantly faster. Chapter 10 shows an example of using setInterval to update text fields.

Attaching code to keyframes instead of code   ActionScript works best when all your code is on one keyframe, but in that one keyframe, the ActionScript attaches itself to events by defining event handlers. If you attach your code to a looping Timeline, not only are you using an old-fashioned (Flash 3 to 4) way of running code, you're also most likely writing inefficient code.

Failing to stop events when they're no longer needed   When an event is no longer needed, make sure you remove it. You can end most events by using the delete keyword.

Creating code that tries to do everything at once   If all your code runs in a single frame, that one frame will cause a noticeable slowdown. It is better to spread code execution so that the Flash Player isn't forced to do a lot of things all at once. Put another way, if you want an animation, A, to run quickly, then stop all other animations that might be running at the same time, and restart them when A is done.

Creating and Scheduling Events

Efficiently choosing and scheduling events is one of the major ways to create responsive and efficient sites. When deciding which event to use, you should consider how often you want your code to run. Your options are usually one of the following:

- Periodically at less than the frame rate
- Periodically at the frame rate
- Periodically at more than the frame rate
- Once

Creating Events That Occur at Less Than the Frame Rate

Running all your code at the frame rate makes for easy-to-write code, since the only event you have to use is onEnterFrame. Although easy to write, such code is usually inefficient, because at least some of your code will be able to perform its intended tasks even if you run it less often.

You can find the following example on the book's CD as checkInteraction.fla.

When you want to run code at a rate slower than the frame rate, you should consider using the setInterval event. To use a setInterval, you should place the code you want to run in a function. Given that you have a function called myFunction that you want to run every period millisecond via a setInterval event called myEvent, you use the following:

```
var myEvent:Number = setInterval(myFunction, period)
```

If your function has arguments, you can add them as parameters to the setInterval definition. The following code runs the function traceArguments(), which accepts two arguments, x and y:

```
function traceArguments(x:Number, y:Number):Void
{
  trace(x+" "+y);
}
var myEvent:Number = setInterval(traceArguments, 1000, 10, 20);
```

Supposing you wanted an animation to start if the user has not done anything for a period of time, the following code checks for no user interaction over a 10-second period:

```
function checkInteraction() {
  var mouseNotMovedX = oldMouseX == _xmouse;
  var mouseNotMovedY = oldMouseY == _ymouse;
  if (mouseNotMovedX || mouseNotMovedY) {
    trace("Hey! Wake up!");
  }
  oldMouseX = _xmouse;
  oldMouseY = _ymouse;
}
var oldMouseX:Number = _xmouse;
var oldMouseY:Number = _ymouse;
var checkUser:Number = setInterval(checkInteraction, 10000);
```

If you test this script, the message "Hey! Wake up!" will appear if you don't move the mouse for 10 seconds. The important point is that the function checkInteraction runs no faster than once every 10 seconds—it needs to run only as often as the thing for which it is checking. If you checked for mouse movement every frame in a movie running at 24fps, the function checkInteraction would run 240 times, making code using setInterval 24,000 percent more efficient than code using onEnterFrame for this application!

Creating Events That Run at the Frame Rate

When you want to create events that run at the frame rate, use an onEnterFrame event. You typically use an onEnterFrame event if you are driving animation. If you're *not* driving animation, then you should consider whether you're using the most efficient code (hint: you probably aren't).

When you create onEnterFrame event handlers, make sure they stop running once your animation has finished. It's amazing how many Flash users complain about the slowness of the Flash Player when it's actually because of lots of animation scripts that never actually stop—that circle may have gone off-screen and no longer be visible, but Flash is still animating it unless you specifically tell Flash to stop!

You can find the following example on the book's CD as stopAnimation.fla.

The following event handler will animate a Movie Clip called clip, moving it left to right. When the Movie Clip reaches the right of the screen, it will stop, *and the event handler controlling it will also stop.*

```
clip.onEnterFrame = function() {
  this._x += speed;
  if (this._x>500) {
    delete this.onEnterFrame;
    trace("clip.onEnterFrame has been stopped");
  }
};
//
var speed:Number = 4;
```

The if statement in the event handler checks whether the Movie Clip has reached the position x = 500. If it has, then the animation is stopped by deleting the onEnterFrame event handler.

Creating Events That Run Faster Than the Frame Rate

Sometimes you will want code to run faster than the frame rate. The only occasion when you may want to do this is when you need ultrasmooth animation for one or more Movie Clip.

When you're using drag and drop, it makes sense to make the dragged Movie Clip animate at the rate the mouse is dragging it rather than at the frame rate. You can achieve this with the onMouseMove event handler.

You can find the following example on the book's CD as smoothDragger.fla.

The following code shows two versions of the standard drag-and-drop animation code. The first onPress drives a Movie Clip called slowBall. This is the black ball in the example FLA. The next onPress animates the Movie Clip called fastBall (the gray ball). If you test the movie, you will see that fastBall drags much more smoothly.

```
slowBall.onPress = function() {
  this.startDrag();
```

```
      this.onRelease = function() {
        this.stopDrag();
      };
      this.onReleaseOutside = this.onRelease;
    };
    //
    //
    fastBall.onPress = function() {
      this.startDrag();
      this.onMouseMove = function() {
        updateAfterEvent();
      };
      this.onRelease = function() {
        this.stopDrag();
        delete this.onMouseMove;
      };
      this.onReleaseOutside = this.onRelease;
    };
```

The faster version is much smoother because of the following lines within the `onPress` event handler for `fastBall`:

```
    this.onMouseMove = function() {
      updateAfterEvent();
    };
```

The `onMouseMove` occurs every time the mouse moves; when this happens, you execute the action `updateAfterEvent()`. This function tells Flash to update the screen at the end of the current event, causing Flash to create many more animation frames than the current frame rate allows.

> The `updateAfterEvent()` action should be the last line in an event handler; otherwise, it will not work. Also notice that you delete the `onMouseMove` as soon as the user stops dragging. The `onMouseMove` event occurs *very* frequently, and you should avoid it running other than when you specifically need it.

What if you wanted to create animations that run faster than the frame rate? You can use `setInterval` with periods faster than the frame rate.

For scripted animations, use a `setInterval` with a period faster than the frame rate. You can find the following example on the book's CD as `fasterFramerate01.fla`.

The following example code uses a `setInterval` to make `fastBall` (again, the gray ball) move at a frame rate of 1 millisecond (1,000fps!). Flash can't actually attain this frame rate, but it will instead try to move `fastBall` as fast as it can. The black ball (`slowBall`)

moves at the standard frame rate—and, boy, will you see a difference…the gray ball will be nothing short of a blur.

```
slowBall.onEnterFrame = function() {
  this._x += speed;
  if (this._x>500) {
    this._x = 0;
  }
};
//
function moveFaster(clip:MovieClip) {
  clip._x += speed;
  if (clip._x>500) {
    clip._x = 0;
  }
  updateAfterEvent()
}
var fastEvent:Number = setInterval(moveFaster, 1, fastBall)
var speed:Number = 6;
```

Here you use a setInterval, fastEvent, to animate fastBall as fast as Flash can move it. Notice that you send the name of fastBall as a parameter. This is because the setInterval isn't scoped to the Movie Clip it is controlling, so you have to explicitly name that Movie Clip.

Each setInterval is assigned a numeric identifier by Flash, and this is why we equate the setInterval to a number. As we will see later, this identifier can be used to stop the setInterval via clearInterval.

What about Movie Clips that aren't driven though code? Such Movie Clips create their animations via tweening and can't be forced to run faster via the previous code, but you can modify the previous concept so that even tweens run faster than the frame rate.

 You can find the following example on the book's CD as fasterFramerate02.fla.

If you add the following code to any Timeline, that Timeline will play not at the frame rate but as fast as Flash can run it:

```
function timelineFaster() {
  nextFrame();
  updateAfterEvent();
}
var tweenFaster:Number = setInterval(timelineFaster, 1);
```

In the example file, fasterFrameRate02.fla, the code is on the first frame of symbol *nested tween 2*.

Amazingly, this trick will even work for the main Timeline, and any keyframes containing code in the faster Timeline will run.

To stop the Movie Clip from moving faster, add the following line on the keyframe where you want a return to normality:

```
clearInterval(tweenFaster);
```

Advanced users will immediately see the possibility of using this code to create a new class of Movie Clips that can have a `frameRate` property, allowing the developer to assign custom frame rates on a per-instance basis. Be wary, though, because your Timelines will become unsynchronized, so we recommend speeding up only one or two Movie Clips.

Creating Events That Run Once

If you want a piece of code to run once, the easiest route is to simply place it on a keyframe that will be played once. If you want a script to run some time in the future on a Timeline that may be halted, you can use any of the events you have used previously, namely, the `onEnterFrame` event or the `setInterval` event.

It is common to have a script on the current frame with the need to delay the script's execution until the next frame. The main reason you would need to do this is because you have dynamically attached a Movie Clip or component onto the current frame, and this Movie Clip/component will not initialize itself (and therefore begin working) until the next frame.

To run a script on the current keyframe at the next frame, simply place that script in an `onEnterFrame`, and then delete the `onEnterFrame` the first time it runs.

The following script will run a function called `delayedFunction()` in the next frame. The function will run only once:

```
var tempClip:MovieClip =
    this.createEmptyMovieClip("tempClip",
    this.getNextHighestDepth());
tempClip.onEnterFrame = function() {
    delayedFunction();
    delete this.onEnterFrame;
    this.removeMovieClip();
};
```

The code creates a temporary Movie Clip, `tempClip`, and attaches an `onEnterFrame` script to it. The `onEnterFrame` will start running on the next frame; when it runs, the last two lines remove the `onEnterFrame` and delete the temporary clip.

If you want to run some once following a delay, you can create a `setInterval` that's deleted after running once:

```
function delayedFunction(anInterval:Number) {
    trace("This line will run once after 5 seconds");
```

```
        clearInterval(delayedCall);
    }
    var delayedCall:Number = setInterval(delayedFunction, 5000);
```

Both the delayed function calls used here are much more efficient than using a count-down timer or than simply counting frames. By using event handlers, you make sure your code runs only once and only when it is needed.

Knowing about the wide range of events that Flash offers, and knowing how to create efficient timers and countdowns, is perhaps the best way to write efficient animation code. We've covered the basic building blocks, but don't forget that Flash contains many specialized events for common actions you want to respond to, from well-known and often-used events such as when the user clicks a button to lesser known but useful events such as when the user resizes the browser or when an XML message is received. Whenever you need to solve a new problem efficiently, always refer to the ActionScript 2.0 Language Reference, available from the Help panel, and pay particular attention to the various methods and events available; many of them will solve your problem quickly with just a few lines!

Creating Scripted Motion

One of the biggest problems new users to ActionScript have is understanding the basic principles of scripted animation. Sure, you can make a ball move by varying its properties, but how do you make it go where you want to, and how do you know when it has go there?

In tweening, it's easy to see what is happening. The Timeline moves from the starting keyframe toward the end keyframe, causing the tweened object to move smoothly between the two end points of the animation.

In scripted animation, the start point and end points aren't even fixed—the object has to move between two points that may not be fully defined. And if they aren't defined, how does the object know when it gets to an end point?

Scripted animation as seen in video games or complex interfaces may seem difficult to define, but the underlying principles are actually simple (and, incidentally, are the same in all motion graphics—they apply as equally to high-end Xbox 2 video games as they do to Flash). These principles are called *target-driven animation*.

Understanding Target-Driven Motion

Consider a ball tied by elastic to a point. If you drag the ball away from the point and let go, the ball will jump back to the point, dragged along by the elastic. If you hold the ball down and tie the free end of the elastic to another point and then let the ball go, the ball will jump to the new point.

Motion has four components:

The target This is the place to which the elastic is tied. It is the place the ball will try to get to when it starts moving.

The trigger   This is the thing that starts the ball moving. In this analogy, the trigger is simply the instant you let the ball go. The trigger is *always* an event. Something has to happen to start the ball moving.

The transition   This is the motion of the ball toward the target. In Flash it is the script that moves the ball toward the target.

The halt condition   At some point, the ball has to stop. Usually, the ball will stop when it reaches the target. Sometimes, the ball may never stop, such as when you tie the free end of the elastic to a fast-moving car. In this case, the ball will keep trying to reach the target but will always be behind some. In this situation, the ball will start following or *tracking* the car.

And that's all the background theory you need to know! It really is that simple.

In Flash, the target is an (x, y) point on the Stage. The graphic you're controlling has to move directly toward the point in a straight line as soon as an event occurs. This event could be the user clicking a button, or it could be the user pressing a key, which is an event that tells you the player is moving. If you want the animation to follow what the user is doing in some way, you *don't* control the ball directly. Instead, you let the user control the target in some way.

If you don't want the ball to be controlled by the user but still want the ball to move in a way that follows rules, you move the *target* every frame in a way that follows your rules, and the ball will dumbly follow it. The intelligence is *always* in the target and not the ball.

As the target moves, the ball moves in a linear fashion toward the target, but as the target changes, the ball may end up tracing a complex *curved path*. To someone who doesn't know what is happening, it looks as if the ball has all the intelligence.

In most animations where you want to give the impression of artificial intelligence, the trick is usually for most of the intelligence to come from the user rather than from your code. You do this by letting the player control the target, but you do it in a way that isn't obvious.

Consider the ubiquitous space invaders game. When an alien dives at the player, the following is true:

- When the alien dives is based on the player's score. The higher the score, the more often the alien dives, creating a progressively more difficult game.

- Where the alien dives toward is controlled by the player, as the target is the player— the alien wants to either shoot or hit the player's ship, so the alien "ball" has a piece of elastic that's tied firmly to the player's ship.

- The transition is the only element the game code really controls. This code will have a certain level of randomness in it to hide that the alien is actually taking its primary control from the player.

- The halt condition is when the alien reaches the end of the screen or when it collides with the player. Notice that the halt condition is simple and well defined. Little or no complexity exists in the halt condition.

In Pac-Man, it's the same, except that the ghosts have some simple rules that stop them looking stupid by crashing into the sides of the maze as they move toward the player target. In Doom, the monsters move toward invisible targets that are set off by triggers that are points in the game world that become active when the user moves over them. When these triggers are set off, the monsters start tracking the player's position in a way that implies they have "seen" the player. Although the game world is in 3D, the enemies in Doom are essentially still dragged toward the player's position by code that simulates a piece of elastic that's attached firmly to the player!

You can see the basic building blocks of target-driven animation in action by testing the file `scriptedAnim_completed.fla`.

You will see two circles when you test the movie. The large gray circle is the Movie Clip you will be moving (the ball), and the smaller black circle is the position of the target. We have also added the elastic as a line connecting the ball and target to complete the analogy.

The black circle is draggable. When you drag it, you're setting the *target*. The ball doesn't follow the target immediately but waits for the *trigger*, which occurs when you release the target. When you release, the ball will move in a straight line toward the target, using its *transition* script to create the motion.

Part of the transition script checks for closeness between the target and the ball. When this occurs, the ball is assumed to have reached its target, and the *halt conditions* are met. The ball will now be stationary at the target.

Notice that if you drag and then release the target but start dragging again before the ball reaches the target, the ball doesn't stop because you're moving the target away from it, and the halt conditions aren't met. Instead, the ball starts following the target. Although the ball always moves in a straight line toward the target, if you move the target as the ball is trying to reach it, the ball will travel in a complex *curved* path as it *tracks* the target.

> Although the transition code of the ball simply moves the ball in a straight line, moving the target in a complex way creates complexity in the ball's motion. If you allow the user to create the complexity associated with the target motion, you can create animations that appear to be doing complex things, when all along it is the user who is introducing the complexity!

Target-driven motion splits the difficult problem of scripted animation into four separate (and simpler) tasks, and this is the main advantage of knowing the concept of target-driven motion. The other big advantage is that you can build each of the four parts of the motion separately.

Creating Scripted Motion in Four Easy Steps

The simplest form of target-driven motion is position. In positional motion, a Movie Clip has to reach a certain place on the Stage. We'll show how this will occur by building each part separately.

Open the file scriptedAnim_simple.fla. This includes a simplified version of the FLA you just tested in the previous section.

The code in this FLA looks like this:

```
function transition() {
  //
  // This is the transition code
  this._x -= (this._x-target._x)/2;
  this._y -= (this._y-target._y)/2;
  //
  //  This is the halt code
  var closeX = Math.abs(this._x-target._x)<1;
  var closeY = Math.abs(this._y-target._y)<1;
  if (closeX && closeY) {
    delete this.onEnterFrame;
    trace("Animation has ended\n");
  }
}
target.onPress = function() {
  //
  //  this code allows the user to set the target
  this.startDrag();
  this.onMouseMove = updateAfterEvent;

  this.onRelease = function() {
    // This event generates the trigger
    trace("Animation has started");
    ball.onEnterFrame = transition;
    this.stopDrag();
    delete this.onMouseMove;
  };
  this.onReleaseOutside = this.onRelease;
};
```

The target.onPress event handler runs when you start dragging the target by clicking it. The target position (x, y) is defined by the _x and _y properties of the target clip. When you release the target, the onRelease near the bottom of the code listing runs. This event handler catches the trigger event (which is when you release the target). You start the transition code with the following line within the onRelease:

```
ball.onEnterFrame = transition;
```

The trigger thus kicks off the transition by making the function transition() an onEnterFrame event. The transition code consists of these two lines:

```
this._x -= (this._x-target._x)/2;
this._y -= (this._y-target._y)/2;
```

This code produces the smooth easing motion that the ball uses as it moves toward the target (we'll cover what this code does in the "Understanding the Different Types of Scripted Animation" section of this chapter).

The halt condition is the `if` statement at the bottom of `transition()`, and it looks like this:

```
// This is the halt code
var closeX = Math.abs(this._x-target._x)<1;
var closeY = Math.abs(this._y-target._y)<1;
if (closeX && closeY) {
   delete this.onEnterFrame;
   trace("Animation has ended\n");
}
```

The Boolean variables `closeX` and `closeY` are true if you're within 1 pixel of the target position. If both are true, you stop the transition by deleting the `onEnterFrame`.

As you set off a number of target-trigger-transition-halt cycles, you will notice that the Output panel looks like Figure 7.5.

Notice that the animation has a definite start and end point per transition. Put another way, *no animation occurs before the trigger, and no animation occurs after the halt condition*. The animation code is efficient because the code that creates the animation never runs when the animation isn't needed.

Many beginners create animations that start when the Flash site starts, and the animations never stop. Alternatively, some animations may start but are never halted. Both of these situations are cases where inefficient animation code is being used, and some users start blaming Flash as the culprit because "the Flash Player is too slow." Using target-driven animation, complete with the trigger and halt conditions, will go a long way toward creating faster sites. Also, because your animations stop when they aren't needed, you can afford to have many transitions in your site, thus building up a complex set of animations from lots of little animations.

Figure 7.5

This is how the Output panel looks during the scripted animation.

Understanding the Different Types of Scripted Animation

Most scripted animations use target-driven animation. The only parts that really change are the trigger and the transition.

Creating Motion with ActionScript

You create movement in Flash by varying the _x and _y properties of a Movie Clip. To move a Movie Clip to the left/right, you decrease/increase the _x property over time. If you want to move a Movie Clip up/down, you decrease/increase the _y property.

If you want to move a Movie Clip in a direction other than directly up/down or left/right, you have to change the _x and _y properties simultaneously.

Open the file `scriptedAnim_linear.fla`.

To use linear motion in the target-driven example, you need to change the transition function as shown here:

```
function transition() {
  //
  // This is the transition code
  direction = Math.atan2(target._y-this._y, target._x-this._x);
  this._x += speed*Math.cos(direction);
  this._y += speed*Math.sin(direction);
  //
  //  This is the halt code
  var closeX = Math.abs(this._x-target._x)<(speed+1);
  var closeY = Math.abs(this._y-target._y)<(speed+1);
  if (closeX && closeY) {
    this._x = target._x;
    this._y = target._y;
    delete this.onEnterFrame;
    trace("Animation has ended\n");
  }
}
```

Linear motion toward a general point requires some knowledge of trigonometry, because you have to know the angle you need to travel in to reach your point. When you test the movie, you will also see a big problem with linear motion—it looks slow and wooden. Most real things accelerate and decelerate as they move because they have mass. The linear example stops and starts suddenly and moves in obvious steps.

For these reasons, linear motion is actually not used often in Flash scripted animation, and when it is used, only motion in the four "easy" directions (up, down, left, and right, as in Figure 7.6) is used. Many designers also find that the trigonometry calculations involved slow the code down if a lot of elements are moving. Of course, many designers also hate trigonometry, which is another good reason to stay clear of linear target-driven motion!

A better set of motion equations use *easing* (also sometimes called *inertia* or *inertial motion*, as named by Joshua Davis, the designer who first popularized its use in Flash scripted motion).

You can create easing in ActionScript by looking at the distance to the target and traveling some fraction of that distance (in both X and Y coordinates) per frame. For example, if you wanted to travel from A to B as per Figure 7.7, you could decide to move half the distance remaining between where you are at A and the target, B, per frame. As you approach point B, the speed of the motion toward B halves as the distance halves, resulting in a deceleration effect.

Figure 7.6

You can move a Movie Clip directionally.

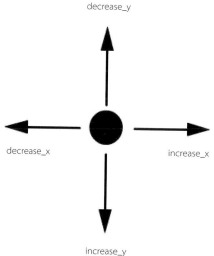

decrease_y

decrease_x   increase_x

increase_y

Figure 7.7

You can simulate easing with scripting.

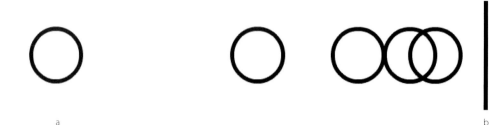

a   b

The ball will never actually reach point B if you keep halving the distance (although it will over time get very close). Usually, the animation is stopped by the code once the ball is within a pixel or so away from the target.

The previous example file, `scriptedAnim_simple.fla`, uses easing/inertia, and you will notice that it appears much smoother than the linear motion whilst at the same time reaching its target position quicker. Because of this smoothness and speed, inertia motion is used more often than any other form of motion in Flash scripted animation.

The equations used in `scriptedAnim_simple.fla` look like this:

```
this._x -= (this._x-target._x)/2;
this._y -= (this._y-target._y)/2;
```

The terms in the parentheses give you the distance from where the Movie Clip is to where it needs to get to, and the `/2` ("divide by two") gives you half that distance. Thus, the Movie Clip will move half the distance between where it currently is (`this._x`, `this._y`) and its target position (`target._x`, `target._y`).

Creating Other Transitions

You can use scripted transitions to change other attributes of a Movie Clip, including scaling, height/width, rotation, or even transparency through using the same equations you used on the position but this time applying the equations of scripted motion to other properties.

For an example of this, refer to `scriptedAnim_width.fla` on the book's CD.

In this FLA, the inertia equations are applied to the `_width` property, allowing the target to control the width of a Movie Clip. You could use such an animation for several parts of a site:

- A volume control bar on a site.

- The loading progress of a preloader. Using easing would soften the fact that the site loads chunks of data by adding easing to the animation.

- The scaling of expanding and contracting of images in an image gallery. Rolling over a thumbnail of an image could make the image grow with an inertia equation applied to the `_xscale` and `_yscale` properties.

As you're probably starting to gather from these examples, scripted animation is much more versatile than tweening because user interaction can control the animation to a much greater degree.

You can also use scripted motion to simulate other effects during motion (and other transitions) such as gravity and friction. ActionScript can also simulate bouncing and rolling objects—in fact, you can describe any kind of motion with equations.

You can find examples of such motion in Chapter 12.

PART II

Interactivity

One of the more elusive terms we hear as developers of digital media is interactivity. This word appears frequently in books, tutorials, and articles, and is usually used to qualify or categorize the media we produce. It has become a sort of buzzword, such that in many circles, interactive equals cool. In its defense, though, many things (digital and otherwise) are interactive and require this cyber-savvy stamp of approval. One fear, however, is that the word is used so often that either it has lost its meaning or its meaning has been diluted.

So what exactly is interactivity? Merriam-Webster's Collegiate Dictionary defines interactive as "of, relating to, or being a two-way electronic communication system…that involves a user's orders (as for information or merchandise) or responses…." Well, that gets us started—a two-way communication between a person and a machine, but how does this relate to Flash? That's where you come in. As a developer of Flash movies, you are the person responsible for determining the nature of communication between your movies and your audience. This part of the book opens the floodgates to the vast world of interactivity. You will begin to understand the techniques that afford communication between your audience and your Flash creations.

CHAPTER 8

Creating Interactive Controls

Building controls in Flash is an essential step toward creating an application that is both great to look at and easy to use. At the most basic level, you can create simple button controls to turn a movie on or off and to skip to different sections. Controls comprise the backbone of any interactive interface and serve as an integral part of the overall design of your movie. For those who are under a tight deadline, or just need to do some rapid prototyping, Flash 8 offers *components*. These ready-made interface elements allow you to quickly build Flash-based applications. As you progress to a more advanced stage, you'll be able to create robust interfaces with flexible navigation options that have a savvy look and feel.

- **Using built-in button controls**

- **Creating complex controllers**

- **Adding functionality to buttons**

- **Creating drag-and-drop interactivity**

- **Using ActionScript to create text**

- **Creating scalable and flexible interactive controllers**

- **Using components for interface development**

Adding Interactivity with Simple Buttons

Flash is capable of managing complex and dynamic interactivity, but it's not always necessary to pull out all the stops for your movie. Sometimes you might find simple elements are just as effective as complex ones. Designing an interactive movie is no exception. Flash offers many options for adding interactive controls that don't demand a lot, and the results can be very satisfying.

Selecting Buttons from the Flash Common Library

Flash has several Common Libraries, which include sounds, Movie Clips, and, yes, buttons. They're resources embedded within the program and thus will be available every time you use Flash. The buttons in the Common Library are great for quick mock-ups or tests.

To open the button Library, select Window → Common Libraries → Buttons (see Figure 8.1). This Library looks like any other in Flash. The only exception is its contents. It contains a wide assortment of buttons designed and ready for use in a movie.

For more information about working with Libraries and shared assets in Flash, see Chapter 4.

This Library consists of a series of individual folders that contain button *families*. Each family contains a group of button graphics that have a similar look and feel. This allows you to use the family as a set and maintain a consistent look for all your navigational or interactive elements.

Figure 8.1

The Common Library for buttons contains ready-made buttons.

To use a Common Library button in your movie:

1. Select Window → Common Libraries → Buttons to display the Library if it's not open already.

2. Open the folders within the Common Library panel to find the button you want. You can open and close folders in the panel by double-clicking the folder icon (see Figure 8.2).

3. Do either of the following:

   • Drag a button from the Common Library to the main Library for your movie. If your movie Library isn't visible, display it by selecting Window → Library (or pressing Ctrl+L / Cmd+L).

   • Drag a button from the Common Library directly to the Stage. It will automatically appear in your main movie Library.

   At this point, the button is a symbol in your movie, either on the Stage or in your main Library.

From here, your button has many options. If you put it directly on the Stage, it becomes an instance in your movie and can have ActionScript attached to it.

Creating Your Own Buttons

Although using buttons in the Common Library is convenient, you'll likely want to create some of your own buttons. By creating your own buttons, you'll get, with some effort, exactly what you want. In other words, you can build a custom button to your exact specifications so it fits the specific design goals of your movie. Because interactive controls are a big part of a Flash movie, it's important to get them right.

A button is a short, interactive movie with only four frames. Each of the frames represents a different appearance, or state, of the button that reflects user interaction. These different states are saved as separate images in keyframes along the Timeline of the button movie. As you move the mouse over the button and click it, it changes states accordingly by displaying the correct keyframe image. By making a button change appearance while it's being manipulated, you show your audience that it's "active" in the movie and that clicking it will produce a change in your movie.

Like Movie Clips, buttons are another kind of symbol. Therefore, you can create a single button and use it repeatedly. Every instance of a button will be treated independently throughout an animation or interactive movie.

The four states of a button are as follows:

Figure 8.2

The Common Library folders hold various buttons.

Open folder
Folder contents (indented)

Closed folder

Up The Up state represents the appearance of the button when the cursor isn't over it. This can also be considered the "inactive" state.

Over The second keyframe of the button Timeline represents the Over state. This creates the appearance of the button when the cursor is positioned over it. Note also that when the cursor moves over a button, the Flash Player changes it from the standard arrow pointer to a hand with a finger pointer.

Down The third keyframe of the button Timeline shows the button graphic when it's clicked and held.

Hit The final keyframe defines the area of the button that will respond to a mouse click. Think of the Hit state as the button's hotspot. It defines the area that must be clicked for the button to execute any scripts or behaviors attached to it.

Table 8.1 describes and depicts the four states of a typical button.

STATE	ILLUSTRATION	DESCRIPTION
Up	▶	Defines the appearance when the cursor is not over the button
Over	▶	Defines the appearance when the cursor is over the button
Down	▶	Defines the appearance when the mouse clicks the button
Hit	▶	Defines the button area that can respond to a click

Table 8.1

The Four States of a Button

To create your own button:

1. Select Insert → New Symbol (or press Ctrl+F8 / Cmd+F8) to display the Create New Symbol dialog box.

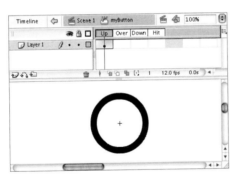

2. Choose Button as the type, and enter a name for the button in the Name field.

3. Click OK, and you'll switch into Symbol Editing mode (see Figure 8.3). Notice the appearance of Flash changes in this mode. For instance, the title of your symbol appears beside a button icon in the Scene and Symbol bar. The frames of the main Timeline disappear and are replaced by the new frames of your button. Also, the frames of the new Timeline are labeled to show the four states of your new button. The first frame for the Up state contains a blank keyframe.

4. Create an Up state for the button by doing any one of the following:

   • Use the Flash drawing tools to create a graphic.

   • Import a graphic file, and drag it onto the button's Stage.

   • Drag an instance of another graphic or Movie Clip symbol to the Stage to create an instance within a button.

   The crosshairs in the middle of the Stage represent the registration point of the button.

It's possible to use Movie Clips within Button symbols, but you're not allowed to put a button within a button. Using a Movie Clip as part of a button creates an animated button. For more on this, see the section "Creating Animated Buttons" later in this chapter.

5. To create a new keyframe for the Over state, click the Over state frame, and then select Insert → Timeline → Keyframe (or press F6). Flash automatically duplicates the previous frame in the new keyframe. Alternatively, if you know the graphic for the Over state is going to be completely different from the one for the Up state, select Insert → Timeline → Blank Keyframe (or press F7).

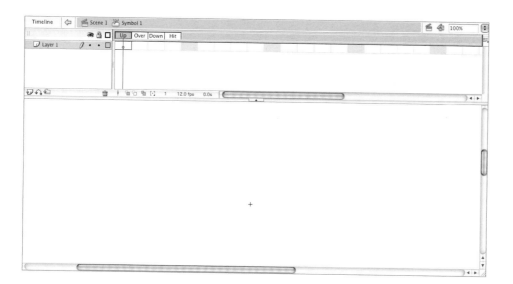

<figure>Figure 8.3

When creating a new symbol, the Timeline in Symbol Editing mode.</figure>

6. Create or make changes to the graphic in frame 2, or use any of the methods outlined previously to alter the appearance of the Over state.

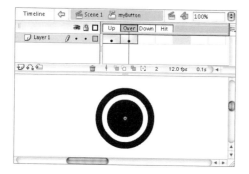

7. Repeat steps 5 and 6 for both the Down and Hit states.

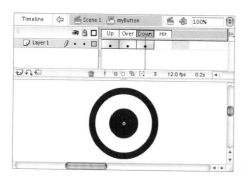
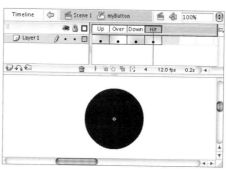

The Hit state has a unique importance. It defines the area that will respond to any mouse clicks on the button. This means it must have a solid graphic so clicks don't "slip through the cracks" in the button, and the graphic must be large enough to be clicked. If it's too small, your audience might have a difficult time trying to click the right spot.

> If you're creating a button that consists solely of text, creating an invisible button for the Hit state, as described in "Creating Invisible Buttons" later in this chapter, is a great way to make sure the button will work.

8. With graphics for the four states in place, your button is ready to go. To leave Symbol Editing mode, either select Edit → Edit Document (or press Ctrl+E / Cmd+E) or simply click the Back button in the Scene and Symbol bar.

9. Drag your button from the Library to the Stage to create a button instance in your movie.

10. As needed, attach ActionScript or behaviors to the button so it can be used to control various elements of your movie.

These are the fundamental steps for creating a simple button for your Flash movie. From this point, the possibilities are virtually limitless. For a discussion of how to add sound to a button in your movie, see Chapter 14. If you want to continue to work with your movie and explore the potential of buttons as interactive control sources, read on. In the next section, we'll discuss the ins and outs of testing your buttons and making any changes or edits to their components.

Creating Complex Buttons

Complex buttons do more than serve as navigational icons. They allow you to give the audience a clear means of moving through your movie while offering visual interest. Once you start to explore the possibilities outlined in the following sections, you'll see the benefit these techniques can bring to your Flash productions.

Creating Multilayered Buttons

Buttons aren't only controllers in your movie—they are graphics that contribute to the movie's overall look and feel. This presents you with several choices. On one hand, you can try to make the buttons as unobtrusive as possible so they're transparently woven into the fabric of your movie. On the other hand, you can play it up and allow the buttons to make a bold visual statement.

In the next example, you'll see how to create a graphically dynamic button with components on several layers. The beauty of a multilayered button is that each graphic layer is independent. In other words, one layer can change without affecting the others. You can find a sample file, `multilayer.fla`, on this book's CD. It was created following these steps to make a button that looks like a squashed tomato.

To create a multilayered button:

1. Select Insert → New Symbol, or press Ctrl+F8 / Cmd+F8. The Create New Symbol dialog box opens.

2. In the Create New Symbol dialog box, choose Button as the type, and give the symbol a name. Then click OK.

3. Flash automatically jumps into Symbol Editing mode. You'll see the button Timeline and the Up, Over, Down, and Hit state keyframes.

4. To add another layer to the button Timeline, select Insert → Timeline → Layer, or click the Insert Layer icon in the Timeline. The new layer appears in the Timeline with an empty keyframe in the Up state frame.

5. Begin by drawing a graphic on layer 1 to represent the Up state of the button. When you're finished, click layer 2, and draw an additional portion of the graphic. Because each part is on its own layer, you have more flexibility to change the various states of the button.

6. If necessary, repeat steps 4 and 5 to create additional layers for the button.

7. When the Up state is complete, select layer 1, and then select Insert → Timeline → Keyframe to add a keyframe for the Over state. When you do this, Flash automatically

inserts a new frame in layer 2 and duplicates the Up state graphics in the new frames (below left).

8. Draw a new graphic for the Over state of layer 1, or make changes to the duplicated frame as needed. Then click frame 2 of layer 2, insert a new keyframe, and adjust this image as needed.

9. Repeat the process outlined in steps 7 and 8 to create the appearance for the button's Down state.

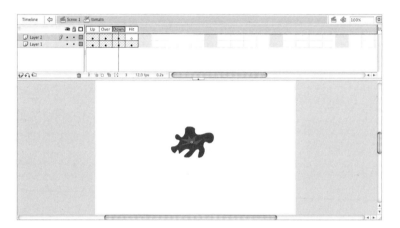

In the example on this book's CD, you can see that the button is a tomato. When it's rolled over, both the stem and the fruit change color. Then, when the tomato is clicked, it's squished and changes to a dark color. You can manipulate each element (stem and fruit) separately because each layer is autonomous and will not directly affect the other.

10. Insert a new keyframe in layer 1 to complete the button, and give it a Hit state. Remember, the Hit state isn't visible; it's what enables the button to respond to mouse interaction. Even though the button has several layers, it's acceptable to put a Hit state keyframe in only one layer.

11. When you've finished creating the button, select Edit → Edit Document to return to the main Timeline. To preview your button, choose Control → Enable Simple Buttons. This option allows you to see how the multilayered button looks when manipulated by the cursor.

Creating Animated Buttons

Buttons are by default a kind of animation. When you roll over them, the graphic changes. When you click them, you see another change. It's not a linear animation but rather one that demonstrates the graphic is somehow significant; the animation begs you to click it. You can take this idea a step further by creating animated buttons. Such buttons use a Movie Clip or small animation to represent one of their states. Generally, this happens at the Over state, although that's certainly not a requirement. However, if you used a Movie Clip for the Up state, the animation could be distracting. If you used an animation as the Down state, a chance exists that the Movie Clip animation wouldn't be seen at the instant the button is clicked. The Over state presents the animation when the button is active (rolled over). It grabs your attention and adds more to the rollover effect than just a change of graphic.

In the next example, you'll see how to create an animated button by using a Movie Clip. You can find an example of the process in the `animated_button.fla` file on this book's CD.

To create an animated button:

1. Create a graphic on the Stage to use as your button. When it's complete, drag around it to select the entire graphic, and either choose Modify → Convert to Symbol or press F8. In the Convert to Symbol dialog box, select the Graphic type, and give the symbol a name in the Name field. Click OK.

2. The symbol appears in the Library. Delete the symbol from the main Timeline Stage. This Graphic symbol will be the starting point for each part of your button. You're using a symbol so that you can use instances of the symbol repeatedly in the button animation.

3. Select Insert → New Symbol, or press Ctrl+F8 / Cmd+F8. This time, choose the Movie Clip type, give the empty clip a name, and click OK. Flash takes you immediately to Symbol Editing mode.

4. You can now create the animation you'll use as the Over state of your button. Drag the Graphic symbol from the Library to the Stage while you're in Symbol editing mode. Use the arrow keys to align the registration point of the symbol with that of the new Movie Clip, using the X and Y coordinate fields in the Property Inspector as a guide.

> Lining up the registration points is a good idea because you'll use the Graphic symbol several times in this process. This ensures each instance of the symbol is positioned in the same place. Alternatively, you can use the Align panel (Ctrl+K / Cmd+K) and have Flash handle the registration for you automatically. To learn more about working with the Align panel, see Chapter 3.

Figure 8.4

The Timeline for the Movie Clip in the file `animated_button.fla`**. You'll see instances of both tweened and frame-by-frame animations in the Timeline.**

5. Create the animation using keyframes, tweening, and any other Flash techniques (see Figure 8.4). If you want the animation to play only once, it's a good idea to add a `stop()` function to the last frame of the Movie Clip's Timeline. Otherwise, it will loop continuously (which might be desirable in certain situations). If you need to change the symbol, you can select Modify → Break Apart (or press Ctrl+B / Cmd+B) and edit its characteristics directly. For more information about keyframes and animation concepts, see Chapter 6.

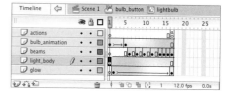

6. When you've finished creating your Movie Clip, select Edit → Edit Document, and return to the main Timeline.

7. At this point, you're ready to create the button. You have a graphic, and you have a Movie Clip; now is the time to bring it all together. Choose Insert → New Symbol, and the Create New Symbol dialog box opens again. This time, choose the Button type, and enter a name in the Name field.

8. Click OK, and Flash jumps into Button Editing mode.

9. Drag the Graphic symbol to the Stage, and use the arrow keys or Align panel to move it into place so the registration points line up.

10. After the Up state graphic is in place, you can move onto the Over state. Select Insert → Timeline → Keyframe to insert a new keyframe. The keyframe appears in frame 2 as the Over state graphic. Flash automatically copies the Up state graphic into the new keyframe. You'll need to swap this with the Movie Clip you created in step 5. Select the graphic in the Over state frame, and then click the Swap Symbols button on the Property Inspector.

    The Swap Symbol dialog box opens and allows you to exchange graphics for the Movie Clip symbol. Be sure the Property Inspector displays the Movie Clip in the Symbol Behavior menu after you've swapped symbols; otherwise, the clip will not animate. For specifics on swapping symbols, see Chapter 4.

11. The bulk of the work is done. You now have an Up state and an animated Over state. The next step presents a choice depending upon your intentions for this button:

    - If the animation is all you need to complete the button, click in frame 3 of the button Timeline, and choose Insert → Timeline → Frame. This will extend the Movie Clip instance one frame and allow it to serve as the Down state as well. This will not cause the animation to replay.

    - If you want an additional change to the button when it's clicked, you need to create a keyframe for the Down state in frame 3 of the button Timeline. Flash will duplicate the contents of the previous keyframe in the new frame. Using any of the previously described techniques, insert a graphic for the Down state in this keyframe.

The example on this book's CD, `animated_button.fla`, demonstrates the results of the first choice. However, you can experiment with this file using the techniques described in the second choice. Look for the Graphic symbol named `light_down` in the movie's Library. This graphic could work well as a Down state graphic for this particular animated button. Try it to see what you think.

12. Click frame 4 of the Button Timeline, and choose Insert → Timeline →
    Blank Keyframe. Use any of Flash's painting or drawing tools to
    create a Hit state that is appropriate to the shape and size of your
    animated button. With keyframes and graphics for each of the
    four states, your animated button is now ready to go.

13. Select Edit → Edit Document (or press Ctrl+E / Cmd+E) to return to the main Time-
    line and save your movie. Because you used a Movie Clip, Flash won't give you a true
    preview of the animated button in authoring mode. To see the button in action, add
    an instance of the animated button to the movie; then select Control → Test Movie to
    give it a spin.

An animated button is a button like any other. Once it's in your Library as a Button
symbol, you're free to use it throughout your movie. You can attach ActionScript to
instances of the animated button and use it as a means of controlling other movie elements
and the movie's playback.

Creating Invisible Buttons

An invisible button is transparent. It has no physical/on-screen attributes; it's purely
functional. It lacks Up, Over, and Down states and has only a Hit state, the state that
defines the active area of the button. This characteristic makes it, in many ways, the most
important state of a button. Invisible buttons use it exclusively to their advantage.

Put another way, an invisible button is a button that has only a Hit state and will
respond to mouse interaction. Invisible buttons will not appear in your final, published
SWF movie. However, they will be present as functional buttons that your audience can
click to make choices and selections while interacting with your movie or application.
Invisible buttons aren't practical in all situations, but they are extremely helpful and can
save a lot of time under certain circumstances.

An invisible button, because it's transparent, can lie on top of any object in your movie
without obscuring or hiding it. And because it's a button positioned over another object,
that object seems to act like a button itself. Invisible buttons thus give you the flexibility
to turn any object into a button.

To create an invisible button:

1. Select Insert → New Symbol, or press Ctrl+F8 / Cmd+F8. The Create New Symbol
   dialog box opens.

2. In the Create New Symbol dialog box, choose Button as the type, and give the symbol
   a name. Then click OK.

3. Flash automatically switches to Symbol Editing mode. You'll see the button Timeline
   and the Up, Over, Down, and Hit state keyframes.

Figure 8.5

The invisible button has only a Hit state graphic that is registered at coordinates (0,0).

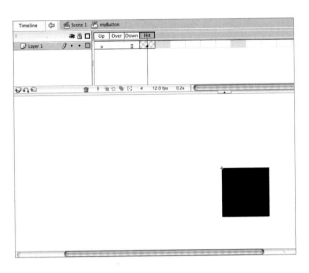

4. Click the fourth frame (the Hit state), and the frame will become highlighted. Choose Insert → Timeline → Blank Keyframe (or press F7) to create a blank keyframe for the button's Hit state.

5. Use the Rectangle tool to draw a square button or the Oval tool to draw a round button. The size isn't all that important, but something around 25 pixels square or in diameter is a good starting point.

6. Use the Align panel (choose Window → Design Panels → Align, or press Ctrl+K / Cmd+K) to position the upper-left corner of the button at the registration point or Stage coordinates (0,0). The Property Inspector can also help with the alignment. For an illustration of the finished invisible button, see Figure 8.5.

7. When your button is aligned and finished, choose Edit → Edit Document to return to the main Timeline's Stage and save your movie.

Creating an invisible button is a snap. It's just like creating a regular button, with the exception that you don't have any Up, Over, or Down states to worry about. After you've created the button, Flash puts it in your movie's Library as a Button symbol for use later. As a symbol, invisible buttons can turn many different graphic and animated elements of your movie into buttons.

To use an invisible button in your movie:

1. Find the layer in the Timeline that holds the object you want to make work as a button. Create a new layer *above* this layer, and name it **buttons**.

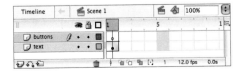

2. Choose Insert → Timeline → Blank Keyframe to create a keyframe for the invisible button in the same frame as the object. If necessary, press the F5 key to extend the number of frames so the new layer has enough frames to match the object.

3. If it isn't open already, open your movie's Library (Window → Library). Click the invisible Button symbol, and drag it into the newly created keyframe in the buttons layer.

4. Return to your movie's Stage. The invisible button appears as a semitransparent blue box. Use your mouse and/or the arrow keys to nudge it into place so it completely covers the object you want to turn into a button.

5. If your button doesn't exactly fit the size and shape of the other object, use the Free Transform tool to reshape or resize the button as necessary (see Figure 8.6).

6. Now that your button is positioned, you're free to attach behaviors or other Action-Script as needed.

Figure 8.6

You can use the Free Transform tool to resize an invisible button. Here, it makes adjustments for a button to fit over the word *Home*, **thus making the word a button.**

Besides allowing you to turn any object into a button, invisible buttons have a few other benefits:

- Invisible buttons are Button symbols, meaning a single button can be reused repeatedly in different instances with unique sizes and positions on the Stage.

- Invisible buttons can make any object—graphic, Movie Clip, text field, bitmap image, you name it—act like a button.

- Making Hit states for text buttons can be tedious. Invisible buttons have a definable shape, making them perfect for text or other objects with irregular or uneven shapes.

To try your hand at invisible buttons, check out `invis_buttons.fla` on the book's CD. This movie has two completed invisible buttons and all the trappings to complete three more. The buttons use ActionScript to navigate to different frame markers of a Movie Clip. To learn more about how to do this, see the next section of this chapter.

Button Scripting 1: Attaching ActionScript to Buttons

Buttons are one of the most basic and intuitive kinds of interactive controls. Their role in an interactive movie is straightforward: you click them and something happens. Like a Movie Clip, a button can have a script attached to it. When the button is clicked, any attached ActionScript statements execute in accordance with the handler managing them.

Here and in the following sections, you'll be working extensively with ActionScript. If you need more explanation of the language elements used, see Chapter 9 for a complete introduction to ActionScript.

At the most basic level, a button will have a single on() handler with an event and a single statement. For example:

```
on(release){
    gotoAndPlay(15);
}
```

When the mouse button is released, the function that sends the movie to play at frame 15 executes. The handler event, (release), sets the function in motion. Refer to the example file invis_buttons.fla to see a button script in context.

While perfectly valid, this button-related ActionScript syntax isn't the most current. It's used occasionally in this book for the sake of example but is considered by Macromedia to be out-of-date. See the next section of this chapter to learn the preferred syntax for scripting and buttons.

Button Scripting 2: Using Event Handler Methods

Event handler methods were first introduced in Flash MX (a.k.a. version 6) and represent the most current ActionScript syntax for associating scripts with buttons. Like regular event handlers, they provide a means to attach scripts to objects such as buttons and Movie Clips. The difference is that event handler methods don't have to be attached to the object. Rather, they can be assigned from a separate location. This makes it easy to centralize all your button- and Movie Clip-related ActionScript in one location.

Defining Event Handler Methods

An event handler method is easy to understand if you examine each word in the name:

- An *event* is an occurrence—something that takes place while a movie is playing. The most familiar example of an event that can occur to an object is a button being clicked.

- A *handler* executes statements (in this case, a function) when the handler's event occurs.

- A *method* is a function associated with an object.

Now let's put it all together. An *event handler method* is ActionScript code associated with an object that performs a function when the prescribed event occurs to that object. It allows you to define specific kinds of object interaction that will set a function into motion and effect changes in your movie. You can use event handler methods to control several of the various objects in a Flash movie, including text fields, Movie Clips, and buttons.

Assigning Functions to Buttons with Event Handler Methods

Buttons have always been objects of a Flash movie, but when Flash MX was introduced, they were given their own object class. As a result, it's now possible to assign a unique instance name to a button and to control its behavior and properties via ActionScript. This feature will not significantly change the way you create Flash movies. It will, however, expand the possibilities of what you can do with a button in your interactive movies.

The Button object has its own set of event handler methods. These are used like the events for the on() handler: they determine which button event must occur for the assigned function to be called.

Like regular buttons, Button objects can be interactive controllers in your movie. The only difference is that the Button object must have a unique instance name assigned to it. This way, the assigned function "belongs" to the button. The function contains a statement that executes when the event handler method occurs and calls the function. The basic syntax looks like this:

```
buttonInstance.eventHandlerMethod=function(){
    statements to be executed when eventHandlerMethod occurs
}
```

The Button object events and their descriptions are as follows:

Button.onDragOut Occurs when the cursor is pressed over the button and dragged outside its bounds.

Button.onDragOver Occurs when the cursor is pressed over the button, dragged outside its bounds, and then dragged back inside.

Button.onKillFocus Occurs when the button loses keyboard focus.

Button.onPress Occurs when the cursor is pressed over the button.

Button.onRelease Occurs when the cursor is first pressed and then released over the button.

Button.onReleaseOutside Occurs when the cursor is first pressed over the button and then released outside the button's bounds.

Button.onRollOut Occurs when the cursor moves outside the bounds of the button.

Button.onRollOver Occurs when the cursor moves within the bounds of the button.

Button.onSetFocus Occurs when the button is given keyboard focus.

As you can see, the Button object's event handler methods and regular button event handlers have many similarities.

Now that you're acquainted with the Button object and its associated events, you're ready to learn how to assign a function to a Button object. First, open a new Flash document and create a Button symbol. (For specifics on creating buttons, see "Creating Your Own Buttons" earlier in this chapter.)

To use an event handler method and assign a function to a Button object:

1. Select the button on the Stage, and open the Property Inspector.

2. In the Instance Name field, type an instance name for the button. For the sake of this example, enter the name **clicker**.

3. Insert a new layer in the Timeline, and call it **code**. Select the first keyframe of the code layer, and choose Window → Actions (or press F9) to open the Actions panel.

4. Enter the following statements:

```
clicker.onRelease=function(){
    trace("clicked");
}
```

This script assigns a function to your `clicker` button instance. The function will print the phrase *clicked* in the Output panel and will execute when the mouse is pressed and released over the `clicker` button instance.

5. Select Control → Test Movie to try your new function. When you click the button, the Output panel should appear with the message *clicked*.

 One advantage of this scripting technique is that rather than having to attach scripts to each button individually, you can assign them to each button from one location in your movie. If you have many buttons and button scripts, this can centralize the task of scripting for all these elements. Be sure that for every Button object script you write, the script's corresponding button instance is on the Timeline at the same frame number. If a script is read on frame 1 but the button isn't encountered until frame 2, Flash won't know where to assign the function, and it will fail. In short, be sure to keep button scripts *and* their buttons in the same frame number at all times. See `clicker.fla` on this book's CD for an example of button scripts that both work and fail.

Introducing Drag-and-Drop Button Interactivity

Using ActionScript, you can create interesting effects and provide fun user interaction with drag-and-drop functionality. This technique is great for:

- Creating games, puzzles, and jigsaws
- Allowing users to organize the screen space
- Creating knobs and sliders

Creating Drag-and-Drop Functionality

To create drag-and-drop functionality, you can employ an Event Handler method. You can also use Button object events to invoke drag-and-drop functions, but in this example, you'll be centralizing your code using event handler methods. For more information about events and event handlers, see "Button Scripting: Adding Actions to Buttons" earlier in this chapter.

The basic structure for executing drag-and-drop functionality using the event handler method is as follows:

```
movieClipInstance.buttonInstance.eventHandlerMethod=function() {
    add a drag and drop function here
}
```

This code employs both Movie Clips and buttons to execute a drag-and-drop function. Although drag-and-drop functionality applies only to Movie Clips, the specific functions will be executed through the use of buttons.

The drag-and-drop functions and their descriptions are as follows:

startDrag(target, lock, left, top, right, bottom) Makes the target Movie Clip draggable while the movie plays. This function has several parameters you can use to further define your drag and drop.

Target is the target path of the Movie Clip to drag. This is required.

Lock is a true/false value specifying whether the draggable Movie Clip is locked to the center of the mouse position (true) or locked to the point where the user first clicked the Movie Clip (false). This is optional.

Left, Top, Right, and Bottom are values relative to the coordinates of the Movie Clip's parent that specify a rectangle for the Movie Clip to be constrained within. These are optional.

startDrag() is also a method of ActionScript's MovieClip class. As a method, it produces the same results but uses a slightly different syntax. To learn the difference, see "Breaking Down a Script" in Chapter 9.

stopDrag() Stops the current drag operation.

_droptarget Although it's not specifically a drag-and-drop function, the _droptarget property of the MovieClip object detects whether the draggable Movie Clip was dropped over a desired location. It returns the absolute path in slash syntax notation of the Movie Clip instance on which the draggable Movie Clip was dropped. The _droptarget property always returns a path that starts with a slash (/). To compare the _droptarget property of an instance to a reference, use the eval() function to convert the returned value from slash syntax to a dot syntax reference.

You must perform this conversion if you're using ActionScript 2.0, which doesn't support slash syntax.

If this seems complex at first, don't worry; as soon as you get into creating a drag-and-drop movie, you'll become accustomed to the process.

Simple Drag and Drop: Creating a Recycle Bin

In this example, you'll learn how to create a drag-and-drop movie that employs both the startDrag() function and the stopDrag() function as well as the _droptarget property.

We'll show how to create a recycle bin, much like you're used to seeing on your computer's desktop. You'll be able to drag a document from your "desktop" to the "recycle bin" and watch the bin change from empty to full.

Open recycle_dragDrop.fla on the book's CD. If you want to see how the finished file looks, or double-check your code, you can open recycle_dragDrop_complete.fla.

1. You'll see several layers already created in the movie for you. One layer contains the title of the project, another includes a bounding box for the desktop, and several blank layers are for you to place the document, the recycle bin, and ActionScript.

2. All the necessary graphics for creating the movie are already in your Library. Open the Library.

3. Select the document layer in the movie. Drag the bitmap document.png to the Stage. This will become the draggable element you'll drop into the recycle bin.

4. Convert the bitmap to a Movie Clip symbol by choosing Modify → Convert to Symbol or by pressing F8.

5. The Convert to Symbol dialog box appears. In the Name field, enter **document**. Make sure you select Movie Clip as the type and set the registration point to the symbol's center. For more information regarding symbols and registration, see Chapter 4.

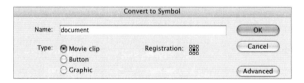

6. The bitmap has been converted into a Movie Clip symbol in the movie. Using the Property Inspector, enter an instance name of **document_mc** for the Movie Clip.

7. Enter Symbol Editing mode by double-clicking the document_mc Movie Clip instance on the Stage. Rename the layer the bitmap is on by double-clicking the layer name and typing **bitmap**.

8. Add a new layer by clicking the Insert Layer icon or by choosing Insert → Timeline → Layer. Rename this new layer to **invis_btn**. This is the layer where you'll place an invisible button that will receive ActionScript to create the drag-and-drop functionality.

9. The invisible button needed for this movie has already been created for you and is in the Library of the movie. Drag it from the Library to your newly created invis_btn layer within the document_mc Movie Clip. Give the button an instance name of **invis_btn** by using the Property Inspector. Center the button over the document graphic by using the Align panel (Ctrl+K / Cmd+K) and pressing both the Align Horizontal Center and Align Vertical Center buttons.

> Remember when using the Align panel to make sure the To Stage button on the panel is enabled. Otherwise, Flash will attempt to align your object to another selected object.

10. Exit Symbol Editing mode, and return to the main Timeline. Select the ActionScript layer in movie, and open the Actions panel by choosing Window → Actions or by pressing F9 / Opt+F9.

11. You'll now assign the drag-and-drop functionality to your movie using the Event Handler method. In the Actions panel, enter the following code:

```
_root.document_mc.invis_btn.onPress=function(){
    startDrag(_root.document_mc, true, 80, 100, 470, 300);
};
```

You've now successfully targeted the button instance. You've told Flash to look on the main Timeline, or _root, for an object instance called document_mc (the Movie Clip instance). Upon successfully finding that instance, Flash looks within that Movie Clip instance for the button instance called invis_btn. It's on that button instance that you place the event method handler, onPress. This tells Flash whenever the invis_btn instance is clicked, execute the function startDrag() with the specified parameters.

Notice how you've used the startDrag() function parameters to define exactly how your drag-and-drop functionality will work. The first parameter defines the target of the drag and drop or, in other words, the path to the Movie Clip you'll be moving. In the example, the Movie Clip is the document_mc instance on the _root Timeline.

The next parameter, lock, is set to true. This ensures that while dragging the document around, you'll always be locked to the center of that Movie Clip and never be dragging it around by its edges.

The last four parameters define the draggable area for the Movie Clip. In this example, this provides the desktop area in which you're able to move the document. The area drawn for the desktop is 450×275 pixels and centered on the Stage with X, Y coordinates of (50,63). These parameters for the Left, Top, Right, and Bottom of the bounding box have been chosen to ensure that the document graphic always stays within the desired area.

At this point, you can test your movie by choosing Control → Test Movie (or by pressing Ctrl+Enter / Ctrl+Return). You can see that when you press and hold the mouse down over your document, you're able to pick it up and move it around on the screen—only there isn't anywhere to drop it yet! And if you try, it only "sticks" to the mouse because you have no way to drop it. Close the Test Movie dialog box, and return to the Flash authoring environment. From here you'll add the drop functionality.

Return to the Flash authoring environment. Click the ActionScript layer, and then click frame 1. Open the Actions panel, and enter the following code:

```
_root.document_mc.invis_btn.onRelease=function(){
    stopDrag();
};
```

What you've done here is tell Flash to stop executing the drag-and-drop code when the button instance is released. You're now able to pick the document graphic up, move it around the Stage within the defined desktop area, and drop it when you release the mouse.

The basic drag and drop is complete! To create a recycle bin:

1. Create a new Movie Clip symbol by selecting Insert → New Symbol. Enter **recycle_bin** in the Name field. Make sure to set the type to Movie Clip.

2. Flash opens Symbol Editing mode. Rename layer 1 by double-clicking the name. Enter a new name of **bitmaps**. Create two more new layers by clicking the Insert Layer icon or by choosing Insert → Timeline → Layer. Name these layers **label** and **ActionScript**.

3. Select the bitmaps layer. Open the Library. Notice two bitmaps, called `empty_bin.png` and `full_bin.png`, inside. Drag the bitmap `empty_bin.png` from the Library to the Stage. Center the bitmap using the Align panel (Ctrl+K / Cmd+K).

4. Insert a new blank keyframe on the bitmaps layer by clicking frame 2 and choosing Insert → Timeline → Blank Keyframe. As in the previous step, drag `full_bin.png` from the Library, and center it on the Stage.

5. Select the label layer, and create a new blank keyframe (Insert → Timeline → Blank Keyframe) in frame 2. Click frame 2, and using the Property Inspector, enter **full_can** in the Frame Label parameter. Repeat this process for frame 1, entering **empty_can** as the Frame Label parameter in the Property Inspector.

6. Select the ActionScript layer, and click frame 1. Open the Actions panel (Window → Actions), and enter the following code:

```
stop();
```

This prevents the Movie Clip from continually playing and rapidly displaying both the empty-can and full-can graphics. The movie will stop at frame 1, displaying only the empty can and waiting for the drag-and-drop functionality to execute.

7. Exit Symbol Editing mode, and return to the main Timeline. Drag `recycle_bin` to the recycle_bin layer of the Stage. If it's not already selected, click the newly created recycle bin Movie Clip. Using the Property Inspector, enter an instance name of **recycle_bin_mc** for the Movie Clip.

> All symbols must have an instance name to be used with ActionScript. Whenever you create a Movie Clip, or any other symbol, it's good to get in the habit of giving that symbol an instance name immediately via the Property Inspector.

You'll now add the final piece of ActionScript to detect whether you've dropped the document graphic on top of the recycle bin. If you do, the recycle bin will change graphics appropriately from empty to full, and the document Movie Clip will disappear, thus placing it in the bin.

On the main Timeline, click the ActionScript layer. Open the Actions panel (Window → Actions), and add the following code to the `onRelease` handler:

```
if (eval(_root.document_mc._droptarget)==recycle_bin_mc) {
    _root.document_mc._visible = false;
    _root.recycle_bin_mc.gotoAndStop("full_can");
}
```

This `if` statement evaluates the `_droptarget` property of the document Movie Clip, checking to see whether the clip has been dropped over the recycle bin. If it has, the next two lines of code execute. The first statement hides the document Movie Clip so it appears to be in the recycle bin. The next statement tells the recycle bin Movie Clip to move to the frame containing the graphic of the full bin, giving you the desired visual result. The completed block of code should read as follows:

```
_root.document_mc.invis_btn.onRelease=function(){
    stopDrag();
    if (eval(_root.document_mc._droptarget)==recycle_bin_mc){
        _root.document_mc._visible=false;
        _root.recycle_bin_mc.gotoAndStop("full_can");
    }
};
```

Congratulations! You've created your first drag-and-drop movie. Select Control → Test Movie to see it in action. By expanding on these principles, you can create highly interactive and fun applications.

Creating Scalable, Flexible Interactive Controllers

You've explored using both Button and Movie Clip symbols in Flash. As you know, you can use these symbols repeatedly to create many instances in your movie. This allows you to create flexible, self-sufficient, interactive controls to use in a variety of ways. In the following sections, you'll create three flexible interactive controllers to use in any Timeline and any movie.

Organizing Information with a Cascading Menu

Creating navigation can be a challenging task. Your navigation should be clear, concise, and intuitive for users. No matter how cool or interesting your menu is, its primary function is to deliver content. A cascading menu is a great way to do this. It allows you to guide the user to lots of information while still keeping an orderly interface.

In the following example, we'll show how to create a cascading menu that is flexible enough to be placed in any movie and to be extended for a variety of purposes. This example assumes you're familiar with creating your own buttons, Movie Clips, and their properties. For more information about buttons, see "Creating Your Own Buttons" earlier in this chapter. For more information about Movie Clips, see Chapter 4.

To see the completed working version of this example, open `cascadingMenu.fla` on the book's CD.

1. Create a new Flash 8 document by choosing New → Flash Document.

2. Use the Rectangle tool to create a rectangle that is 150×20 pixels. Convert this rectangle into a Button symbol by pressing F8. Set the type of this symbol to Button, set its registration point to the rectangle's upper-left corner, and give your symbol the name **button_item**. Press OK, and then double-click the new Button symbol to enter Symbol Editing mode.

3. Now in Symbol Editing mode, insert a keyframe in your button's Over state by choosing Insert → Timeline → Keyframe. In your newly created Over state, change the color of your button to indicate a highlight when the user rolls over the button. In the example on the CD, the rectangle has a dark-green stroke and a light-green fill.

4. Insert frames in both the Down and Hit states of your button by clicking in each name and pressing F5.

5. Exit Symbol Editing mode, and return to the main Timeline. Select your newly created button, and enter an instance name in the Property Inspector of **button_item_i**. Then, select the `button_item_i` instance, and convert it into another symbol by pressing F8.

6. Select Movie Clip as the type for this symbol, set its registration point to the button's upper-left corner, and enter **menu_item** in the Name field.

7. Double-click the new symbol to enter Symbol Editing mode. You'll see your `button_item_i` instance on Layer 1. Double-click this layer's name, and change it to **button**. Create a new layer by pressing the New Layer icon or by choosing Insert → Timeline → Layer. Name this new layer **label**.

8. Create a Dynamic Text box on your label layer. Choose _sans for the font, 14 points for the size, and enter an instance name of **menu_label** in the Property Inspector. Enter **Label** in the new text box, and position it over the button on the button layer. For more information about creating Dynamic Text or manipulating text properties, see Chapter 3.

9. Exit Symbol Editing mode again, and return to the main Timeline. Select your Movie Clip on the Stage. In the Property Inspector, enter **mainMenu** in the Instance Name field.

10. Convert your `mainMenu` Movie Clip instance to another symbol by pressing F8. Choose Movie Clip as the type, set the registration point in the upper-left corner, and enter **cascadingMenu** in the Instance Name field. Click OK to return to the main Timeline, and then double-click the instance of `cascadingMenu` to enter Symbol Editing mode.

11. You'll now see your `mainMenu` Movie Clip instance on layer 1. Double-click the layer name to change it to **menu**. Create three more layers using the Insert Layer icon or by selecting Insert → Timeline → Layer. Name them, from top to bottom, **ActionScript**, **frameLabel**, and **subMenu**.

12. Select frame 1 of your frameLabel layer. In the Property Inspector, enter **mainMenu** in the Frame Label field. Insert a blank keyframe in frame 2 of this layer by selecting it and choosing Insert → Timeline → Blank Keyframe. Enter a frame label of **subMenu** for frame 2. This will be used in a later step.

13. Select frame 1 on your ActionScript layer. Open the Actions panel by choosing Window → Actions. Enter the following code:

```
stop();
mainMenu.menu_label.text = "Show Options";
mainMenu.button_item_i.onPress = function() {
    gotoAndStop("subMenu");
};
```

The first line contains the `stop()` function. This tells Flash to stop on this frame. If this function weren't here, the movie would rapidly jump between frames 1 and 2 of the `cascadingMenu` Movie Clip.

The second line of code sets the text for the menu. By using Dynamic Text, you're able to assign text to the field via ActionScript using the `text` property. You're telling Flash to look for the `mainMenu` Movie Clip instance. Upon finding it, Flash looks inside that symbol for a text field instance called `menu_label` and manipulates its `text` property. For more information about assigning Dynamic Text via ActionScript, see Chapter 3.

In the example, you assigned the text *Show Options* to the top-level navigation. When this is clicked, the subnavigation menu will display. The third line of code does just that. It contains the event method handler for an `onPress` event, telling Flash to once again look for the `mainMenu` Movie Clip instance and, upon finding it, look inside for a button instance called `button_item`. This `button_item` instance has a function applied to it so that, when pressed, the `cascadingMenu` Timeline will move to the frame label `subMenu`.

If you test your movie at this Stage it will appear to not work, but don't worry; you're not finished. With these statements in place, you can complete the ActionScript that defines the functionality of the menu:

1. Select frame 2 of the menu layer. Choose Insert → Timeline → Frame (or press F5) to insert a new frame. This extends the `mainMenu` instance into frame 2.

2. Select frame 2 of the subMenu layer. Insert a blank keyframe by choosing Insert → Timeline → Blank Keyframe. It's on this frame that you'll create the subnavigation menu.

3. Drag three instances of the `menu_item` symbol from the Library. Line them up however you want, but keep in mind you should have a correlation for the user between your main menu and submenu options. Give each `menu_item` symbol an instance name in the Property Inspector. In the example, we used **menu1**, **menu2**, and **menu3**, respectively.

4. Select frame 2 of the ActionScript layer. Insert a blank keyframe by choosing Insert → Timeline → Blank Keyframe. Open the Actions panel by choosing Window → Actions. Enter the following code:

```
stop();
mainMenu.menu_label.text = "Hide Options";
menu1.menu_label.text = "Menu Item 1";
menu2.menu_label.text = "Menu Item 2";
menu3.menu_label.text = "Menu Item 3";
mainMenu.button_item_i.onPress = function() {
    gotoAndStop("mainMenu");
};
menu1.button_item_i.onPress = function() {
    // Add actions here
};
```

```
menu2.button_item_i.onPress = function() {
    // Add actions here
};
menu3.button_item_i.onPress = function() {
    // Add actions here
};
```

Once again, a stop() function prevents the movie from jumping to another frame in the movie. The next line reassigns the previous label of *Show Options* to the new label of *Hide Options*. This reflects how the menu will behave depending on whether the subnavigation is visible.

Following the same procedure for assigning Dynamic Text via ActionScript, lines 3 through 5 assign labels to the three subnavigation items.

Line 6 follows the previous model of moving the Timeline when the mainMenu item is clicked. The cascadingMenu Timeline is now sent to the frame label mainMenu.

In lines 9 through 17, the correct Event Handler method has been set up for the onPress event. Replace the // Add actions here lines of code in each function with your own commands. These could be such commands as launching a web browser and going to a specified web address, navigating to another section in your movie, or triggering an animation. For example, in the demo file cascadingMenu.fla on the CD, selecting the first menu item will play a short animation.

Test your movie by choosing Control → Test Movie.

Congratulations! You've successfully created a basic cascading menu. This menu works independently and can be placed in any Timeline of any movie. To reuse this interactive control, drag the cascadingMenu item from the Library to any new Library in any movie. All the required Movie Clips and button instances will move along with it.

Movable Content: Creating a Draggable Pop-up Window

Another useful interactive control is the pop-up window. It allows you to display graphics, animations, and text messages. However, users appreciate having the capability of dragging this window around to a desired location, rather than simply opening and closing it.

In the following example, we'll show how to create a draggable pop-up window as a reusable element in any movie. This example assumes you're familiar with invisible buttons, Movie Clips, and drag-and-drop functionality.

Open the popWin.fla file on the book's CD. We've create all the necessary graphic files for you; they reside in the Library (Ctrl+L / Cmd+L). To see the completed, working version of this example, open popWin_complete.fla.

1. The document has three layers on the main Timeline: ActionScript, pop, and open-Win. Click the pop layer. Open your Library (Ctrl+L / Cmd+L), and drag an instance of the popWin symbol to the Stage.

2. Click the instance of the popWin Movie Clip symbol, and give it an instance name of **popWin_mc** in the Property Inspector.

3. Double-click the popWin_mc instance to enter Symbol Editing mode. You'll notice several layers have already been created: ActionScript, drag_btn, text, outline, close, and win.

4. Select the drag_btn layer. Drag an instance of the invis_btn symbol from the Library. Enter an instance name of **drag_btn** in the Property Inspector. Align this instance to an X, Y value of (0,0). Set the width to 178 pixels and the height to 20 pixels. This invisible button will receive all of the drag-and-drop commands.

5. Select the text layer. Create a Dynamic Text field instance, and position it on the silver area within the bounds of the popWin symbol. Set the following in the Property Inspector: __sans for the font, 16 points for the size, Multiline for the line type, and windowText for the name. For more information about working with Dynamic Text, see Chapter 3.

6. Select the Close layer. Drag an instance of the close_btn symbol from the Library (Ctrl+L / Cmd+L), and place in on the Stage. Assign the instance name **close_btn** in the Property Inspector. Place your close_btn instance at the X, Y position of (182,2).

7. Select frame 1 on the ActionScript layer. Open the Actions panel by choosing Window → Actions. Enter the following code in the Actions panel:

```
windowText.text="This is a pop-up window";drag_btn.onPress=function()
    startDrag(_parent.popWin_mc);
};
drag_btn.onRelease=function() {
    stopDrag();
};
drag_btn.onReleaseOutside=function() {
    stopDrag();
};
close_btn.onPress=function() {
    _parent.popWin_mc._visible=false;
};
```

The first line sets the text property of the Dynamic Text field to display the pop-up message. Since you've set the Dynamic Text field to a line type of Multiline, you can assign multiple lines of text here to display when the window pops up. The functions that pertain to drag_btn should look familiar. (They're the drag-and-drop functions discussed earlier in this chapter.) The onPress event for drag_btn tells Flash to look up one level from the current Timeline to find the Movie Clip instance popWin_mc and to use that instance as the target for the drag and drop. Since you want to freely drag this Movie Clip instance around, you don't need any other parameters to restrain the boundaries for dragging and dropping. The onRelease event stops the drag function. Additionally, you'll see an onReleaseOutside event. This is a "safety net" to catch those few instances when someone's mouse isn't actually over the item they want to drop (see Figure 8.7).

The onPress function associated with close_btn will manipulate the visibility of the pop-up window. This functions tells Flash that when the close_btn instance is clicked, the _visible property of the popWin_mc Movie Clip instance, residing one Timeline up from the current location, should be set to false, thus making the Movie Clip instance invisible to the viewer.

8. Exit Symbol Editing mode, and return to the main Timeline. Select the first frame of the ActionScript layer, choose Window → Actions to open the Actions panel, and enter the following statement:

    ```
    popWin_mc._visible=false;
    ```

    This tells Flash to set the visibility of popWin_mc to false, which sets the initial state of the pop-up window, rendering it invisible until it's requested.

9. Select the openWin layer. Drag another instance of the invis_btn symbol from the Library (Ctrl+L / Cmd+L). Give this instance the name **open_win** in the Property Inspector. Size and position this instance appropriately over the text *To open the pop-up window, click here*. This is the button you'll use to trigger the pop-up window.

10. Select the ActionScript layer, and open the Actions panel (Window → Actions). Enter the following code:

    ```
    open_win.onPress=function(){
        popWin_mc._visible=true;
    };
    ```

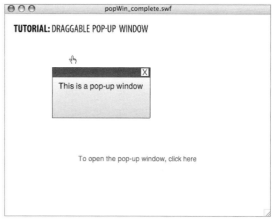

Figure 8.7

When a user's mouse moves too fast, it can leave the bounds of the draggable window, rendering the window "undrop-pable." The onReleaseOutside() event provides function-ality to avoid this because it registers specifically when the mouse is outside the draggable object.

This function executes as soon as the invisible open_win button instance is clicked. It tells Flash to set the _visible property of the popWin Movie Clip instance to true, allowing you to see the pop-up window.

11. Test the movie by selecting Control → Test Movie.

Success! You've created a draggable pop-up window! This window can display any text you'd like and acts as an alert or information box to users. You can use this pop-up window independently in any Timeline or movie provided that you repeat steps 9 and 10 every time you move the popWin_mc instance to a different location. To reuse this pop-up window, drag the popWin symbol from your Library (Ctrl+L / Cmd+L) to any other movie's Library. All the necessary symbols will automatically be copied as well.

The example file, popWin_complete.fla, has some additional code that sets boundaries for the draggability of the pop-up window. Limiting the range of motion for a pop-up window may be useful in your projects.

Using Buttons to Scroll Text

Scrollable text fields are an integral part of any interactive toolset. They provide a great functional benefit by allowing designers and programmers to display lots of text in a confined, manageable area. By creating your own interactive controls for scrolling text, you not only have that same great function benefit but also complete control over the look and feel over your controls, allowing them to fit into a tighter, more integrated design scheme.

In the following example, we'll show how to create a scrollable text field that you can reuse across any Timeline and any movie. This example assumes you're familiar with Common Libraries for buttons, Movie Clips, and Dynamic Text fields.

 Open the file `customScroll.fla` on the CD. This file contains all necessary graphic elements needed to complete this example. (To see the final results of this example, open `customScroll_complete.fla`.)

1. You'll notice a Movie Clip instance on the main Timeline called `customScroll`. Double-click it to enter Symbol Editing mode. You'll see that the Movie Clip instance has three layers: ActionScript, controls, and text.

2. Let's examine the text layer. Click the text box that resides on the text layer. From the Property Inspector, you'll see that this is a Dynamic Text field with the following properties: the font is set to _sans, the size is set to 12 points, the line type is set to Multiline, and both the Selectable and Show Border Around Text buttons have been enabled. For more information about Dynamic Text fields and their properties, see Chapter 3.

The "dummy" text for this example was provided by `www.lipsum.com`.

3. Enter an instance name of **scrollText** in the Property Inspector.

4. While the `scrollText` text field instance is selected, choose Text in Flash's main menu bar. You'll notice the Scrollable option is checked. This allows the text field to be contained in an area you define, and any text that doesn't fit in this area will be visible only when scrolled.

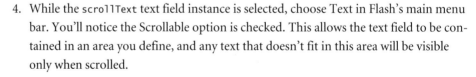

If the Scrollable property of the text field isn't enabled, the text box will resize to accommodate all text inside it, and the scroll bars will have no effect.

5. Select the controls layer. Drag an instance of the `scroll_button` symbol from the Library to the Stage. This Button symbol was taken from Flash's Common Library (Window → Common Libraries → Buttons).

6. Name your new button instance **upArrow** in the Property Inspector. Drag another instance of the `scroll_button` symbol to the Stage. Flip this instance vertically by choosing Modify → Transform → Flip Vertical. Name this instance **downArrow** in the Property Inspector. Place both instances next to the text field as you see fit.

7. Select frame 1 of the ActionScript layer. Open the Actions panel by choosing Window → Actions. Enter the following code in the Actions panel:

```
upArrow.onPress=function(){
    scrollText.scroll-=1;
};
downArrow.onPress=function(){
    scrollText.scroll+=1;
};
```

These two functions control all the scrolling for the text field. They both execute when the `upArrow` and `downArrow` button instances are clicked. Upon executing, the `scroll` property of the text field object is manipulated.

Both of these functions use the subtraction assignment operator and the addition assignment operator. These operators are handy for an array of tasks, but in particular for scrolling text.

Addition assignment operator (+=) Assigns `expression1` the value of `expression1 + expression2`. For example, the following two statements have the same result:

```
x+=y;
x=x+y;
```

Subtraction assignment operator (-=) Assigns `expression1` the value of `expression1 − expression2`. For example, the following two statements are equivalent:

```
x-=y;
x=x-y;
```

What this means for the scrollable text field is that each time the `upArrow` button instance is clicked, the `scroll` property of the text field is set to the current `scroll` property value minus 1. That is, the text field will scroll up one line. Similarly, each time the `downArrow` is clicked, the `scroll` property for the text field is set to the current `scroll` property value plus 1, thus scrolling the text field down one line.

Test your scrollable text field by choosing Control → Test Movie.

Congratulations! You've created a scrollable text field! You can place any amount of text in the text field instance, and your interactive controls will automatically scroll it up and down. To reuse this scrollable text field, drag the `customScroll` symbol from your Library (Ctrl+L / Cmd+L) to any other movie's Library. All necessary symbols will automatically be copied as well.

Using Components for Interface Development

Components are drag-and-drop building blocks for interactive Flash applications (see Figure 8.8). They provide instant functionality for a wide variety of interface elements common to applications: scroll bars, text input fields, list and check boxes, radio buttons, and so on. Components help make Flash an ideal environment for prototyping web-based forms and applications.

Components are a means of combining the visual appeal designers want with the flexibility and functional robustness programmers want. They are well designed and you can customize them to fit specific needs. The components that ship with Flash 8 all have the same graphic *theme* known as Halo, which will give your component-based applications a unified appearance. From a technical perspective, Components have flexible yet solid code to make them work in a variety of settings.

As great as components sound, we don't want to give you the impression they're the answer to all your application development wishes. Yes, they're useful, and yes, they save time. However, with the prior release of version 2 components in Flash MX 2004 and MX Pro 2004, many of the components are targeted to the high end of the application development community. To get version 2 components to deliver their best or most useful functionality, you need to be comfortable writing ActionScript 2.0. For those of you who aren't interested in developing applications or ready to leap into advanced ActionScript, this is probably disappointing. We understand these concerns and offer as much guidance about each new component as space allows in the following sections.

Introducing Flash Components

Figure 8.8

You can select components from the Components panel (Ctrl+F7 / Cmd+F7).

In Flash 8, components are divided into three categories: data, media, and user interface (UI). Data components require advanced ActionScript beyond the scope of this book and will not be covered. You can learn more about these components by using the Help panel (F1). We'll discuss media components for streaming audio and video in Chapter 16. This topic is limited to Flash 8 Professional users. To learn about other ways to incorporate streaming audio into a Flash movie, see Chapter 15. You'll find you still have loads of options that aren't limited to the Professional version of Flash and that often provide much simpler solutions. We'll cover the basics of the UI components in the following sections.

Introducing the UI Components

If you've used components in previous versions of Flash, then you should be right at home with many of the new components in Flash 8. The UI components provide a wide array of options for building interfaces for Flash applications. This set includes most of the widgets you'd find in any kind of software application, including radio buttons, list boxes, text fields, and so on. The UI components are as follows:

- Accordion
- Alert
- Button
- CheckBox
- ComboBox
- DataGrid
- DateChooser
- DateField
- Label
- List
- Loader

- Menu
- MenuBar
- NumericStepper
- ProgressBar
- RadioButton
- ScrollPane
- TextArea
- TextInput
- Tree
- UIScrollBar
- Window

Combining Version 1 and Version 2 Components

If you used components in Flash MX, then you were using version 1 (v1) components. Flash 8 ships with version 2 (v2) components. The v2 components represent the next step in Flash components and component architecture. Because they're fundamentally different from v1 components from a programming perspective, Macromedia strongly discourages you from creating applications that use both v1 and v2 components, claiming it will lead to "unpredictable behavior." This means it's a bad idea to use older, Flash MX (or v1) components in an application you build in Flash 8 where you plan to *also* use v2 components. However, if you have a few v1 components you just can't live without, you're in luck. You can use them in an application that meets the following criteria:

- The application uses only v1 components.
- The final SWF is published for Flash Player 6.
- The application uses ActionScript 1.0.

The application will be able to run correctly if your audience is using Flash Player 6, and the functionality of your v1 components will remain intact. To learn how to publish movies for Flash Player 6 and ActionScript 1.0, see Chapter 17. If you want to ensure compatibility between v1 components and Flash Player 7, you can download updated components from Macromedia Flash Exchange (www.macromedia.com/go/v1_components). For more details on components and Flash Player version compatibility, choose Help → Components → Using Components → Working with Components → Upgrading Version 1 Components to Version 2 Architecture.

Employing UI Components in Your Flash Applications

The UI components are representative of the most common elements of computer software. They will enable the users of your application to make choices, get and provide information, monitor the status of an application as it's loading, and scroll through large text files and graphics.

To add a component to your application:

1. Select the component in the Components panel.

2. Drag the component to the Stage and position it. If necessary, you can use the Free Transform tool to change the size and dimensions of any component (see Figure 8.9).

3. Enter any required parameter values in the Property Inspector (see Figure 8.10).

Some components (such as the ComboBox and List) require multiple values for one parameter. It's easy to enter these values using the Values dialog box. To enter multiple values:

1. Click the value column for the parameter you want to edit.

2. Click the Magnify button at the right side of the column. The Values dialog box opens (see Figure 8.11).

3. Use the Add button (+) to add a value. Use the Remove button (−) to clear a value. Use the up and down arrow buttons to reorder values in the list.

4. When you're finished, click OK.

5. Attach a behavior or write ActionScript to make the component do something.

6. Save your movie and test it to confirm the component works.

Live Preview allows you to see the changes made to a component while you're building your application. Not all changes will appear in Live Preview, but it gives you an idea of what the component will look like in your published application. Choose Control from the main menu bar, and look near the bottom for the Enable Live Preview option. If it's checked, Live Preview is turned on. To change this, select Enable Live Preview, and it will be disabled. Live Preview can be helpful; we recommend you take advantage of it and leave it enabled.

Figure 8.9

Use the Free Transform tool to resize a component. Here, you see it adjusting the dimensions of a Button component.

Figure 8.10

When a component is selected on the Stage, the Property Inspector's Parameters tab shows two columns, one for specific parameters and another for parameter values. Enter a value for each parameter in the field beside its name.

Retrieving Information from Components Using ActionScript

As you'll soon discover, it's easy to add components to your application and customize them to fit your needs. What can be difficult, however, is getting them to do something useful once you've configured them to work in the context of your Flash movie or application. For this task, you have two choices: ActionScript and behaviors.

For simple Components, such as the Button and CheckBox, behaviors can make it easy to navigate to a new frame number or label or open a link on the Web. If your application calls for this kind of functionality, the most straightforward choice is to use behaviors. However, ActionScript behaviors are one of the more poorly implemented features of Flash. Consequently, this book doesn't cover them in detail. If you're interested to know whether they're useful for what you need to do, choose Help → Flash Help (F1).

For more advanced functionality, you'll need to go a little further into ActionScript. Again, if this is your first exposure to the scripting language, study Chapter 9 before trying the techniques covered here.

Consider the following statements:

```
listenerObj=new Object();
listenerObj.event = function(eventObj){
    statements;
}
eventSrc.addEventListener("event",listenerObj);
```

This ActionScript will not actually run. It's a kind of "script template" that will allow you to retrieve information from many of the UI components. Here's how it works. The first line creates a listener object, an element that waits to respond to events that take place in your movie:

```
listenerObj=new Object();
```

The next three lines create a function for the listener object:

```
listenerObj.event = function(eventObj){
    statements;
}
```

The function represents what the listener should do when the events it's waiting for actually happen. The tasks the function performs would be written where you see the placeholder, *statements*.

The last line brings this all together:

```
eventSrc.addEventListener("event",listenerObj);
```

`eventSrc` is the instance name of a component in your Flash application. When event happens to the component (`eventSrc`), the event (such as "click" or "change") is broadcast to `listenerObj`, which then performs the function you associated with it.

Figure 8.11

The Values dialog box allows you to enter multiple values for a single parameter.

Use this basic structure to help retrieve information from a UI Component. It's by no means the only way to use ActionScript in conjunction with components. It will, however, provide a means for you to retrieve the information selected or entered by the users of your applications.

During the development process, use the trace() function in the *statements* line. This causes Flash to print information to the Output panel. It isn't especially relevant to the final, published application, but it's extremely helpful while you're in the building stage because it allows you to track information passed to and from your application in real time. In lieu of trace(), a more concrete method would be to assign the output of a component to a variable where it can be stored temporarily and retrieved later. To learn more about trace() and variables, see Chapter 9.

Stepping Beyond Components

Components allow you to work quickly when creating applications in Flash. Through a simple drag-and-drop process, you can easily add interface elements that bring your applications to life. After using components and putting them to work in your movie, it might seem you have run the gamut of possibilities, but you can still do much more with them. In the following sections, you'll learn how to *skin* a component, giving it an entirely new look. You'll also learn where to get additional component resources and how to install them so that they're available alongside the others in the Components panel.

Skinning Components with Custom Themes

In the computer software world, the term *skin* refers to a piece (or pieces) of art that changes the appearance of an application. For example, by applying a skin to an MP3 player, you can get rid of the default appearance (usually bland and monotone) and replace it with something that looks like a furry animal, a brick wall, some viscous fluid— just about anything. The skin graphics *become* the appearance of the application and establish an entirely new look and feel. The process of changing an application's appearance in this manner is known as *skinning*.

Ever since v1 components were released in Flash MX, it has been possible to skin them. Now, with v2 components, it's still possible, though the process has changed a bit. Component skins in Flash are called *themes*. Themes reside in the Libraries of FLA files (see Figure 8.12). You can open these files to see all the parts that comprise the theme of any given component. The default theme for v2 components is Halo. To skin a component, all you need to do is replace the Halo theme with a new theme. If you don't have a theme, you can create one.

To learn the steps involved in skinning a component, choose Help → Flash Help (F1) and navigate to Components → Using Components → Customizing Components → About Skinning Components.

Finding Additional Resources for Components

The set of v2 components that shipped with Flash 8 is helpful for most general interface needs. However, you might find you have a need beyond the default set of UI components. Plenty of resources are available for getting additional components. Some of the following sites charge a fee for their components; others don't. Visit each site to see their current offerings and pricing information.

Macromedia Flash Exchange This is the official component source. Macromedia Flash Exchange always has a huge list of downloadable components and other tools to extend the abilities of Flash. Many downloads are free; others cost money. If you're interested in developing your own components and sharing them, Macromedia Flash Exchange provides a forum for this as well. Visit the Macromedia Flash Exchange at www.macromedia.com/exchange/flash.

Eyeland Studio Eyeland Studio is run by components guru J. Scott Hamlin. Eyeland has lots of components from which to choose. Many are available via subscription, but a few freebies exist. Visit www.eyeland.com to see what the site has to offer, follow the links to Flash Foundry → Flash → Components.

The Flash Components Network This site is probably one of the best-known resources for Flash components. The Flash Components Network is an open forum of exchange for components, discussions, tutorials, and information about Flash development. Visit this great resource at www.flashcomponents.net.

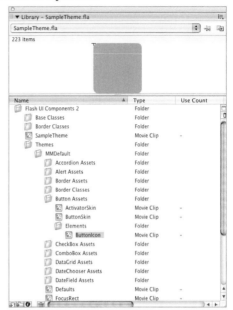

Figure 8.12

After opening a theme FLA file, the Library will allow you to view and edit the Movie Clips that make up a component theme.

Installing Additional Components

Once you've picked up a new component or two, you need to install them to use them in your applications. You have two ways to do this: by importing the component's FLA file as an external Library or by using the Macromedia Extension Manager application.

INSTALLING COMPONENTS AS EXTERNAL LIBRARIES

You can install Flash components as an external Library when the components are distributed in FLA files. This process is somewhat similar to applying a new theme to an existing component in your movie.

To install a component from an FLA file:

1. Open the Flash document where you want to add the new component. Open the document's Library (Window → Library).

2. Choose File → Import → Open External Library, and select the FLA file that contains the new component.

3. The FLA file opens as an additional Library. Click the component's icon in the external Library, and drag it to the Library of the movie with which you're working.

4. Click the menu in the title bar of the external Library panel, and choose Close Panel.

5. To implement the new component in your movie, drag the component from the Library to the Stage, and edit its parameters in either the Property Inspector or Components panel.

INSTALLING COMPONENTS WITH THE EXTENSION MANAGER

When you install Flash, a little application called the Extension Manager is also installed. This utility allows you to install software that extends the functionality of various Macromedia applications including (of course) Flash 8. If you download third-party components saved as MXP files, the Extension Manager will allow you to install them.

To install components with the Extension Manager:

1. Launch the Extension Manager. In Windows, navigate to Macromedia\Extension Manager\Extension Manager.exe. On a Mac, go to Applications → Macromedia Extension Manager → Extension Manager. You can also choose Help → Manage Extensions.

2. Choose Flash 8 from the Product menu (see Figure 8.13).

3. Choose File → Install Extension (or press Ctrl+O / Cmd+I).

4. Navigate to the component file you want to install. It should be named with an .mxp extension. Select this file, and click Install/Choose.

Figure 8.13

Use the Macromedia Extension Manager application to extend the functionality of Flash.

5. As installation starts, you'll see a disclaimer. Read it, and click Accept if you agree with the message. Installation will then commence.

6. Once installation has finished, click OK to confirm that it has completed.

At this point, the Extension Manager will show the name of the component you just installed in its main window. If you want to install additional components, repeat steps 3–6.

After installing a component with the Extension Manager, open Flash, and choose Window → Components. The newly installed component should be ready to use. If you opened the Extension Manager from within Flash, you'll need to quit and restart Flash.

CHAPTER 9

Using ActionScript in the Flash Environment

In the past few chapters you've dabbled in ActionScript and you've begun to see the power of issuing commands to control your Flash movie. Now you're ready to take the plunge into scripting. Congratulations! You'll find that becoming competent with Action-Script allows you to do much more with your Flash creations than you could ever do by selecting behaviors. Whenever you find yourself getting stuck with behaviors, hand-coded ActionScript offers a new world of possibilities. This is one of the most exciting and rewarding aspects of working in Flash—but it can also be the most difficult and demanding.

Learning ActionScript and becoming comfortable with the language is a challenge. Getting to the point where you can use the language with fluidity can be even more tenuous. However, none of this is impossible. What is most important is that you practice diligently. Learning ActionScript (or any programming language, for that matter) is like learning to speak a foreign language: to use it fluently, you have to practice every day. Practice can be as basic as trying to create simple movies that perform tasks using capabilities of the ActionScript language. Repeated exposure to the language through this kind of routine will give you a good feel for the language in context. The more you practice, the more of the language you'll learn and the more comfortable you'll become with its elements.

This chapter covers fundamental ActionScript terms and concepts and gets you started with some advanced scripting techniques.

- Learning ActionScript, an object-oriented language
- Using components of a script in the context of a simple movie
- Learning how scripts flow
- Planning scripts before you create your movie
- Getting familiar with ActionScript terms, vocabulary, and syntax
- Using the Actions panel: your scripting interface
- Picking up troubleshooting tips and debugging techniques

Exploring the Anatomy of ActionScript

ActionScript is most similar to the programming language JavaScript. In fact, ActionScript is derived from the JavaScript specifications set forth by the European Computer Manufacturers Association (ECMA).

For more information about the ECMA, visit `www.ecma-international.org`.

As an object-oriented scripting language, ActionScript has components that follow a particular organization. Elements of a movie are organized into *classes*. Classes can then be expressed as independent parts called *objects*. An object is an *instance* of a class.

A class has information it passes to each object it creates. This information comes in the form of *properties*, which are the qualities of an object, and *methods*, which are the "tasks" an object can perform. In Flash, several predefined classes create objects, such as Date objects and Sound objects. One of the most common predefined objects, the Movie Clip, has properties such as `_framesloaded` and methods such as `play()`.

It's also possible to create your own objects using ActionScript. For example, you could use a *constructor* function to create the class Dogs, with properties such as `_spotted` and `_scruffy` and with methods such as `fetch()` and `bark()`.

Breaking Down a Script

One way to understand how scripts work is to dissect a script that is functioning in the context of a movie. Once you grasp what's happening on the movie's Stage, you can peek behind the scenes and see what kind of script is making the movie act a certain way or perform a certain task.

In Figure 9.1 (`coffee_break.fla` on this book's CD), the audience's standard pointer cursor is replaced with a jittery, caffeine-deprived custom cursor. When someone clicks to "fill" their coffee mug, the jitters disappear and steam rises as coffee is poured into the mug. This movie consists of a single frame in the main Timeline (although the jitter and steam Movie Clip animations are nested in this Timeline and take about 100 frames). The hand holding the mug is an instance of a Movie Clip; the jitters and steam animations are also Movie Clip instances inside the mug clip.

The most important script in this movie is a series of statements on the main Timeline directed at the `coffee_mc` Movie Clip instance. This script is responsible for attaching the custom cursor, cueing the animations, and playing the sound.

Open and play the movie so you can see exactly what it does. Also, select the keyframe in the code layer, and open the Actions panel (by pressing F9 / Opt+F9) to see the scripts that control the instance's behavior as a custom cursor. For a breakdown of the scripts in this movie, refer to Figure 9.2.

When this movie loads into the Flash Player, these statements on the main Timeline execute:

```
Mouse.hide();
coffee_mc.startDrag(true);
sfx = new Sound();
sfx.attachSound("pour");
```

The Mouse object hides the pointer cursor, and the `startDrag()` method makes this coffee mug Movie Clip draggable. These statements make the mug a kind of custom cursor by replacing the pointer with the mug. The next two lines create a Sound object using the `new Sound()` constructor and attach the sound `pour` to a sound instance named `sfx`.

> In this example, `startDrag()` is used as a method of the MovieClip object and uses a slightly different syntax than discussed previously. You can read more about drag and drop functionality in Chapter 8 and the ActionScript reference on the CD.

The next function is called whenever the mouse moves:

```
coffee_mc.onMouseMove = function() {
    coffee_mc._x = _root._xmouse;
    coffee_mc._y = _root._ymouse;
}
```

The statements inside the function lock the horizontal and vertical positions of the mouse to the registration point of the `coffee_mc` Movie Clip instance.

Figure 9.1

Give me some more coffee!

Figure 9.2

This Actions panel shows scripts for the `coffee_mc` instance.

Finally, one last function is called when the mouse is clicked, or more specifically, pressed down. This function is called by the onMouseDown event and runs through a conditional statement:

```
fillerUp_mc.onMouseDown = function(){
    if (coffee_mc.hitTest(fillerUp_mc)){
        coffee_mc.jitters_mc.gotoAndPlay("fade");
        coffee_mc.steam_mc.gotoAndPlay("fill");
        _root.sfx.start();
    }
}
```

The conditional if statement asks whether the coffee_mc clip instance has collided with or is over the fillerUp instance. If the instances intersect, the conditional returns a true value, sends the jitters_mc instance to play at the frame labeled fade, and sends steam_mc to play at the label fill. After doing this, the script plays the Sound object sfx that was created when the movie first loaded. The conditional has no else, or alternative statement. This means if the two clips don't intersect when the mouse is clicked, the if statement returns a false value and nothing is done. Without the conditional statement to check whether the mug is in the fillerUp area, any mouseDown event would cause the animation and the sound to play. To experiment with this script, try changing the parameters to see what kinds of behavior you can create.

> This movie has two other scripts. In the jitters_mc and steam_mc Movie Clip instances, a stop() function appears at frame 1 of each clip's Timeline. This prevents the clip from playing until it receives a message that tells it to jump ahead to a frame label and begin the animation.

Understanding How Scripts Flow

Understanding the *flow* of a language is almost more important than understanding its elements. Flow refers to the way a script is read and processed while your movie is running. When scripts don't work properly, the cause is often a mistake in the flow, or order of the script, rather than a misuse of terms or incorrect syntax.

Like most programming languages, ActionScript follows a logical, step-by-step flow. This means lines execute in sequential order, starting at the top and working down through the script.

For example, in the following script, the playback head stops, sets the _alpha property (or transparency) of a Movie Clip named plane to 50 percent, and then continues playing at frame 11:

```
stop();
_root.plane._alpha=50;
gotoAndPlay(11);
```

The actions take place specifically in the order they're listed.

But a script can take several diversions as it travels along in your movie. In ActionScript, statements known as *conditionals* will reroute your script flow. This detour in the flow of the script is usually for testing a condition and then doing something as a result of the test.

One of the most common conditionals is an `if` statement. Here's its basic structure:

```
if(thisStatementIsTrue){
    do thisStatement
}
```

The `if` statement tests a condition, which can be evaluated as either `true` or `false`; and if the evaluation is `true`, the statements in the body of the `if` statement execute. The `if` statement can provide an `else` alternative. This way, if the condition tested is `false`, the script executes a separate action—the statements in the body of the `else` part of the statement (see Figure 9.3).

For example:

```
if(thisStatementIsTrue){
    do thisStatement
}else{
    do aDifferentStatement
}
```

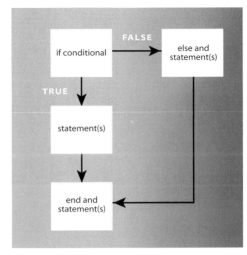

Figure 9.3

Consider the flow of this `if…else` statement.

In a script where the `if` statement evaluates to `false` and no `else` alternative exists, the statements in the body of the `if` are skipped entirely.

Figure 9.4

Consider the flow of this `while` loop.

These structures are useful for testing different parameters in your movie and telling Flash to act accordingly.

Related to the conditional script structure is the *loop* structure. It performs a task or process repeatedly until a value is achieved to satisfy the loop's condition (see Figure 9.4).

For example:

```
i=0;
while(i<3){
    trace("i is "+i);
    trace(i+" is less than 3");
    i++;
}
trace("loop completed!");
trace("i is "+i);
trace(i+" equals 3");
```

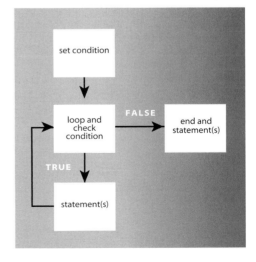

This script executes in the same step-by-step fashion as the `if` conditional. However, a slight delay takes place before the script makes it to the last line. This script uses a `while` loop and detains the script flow while it runs the variable `i` through an increasing series of values. This script methodically increases the value of `i` by 1 as long as it's less than 3, and the `trace()` function prints the results to the Output panel. When the script has completed this task, it continues down the line to execute the last statements and print a final evaluation.

The entire loop prints the following:

```
i is 0
0 is less than 3
i is 1
1 is less than 3
i is 2
2 is less than 3
loop completed!
i is 3
3 equals 3
```

Loops such as this are especially helpful for repetitive actions and information processing. For more information about loops and loop syntax, see Chapter 10, as well as the ActionScript Reference on this book's CD. You'll learn more about the `trace()` function in " Monitoring Scripts with `trace()` and the Output Panel" later in this chapter.

Planning and Assigning Scripts

Every designer or animator knows that essential parts of the development process are planning and storyboarding. Planning is crucial. It allows you to think through your movie before committing to a final version. Planning answers the most important question: what am I creating?

Planning is common practice for design and animation, and it should be equally important for scripting. Before writing a single line of ActionScript, you should know the purpose of every script and how it will work toward a goal in your movie.

To begin the process, you need to start at the top and decide what you need the movie to do. Then, take this a step further: what movie elements are needed to accomplish this? When the various movie components are clear, you should decide how they work and whether they interact. At that point, you'll have a good start toward defining the purpose of ActionScript in your movie. The next step is, of course, to start writing scripts.

The best strategy for writing scripts is to start simply. Get one element of the movie working before you move on to the next one. This technique allows you to isolate problems as they occur. It's also good to get in the habit of saving your work often and saving multiple versions of a project. This way, if something goes awry, you can return to the last working version and pick up where you left off, rather than having to rebuild the movie from scratch.

As you study ActionScript references or the built-in Help panel (F1) looking for the language elements you need to build your scripts, you'll encounter features that might be helpful in the future. On these occasions, it's a good idea to keep a list or journal of the terms you discover. That way, when the time comes and you need a term, you can reference your notes rather than dig through the reference again.

Getting Familiar with ActionScript Terminology

A powerful and flexible scripting language, ActionScript has many components. It's important to understand these terms and how they fit together in the ActionScript family. The following list, organized alphabetically, is a breakdown of the key ActionScript terms and their general descriptions:

Actions is a generic name for a term that tells a movie or one of its components to do something while the movie is running. In previous versions of Flash, ActionScript "commands" were called *actions*. It's more accurate to call them *functions* because they do something or *statements* because they give your movie instructions. Macromedia and the Flash community seem to agree the term *actions* is no longer appropriate.

Arguments (or **parameters**) are containers that hold information and pass it on to statements or functions. For example, the custom function `newUser` has two arguments, `userName` and `userID`:

```
function newUser(userName,userID)
```

These arguments are stored and used later in the function. Similarly, ActionScript functions can take arguments. For example:

```
gotoAndStop(5);
```

The `gotoAndStop()` function requires an argument so it knows where to stop the Timeline.

Classes are categories of information in your movie. Each object belongs to a class and is an individual *instance* of that class. To define a new object, you must create an instance of the object based on its class. You can do this with the help of a constructor function.

Constants are script elements that don't change. For example, an integer (whole number) is a constant and can be used to check the value of an expression. SPACE is a constant because it always refers to the spacebar.

Constructors are functions used to create objects based on classes. The function, in turn, has arguments that can give each object its own set of properties specific to the object's class.

Data types describe the kind of information that a variable or ActionScript element can communicate. In ActionScript, the data types are string, number, Boolean value (`true` and `false`), object, Movie Clip, Array, undefined, and `null` (no data).

Events happen while your movie is running. They're generated by such things as mouse clicks, the loading of Movie Clips, and keystrokes. You'll use events to trigger functions and other ActionScript statements.

An **expression** is any chunk of information that can produce a value. For example:

```
gotoAndPlay(_currentframe+1);
```

This statement sends the movie to the frame number equal to the value of the expression _currentframe+1.

Functions are information processors, the "worker bees" of any Flash movie. They can be passed information in the form of arguments and return a value or perform a task. You can also create custom functions, which are great if you want to create a unique ActionScript routine or task that will be used repeatedly throughout a movie.

Handlers perform functions in response to events. In ActionScript, handlers exist for both mouse and Movie Clip events.

Identifiers are unique names assigned to functions, methods, objects, properties, or variables. The first character of an identifier must be either a letter, dollar sign ($), or underscore (_). A full identifier name can use numbers as well as these characters. For example, you can have a Movie Clip instance named `code_mc` or a function called `routine1`.

Instances are individual objects that belong to a class. For example, the `today` instance could belong to the `Date` class.

An **instance name** is a unique name used to refer to a specific instance of an object in your movie. This could be an instance of a TextField, Sound, or Array object. Movie Clips are treated like objects but are fundamentally different because we create Movie Clips in Flash and save them as symbols. However, to control them with ActionScript, Movie Clips (like objects) require an instance name. For example, you can use a Movie Clip symbol named `logoMovie` repeatedly throughout a movie. You must give each instance a unique instance name, such as `logo1` or `logo2`. Each instance in the movie must be referred to by its unique instance name. This distinction allows ActionScript to control each instance of a Movie Clip symbol independently.

Keywords are words with special meaning in the ActionScript language and are unavailable for use as variables, functions, and so on. See the list of ActionScript keywords later in this chapter.

Methods are functions that belong to and can be performed by objects. For custom objects, you can create custom methods. In ActionScript, each predefined object (such as the Sound object or MovieClip object) has its own methods. For a list of object methods, choose Help → Flash Help (F1), or see the ActionScript Reference on this book's CD.

Objects are instances of a class. ActionScript has several built-in classes that are called *objects*; these include the Sound object, the Date object, and the MovieClip object.

Operators are elements that calculate and compare values. For example, the forward slash (/) operator divides one number by another.

A **property** is any kind of quality that belongs to an object and can define an instance of an object. For example, the _x property determines the X coordinate of a Movie Clip on the Stage.

Target paths pass information along the chain of Movie Clip instance names, variables, and objects in a movie. For example:

```
menuBar.item1.selected
```

This is the target path to the variable `selected`, which is inside the Movie Clip `item1`, which is inside the Movie Clip `menuBar`. For more details on the hierarchy of Movie Clips, see Chapter 12.

Variables are storage locations that hold information and values. You can use variables for permanent or temporary storage. You can set, modify, and retrieve the value of a variable and use it in scripts while a movie is playing.

Using the Actions Panel for Scripting

As you learned in Chapter 8, The Actions panel is your interface for adding ActionScript statements to a Flash movie. It provides several components that allow you to select ActionScript elements, arrange and order them as you see fit, and edit any individual parameters as needed.

In Flash 5 and Flash MX, the Actions panel had two modes of operation: Normal and Expert. Normal mode provided a menu-driven interface that allowed users to create their scripts with a minimum of typing. Flash MX 2004 replaced Normal mode with ActionScript behaviors, so it has since been absent. However, Flash 8 has reintroduced Normal mode with the new title Script Assist mode.

Where ActionScript behaviors were limiting and downright frustrating, Script Assist mode is straightforward and actually useful. When you work with Script Assist mode, the Actions panel becomes a sort of form that you fill in to generate ActionScript. You check boxes, choose from menus, type into fields, and *voilà!*—your script is assembled. Alternatively, hand-coding ActionScript in the Actions panel gives you enormous freedom and flexibility. Certain scripts can't be written using Script Assist mode and must be hand-coded. Which is right for you? This depends on many issues. If you struggle with the syntactical conventions of ActionScript and find it's easy to forget closing parentheses, quotation marks, and the like, you may find Script Assist mode helps you avoid most of these common errors. On the other hand, if you're already writing complicated scripts that depend on built-in objects and classes or custom functions, a hand-coded approach will probably allow you to work more efficiently. We recommend that for most of the examples in this book, you avoid using Script Assist mode. However, for quick `gotoAndPlay()` or `stop()` functions, Script Assist mode can be efficient.

Scripting with the Actions Panel

As mentioned, the Actions panel is your interface for creating scripts that will execute in a Flash movie (see Figure 9.5). It's a window where you can create and modify the interactivity of your movie. To help with this process, the Actions panel provides several tools that can automate different aspects of scripting, provide help when needed, and organize the scripting workspace.

The following list describes the Actions panel's features:

Check syntax Click this button to confirm that all ActionScript terms have been implemented properly.

Find This opens a dialog box to find and replace terms within the Script pane.

Help button This context-sensitive button will direct you immediately to an ActionScript-related Help topic. Simply select a term in the ActionScript Toolbox, and click the Help button. The Help panel will open to the topic you require.

Script Assist mode toggle Toggle this button to enter Script Assist mode. You can learn more about composing ActionScript with Script Assist mode later in this chapter.

Figure 9.5

The Actions panel is filled with unique and useful features for composing ActionScript.

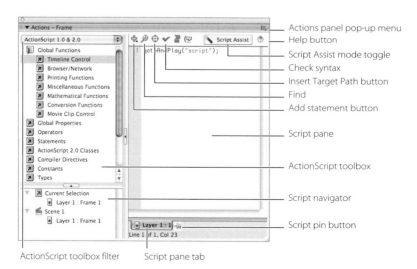

Actions Toolbox This menu is one location where you can access an ActionScript Library. You can select actions in this area of the panel and drag them into the Script pane.

Actions Toolbox Filter drop-down menu Use this drop-down menu to sort the Action-Script Library into publishing- and platform-related categories: ActionScript 1.0 & 2.0, Flash Lite 1.0, and Flash Lite 1.1.

Script Navigator The Script Navigator allows you to locate a script anywhere in your movie and immediately call it up in the Script pane.

Script pane Scripts appear in their entirety here. This is the area where you compose ActionScript.

Add a Statement button Click this button to add an ActionScript statement. Clicking this button opens a cascading series of menus. When an item is selected, it appears in the Script pane.

Actions panel pop-up menu This menu provides access to many additional Actions panel features such as panel preferences and options for script formatting.

Script Pin button The Script Pin button allows you to "stick" a script to the panel. This is the digital equivalent of a pushpin corkboard: once you pin a script to the panel, it stays there. This feature allows you to make one script viewable at all times while selecting other objects in your movie.

Script pane tabs Once you pin a script in place on the Script pane, it's assigned a tab. The Actions panel can hold many tabs, giving you instant access to the most important scripts in your movie.

Working with the Actions Panel's Features

The Actions panel is stocked with tools to help make writing ActionScript easier. It can provide assistance with writing and editing, keep your scripts organized, and control the way scripts appear in the panel. You're able to search scripts and perform find-and-replace edits for ActionScript terms that appear more than once. It's also possible to write your scripts outside Flash and include them in your movie from an external location. Additionally, the Actions panel allows you to print scripts and check for errors before testing your movie.

SCRIPT PIN AND SCRIPT PANE TABS

Script pane tabs provide an easy way to organize your scripts. Each pinned script is given its own tab that appears below the Script pane in the Actions panel. You can navigate from one pinned script to the next by simply clicking these tabs. To pin, unpin, or change tabs for a script:

1. Choose Window → Actions, or press F9 / Opt+F9 to open the Actions panel.

2. Select the script you want to pin. Either click the frame or object attached to the script or use the Script Navigator to display the script.

3. Do any of the following:

- To pin a script in place, click the Script Pin button. The script gets a new tab, which is highlighted at the left edge of the Script pane (see Figure 9.6).

- To unpin a script, click the Script Unpin button. The script's tab disappears when a script or different frame or object is selected. Alternatively, right-click / Ctrl+click on a tab, and choose Close Script to remove a script's tab.

- To navigate to a new script, click the tab for the script you need to see.

Figure 9.6

When a script is pinned to the Actions panel, a new tab is created and stored in the panel. You can use these tabs to navigate between other pinned scripts in your movie.

This functionality provides a great way to both organize and edit ActionScript in your movie.

LINE NUMBERING

The Actions panel's line-numbering feature allows you to better manage long scripts. Line numbering gives each line in your script an "address" of sorts so you can easily refer to each script element by number. To activate or deactivate line numbering:

1. Choose Window → Actions, or press F9 / Opt+F9 to open the Actions panel.

2. Select the Actions panel pop-up menu, and do either of the following:

- To display line numbering, select Line Numbers, or press Shift+Ctrl+L / Shift+Cmd+L. A check appears beside the menu option in the menu.

- To hide line numbering, select Line Numbers again. The check beside the menu option disappears.

When line numbers are on, they appear in the vertical strip between the Actions Toolbox and the text box (see Figure 9.7). When the option is off, the strip is empty.

ACTIONS PANEL TEXT DISPLAY

In Flash 8 you can control the display (font, size, text color, and spacing) of actions in the Actions panel by using the ActionScript category of the Preferences menu. To open this menu, do either of the following:

- Select Edit → Preferences / Flash → Preferences, and choose the ActionScript category.

- Click the Actions panel pop-up menu, and select Preferences (Ctrl+U / Cmd+U). Once you have this menu open, you can set several options:

Spacing Check the Automatic Indentation box, and Flash will automatically indent your scripts. To set the amount of indentation, type a number in the Tab Size field.

Imported/exported text encoding Flash 8 supports Unicode text encoding for Action-Script. This means you can import text in languages other than your system default language. To take advantage of Unicode support, select UTF-8 in the Open/Import and Save/Export drop-down menus. To work only with the system default language, select Default Encoding.

Text Use the text menus to select a font and size for your actions. Because ActionScript must be entered with specific syntax, it's better to choose a legible screen font than your favorite deconstructed display typeface.

Color Syntax coloring can make it easier to visually organize your scripts based on the color of individual script entries. Flash allows several options for the display color of ActionScript in the Script pane. When the Syntax Coloring box is checked, you can set a specific color for the following ActionScript elements: foreground (text), background (window color), keywords, comments, identifiers, and strings. Use the color swatch next to each element to choose a display color. To view your scripts without the syntax coloration, deselect the Syntax Coloring option, and choose appropriate foreground and background colors.

SYNTAX VERSION TRACKING

Although you're working in Flash 8, you can still publish your movie for older versions of the Flash Player. Previous releases of Flash published movies for Flash Player 7 (and below), ActionScript 2.0 (Flash Player 6 and 7 only), and ActionScript 1. Alternately, you may need to publish a mobile application for Flash Lite 1.0 or 1.1. Whatever your situation may be, certain terms are restricted in various versions of the Flash Player. It can be hard to keep track of which terms are available in which versions, so the Actions panel makes it easy for you. Any terms that are unavailable in the version for which you're publishing (which you've chosen in the movie's publish settings) will be highlighted in bright yellow. You can't use these terms unless you switch your publish settings to a different version number. You can read more about publishing movies in Chapter 17. Also, choose Help → Flash Help (F1) or see the ActionScript Reference on this book's CD for individual terms and their compatible Flash Player version.

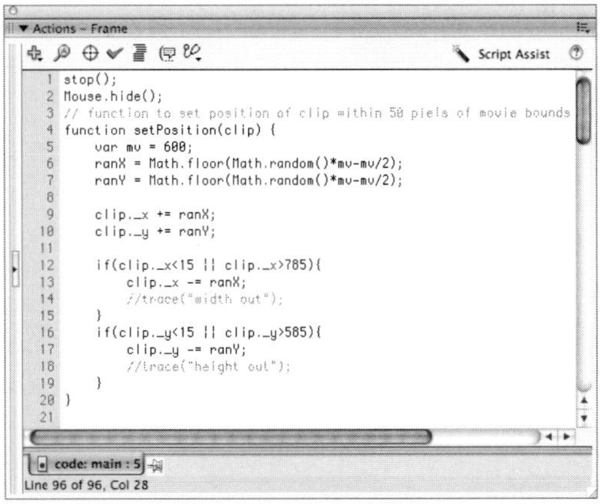

Inserting a Target Path

If you want to direct ActionScript statements to affect specific Movie Clip instances or other objects in your movie, use a target path. A *target path* is the specific address for a Movie Clip or other object. Without target paths, your scripts can't locate the objects you want to control. Target paths were required for behaviors, and they're equally important when you write ActionScript by hand. To learn more about target paths, see Chapter 12.

Figure 9.7

This Actions panel has the line numbering option turned on.

Often, target paths can be long and complex, and if you make a mistake when you type one, your movie will not perform properly. Luckily, the Actions panel provides an additional tool, the Insert Target Path dialog box, to help you avoid errors.

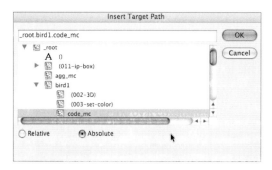

To enter a target path using the Actions panel:

1. Click the Insert Target Path button ⊕ . The Insert Target Path dialog box opens and displays an outline of the Movie Clips in your movie.

2. Select the clip you want to target, and the instance name appears in the Target field.

3. The Mode setting allows you to choose how you compose the path:

   - Relative writes the path starting from the current Timeline.

   - Absolute writes the path starting from _root (at the top of the outline) and shows the path to the clip from the main Timeline.

   Although either mode works, you'll find that relative paths are more concise and can sometimes be easier to understand. Click OK to return to the Actions panel. Your target path is added to the Script pane.

The Insert Target Path dialog box shows you only Movie Clip Timelines. If you need to insert a target path to a different kind of object (such as an Array or Sound), you can still use the dialog box. Simply follow the previous steps, locate the Timeline where the object resides, and following the target path that was generated in the Script pane, type a period (.), followed by the name of the object you want to target. For more details about target paths, see Chapter 12.

Navigating, Searching, and Replacing ActionScript

To look for specific portions of ActionScript, click the Actions panel to give it focus, and use the pop-up menu in the upper-right corner of the Actions panel:

- Select Go to Line (Ctrl+G / Cmd+,) to skip to a particular line in a long script.

- Select Find and Replace (Ctrl+F / Cmd+F) or click the Find button 🔎 to locate a particular word or phrase. In the Find and Replace dialog box, use the Replace With field to swap the found bit of text with something new. Clicking Find Again (F3 / Cmd+G) will locate the next occurrence of that text.

The Actions panel's Find and Replace option searches the entire script body but only in the immediate script window. To do a moviewide search, go to the main menu bar, and choose Edit → Find and Replace. (For more information about this feature, see Chapter 5.)

Getting Files In and Out of the Actions Panel

You have several ways to move data in and out of the Actions panel. Use the pop-up menu in the upper-right corner of the panel to handle these tasks.

Importing a script The Import Script option is particularly useful if you prefer to write scripts in a text- or script-editing program and want to integrate them directly into your movie.

To import an external ActionScript (.as) file:

1. Click the Script pane where you want the imported file to begin.

2. Select Import from File or press Shift+Ctrl+I / Shift+Cmd+I, and browse to a text file composed of ActionScript (see Figure 9.8).

3. Click OK. Flash drops the imported file into the Actions panel starting from the position of the cursor.

Exporting your script Select Export Script or press Shift+Ctrl+X / Shift+Cmd+X, give the file a name with the extension .as, and click Save. Flash exports a text file containing your script.

Printing a script Select Print, pick your print options, and click Print.

Figure 9.8

You can import this ActionScript text file (composed in TextEdit) directly into the Actions panel.

> When you print scripts from the Actions panel, Flash doesn't include any information about the file that contains the script or the script's location in the movie. If you plan to print several scripts, it can be helpful to include comments that note where each script resides in your movie. For more information see "Using Punctuation Marks in ActionScript" later in this chapter.

Using Script Assist Mode

Script Assist mode is a what-you-see-is-what-you-get (WYSIWYG) ActionScript-writing interface for the Actions panel. Script Assist mode, which originally appeared in Flash 5 and then disappeared, enables you to easily create scripts without having detailed knowledge of ActionScript syntax. It helps you build scripts by selecting items from the Actions Toolbox in the Actions panel. It provides an interface of text fields, radio buttons, and check boxes that prompt you for the correct parameters and other script elements required for each ActionScript term.

To add a function or ActionScript statement to a Flash document, you attach it to a button, Movie Clip, or frame in the Timeline. The Actions panel lets you select, drag and drop, rearrange, and delete lines of script attached to these objects. Script Assist mode allows you to go through this process by selecting from preset menus. The idea is that if you have less to type, you'll have less possibility of error in the finished script. Less error means fewer headaches for you and more deadlines met on time.

To attach ActionScript using Script Assist mode:

1. Select the frame, button, or Movie Clip where you'd like to attach a script.

2. Select Window → Development Panels → Actions (or press Alt+9 / Opt+F9). The Actions panel appears.

3. Click the Script Assist button, and the Actions panel enters Script Assist mode (see Figure 9.9).

> If the Actions panel contains ActionScript statements when you click the Script Assist button, Flash compiles the existing code. If there are errors, you won't able to use Script Assist mode until you fix the current selection.

When Script Assist mode is enabled, the Actions panel interface changes in the following ways:

- The Add (+) button allows you to choose ActionScript statements and functions from a menu. (You'll then see menu options that allow you to choose specific parameters for that statement or function.) New lines of script are added *after* the line where the cursor or a selection sits.

- The Remove (–) button lets you remove the current selection in the Script pane.

- The up-arrow and down-arrow buttons let you move the current selection in the scrolling text area forward or backward within the code. Continue to click the up-arrow or down-arrow button until a script's lines are in the order you require.

- Check Syntax and other buttons normally available in the Actions panel are disabled, because they don't apply to Script Assist mode.

- The Insert Target Path button is disabled unless editing a field in Script Assist mode. Click it to place a target path in the current edit field.

To add an action to the Script pane, do one of the following:

- Click a category in the Actions Toolbox to display the actions in that category. Then, either double-click an action and drag it to the Script pane or right-click / Ctrl+click and select Add to Script.

- Click the Add (+) button, and select an action from the pop-up menu.

In either instance, the script element is added to the Script pane, and any parameters appear in Script Assist mode. Working with parameters is easy. However, it's essential you understand the parameters of the Action-Script term you're using. Consult specific entries in Chapters 8–13 in this book and the ActionScript Reference on the CD. Once you know how various parameters can affect a particular ActionScript term, configuring it is just a matter of choosing the right radio button/menu item or entering the correct bit of text.

To delete an action, select the statement in the Script pane. Then, either click the Delete (–) button or press the Del key. The statement will disappear and can be replaced with a new statement or left blank.

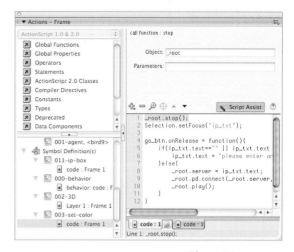

Figure 9.9

Script Assist mode reconfigures the options within the Actions panel and allows you to change parameters for individual statements using menus, buttons, and text fields.

Checking for Syntax Errors

Outside Script Assist mode, the Actions panel gives you complete control over what is entered in the text box, but you have no way to check automatically for errors as you input the statements. To ensure your scripts are syntactically correct before testing your movie, you can check the syntax in the Actions panel by doing one of the following:

- Click the Check Syntax button ✔ near the top of the Actions panel. This button looks like a check mark.

- In the pop-up menu in the upper-right corner of the Actions panel, click Check Syntax.

- Press Ctrl+T / Cmd+T while the Actions panel is active.

Whichever option you choose, if the script is free of syntax mistakes, you'll get an OK message. If there are errors, you'll be alerted, and any errors appear in the Output panel.

Working with an External Script Editor

Although the Actions panel gives you total control, you might find it helpful to take advantage of an external editor and do your scripting outside Flash. To incorporate code you've written this way, all you need to do is replace any chunks of ActionScript with this line:

```
#include "actionScriptFile.as"
```

Here, `actionScriptFile.as` is a text file containing all the necessary code for the frame or object where `#include` is attached. The `#include` directive imports the lines of Action-Script from the external AS file and runs it in the movie as though it were written directly in the Actions panel. To use this technique to import ActionScript from an external file:

1. Write your script in an external editor, and save it with an `.as` extension.

2. Type `#include` in the Script pane.

3. After the `#include` directive, enter the path to the external script file. Use the slash character (/) to delimit the path. For example, if `movie.fla` and `extScript.as` were in the same folder, the path would be `extScript.as`. If the script file were in a subfolder named `scripts`, the entire statement would be as follows:

```
#include "scripts/extScript.as"
```

Once you publish a movie that uses external scripts, those scripts become a permanent part of the movie. To make any changes to the script, you'll have to change the Action-Script in the `.as` file and republish your movie.

You can write external ActionScript files (`.as`) in the Script Editor if you use Flash 8 Professional (see Figure 9.10). The Script Editor is simply an oversized version of the Actions panel that is used solely to compose external files. To open the Script Editor, choose File → New, and select the ActionScript file. Later, you can import these scripts directly into the Actions panel or include them in projects that use ActionScript 2.0.

Learning ActionScript Syntax

Like spoken languages, computer languages such as ActionScript follow a particular set of rules, or *syntax*. These rules define how all the terms are used and how they work together as a language. It's crucial to understand the syntax of the language so you can use it to say something meaningful. After all, the purpose of a language is to communicate, and ActionScript provides you with a communication link to Flash.

Using Punctuation Marks in ActionScript

In ActionScript you can use punctuation to issue a command, track the path to a movie or variable, and help annotate your scripts to provide both explanation and instruction. Mainly, the purpose of punctuation is to bring order to your scripts and organize their contents so Flash can understand how the scripts should be executed.

ActionScript Dot Syntax

The ActionScript *dot syntax* was introduced when Flash evolved to version 5. The dot syntax makes ActionScript look similar to JavaScript. If you're comfortable with JavaScript, learning ActionScript will put you in familiar territory. The construction for the dot syntax is shown here:

```
object      target path
instance    property
timeline    function
            variable
            object
```

The left side of the dot can refer to an object, instance, or Timeline in your movie. The right side can be a property, target path, variable, function, or even another object that is directed at or found within the element on the left side. Here are three examples:

```
myClip._visible=0;
menuBar.menu1.item3=152;
_root.gotoAndPlay(5);
```

In the first example, a Movie Clip named myClip is made invisible by setting the _visible property to 0 with the dot syntax. The second example shows the path to the variable item3 through menu1, a nested Movie Clip in the Movie Clip named menuBar. The variable is assigned a value of 152. The third example uses the _root reference to command the main Timeline to jump to frame 5 and play. In each example, you can see how the left side of the dot names or references an object, and the right side contains either a new object or some kind of instruction or parameter that defines or manipulates the first object to the left of the dot.

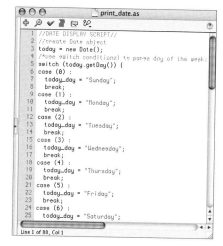

Figure 9.10

The Script Editor is similar to the Actions panel and allows you to compose ActionScript that will reside outside your Flash movies.

> The dot is also known as the *dot operator* because it can issue commands and modify properties. For more information on other ActionScript operators, see the "Operators" section later in this chapter.

Comments

It's a good idea to make notes, known as *comments*, as you write your scripts. Comments can provide guidance or instructions to someone who has to edit your scripts. They can also be helpful if you're forced to abandon a project for a period of time; when you return to the code, your notes will remind you what each part of the script is doing.

To insert comments in ActionScript, type two forward slashes (//), and enter your notes after them. For example:

```
// checks to see if all movie frames are loaded
if(_framesLoaded>=_totalFrames){
// if TRUE, then it starts the move at frame 6
   gotoAndPlay(6);
}else{
// if FALSE, it loops back to frame 1
   gotoAndPlay(1);
}
```

In ActionScript, Flash will ignore anything on the same line that follows the double slash. This means you can type anything you like after the slashes because Flash won't interpret the comments as ActionScript. Comments also allow you to "turn off" parts of a script. If one or more lines are causing problems, you can comment them out and run the script without those lines. Flash will ignore the commented lines and run everything else in the script.

> To insert large notes or blocks of text within your ActionScript, you can use multiline comments (/*). Simply begin the note with the opening character sequence (/*) and end with the closing sequence (*/). The Flash Player ignores all statements between these markers.

When the ActionScript editor preferences are set to default, comments appear in the Script Editor in a light-gray color so you can distinguish them from other parts of your script. As described earlier, you can change this and other syntax colors using preferences.

Curly Braces

ActionScript organizes the elements of a script by using the curly brace characters ({}). (These characters are also called *curly brackets*.) In the following script, the statements within the pair of curly braces will execute when the mouse is pressed:

```
nav_btn.onPress=function(){
    gotoAndStop("main");
    container_mc.loadMovie("menu.swf");
}
```

A script can also include multiple sets of curly braces:

```
fish_btn.onRelease=function(){
    with(fishClip){
        gotoAndStop(50);
    }
}
```

In this example, the curly braces organize the script into two parts. The onRelease event method handler executes the with statement, and then with targets the instance fishClip, sends it to frame 50, and stops it.

> Statements within curly braces are often referred to as *blocks* of a script. This often makes it easier to refer to a specific portion of the script, for example "the with block."

Parentheses

You can use parentheses in ActionScript to assign arguments for functions or to set the order of operations in an expression. For example, the duplicateMovieClip() function has three arguments: *target, instance,* and *depth*. Here you use the parentheses to list the arguments after calling the action:

```
duplicateMovieClip("alien","alien_copy",1);
```

This statement duplicates (makes a copy of) the clip alien, names the duplicate alien_copy, and sets it at a depth of 1 above the original.

You can also use parentheses to alter the order of operations. The expression 2 + 3 * 4 evaluates to 14, and the expression (2 + 3) * 4 evaluates to 20, because the parentheses force you to do the addition first.

Semicolon

In ActionScript, the semicolon (;) marks the end of a statement. For example:

```
menu1.onPress=function(){
    introClip._visible=0;
}
```

Here, the statement making the instance introClip invisible terminates with a semicolon. If you forget to use the semicolon, Flash will still compile the script correctly. However, it's good practice to follow correct syntax conventions and always terminate statements with the semicolon character.

Semicolons also can separate the parameters in a for loop structure. To learn more about this ActionScript convention, see the discussion of conditionals in Chapter 10.

Understanding Other ActionScript Syntax Conventions

Aside from the mechanics of ActionScript, a few other conventions are important to understand so you can work flexibly with the language. Certain terms in the language are "protected" (*reserved*) because they have a specific meaning in ActionScript. Other terms must follow a specific uppercase or lowercase structure so Flash will know how to interpret them.

Constants

Constants are terms or properties that retain a specific, unchanging value in ActionScript. In a script, they are (with a few exceptions) written in all-capital letters. Constants are part of three ActionScript objects: the Key object, the Math object, and the Number object.

The following script uses the Key object to test whether the spacebar has been pressed:

```
if(Key.isDown(Key.SPACE)){
    laser.shoot(1);
}
```

The spacebar has a constant value, and it's a property of the Key object. When it's pressed, the statements below it execute.

In the next example, the Math object uses the constant value of PI to evaluate the area of a circle:

```
area=Math.PI*(radius*radius);
```

In the following example, the MAX_VALUE constant sets the variable duration to the highest possible positive number value in ActionScript (1.79769313486231e+308):

```
duration=Number.MAX_VALUE;
```

Keywords

Keywords are ActionScript terms reserved for a specific purpose in the language. These terms are used only in a specific context and aren't available as names of variables, functions, objects, or instances. These are the ActionScript keywords:

add	and	break	case	catch	class
continue	default	delete	do	dynamic	else
eq	extends	finally	for	function	ge
get	gt	if	ifFrameLoaded	implements	import
in	instanceof	interface	intrinsic	le	lt
ne	new	not	on	onClipEvent	or
private	public	return	set	static	super
switch	tellTarget	this	throw	try	typeof
var	void	while	with		

In addition to these reserved words, Macromedia has flagged other terms as "potential" reserved words in the future. For a list of these terms, choose Help → Flash Help (F1), and navigate to Learning ActionScript 2.0 in Flash → Syntax and Language Fundamentals → About Constants and Keywords → About Reserved Words.

ActionScript Case Sensitivity

In older versions of Flash (6 and older), ActionScript 1.0 was fairly forgiving when it came to uppercase and lowercase letters. You can see this when working in the Script pane. Notice that the color for a term will change if it isn't entered in the preferred upper-case or lowercase syntax. For example, `stop()` is usually blue. If you were to enter it as `Stop()` (note the capital *S*), it would change to black to show that the term has been entered incorrectly. However, in Flash Player versions 6 and older, your scripts could be interpreted without error.

Using ActionScript 2.0 with Flash Player 7 and newer slightly changes the rules of case sensitivity. Movies using ActionScript 2.0 that are published for Flash Player versions 7 and 8 will implement case sensitivity. This means names of functions, keywords, variables, objects, and so on, will be held to strict case sensitivity. For example:

```
var count=0;
var Count=0;
```

Here, a Flash 8 movie would consider these to be two different variables: `count` (with a lowercase first letter) and `Count`. Similarly, the following statement, which would cause errors in Flash 6 and older, is acceptable in Flash 8:

```
sound = new Sound();
```

Correct syntax demands that the constructor function for a Sound object use a capital *S* for the word *Sound*. In Flash 6, where case sensitivity was looser, `sound` and `Sound` were interpreted as the same, so this statement produces an error. However, because Flash 8 uses strict case sensitivity, sound and Sound are considered to be different and no error occurs. And although no error occurs, this leads to a potentially confusing situation. The following statement demonstrates the correct way to create a Sound object in Flash 8:

```
mySound = new Sound();
```

To be safe, it's best to follow proper ActionScript syntax at all times. Capitalize anything that should appear in uppercase; keep all lowercase terms free of capital letters; and use unique names for variables, objects, instance names, and functions. If you're consistent and adhere to the rules, you can avoid these issues. Keep reading to explore these practices further.

Learning ActionScript Language Elements

So far, you've learned the conventions of ActionScript and how the pieces of the language fit together to create scripts. Now it's time to look at those individual pieces and see exactly what constitutes ActionScript. The language has many components, some of which will be familiar based on what you already know. Luckily, most of the terms have reasonably descriptive names. The most important step in learning to write ActionScript is understanding the *role* a particular term plays in the language. As the duties of these terms become clearer, you'll begin to see how to fit pieces of the puzzle together to suit your needs.

Understanding Data Types

As you learned earlier, data types define the kind of information that can be represented by elements of ActionScript. Eight types of information are used in a script: strings, numbers, Booleans, objects, Array, Movie Clips, undefined and null. We'll discuss the specifics of each type in the following sections.

Strings

Strings are literal chunks of information that hold a textual value. They're composed of any combination of letters, punctuation, and numbers. String data is enclosed in quotes (" " or ' ') and treated as a single piece of information. Because strings are literal, they're case-sensitive; so, for instance, the strings "one" and "One" are different. In the following example, "Joe" is a string stored in myName:

```
myName="Joe";
```

You can combine, or *concatenate*, strings to link string information together. For example:

```
fullName=myName+" Smith";
```

The addition operator (+) concatenates string data. Note that in the preceding example, the string " Smith" contains a space. This is to prevent the two string elements from getting closed up when they're concatenated. When the strings are combined, fullName will contain the string 'Joe Smith'.

You can also organize strings alphabetically by using the comparison operators: <, >, =<, and >=. Flash uses the Unicode (UTF-8) character set. When evaluating strings alphabetically, the letter *z* holds the highest value, and *A* holds the lowest. Note the following expression:

```
"alligator"<"zebra"==true
"alligator">"Zebra"==true
```

Lowercase letters hold a higher value than uppercase ones. For more information about operators and comparisons, see the "Operators" section later in this chapter.

Numbers

Numbers are characters that hold a specific numeric value. In ActionScript, you can manipulate number values in expressions using mathematical operators such as addition (+), subtraction (–), multiplication (*), division (/), modulo (%), increment (++), and decrement (––). You can also use ActionScript's predefined Math object to evaluate numbers and expressions.

Booleans

A *Boolean* is a value that is either `true` or `false`. Booleans are used in conditional statements to evaluate an expression and see whether conditions have been met or values initialized. The following statements evaluate whether all a movie's frames have been loaded into memory:

```
if(_framesloaded==_totalframes){
    introMovie.gotoAndPlay(2);
}
```

If the current number of loaded frames (`_framesloaded`) is equal to the total number of frames (`_totalframes`), the statement inside the parentheses returns a Boolean value of `true`. If not, it returns `false`. For more specifics on this, see the "Conditionals" section later in this chapter.

Objects

An *object* is a collection of information organized into properties. These properties have names and values that can be accessed in a Flash movie. The object data type allows you to manipulate the properties assigned to a particular object. In the following statement, the object `money` has a property named `myAccount`, which is assigned the value 5000:

```
money.myAccount=5000;
```

Flash allows you to create your own objects or use one of the built-in objects such as Date and Color. You can explore these scripting techniques in Chapter 11.

Array

An *array* is a data type that allows you to manage lists or complex sets of information. You can read more about Arrays in Chapter 11.

Movie Clips

Movie Clips are self-contained animations that run independently in a Flash movie. They're self-contained in that they have their own Timelines. Movie Clips have properties such as _alpha or _rotation that can be assigned values in ActionScript. Here, a Movie Clip instance is rotated to 180°:

```
spinClip._rotation=180;
```

Movie Clips also have methods that you can use to control them. In this example, a clip is instructed to stop on the first frame of its Timeline:

```
audioClip.gotoAndStop(1);
```

> Movie Clips are one of the most interesting, complex, and useful data types in a Flash movie. In fact, they're so important that we've dedicated an entire chapter to them. See Chapter 12 for more details about Movie Clips and their role in Flash.

Undefined and Null

Undefined exists to represent a lack of data or no data. A variable that has no value returns undefined. A variable with no value can't be considered an "empty" variable. Without a value, it doesn't exist and is therefore undefined. For example, the following statement returns nothing; as a nonexistent container, the variable is declared but has no value:

```
var one;
```

Here, one is undefined and is relatively useless to you.

If you want to create an empty variable, you can set the value of the variable to be null. Rather than containing no value (undefined), the variable exists but has an "empty," or null, value.

The next statement returns null; the variable is an empty but *existing* container:

```
var two=null;
```

If you want to erase a variable's value, or create a variable and make it empty, null is a helpful term. To learn more about variables, see the next section.

Understanding Variables

Variables serve as storage locations for information you need in a script. Variables are like pockets where you can put something, keep it there for a while, and then retrieve it when you need it later in your movie. To use a variable, you have to first *declare*, or state, the variable. Then you must *initialize* the variable to let Flash know you're going to store something in it. Once you've initialized the variable with a starting value, it will hold that value until it changes. To change the value of a variable, all you have to do is add to it, subtract from it, or reinitialize it.

You can use variables to hold any type of data: string, number, Boolean, object, Array, Movie Clip, undefined or null. For example, you can initialize the variable *x* to either a numeric value or a set of string data:

```
x=24;
x="myName";
```

You can also use variables in conditional loops to serve as the loop counter. For example:

```
j=2;
while(j>0){
    duplicateMovieClip(_root.ship,"ship"+j,j);
    _root["ship"+j]._y=_root.ship._y+50*j;
    trace("duplicated"+j);
    j-;
}
```

In this example, the variable *j* is initialized to 2. Every time it passes through the while loop, it's reduced by 1 or reinitialized until it no longer meets the conditions of the loop. The variable *j* also helps name the duplicated Movie Clips and assigns the level of each new clip in the duplicateMovieClip statement. In the next statement, *j* is used in an expression to position the new Movie Clips at a location that is 50*j* pixels away from the original clip. That's a lot of work for one variable! The important fact to realize is that you can use a variable repeatedly in your scripts to help perform a variety of tasks.

When you use a variable, it's important to give it an appropriate name. This has a few rules, though. First, a variable must be an identifier—a combination of letters, numbers, underscores (_), or dollar sign characters ($). Second, a variable can't be an ActionScript keyword, and it must be unique within the Timeline where the variable was created.

It's good practice to name a variable something meaningful that relates to the job it will perform in your movie. For example, if you use a variable to store the name of a visitor to your website, name the variable something like siteVisitor to keep things simple. If visitors enter their names in an input text field, give the field the variable name siteVisitor. This way, anytime you want to use a visitor's name, you can just call on the variable, and the name will be available immediately. If you wanted to print a farewell message in the text field goodbye, you would write this:

```
goodbye.text="Thanks for visiting "+siteVisitor;
```

We already mentioned that movies using ActionScript 2.0 published for Flash Player 7 and newer implement strict case sensitivity. This is especially important to consider when naming variables. Here are a few additional naming strategies you can employ to help ensure consistency:

Using lowercase and uppercase Multiword names can be more descriptive, but of course a space isn't allowed in the names of ActionScript objects and variables. You can work around this by using "camel notation"—an uppercase first letter for any additional words in the name. For example:

```
firstSecondThird=0;
```

Using underscore characters You can use the underscore character (_) to separate individual words written in all lowercase, for example:

```
first_second_third=0;
```

Using an alphanumeric strategy Use a combination of letters and numbers to give similar or related variables unique names. For example:

```
item1=0;
item2=1;
```

Whatever method you choose to use, be consistent! It will save you headaches and frustration.

Using the *trace()* Function with Variables

In the previous conditional loop script example, you might have noted the trace("duplicated"+j); line. trace() is a special function of ActionScript that allows you to monitor different elements of your script. In this line, the script will trace the word duplicated and concatenate it with the current value of *j*. This function is helpful because it allows you to track the value of your variables as they change while your script executes. trace() is also extremely useful for debugging scripts. You'll learn more about it in "Monitoring Scripts with trace() and the Output Panel" later in this chapter.

Setting Variable Scope

One of the most important aspects of variables is their availability, or *scope*. A variable's scope determines how it's available to other portions of your movie. Because you use variables to store and retrieve information, giving them appropriate availability is important. In ActionScript, you can define a variable's scope to be global, Timeline-specific, or local.

If a variable is global, it's shared by all Timelines in your movie and is available at any time. Any script in any part of your movie can access or change the value of a global variable. You declare a global variable by using the reference _global. For example, the following statement will create a global variable named store1 and initialize its value to 1:

```
_global.store1=1;
```

You can retrieve the value of *store1* at any point in your movie with this statement:

```
trace(store1);
```

Because the variable is global, it's always available, by name.

A Timeline-specific variable is also available throughout your movie. However, you must always use a target path when working with the variable; otherwise, Flash won't know where to find the information the variable is storing. Declare a Timeline variable by giving it a name and assigning it a value. For example, to create a Timeline-specific variable named `store2`, you would enter the following statement on any Timeline (Movie Clip, main Timeline, and so on):

```
store2=2;
```

If you created this variable on the main Timeline, you could create its value at any point in your movie with this statement:

```
value=_root.store2;
```

If you created `store2` on the Timeline of the Movie Clip instance `sprocket`, you would access it by using this target path:

```
value=_root.sprocket.store2;
```

Because the variable is scoped to a particular Timeline, you must refer to it using a target path, or the "address" of the variable in your movie. Timeline variables are usually your best choice because they aren't as general as global variables and have greater flexibility than local variables.

A local variable is different. Local variables are scoped to functions and can be changed only within the block of script or function where they reside. This can be helpful if you have a value that needs to exist for only a brief period of time. To make a variable local, you must use the `var` action when you declare and initialize the variable. For example:

```
function init3(){
    var store3=3;
}
```

This script declares the variable `store3` as a local variable and initializes its value to 3. As a local variable, `store3` is available only within the curly braces (`{}`) of the function where it resides, and it will be "alive" (contain a value) only while the function is executing. To summarize:

- To create a global variable, type __**global.name**=**value**, and assign a name and value.
- To create a Timeline-specific variable, type the name of the variable, and use the assignment operator (=) to assign a value.
- To create a local variable inside a function, type **var**, followed by the variable name, and use the assignment operator (=) to assign a value.

Understanding Operators

Operators are characters that instruct ActionScript how to combine, remove, or compare the values in an expression. On both sides of the operator, you have the values, known as the *operands*. The operator takes the operands, performs its function on them, and leaves a final value for the expression.

If an expression has more than one operator, they execute in a specific order, or *precedence* (just like the order of arithmetic operations you learned in grade school). Operators with the highest precedence execute first, followed by others in order of highest to lowest precedence. For example:

```
total = 3 + 4 * 5
total = 23
```

According to the rules of precedence, the 4 and 5 are multiplied first, and then the 3 is added. Tables 9.1–9.4 list some of the ActionScript operators in order of precedence, from highest to lowest. Where operator precedence is equal, operations are performed from left to right.

Numeric Operators

Numeric operators add, subtract, multiply, and divide the operands of an expression. Table 9.1 lists the ActionScript numeric operators. Operators with the highest precedence are listed first; precedence decreases as you move down the table.

OPERATOR	OPERATION
++	Increment by 1
– –	Decrement by 1
*	Multiplication
/	Division
%	Modulo
+	Addition
–	Subtraction

Table 9.1

The Numeric Operators

Comparison Operators

The comparison operators compare the value of two operands and return a Boolean (true or false) value based on the comparison. Table 9.2 lists the ActionScript comparison operators. Comparison operators have equal precedence and are read from left to right.

OPERATOR	OPERATION
<	Less than
<=	Less than or equal to
>	Greater than
>=	Greater than or equal to

Table 9.2

The Comparison Operators

Logical Operators

Logical operators compare two Boolean values and return a third Boolean value. Logical AND will evaluate to true if all conditions are true. Logical OR will evaluate to true if one of the

OPERATOR	OPERATION
!	Logical NOT
&&	Logical AND
||	Logical OR

Table 9.3

The Logical Operators

conditions is true and `false` if all conditions are false. Logical NOT inverts the value of an expression—for example, `!false==true`. Table 9.3 lists the ActionScript logical operators. Operators with the highest precedence are listed first; precedence decreases as you move down the table.

Equality and Assignment Operators

The equality operators test for equality between two operands. The operation will return a Boolean value based on the operands. The assignment operators make assignments and initialize variables. Table 9.4 lists the equality and assignment operators. Operators with the highest precedence are listed first; precedence decreases as you move down the table. All compound assignment operators (+=, –=, *=, and so on) have equal precedence and are read from left to right.

ActionScript's bitwise operators, which are used to set and evaluate values at the bit level, are beyond the scope of this book and will not be covered. To learn more about them, refer to the Flash documentation.

Understanding ActionScript's Global Functions

The ActionScript language incorporates many built-in, or *global*, functions. These functions are part of the language and perform many of the common tasks in a Flash production. In the past, Macromedia and many users referred to these global functions as *actions*. Whatever you prefer to call them, the global functions are statements in ActionScript that issue commands to a movie or one of its components, telling it to do something. For example:

```
gotoAndPlay(5);
```

The `gotoAndPlay()` function tells the current Timeline to go to frame 5 and continue playing when it gets there.

Table 9.4

The Equality and Assignment Operators

OPERATOR	OPERATION
==	Equality
===	Strict equality
!=	Inequality
!==	Strict inequality
=	Assignment
+=	Addition and assignment
–=	Subtraction and assignment
*=	Multiplication and assignment
/=	Division and assignment
%=	Modulo and assignment

Here's another example:

```
duplicateMovieClip("myClip","myOtherClip",1);
```

This action makes a copy of the Movie Clip myClip, names the copy myOtherClip, and sets it at stacking level 1 above the original clip.

Global functions are one of the largest portions of the ActionScript language and can be thought of as the "nuts and bolts" of any Flash project. You can find them in the Actions Toolbox section of the Actions panel. Click the Global Functions icon to display a list of categories. Each category contains a set of functions available to you:

Timeline Control Regulates the flow of the main Timeline and Movie Clip Timelines

Browser/Network Communicates and accesses resources outside the Flash Player

Printing Functions Prints portions of a movie or application

Miscellaneous Functions Performs conversions, sets timers, and retrieves information

Mathematical Functions Uses mathematical routines to evaluate data

Conversion Functions Changes information into a specific data type

Movie Clip Control Controls the interactive behavior of Movie Clips

You can find examples of these functions in nearly every chapter of this book.

Understanding Conditional Statements and Custom Functions

Conditionals (if) statements and user-defined functions are among the most important aspects of ActionScript. They regulate the flow of a script and provide options for powerful customization. We'll discuss these important topics in Chapter 10.

Understanding Objects

Objects are one of the many data types in Flash, and as such, they can be referred to directly in an ActionScript statement. They're also an important element of the language because they hold chunks of information that affect different elements of your movie. Objects have properties that can be set and reset as needed within a movie. They also have methods, which are built-in functions specific to each object. You can use methods to produce values or perform tasks.

For a list of the predefined objects in ActionScript, consult the Actions panel (Alt+9 / Opt+F9). Look for the category named ActionScript 2.0 Classes in the Actions Toolbox (see Figure 9.11). You can choose a category and double-click the icon beside each object to reveal the properties and methods belonging to it. For specifics on each class, choose Help panel (F1) → Using Flash → ActionScript 2.0 Language Reference → ActionScript Classes. We'll discuss specific objects, along with their associated properties and methods, in Chapters 10–12.

Figure 9.11

The names, properties, and methods of ActionScript's predefined objects are in the ActionScript 2.0 Classes category of the Actions panel.

Scripting and Working Smart: Some Suggestions

Even the most proficient and knowledgeable ActionScript gurus get stuck in technical ruts. The experts, however, know how to get out of these ruts. Experience has taught them how to step away from the problem, evaluate the situation, and dive in again with an appropriate solution. Often, you can solve technical problems not through scripting wizardry but through a logical and methodical reevaluation of your code. Moreover, by practicing good, consistent techniques while planning and writing your scripts, you can avoid many problems altogether.

Good scripting form means good habits that minimize the possibility of errors. Good form ultimately means working smarter. It can also help you flush out problems and find solutions when they do pop up. The following are tips for avoiding problems while working on your Flash projects and writing ActionScript:

Use appropriate variable names. Variables are storage locations for many kinds of information: values, properties, Movie Clip instances, frame labels—just about anything in a movie. When you initialize a variable, try to select a meaningful name—ideally a name that references the role or purpose of the variable. A variable name must also follow the rules for an identifier.

Use ActionScript terms correctly. Some elements of ActionScript are read-only, which means they can be checked but not set. Many terms use a specific configuration of uppercase and lowercase letters and punctuation. When in doubt about a particular term, consult this book's ActionScript Reference (on the CD) or the ActionScript Dictionary section of the Help panel (F1).

Work deliberately; test movies and scripts often. While you're creating a Flash movie, it's easy to be swept away by the pure joy of creativity and forget about the technical feasibility of what you're doing. Without compromising your work style, try to approach the creative process by taking small steps. With every little accomplishment or scripting victory, test the movie to ensure *every* element is still working properly.

Save multiple versions, and back up your files. Everyone knows about frequent saves, but everyone forgets occasionally, too. Backup files are essential to ensure against disk errors, hard-drive crashes, and other anomalies that can plague the citizens of a digital world. Saving multiple versions of a file helps protect against major mistakes, lost data, corrupted files, and so on. If a newer version has problems or is altered beyond repair, it can be helpful to return to a previous version and start afresh.

Use the `trace()` function to track variables and properties. The `trace()` function is one of the most helpful parts of ActionScript. It allows you to get feedback from the Flash Player and tells you what is *really* going on in your movie with variables, loops, and other script elements. To learn more about this, see the section "Monitoring Scripts with `trace()` and the Output Panel" later in this chapter.

Use comments to mark up your code. Comments, created by typing a double forward slash (//), tell Flash to ignore whatever is written after the slashes. For blocking out large chunks of code, don't forget the multiline comment characters (/* and */). Use comments to write notes to yourself or another member of your team, to make citations about the portions that work and the portions that don't, and so on. Comments can also help keep script sections organized.

Storyboard a script to check the logic and flow. If you're going to tackle a large project involving a lot of ActionScript, it can be helpful to start by working on paper. You can plan and conceptualize your script outside Flash and then step into the program once you're ready to begin development. It can also be helpful to plan complex loop structures on paper, where you can do all the computations and logic in a medium that shows the flow of information.

Build your movie in small chunks. It can be advantageous to break a project into sections and tackle them one by one, a kind of divide-and-conquer approach. Get one portion of your movie working before moving on to the next.

Identify problems as they arise. If something seems to be amiss, chances are it is. It's always better to deal with problems right away than to let them linger. Also, as you try different solutions, think about how temporary fixes might negatively impact other movie elements in the future.

It's often better the second time around. If you have the time, try re-creating a project you just finished. In other words, develop the movie or application, and then build it again. You might find that in the second round, you intuitively find more elegant solutions to problems that were frustrating in the first round of development.

Troubleshooting: Tips and Techniques

Try as you might, you simply can't avoid some problems. When they occur, they're like sand in the gears of your scripting machine. Technical scripting errors can bring your productivity to a screeching halt and create frustration in the ranks of your development team. But you can overcome technical errors. They're simply *errors*. All you have to do is set things straight; in other words, change them and make them the way they ought to be.

Sound too easy to be true? Well, probably, but it does feel good to think about problems so confidently. Attitude can be a great asset in overcoming technical problems. When you're calm and collected, it's easier to examine the situation at hand logically. To do this, you must look at your scripts from every possible angle to try to discover what portion or component is causing the problem and why.

Getting Self-Help: Queries for Troubleshooting Common Mistakes

To get to the bottom of an ActionScript-related problem with your movie, ask yourself these questions:

Is the syntax correct? Many ActionScript elements exist: functions, properties, methods, statements, and so on. It can be easy to confuse one syntax for another, so be sure you're using each term properly.

- Make sure you correctly spell each term and use the right uppercase and lower-case characters where they're needed (for example, `onMouseUp`, not `onmouseup`).

- Be sure to include a semicolon (`;`) at the end of statements, and be sure to use curly braces (`{}`) to enclose the block statements of handlers and loops. Action-Script is often forgiving when it comes to missing semicolons, but a misplaced or forgotten curly brace will stop the Flash Player dead in its tracks when it's trying to read and process your scripts.

If you're not sure of your syntax, Flash will tell you! While working in the Actions panel, simply click the Check Syntax button or press Ctrl+T / Cmd+T to verify the "correctness" of your ActionScript statements.

- Watch your operators carefully! For example, the assignment operator (`=`) and equality operator (`==`) have very different uses. The assignment operator is used to *assign* a value:

  ```
  var i=0;
  ```

  The equality operator tests whether two expressions are equal and will return a Boolean value:

  ```
  if(this._x==bounds._x){
      //statement(s) if expressions are equal (returns True)
  }
  ```

  The Check Syntax feature of the Actions panel won't catch these kinds of mistakes, so it's especially important to confirm you've specified the correct operators for loops and conditional statements.

Did you specify the arguments correctly? Many ActionScript elements (functions and methods, in particular) can take arguments. Make sure you enter all arguments properly. For example, if you enter a variable or identifier where there should be a string, your script will not run properly. The following statement won't execute properly because the `gotoAndPlay()` function dictates that the name of a target frame label must be specified as a string:

```
gotoAndPlay(intro);
```

The correct syntax is as follows:

```
gotoAndPlay("intro");
```

Here, using the right syntax, the frame label `"intro"` is specified as a string, and the statement will execute properly. Without the quotes, `intro` is interpreted as a variable that contains a value. If no such variable exists, the statement won't execute properly because it has no value to use for the target argument of the `gotoAndPlay()` function.

Is the handler getting executed? Every script is called from some kind of handler. However, if a handler doesn't get executed, its scripts will not be called. Use the `trace()` function to test for handler activity. For example, to see whether a Movie Clip is responding to a mouse click event, you could write this:

```
block_mc.onPress=function(){
    trace("clicked");
    //other statements...
}
```

Did you use the correct target path? When you're creating a movie with multiple Movie Clip instances and Timelines, it can be easy to get confused and forget which clips and movies reside where. Check to see you've correctly specified all your target paths to functions, objects, Movie Clips, and their properties. For more details, see the section "Monitoring Scripts with trace() and the Output Panel" later in this chapter.

What's the scope? Global (`_global`) variables are available at any time throughout an entire movie, but others aren't. You must make reference to Timeline-specific variables using a target path to the Timeline where they were created.

Does your math check out? How many expressions are you using in a script? Do they add up correctly to achieve the results you desire? If it's helpful, you can use the `trace()` function to help with some in-context number crunching.

Are loops and conditionals executing properly? When you use a loop or conditional, you set the parameters to test a condition and then have ActionScript do something as a result of that condition. If a script isn't behaving properly, check to see its loops and conditional statements are executing correctly.

Are all Movie Clips and Button objects instances? Unless a Movie Clip or Button object is an instance, you won't be able to target (control) it with ActionScript. Consult the Property Inspector to be sure each Movie Clip or Button object you want to target has a unique instance name.

Do all variables and functions have unique names? It's essential that all variables and functions follow the rules for identifiers. They must have unique names so they won't be confused with other elements in your movie. To learn the proper syntax for creating an identifier, see "Getting Familiar with ActionScript Terminology" earlier in this chapter.

Using the Flash Troubleshooting Tools

It's good to be able to look at a script, walk through it slowly step by step, and uncover the problematic statements. However, sometimes this can prove to be an enormous task! In the same way it's helpful to create a movie in small, deliberate steps, it can be equally beneficial to troubleshoot in the same manner. You can hunt for problems carefully and make sure one area of the movie is trouble free before moving onto the next.

Flash provides a set of tools that can make this process easier. Using these as part of your troubleshooting strategy can help you break a problem down by isolating different parts of a script and testing them individually. Some of these tools are formalized; others are more like scripting techniques. All the tools will help you work through ActionScript problems and get your scripts running smoothly.

Writing Comments   We discussed comments earlier as a means of leaving notes and reminders within the body of a script. You're able to do this because Flash ignores anything that follows the double slash (//). This feature makes comments the perfect tool for turning certain parts of a script on and off.

By "turning off" a portion of a script that works correctly, you can isolate script elements that are problematic or force the script to not run particular statements.

Using the Output Panel   You can use the Output panel in several ways in your movie. It's involved anytime you use the trace() function. All items that you ask to trace will be printed in the Output panel. Additionally, you can use it to provide information about any objects and variables that are active in your movie.

Using the Debugger   The Debugger was introduced with Flash 5 and has been a valuable asset ever since. It offers a series of menus you can use to monitor Movie Clip instances, variables, properties, and in general, all of the technical happenings of your movie. To learn more about the Debugger, see the "Using the Debugger" section of this chapter.

Monitoring Scripts with *trace()* and the Output Panel

The trace() function is every ActionScripter's best friend. It enables you to ask Flash to report specific bits of information about your movie. Flash answers your queries by printing information to the Output panel each time you ask for it. This question-and-answer routine can allow you to gather all kinds of information about your movie and to track things such as event handlers that don't fire, Movie Clip parameters, target paths, variable values, results of functions, and so on. Once you get started using trace(), you'll wonder how you ever created scripts without it.

Because it's a function, you enter trace() in the Actions panel alongside all your other script statements. The syntax is as follows:

```
trace("literal info in quotes"+variablesOrProperties);
```

You can see that `trace()` will accept several kinds of information. It can be helpful to use literal statements when you use `trace()`, especially if you're tracking multiple parameters, for example:

```
trace("loopcount: "+i);
trace("horizLoc: "+_root.ball._x);
trace("vertLoc: "+_root.ball._y);
trace("instance: "+_root.newBall+i);
```

This example demonstrates the fundamental techniques involved in using `trace()`. Place quotes around all information that you want to appear in the Output panel exactly as it appears in the `trace()` statement (such as the name of the thing you want to trace). Flash interprets this as a literal string and prints it verbatim. This is extremely useful for creating labels for your information. The labels `loopcount:`, `horizLoc:`, `vertLoc:`, and `instance:` will appear in the Output panel exactly as they appear in the `trace()` statement because they were entered as strings, including a space following the colon character. Each label is followed by useful information, in this example the value of `i`, the horizontal and vertical position of the `ball` instance, and the current instance number. The addition operator (+) concatenates information so it appears as one "thought" in the Output panel (see Figure 9.12).

You can enter `trace()` anywhere within a script, although you might find some locations are better than others. For instance, to track a variable that increments while a loop is executing, you want to put the `trace()` statement inside the loop so it monitors the loop value each time it cycles through.

Additionally, the Output panel displays scripting errors as they arise. If you script something Flash doesn't understand, it will use the Output panel to tell you where the problem lies.

You can also sometimes get information from the Output panel without asking it a question directly. The List Objects and List Variables functions provide information about the objects and variables in your movie via simple menu options.

In movie-editing mode, the Output panel is usually hidden and unnecessary. That's because its role deals more with testing movies than with creating them. As you compose ActionScript and check its syntax, the window might pop open if it has an error to report.

In Test Movie mode, Flash will open the Output panel whenever it has something to tell you; it will either report an error or display `trace()` output.

To open the Output panel on your own, select Window → Output, or press F2. The Output panel will appear, and its contents will be blank.

Figure 9.12

The Output panel prints the value of variables, properties, and any other information requested within a `trace()` **function.**

The List Objects Command

In Test Movie mode, you can call upon the Output panel to give you specific information about the objects in your movie. This information is delivered in a cascading, outline form to show you the hierarchy of objects as well. List Objects will tell you the level number, frame number, type of object (MovieClip, Button, or shape), and absolute target path to each Movie Clip instance. This feature can be especially handy when taking stock of a movie's "cast" or tracking down an errant target path.

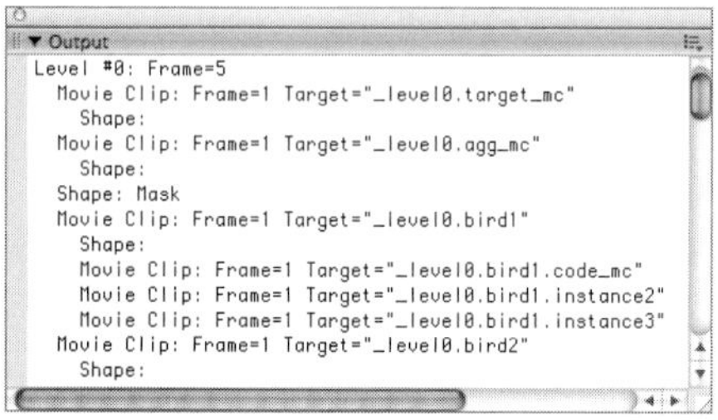

To list the objects in a Flash movie:

1. Save your movie, and then select Control → Test Movie to jump into Test Movie mode. (The List Objects feature isn't available in regular movie-editing mode.)

2. Choose Debug → List Objects (or press Ctrl+L / Cmd+L). The Output panel opens and prints the information for all movie objects in the window. For an example, see Figure 9.13.

Figure 9.13

The Output panel can list all the objects in a movie while Flash is running in Test Movie mode.

The List Variables Command

List Variables is another function available only in Test Movie mode. When selected, List Variables uses the Output panel to print all the variables in a movie, the target path to their locations, and their values when the function is called.

To list the variables in a Flash movie:

1. Save your movie, and then select Control → Test Movie to jump into Test Movie mode. (The List Variables feature isn't available in regular movie-editing mode.)

2. Choose Debug → List Variables (or press Ctrl+Alt+V / Cmd+Option+V). The Output panel immediately prints all the variables in your movie, their target paths, and their values at the time they're printed. The display is similar to the results of the List Objects command.

Variables and objects aren't tracked dynamically when you use List Variables or List Objects. Instead, the Output panel prints the specified information at the instant it receives the command. To monitor variables or objects in your movie continuously, it's best to use either the Display List in the Debugger's Variables tab or the `trace()` function.

Using the Debugger

The Debugger is your window to all the inner workings of your movie. It displays all the Movie Clip instances and levels in your movie, as well as the properties of each. The Debugger will also track all the variables that are active within a given Timeline in your movie. It's an extremely useful and efficient tool because it presents all the technical elements you need in order to monitor a movie within a single window. Use the Debugger to isolate errors in your scripts and look "under the hood." A close examination of your scripts and how they're executing can be invaluable when your movie isn't running properly.

To run, the Debugger requires a tool known as the Flash Debug Player. This is a special version of the Flash Player that is automatically installed with the main Flash authoring application. It allows Flash to load information about your movie into the Debugger as you test a movie.

Activating the Debugger

In Test Movie mode, when you select Window → Debugger or press Shift+F4, the Debugger opens. To initiate debugging in your movie, however, you must *activate* the Debugger. This launches the Flash Debug Player component and allows the Debugger to receive information.

To activate debugging in your movie, choose Control → Debug Movie (or press Shift+Ctrl+Enter / Shift+Cmd+Return). Flash automatically jumps into Test Movie mode. The Debugger pauses by default. To initiate debugging, click the green Continue button in the Code View menu.

Using Debugger Elements

While activated and running in Test Movie mode, the Debugger has several components, all of which give you insight into the workings of your movie. Figure 9.14 shows the Debugger in an active state.

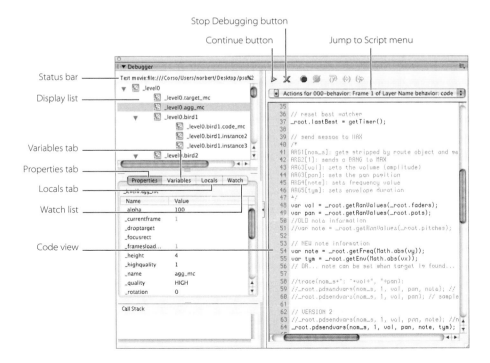

Figure 9.14

When the Debugger is activated, it displays information about various components of your movie.

The following are some of the Debugger's tools:

STATUS BAR

At the top of the Debugger is the status bar. It shows whether you're working in Test Movie mode from your local computer or in Remote Flash Player while debugging from a remote location—and the movie's local file path or uniform resource locator (URL).

DISPLAY LIST

When the Debugger is activated, the Display list shows you a breakdown of each movie level and Movie Clip instance, including a separate clip level for global variables (_global). This list is updated as movies are duplicated, removed, loaded, or unloaded from the main Timeline. The Display list shows these items in a format similar to the Movie Explorer so that you can see the hierarchical relationship between clip instances. If your movie contains lots of clips, you can resize the dimensions of the Display list so it's taller and can show more information.

PROPERTIES TAB

You can use the Properties tab to monitor and change properties of a given Movie Clip instance. You can monitor a clip's properties while you test a movie and change them directly from the Debugger. Any changes you make in the Properties tab will not permanently affect your movie. They can only temporarily alter clip parameters while you test the movie.

To display the properties for a Movie Clip, select the clip in the Display list, and then click the Properties tab. The tab will show a long list of clip properties. Depending on the clip and the way you use it in your movie, some properties might be constantly updating and changing in the Properties tab window.

To change the values for a property, select the clip instance you'd like to modify from the Display list. Double-click the property value, and then enter a new value in the field. Press Enter/Return, and your movie will update itself accordingly.

VARIABLES TAB

The Variables tab gives you access to a live display of all the variables currently active on a given Timeline. You can select a Movie Clip instance in the Display list, and the Variables tab will list the current values of the variables that the instance contains. Selecting the _global clip in the Display list will show any global variables your movie contains.

It's also possible to change variable values as you're testing your movie. Simply select the variable in the list, double-click its value, and enter a new value. Press Enter/Return, and your movie will respond accordingly.

WATCH LIST

The Watch list provides an easy way to monitor a set of variables from one location. For example, if you wanted to simultaneously monitor the variables in two different Movie Clips, you'd have to jump back and forth between them in the Display list while watching the Variables tab. The Watch list allows you to select these variables and put them in one location so you can easily monitor them within a single window. To do this, you must add the variables to the Watch list.

To create a Watch list, you can do one of three things:

- Select a variable in the Variables tab. Right-click / Ctrl+click, and select Watch from the context menu. Alternatively, you can select the variable, and choose Add Watch from the Debugger pop-up menu. Any variables selected for a watch will be marked with a blue dot in the Variables tab.

- Right-click / Ctrl+click in the Watch list.

- Double-click on a new line, and enter the target path to the variable you want to watch.

It isn't possible to directly assign an item from the Properties tab (such as _alpha or _currentframe) to the Watch list. Flash allows you to watch variables only. As a workaround, initialize a variable to the property you want to watch, and then use the Debugger to set a watch for that variable. For example, if you need to constantly monitor the horizontal position of a Movie Clip, create a variable for the _x property:

```
Block_mc.onEnterFrame=function(){
    Block_hPos=block_mc._x;
}
```

Then use the Variables tab to set a watch for the variable Block_hPos.

You can remove an item from the Watch list by right-clicking / Ctrl+clicking the item and then deselecting Watch in the context menu. You can also highlight the item, and select Remove Watch from the Debugger pop-up menu.

CHAPTER 10

Understanding the Fundamentals of the ActionScript Language

Interactive content is one of the effects Flash does well. Not only can you add simple button controls with Flash, but you can also create any number of user interfaces that include animation, sound, and more advanced multimedia such as video. In this chapter, you'll look at the code building blocks you need to know before you can create interactive Flash content.

- **Controlling Timelines though scripting**

- **Creating Timeline-based navigation schemes**

- **Creating code that can make decisions**

- **Creating functions**

- **Creating links with Flash**

Targeting Movie Clip Timelines to Control Playback

So far you've looked at Timelines that perform one action—play. Many reasons exist why you'd want your Timeline to do otherwise, but the main reason is that you want your Flash movies to be *interactive*. In fact, three levels of interactivity exist. We'll begin by describing each level and covering what each requires.

Understanding Linear Content

At the moment, you can make Flash act like a regular television channel. You can decide what you want to watch, but once the content starts, you have only two choices: you can watch what's offered in the order it's offered, or you can switch off the television. This type of movie is called *linear content.*

You produce linear content in Flash via Timelines that contain tweens and no Action-Script. The whole content plays from start to finish, and the user has no control over it.

Linear content is fine for animated cartoons, but much of the content a typical Flash designer is asked to produce is far from linear. Even if you're purely a Flash animator, you'll still need to add *some* control to your online work, such as a menu system that allows the user to choose between different cartoons, choices that allow the user to view different bandwidths of content, or a pause button.

Understanding Nonlinear Content

The first level of sophistication you can add in Flash is rather like adding a video recorder or DVD player to your television setup. With a DVD player, you can skip sections of content or play the content in the order you choose. You can also add pauses to your playback and delay watching sections of the content until you're ready to do so. Although you're still watching linear content, the content is broken up into sections that you can watch in the order of your choosing. This order can be something other than simply watching each section in the normal, linear order, and hence this form of movie is called *nonlinear content.*

To create nonlinear content in Flash, you need to add basic controls to your movies that allow the user to move the Timeline playhead backward, to move it forward (usually to specific sections of your Timelines), or to stop the Timeline altogether. In short, you need to add the same sort of controls that are available on a DVD player so that the user can *navigate* within the content and choose what to see.

Understanding Interactive Content

The next level of sophistication is *interactive content*. Rather than sitting in front of the television, interactive content is like going out and engaging in participative entertainment. Playing sports and physical games, gathering for social events, and playing video games with your buddies are events where your entertainment comes through interaction with other people and/or objects. To provide interaction within Flash, you need to be able to stop the Timelines from playing content in a linear way and instead make everything that Flash does link to something the user does.

The defining feature of interactive content is that it doesn't just blindly skip between linear content segments. Instead, interactive content makes *conditional decisions*. Examples of conditional decisions include the following:

- Flash remembers what has happened previously and uses that information to decide what happens next. Flash stores previous information via *variables* and can use this information to create context sensitivity, complex navigation schemes, or interfaces that respond in cool or novel ways.

- Flash starts additional animations other than the ones the user requests. This allows a Flash site to animate *itself* at the same time as performing the actions the user specifi- cally requests. This is how many sites are able to transition into the requested content via a number of effects and animations that the user did not request.

- Flash performs actions the user doesn't expect. Flash is able to make decisions on its own, and these may be actions the user doesn't expect or doesn't even know are hap- pening. For example, in a game, Flash could control the space invaders that fight against the user or do more mundane tasks such as load content seamlessly behind the scenes (in a way that the user doesn't even notice).

Interactive content requires that the Flash designer start to move away from the concept of keyframes and toward the use of *events* and *event handling*. When Flash performs com- plex responses to user interaction or is managing its own tasks internally, it usually performs these tasks via code that's attached to events rather than to keyframes. Events are impor- tant in intermediate/advanced Flash, and we discuss them in this chapter, in Chapter 7, and in Chapters 11 and 12.

You've already looked at linear Timelines in the chapters about non-ActionScript- based animation earlier in the book. For the rest of this chapter, we'll show how to create nonlinear and interactive content.

Controlling Timelines Nonlinearly

Nonlinear Timeline control allows you to move between frames of your Timeline in any order, as well as to stop a Timeline completely. You can use the following actions (or to give them their correct name, global functions) to control Timelines in your Flash movie:

`gotoAndPlay()` Skips to a frame, frame label, or scene and plays from that location

`gotoAndStop()` Skips to a frame, frame label, or scene and stops at that location

`nextFrame()` Skips ahead one frame and stops

`prevFrame()` Skips back one frame and stops

`play()` Plays through the frames of a Timeline, starting from the current frame

`stop()` Stops the playback of a Timeline at the current frame

You can also control nested Timelines using the *method-based* versions of the previous actions, which will be discussed in Chapter 12. Also, Chapter 11 discusses the concept of methods and how they differ from actions.

The easiest way to show how these actions work is to set up a simple animation and then control it via actions (or use the finished file, nonLinear_start.fla on the book's CD, and skip the next four steps):

1. Using the Oval tool, draw a circle about 50 pixels in diameter. Holding down Shift while you drag the oval constrains it to a circle. If you want a circle that's exactly 50 pixels in diameter, open the Property Inspector, and set both the height and width to 50 pixels using the H and W fields.

2. Either double-click (if you haven't used Object Drawing mode) or single-click (if you have used Object Drawing mode) to select the circle. Press F8 to open the Convert to Symbol dialog box. Make the circle a Graphic symbol, and call it **circle**.

3. Place the circle to the far left of the Stage. On the main Timeline, add a keyframe at frame 20. With the new keyframe selected, move the circle so it's at the same vertical position but to the far right of the Stage (hold Shift as you move the circle to force Flash to move the circle horizontally in a straight line for you). Select the keyframe at frame 1, and select Motion in the Tween drop-down on the Properties tab of the Property Inspector.

4. Change the name of the layer from Layer 1 to **tween**. Add a new layer above tween. Call it **actions** (see Figure 10.1).

You've now created a motion tween of the circle moving from left to right across the screen. Save the FLA, because you'll be using it several times throughout this chapter. In fact, you can change this rather boring and linear animation in several ways.

Figure 10.1
**Create a tween layer
and an** actions
layer.

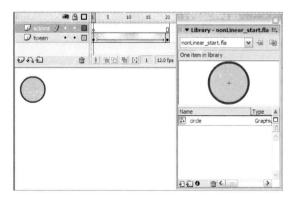

To make the tween stop after it has completed its animation once:

1. Starting with the file `nonLinear_start.fla`, create a keyframe at frame 20 of layer `actions`. With this keyframe selected, open the Actions panel (press F9, or select Window → Actions), and add the following script:

   ```
   stop();
   ```

   If you test the movie, the Timeline will play normally until it hits the stop action at frame 20, and this halts the Timeline (see Figure 10.2).

Figure 10.2

The circle tween looks like this after step 1.

To make the Timeline skip frames 6 to 14:

2. Reload `nonLinear_start.fla`; alternatively, select File → Revert, and click Revert on the rather scary-looking warning that appears.

3. Add a keyframe at frame 5. Using the Actions panel, add the following script:

   ```
   gotoAndPlay(15);
   ```

   The animation will now skip frames 6 to 14, giving you the tween shown in Figure 10.3.

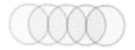 

Figure 10.3

The circle tween looks like this after step 3.

Jumping to numbered frames isn't usually good practice. Say you added `gotoAndStop(15);` and then added frames between frames 5 and 15. Doing so would move the frame you want to jump to; in other words, it would now be a frame other than frame 15. Your only option would be to change the script every time you changed the Timeline, which isn't really a good idea if you have lots of tweens and lots of scripts to manage!

A better way is to jump to a *named keyframe*:

1. Continuing with the FLA from the previous exercise, change the line on frame 5 to the following one:

   ```
   gotoAndPlay("skipTo");
   ```

2. Make sure the keyframe on frame 5 is still selected. In the Property Inspector, you'll see a field with *<Frame Label>* in it. Click inside this field, and enter the text **skipFrom** (see Figure 10.4). Leave the Label Type option as Name.

Figure 10.4

Add a label using the Property Inspector.

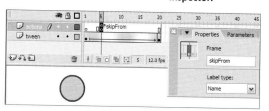

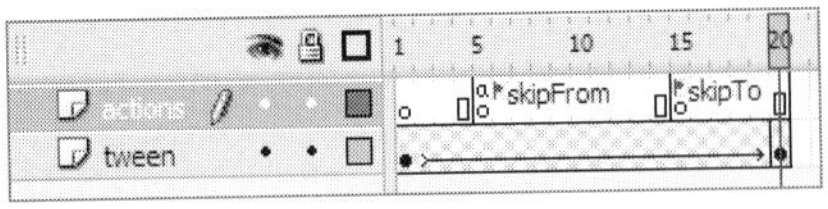

Figure 10.5

The completed Timeline looks like this.

Figure 10.6

You can add frames too.

3. Create a keyframe at frame 15 of layer `actions`. Using the same process as step 2, attach a label to this keyframe called **skipTo**. Your Timeline will now look like Figure 10.5.

4. You can see why labels are better than adding frames to the Timeline (see Figure 10.6). Click any frame on layer `actions` between frames 5 and 15. Shift+click the frame directly below the layer `tween`. (You can also simply click the first frame and drag it to the second frame.) Press F5 a few times to add frames to both layers. As you do so, the `skipTo` frame moves to the right. The frame moves to reflect your changes.

The `play()`, `prevFrame()`, and `nextFrame()` actions are best used with interaction. The following examples will use *event handlers* to run the three actions.

Chapter 8 discusses event handlers and their relationship to interactivity, and Chapter 12 expands on the topic.

The `nonLinear_controls.fla` FLA on the book's CD contains an embedded video object and buttons to control the video's playback. Clicking each of the buttons changes the way the video plays (see Figure 10.7). From left to right, the buttons are as follows:

- The rewind-to-start button moves the video to the start.
- The rewind button plays the video backward at twice the normal speed.
- The play button plays the video at normal speed.
- The fast-forward button plays the video at twice the normal speed.
- The forward-to-end button moves the video to the end.
- The pause button stops the video. If you click it again, it restarts the movie.
- The stop button stops the video.

The `nonLinear_controls.fla` file contains video; you might feel more comfortable looking at the simpler FLA `nonLinear_controls_tween.fla`.

Also notice the empty Movie Clip to the left of the rewind-to-start button. The code uses this Movie Clip to attach an `onEnterframe` event handler.

The code to drive these controls is on the first frame of layer `actions`.

The code for the rewind-to-start button looks like this:

```
backToStart_btn.onRelease = function() {
  gotoAndStop(1);
};
```

When you click the rewind-to-start button, the second line of this code makes the Timeline jump to frame 1 and stop.

The code for the forward-to-end button does something similar except it moves to the last frame in the movie:

```
forwardToEnd_btn.onRelease = function() {
  gotoAndStop(_totalframes);
};
```

Figure 10.7

Use the video's buttons to control the movie.

The _totalframes property contains the total number of frames in a Timeline, and it therefore always contains the frame number of the last frame. Jumping to this frame therefore goes to the last frame.

You can also add labels at the first and last frame and jump to them.

The play and stop buttons have short and uncomplicated scripts attached to them. These scripts simply run play() and stop() actions when you click the appropriate button:

```
play_btn.onRelease = function() {
  play();
};
stop_btn.onRelease = function() {
  stop();
};
```

The rewind and fast-forward buttons can't be driven by single-clicks but a click-release pair. When you click, the rewind/fast-forward should start, and it needs to stop when you release. Between the press and release, you want to run a script every frame. The way you do this in Flash is via an onEnterFrame event handler that runs during the period between the click-release events. You need to attach the onEnterFrame to a Movie Clip (because it's an event associated with Movie Clips, not buttons), and this Movie Clip is the empty one you noticed to the left of the buttons.

Here are the event handlers for the rewind button:

```
back_btn.onPress = function() {
  emptyClip.onEnterFrame = function() {
    prevFrame();
    prevFrame();
  };
};
back_btn.onRelease = function() {
  delete emptyClip.onEnterFrame;
};
```

When you click the button, the onPress event handler sets up the onEnterFrame. The onEnterFrame event moves the Timeline forward by two frames every frame. It does this via two prevFrame() actions. This onEnterFrame event runs until you release the button, whereupon the onRelease event deletes the onEnterFrame.

Similarly, you can do this with the fast-forward button, except that here you use two nextFrame() actions:

```
forward_btn.onPress = function() {
  emptyClip.onEnterFrame = function() {
    nextFrame();
    nextFrame();
  };
};
forward_btn.onRelease = function() {
  delete emptyClip.onEnterFrame;
};
```

The pause button is another tricky one to set up. The pause button should stop the Timeline if the Timeline is playing and not do anything if the Timeline isn't playing. If the Timeline is playing, the pause button should stop it, and pressing the pause button again should restart the Timeline. Here's the code that does this:

```
function pause1() {
  stop();
  pause_btn.onRelease = pause2;
}
function pause2() {
  play();
  pause_btn.onRelease = pause1;
}
pause_btn.onRelease = pause1;
```

The first time the button is clicked, function pause1() is the event handler that runs because of the last line in the previous code. This function stops the Timeline. If the Timeline is playing, it stops; if it was stopped already, nothing happens. Function pause1() sets the onRelease event handler to pause2() as its last line, and this function does much the same as pause1() except that it starts the Timeline and sets pause1() as the event handler. Thus, the pause button toggles between stopping the Timeline and playing it.

Using Timeline Controls to Create Navigation

One of the most important uses for Timeline-controlling actions is to provide simple navigation controls.

The file nav.fla on the book's CD shows some basic site navigation. If you click any of the three buttons at the top, you'll see a content placeholder appear below the menu corresponding to that button. Each button thus takes you to the corresponding content

That's a cool set of abilities Flash has once you implement decision making, but this has a downside—the decision-making code itself tends to look a little underwhelming and pointless until you actually start to use it with graphics. So, although the next section will seem totally unrelated to web design, persevere, because conditional logic is *very* important for truly interactive content.

Introducing Conditional Statements

A *conditional statement* is ActionScript's way of running code based on whether something is true. Consider a real-world example: if you were out on the road in your vehicle, when would you stop for gas? The simplest reason would be if you didn't have enough gas in the car to complete your journey. In code, the decision would look something like this:

```
if (not enough gas) {
    stop at the next gas station;
    fill up the tank;
}
```

The text between the parentheses is called the *conditional*. It is what defines the decision. The lines between the curly braces are a *code block*. The code block will run only if the conditional above it is a true statement.

Normally, we're not so cavalier with when and where we get our gas. Most people stop to fill up when they have some time to kill or simply because they need a short break from driving. We rarely leave it until such time as "Well, if I don't fill up now, I'll be getting out and pushing the damn car for the last three miles…!"

So, true-life decisions are much more complex. You might want to stop for a number of reasons, any of which would cause you to stop and fill up:

```
if ((not enough gas) or (need a break) or (have the time to stop now)){
    stop at the next gas station;
    fill up the tank;
}
```

You have three conditionals, and the first *or* the second *or* the third needs to be true for the code block to execute. In this context, *or* means at least one of the three needs to be true.

What if you didn't have enough money to fill up? If you didn't have enough money, you could turn around and go home. If you didn't have enough gas left to do even that, then you might have to get help from someone who can bail you out of the situation. In code, this kind of decision making looks something like this:

```
if ((I need gas) and (I have enough money)) {
    stop at the next gas station;
    fill up the tank;
}else if (I have enough gas to turn around and go home) {
    turn around;
    go home;
}else{
```

page—the portfolio button takes you to the portfolio content page, and so on. Each button's onRelease event handler includes a gotoAndStop() to the keyframe that contains the corresponding content.

> Chapter 12 discusses more advanced navigation schemes that use dynamically loaded content, and this type of content delivery is closer to the navigation systems used by most commercial sites. However, understanding Timeline-based systems is a prerequisite before you can tackle dynamic loading content, so stay right here!

Understanding Conditionals

The SWFs you've seen so far in this chapter involve the user simply clicking a button and Flash doing something in direct response. To relate this to a real-life analogy, think of a light switch. You can switch the light on and off via the button, so the light has a level of user interaction. It would take a lot of imagination to see this as *interactive* in the same sense as interactive web content, though: just because something has a button doesn't make it interactive.

Early Flash sites were exactly like the light switch—you pressed a button, and something happened in direct response. Times have changed, and what constitutes interactive content has increased considerably. If a client asks you for a site that presents the user with an interactive experience, they most likely want something with an interface that's seamlessly embedded with the content, fully controllable multimedia, novel ways of presenting the content though animated transitions, or other effects…the list goes on.

More recent interactive content includes *web applications*. These are Flash SWFs that act as the front end to a large (and usually data-driven) application running on a remote server. The Flash front end now performs three tasks—it takes requests from the user, requests content from the server, and displays it. Web applications are usually far more complicated than most traditional Flash sites simply because they have far more to do.

To create such content, you need Flash to be able to perform more complex tasks behind the scenes. The major building block that Flash needs to achieve this complexity is *decision making*. Once you have decision-making abilities in a SWF, the following features become available:

- Animations are no longer fixed tweens but are totally code driven. User interfaces no longer simply act as buttons but are now *contextual*. Buttons can appear or disappear so that they show up only when they are actually needed.

- More complex controls are possible, such as drop-down menus, where clicking a control contextually reveals further options.

- Flash video games and other high-end content that requires decision making from the SWF are possible.

```
    ring for help;
  }
```

The first code block will run if I need gas *and* I have enough money. Because of the and in the middle of these statements, both conditionals have to be true.

If both conditionals are true, then you run the first code block:

```
stop at the next gas station;
fill up the tank;
```

What if the first code block doesn't run? Flash looks at the next part of the code, the else if. An else if conditional is checked when the if block doesn't run.

The else if tests whether you have enough gas to chalk it all up to experience and head home. If you're able to turn back (that is, you have enough gas to get home), the following code block runs:

```
turn around;
go home;
```

If an else if block doesn't run, you have one last chance, the else. The else always runs if none of the code blocks above it runs. The else block contains the following code:

```
ring for help;
```

So, if all else fails, you can ring your partner at home, or if you're really desperate enough to live with the story being told at every family get-together for the next 20 years, you can always ring Mom.

Introducing *if* Statements and ActionScript

The general structure of an if is as follows:

```
if (conditional) {
  do this;
}
```

If conditional works out to be true, you run the code between the curly braces:

```
do this.
```

You can also add any number of else if branches:

```
if (condition1) {
  doThis1;
} else if (condition2) {
  doThis2;
}else if (condition3) {
  doThis3;
}
```

If condition1 isn't true (that is, if it's false), then condition2 is tested. If condition2 is true, then doThis2 will run. If both condition1 and condition2 are false, then condition3 will be tested. If it is true, then doThis3 will run. If all of the conditions are false, then none of the code will run.

Note that the order of the else if blocks is important. If both condition2 and condition3 are true, only doThis2 will run because only one block is allowed to run.

You can make sure one code block runs by making that code block an else:

```
if (condition1) {
  doThis1;
} else if (condition2) {
  doThis2;
}else {
  doThis3;
}
```

If condition1 and condition2 are false, then doThis3 will run. This means that at least one block will always run (the else).

It's important to use an else properly, and it must always appear at the end of an if…else if… chain. If you do this:

```
if (condition1) {
  doThis1;
} else{
  doThis2;
}else if (condition3) {
  doThis3;
}
```

then doThis3 will *never* run because doThis2 will *always* run if condition1 is false.

Introducing Booleans

A *Boolean* is a variable that has only two values: true or false. A Boolean is useful because it allows you to store the result of a conditional. For example, if you had some code that worked out whether your tank was empty, you could assign the result to a Boolean called gasTankIsEmpty, and this Boolean would be true if your tank is indeed empty and false if your tank isn't empty.

If your tank is empty because the gas meter on the dashboard reads less than 10 percent full, or less than 0.1, you could use the following conditional:

```
gasLevel<0.1
```

where gasLevel is a number from 0 (the gas tank is so bone dry) to 1 (the gas tank is full).

You could use this condition directly in an if condition as follows (you can type this code, attaching it to the first frame of a new Flash document if you want to try it for yourself):

```
var gasLevel:Number = 0.05;
//
if (gasLevel<0.1) {
  trace("Your tank is empty!");
}
```

If you were to run this code by testing the SWF, you'd see the output in the Output panel, as shown in Figure 10.8.

This is the code most Flash developers would use, but some Flash beginners need a little more feedback. For example, in a longer piece of code, you might not know what the value of the conditional gasLevel<0.1 actually is, so you wouldn't immediately know what was wrong if the "Your tank is empty!" message didn't appear.

The following code fixes this issue:

```
var gasLevel:Number = 0.05;
var gasTankIsEmpty:Boolean = gasLevel<0.1;
//
if (gasTankIsEmpty) {
  trace("Your tank is empty!");
}
```

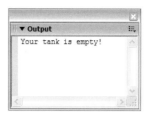

Figure 10.8

This is the Output panel after using gasLevel<0.1 **in an** if **condition.**

If you debug this code (press Control+Shift+Enter / Cmd+Shift+Enter, or select Control → Debug Movie to test the movie in debug mode) and then click the Continue icon in the Debugger (the green triangle to the top-right of the Debug panel), you can now see the value of gasTankIsEmpty directly. To do this, click the _level0 icon in the top-left pane (the Display list), and select the Variables tab in the tabbed pane below the Display list (see Figure 10.9).

As well as allowing you to see whether a conditional is true or false, the resulting code is more readable. You'll find that it is easier to see what the if statement is actually checking because the following:

```
if (gasTankIsEmpty) {
```

indicates that you're checking whether the gas tank is empty than it is to use the following:

```
if (gasLevel<0.1) {
```

Introducing Boolean Operators

You can combine Booleans to create complex conditions using the Boolean OR, AND, and NOT operators.

To test for two conditions, a and b, use the logical AND operator (&&):

```
a && b
```

This is true if both a and b are true.

To test for two conditions, a or b, use the OR operator (||):

```
a || b
```

This is true if either a or b is true.

The final operator, NOT, inverts a condition, changing true to false and changing false to true. To invert a variable a, use the logical NOT operator (!):

```
!a
```

Figure 10.9

View the Boolean value via the Debugger.

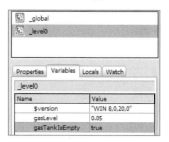

Making Decisions

It's time to tie everything together via an example. Open the file `conditionalExample.fla` on the book's CD. This FLA contains a code version of the gas tank analogy. It consists of code on the first keyframe of the only layer. The code looks like this:

```
// values
var gasLevel:Number = 0.6;
var money:Number = 0;
//
// conditionals
var INeedGas:Boolean = gasLevel<0.2;
var IHaveEnoughMoney:Boolean = money>20;
var IHaveEnoughGasToTurnBack = gasLevel>0.5;
//
// logic
if (INeedGas && IHaveEnoughMoney) {
  trace("Stop at the next gas station");
} else if (IHaveEnoughGasToTurnBack && !IHaveEnoughMoney) {
  trace("Turn back now!");
  trace("You might at least make it back home.");
} else if (!IhaveEnoughMoney && !IHaveEnoughMoney) {
  trace("You're in trouble now!")
  trace("Better ring for help");
} else {
  trace("Keep on driving...");
  trace("You're good to go for now!");
}
```

Lines below the `values` comment set up the numeric values for the comparison. You use the following:

- The gas level in the gas tank, `gasLevel`. This varies from 0 (totally empty tank) to 1 (totally full).

- The amount of money you have, `money`.
  You then set up three conditionals:

- `INeedGas` is `true` if the tank level is below 0.2 (that is, if the tank is ever less than 20 percent full).

- `IHaveEnoughMoney` is `true` if you have enough money to fill up enough to reach your destination.

- `IHaveEnoughGasToTurnBack` is `true` if you have enough gas left to turn back and get home.

The third section of the code is an `if…else if…else if…else` that decides what you should do.

As it stands, you have a 60 percent full gas tank and no money (see the top of the listing that sets gasLevel to 0.6 and money to 0). You can see what Flash thinks you should do by testing the movie (see Figure 10.10).

If you change the three lines at the top of the listing as follows so that you now have $23.50 as well as a 60 percent full gas tank, Flash knows you have enough money and gas to get to your destination safely and tells you so (see Figure 10.11):

Figure 10.10

Flash tells you it's better to turn back and go home.

```
// values
var gasLevel:Number = 0.6;
var money:Number = 23.50;
```

It's worth seeing how the Boolean values are set to true or false via the Debugger; therefore, to see this in action, set different values for gasLevel and money, and then refer to the Debugger.

Using Decisions in Design

You'll need to use conditionals and if…else if…else structures in Flash design in numerous places. Good examples of this include the following:

Figure 10.11

Flash tells you that you have nothing to fear.

- Code-driven animation (see Chapter 7). You'll use conditionals to produce the basic building block of scripted animation, *target-driven animation.*

- Collision detection (see Chapter12). You'll use the MovieClip.hitTest() method as a conditional that tells you whether a collision between two moving Movie Clips has occurred.

- Preloading (see Chapter 12). Here, you'll use code that tests whether a loading file has finished loading and is ready to be used.

Simplifying *if…else* with the *switch* Statement

The switch statement is a conditional structure that provides an alternative to if…else statements. switch statements and if statements are closely related because both get compiled to the same instructions in the final SWF (they both actually get compiled into if statements), but switch statements can be easier to read when you have long decision-making branches.

The following conditional structure presents a script with a series of cases, each of which will be executed depending on the value of the condition to be tested:

```
var num:Number=1;
switch(num){
    case 1:
        trace("case 1 was true");
        break;
    case 2:
        trace("case 2 was true");
        break;
```

```
    case 3:
        trace("case 3 was true");
        break;
    default:
        trace("no case was true")
}
```

In the preceding switch statement, the value of num is tested over several conditions, or *cases*. If a case statement returns true, meaning that the value of the case statement equals that of the variable running through the conditional, its statements are executed. In this example, the Output panel would print "case 1 was true" because the value of num happens to be 1. If the first line read num=3, you would see "case 3 was true" in the Output panel. If no cases evaluated as true, the default case's statement(s) would be executed.

Notice that each case statement contains a break action. This ensures that only a single condition's statements are executed. If you ran this script but removed break, it would print the following:

case 1 was true

case 2 was true

case 3 was true

no case was true

break causes a script to quit executing statements in the current block. This is defined by the pair of curly braces ({}) that contain the switch statement's case conditions. Without the break statement, the remaining conditions in the body of the switch statement will be evaluated as true.

You can use case statements with Booleans in the same way as ifs. The following if and switch statements will both correctly tell you whether aBoolean is true or false:

```
var aBoolean:Boolean = false;
//
//
if (aBoolean) {
  trace("if: The conditional is true");
} else {
  trace("if: The conditional is false");
}
//
//
switch (aBoolean) {
case true :
  trace("case: The conditional is true");
  break;
default :
  trace("case: The conditional is false");
}
```

Looping Scripts with Conditional Statements

You can use ActionScript conditionals to loop repetitive tasks that perform an action (or actions) a certain number of times. You create a loop with the `while` loop, the `do...while` action, or the `for` action. Each of these loop structures has some kind of *counter* that monitors the number of times the loop should be executed. Generally, the counter is initialized as a variable at the outset of the loop and is either decremented or incremented (decreased or increased by one) with every loop cycle. The function of each loop structure is identical, but the way each performs its function is unique.

The `while` loop establishes a condition and then executes statements within the curly braces until the condition is no longer true. In the next example, the variable k is used as the loop counter and is decremented each time the loop statements are executed. This loop will execute three times:

```
var k:Number=3;
while(k>0){
    duplicateMovieClip("spotClip","spot"+k,k+1);
    k--;
}
```

The `do...while` loop executes its statements first and then tests the condition to see whether the loop should continue. If the condition evaluates to `true`, the loop continues. With this kind of loop, the statements are always executed at least once, even if the condition is `false`. For example:

```
k=3;
do{
    duplicateMovieClip("spotClip","spot"+k,k+1);
    k--;
} while(k>0);
```

The `for` loop puts all of the necessary loop information in the first statement: the counter initialization, the condition, and the count expression. For example:

```
for(k=3;k>0;k--;){
    duplicateMovieClip("spotClip","spot"+k,k+1);
}
```

Here you can see that the loop conditions and the count are the same as in the `while` and `do...while` examples. However, all of the information to establish and control the loop has been economically placed in the first line of the loop.

> You can see several listings that use looping in Chapter 12.

Another loop structure, `for...in`, loops through the properties or nested objects of an object. This action can modify properties or use methods to control multiple nested Movie Clips or multiple objects. To learn more about `for...in` loops, see the ActionScript Reference on this book's CD.

Using Custom Functions

Functions are often doers and information processors. You call them or give them a set of arguments, and they perform a specific task using those arguments. ActionScript's global functions are powerful but limited to an array of prescribed routines for common tasks. You can exercise this same kind of power for tasks of your own. ActionScript allows you to create custom functions. These can be useful if you have a series of tasks or operations that need to be performed repeatedly in your movie. For example, if you need to frequently scale a Movie Clip to 50 percent of its original size, you can write a function. Rather than having to use both the _xscale and _yscale properties every time you want to scale a clip, you can call the function, and it will do all the work for you.

First, you must define the function. The syntax for defining a function is as follows:

```
function functionName(arguments){
    statement(s);
}
```

If you want to create fully typed ActionScript (recommended if you want to use ActionScript 2.0 to the fullest), use the following:

```
function functionName(arguments):returnType{
    statement(s);
}
```

Chapter 11 discusses typing.

The following is a function named half that reduces the horizontal and vertical scale of a Movie Clip by 50 percent and moves it 100 pixels up and to the left:

```
function half(myClip) {

    myClip._x-=100;
    myClip._y-=100;
myClip._xscale=50;
    myClip._yscale=50;
}
```

In this function, the term myClip is used as an argument. When the function is called, the Movie Clip listed within the parentheses (an argument to the function) will be scaled down accordingly. When you create a function, it's best to put the script that declares the function in a frame at the beginning of your movie. If ActionScript hasn't read your function, it won't know what to do when you call it later.

When creating a function, it's essential to give it a unique name within your movie so no confusion exists between functions, variables, and instances. For example, if you had a function named half and a variable named half, you'd open the door to possible error and confusion with the ActionScript in your movie. If you can't use any other name, append the name with a prefix such as funHalf for the function and varHalf for the variable.

Once you've created the function, you're free to call it whenever you need it in your movie. You can call a function in any script or in any handler and from any level or Timeline of your movie. In the following example, the half function is called when a button (with the instance name myButton) is clicked and released:

```
myButton.onRelease = function() {
  _root.half(invaders.rogue_1);
};
```

In this script, the clip rogue_1 (nested inside the clip invaders) is moved and sized down by 50 percent using the half function. The target path to rogue_1 is passed as an argument to the function, and the clip is scaled. Because the half function was created on the main Timeline, it's necessary to include the target reference _root when the function is called from a different Timeline.

Code created via functions has a number of advantages over other routes, including the following:

- Functions have their own *scope* within which they can contain their own variables locally. These variables are called *local variables*, and we'll look at them in a moment.

- Code written using functions is usually more modular and reusable than code that doesn't use functions.

- Code written using functions can be easily converted to class-based code, because the code uses a function-based structure.

- ActionScript is optimized to use functions. The virtual machine within the Flash Payer (that is, the software that executes each line of your ActionScript when the SWF is played in the Flash Player) is written such that it can make significant optimizations when running code with functions that pass parameters and that use local variables. Using well-written functions can actually increase the speed of execution of your ActionScript.

Code that's written using modular functions is usually called *structured code*. It tends to be easier to read, update, and maintain than non-function-based code. The Flash Player virtual machine is optimized for code that uses functions when you use Flash Player 7 and later.

Writing General Functions

Functions become useful when you write *general functions*, which are functions that can be reused often because they are written to be flexible.

The generalButtonEvt.fla file on the book's CD contains a simple navigation system. Each button sends the main Timeline to a keyframe every time the button is clicked. Normally, the code to do this would look something like this for each button:

```
buttonx.onRelease = function(){
    gotoAndStop("someLabel");
}
```

And you'd repeat this code for every button. When you have to repeat similar code several times, it's a sure sign that you'd be better off writing a general function that can be used several times.

The code in generalButtonEvt.fla looks like this:

```
function buttonEvt(aButton:Button, gotoLabel:String) {
    aButton.onRelease = function() {
    gotoAndStop(gotoLabel);
  };
}
//
buttonEvt(button01, "home");
buttonEvt(button02, "about");
buttonEvt(button03, "portfolio");
buttonEvt(button04, "contact");
```

Instead of writing four onRelease event handlers, you call the function buttonEvt four times. This function generates the individual button event handlers for you, using the parameters aButton and gotoLabel to decide to which button the onRelease needs to be attached and to which label the button needs to send the Timeline.

Introducing Function Scope and Local Variables

When you create a variable within a function, that variable is available only within the function and only for as long as the current function call. Such a variable is called a *local variable.* Local variables are useful because they allow you to treat code within a function as separate from any code outside the function.

Consider the following code:

```
function aTestFunction() {
    var a:Number = 5;
    trace("local version of a = "+a);
}
var a:Number = 1;
aTestFunction();
trace("timeline version of a = "+a);
```

This creates two versions of variable a. One is created within the function aTestFunction(), and the other is created on the current Timeline.

If you test this code, you'll see output shown in Figure 10.12.

The values of a are different because the two versions of a are themselves different.

You have to use the var keyword when creating local variables; otherwise, you'll create a variable on the current Timeline rather than as local to the function. This is a good enough reason to *always* use var when you create variables.

The following example is an advanced example of localization within functions. Don't worry too much if you don't get the concept the first time around, because it isn't well known (although it is useful to know!).

Flash is different from some other languages in that you can extend the lifetime of local function variables to well beyond the end of the function call's lifetime. This is because you can create event handlers within a function, and these event handlers can keep a local variable "alive."

Consider the following code (menu.fla on the book's CD):

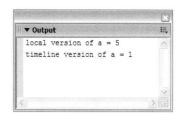

Figure 10.12

This is the result in the Output panel of testing the previous code.

```
function moveTo(clip:MovieClip, moveX:Number, moveY:Number):Void {
  function mover():Void {
    clip._x -= (clip._x-moveX)/4;
    clip._y -= (clip._y-moveY)/4;
    xIsNear = Math.abs(clip._x-moveX)<nearTo;
    yIsNear = Math.abs(clip._y-moveY)<nearTo;
    if (xIsNear && yIsNear) {
      clip._x = moveX;
      clip._y = moveY;
      delete clip.onEnterFrame;
      trace(clip._name+" has reached its position");
    }
  }
  var nearTo:Number = 1;
  var xIsNear:Boolean;
  var yIsNear:Boolean;
  //
  clip.onEnterFrame = mover;
}
```

The function moveTo() is a general function that you can use to move a Movie Clip to the point (x, y). Inside moveTo(), you define *another* function called mover(). Like variables created within a function, this new function is also local. It is accessible only from within function moveTo(). However, function mover() is used as an onEnterFrame for a Movie Clip, and this means it will continue to run well after the function call has ended. Even some advanced Flash developers will be surprised to know that Flash doesn't care—it's intelligent enough to keep the local variables alive until the onEnterFrame stops.

The function `moveTo()` is actually a useful piece of code; it allows you to define eased tweens *at runtime*. The code in `menu.fla` drives a simple menu system. If you click the red (topmost) button, more buttons appear as suboptions, moving in smoothly via an easing effect (also called *inertia* in Chapter 7). If you click the top button again, the suboptions move off screen again.

The cool part of this is that you could have a row of red buttons, each with its own submenu, giving the user loads of options in a simple and clean interface. If you tried to create this effect without using the trick of function scope, you'd end up with some very long code!

Monitoring Time

You have three ways to refer to time in Flash:

- The frame rate. This is usually too inaccurate for all but the most approximate time measurements because the frame rate depends highly on how much Flash is being asked to do.

- The `getTimer()` action (global function). The `getTimer()` action returns the number of milliseconds that have elapsed since the current movie started. It's very accurate but generates no events, so the usable accuracy is limited by how often you read the value.

- The `setInterval()` timed event. A `setInterval` is an event handler that runs at a defined rate. It can be useful when you want code to run periodically, such as every second. It can be much more useful than `getTimer()` because it generates events, making it easy to use, but it can also be less accurate if you use periodic intervals that are much less than the frame rate.

> The frame rate is the *maximum* rate at which Flash will run. If Flash is asked to do too much, the frame rate will drop from the requested frame rate considerably. Even if your movie isn't doing anything difficult, if the user opens another SWF, the other SWF may affect the frame rate in your SWF!

Open `questions01.fla` on the book's CD. This file contains a timed questionnaire. You have 20 seconds to answer four questions, starting from when you test the movie.

The code looks like this:

```
function counter() {
  var elapsedTime = 20-Math.floor((getTimer()-startTime)/1000);
  countdown.text = elapsedTime;
  if (elapsedTime == 0) {
    delete this.onEnterFrame;
    marker();
```

```
      }
    }
    //
    function marker() {
      var mark:Number = 0;
      for (var i = 0; i<answers.length; i++) {
        if (this["a"+i].text.toLowerCase() == answers[i]) {
          mark++;
        }
        title.text = "Times up! You got "+mark+" questions correct";
      }
    }
    //
    //
    var startTime:Number = getTimer();
    var questions:Array = ["Who bought Macromedia in 2005",
        "What is Flash's scripting language called",
    "What is the default stage width (in pixels) in Flash",
        "Is setInterval() an event or global function"];
    var answers:Array = ["adobe", "actionscript", "550",
    "event"];
    for (var i = 0; i<questions.length; i++) {
      this["q"+i].text = questions[i]+"?";
    }
    this.onEnterFrame = counter;
```

If you test the movie, you'll see a countdown from 20 to 0, and you'll be marked on how many questions are correct when the counter reaches zero. The main code (the bottom of the script) initializes the variables. startTime holds the starting value of getTimer(). The questions and answers arrays hold exactly what their names suggest. The loop that follows the initialization shows the questions by populating the question text fields with the questions values. The last line of the script sets up a function counter as the onEnterFrame of the current Timeline (that is, the root Timeline).

> You can't assume that getTimer() will give you zero on the first frame of the movie because Flash may take a few milliseconds (around 10–20ms) to set itself up. This is why you read the value of getTimer() at the start of the code and hold this value in startTime rather than assume zero.

Every time the function counter runs, it reads the getTimer() value, converting it to whole seconds. The if statement in counter checks whether you have counted down to zero; if you have, the onEnterFrame is deleted, and you jump to the marker function to see how many correct answers were given.

Although this code works, it is inefficient. The counter updates every second, but you change it at the frame rate, and that means you update the timer 12 times a second. Updating a text field at the frame rate is guaranteed to make Flash run slowly, especially when the field contains a lot of text or when the text is large.

A more efficient solution is to use a `setInterval` event that runs every second. To set up a `setInterval`, you create a numeric variable and assign it to a `setInterval` using the `setInterval()` action (the number is the `setInterval`'s ID). This has at least two parameters: the function you want to call and the period at which you want to call it (in milliseconds). If you wanted to create a `setInterval` that ran your function, `counter`, every second, you'd use the following line to set it up:

```
var countInterval:Number = setInterval(counter, 1000);
```

To delete a `setInterval` event, you use `clearInterval()`, with the ID as the argument. Therefore, to delete `counterInterval`, you'd use this:

```
clearInterval(countInterval);
```

A modified version of the questions FLA is available for you as `questions02.fla` on the book's CD.

> You can use a `setInterval` event in animation when you want to make graphics move at a rate other than the frame rate, as discussed in Chapter 7.

Creating Links

One final feature of interactivity is the link, or *hyperlink*. In an HTML-based site, you create hyperlinks via the HTML <a>, or *anchor*, tag, and each link allows you to navigate to another web page.

Flash uses the `getURL()` action to perform much the same function as the HTML <a> tag. The `getURL()` action is usually included within the `onRelease` event of a button that you want to act as a link to an external web document or other file.

If you have a button on the current Timeline called `myLink_btn`, the following code will make it act like a link to the Sybex site:

```
myLink_btn.onRelease = function() {
  getURL("http://www.sybex.com/");
};
```

> The preceding code will work if you select the Test Movie option within the Flash authoring environment. If, however, you test this code in your default browser, the Flash 8 security model will not allow the link to work. You can get around this during local testing by exporting a Flash 7 SWF. Of course, this problem doesn't apply if you upload the SWF and test it online.

The preceding code will replace the current web page with the Sybex site. If you actually want the Sybex site to appear in a new browser window, you can use the following code:

```
myLink_btn.onRelease = function() {
    getURL("http://www.sybex.com/", "_blank");
};
```

As well as _blank, you can use _parent or _top. _parent opens the link in the parent to the current HTML frame, which is useful if your SWF is in a frameset and you want the new content to appear in the parent frame; however, it's usually unlikely you'd ever want this to happen. _top replaces the current top-level window in the current browser with the link, which is useful if your SWF is embedded within a frameset or other low-level subdocument, and you want the whole document to be replaced with the linked web page.

Figure 10.13

This code automatically fills an e-mail.

You can use the getURL() action to perform many of the tasks that a standard HTML <a> link can perform, including calling a JavaScript function or issuing a mailto request. A mailto request allows you to open an e-mail in the user's default mail program. The following event handler would make clicking myLink.btn open a blank e-mail addressed to the author of this chapter:

```
myLink_btn.onRelease = function() {
    getURL("mailto:boy@futuremedia.org.uk");
};
```

You can also add a message title and message body to the e-mail. The following code produces an e-mail with the default e-mail address, title, and message body that you'll see if you click the contact button on the www.futuremedia.org.uk website (see Figure 10.13):

```
myLink_btn.onRelease = function() {
    getURL("mailto:boy@futuremedia.org.uk?subject=howdy&body=Hi there
handsome...");
};
```

Working with Objects and Classes

In this chapter, you'll see what classes, objects, methods, and properties are in Flash ActionScript, and you'll learn how to use them in your code.

Although you can create code without knowing anything about classes, understanding what classes are will give you some insight into how ActionScript works internally (as well as give you some insight into how ActionScript is arranged, because it's arranged around classes), and in doing so, your understanding of ActionScript will increase considerably.

- Using ActionScript classes

- Creating and using objects

- Using methods and properties to work with objects

- Understanding the relationship between objects, methods, and properties

Classifying Elements in the Real World

If a friend were to tell you he has a dog, both of you would know he was talking about something that has fur, four legs, and a tail. How do you both know this?

You both know what a dog is because you have seen dogs before.

This is a good, sensible answer, but it doesn't explain how you both know that a cat is *not* a dog. After all, a cat has fur, four legs, and a tail. It's time for a better answer....

From the moment you are born, you classify everything you see so that you are able to build an internal model of the reality around you. This model may include a general template called Dog and another one called Cat. Whenever you see a four-legged animal, you compare that specific animal against the templates you already know in order to see which one fits best. This is how you can differentiate between cat and dog when you see a four-legged, furry animal with a tail.

Think about this model in relation to children; for example, children who have never seen horses may call them big dogs. The child is trying to classify the new animal using only the templates they already know.

As well as allowing you to recognize objects, internal templates also specify how things tend to *act* or *work*, so the Dog template usually tells you that dogs bark.

Computers need to interact with us, and to do that, they have to have enough knowledge of our reality to solve the questions we ask them. They may never need to know what cats, dogs, and horses are, but computers will need to answer other questions: What is a bank account? What is a number? What is a Movie Clip? Since computers can't learn these templates in the same way we can, we have to teach them what the elements that they need to interact with are.

Rather than allow the computer to learn these templates in the same way a child would, we create the templates for the computer through code definitions. With these templates, the computer can recognize everything it needs to solve the tasks we set for it. The computer thus uses the templates to recognize, create, and work with things such as bank accounts, numbers, and Movie Clips.

This process of using templates is called *classifying*, and each template is called a *class*. Each individual bank account or number would be an *object*.

Each object has two main parts:

- *Methods* are the code that specifies how the object *works* or *interacts* with other objects. For a bank account, methods can tell you how to open new bank accounts, add or remove money from the bank account, and how to lock a bank account if you suspect that illegal withdrawals are being made.

- *Object properties,* or simply *properties*, tell you what an object consists of or how it appears to you. For a bank account, such properties would include the bank account number and the bank account balance.

Understanding Programming Concepts

Although you can get by in Flash without knowing what an object or class is, understanding these core concepts will make learning ActionScript much easier. The reason for this is that Flash uses classes and objects to control most movie elements that are accessible through ActionScript.

Introducing Classes

A *class* describes (or *classifies*) a group of related elements. For example, the term *Aircraft* describes the set of man-made machines that can fly, hover, or glide. The class Aircraft is a template (class) that describes what an aircraft is and will tell you what wings, fuselages, cockpits, rotors, aero-engines, and flaps are. More generally, the class Aircraft might tell you the following:

- How to make an aircraft
- What an aircraft will look like
- What an aircraft can do once we have built one, how it will behave, and how well (or otherwise) it will fly

It's important to realize that the Aircraft class describes what an aircraft can do and what it consists of. The class isn't itself a real aircraft. You'll never see something named *aircraft* on a runway but will instead see individually named aircraft, such as *airforce1* (the U.S. president's jet) or *flight 324* (departing from JFK International Airport at 2:05 P.M. today). These individual aircraft are synonymous with objects.

Another important point is that computer languages are based around instructions—code tells a computer what to do. Thus, a typical computer's Aircraft class will mostly specify how to model an aircraft performing tasks. The templates (classes) you have in your head relating to Aircraft are much richer than the ones a computer needs, because you need to know what an aircraft actually is; a computer won't, for example, need to know how the Wright brothers are related to aircraft, and a computer will not know you don't need to use an aircraft to travel to the local grocery store.

Introducing Objects/Instances and Type

An object is a single "thing." If you were creating objects through the Aircraft class, your "thing" would be an Aircraft object.

Flash often uses the term *instance* instead of *object*. Both have the same meaning (and you can use either), but in Flash it's usually better to use the term *instance* unless you have a compelling reason to do otherwise.

It's better to use the term *instance* in Flash instead of *object* for at least two reasons. First, the object name is always called the *instance name* in Flash, and "an instance with the instance name myClip" sounds more logical than "an object with the instance name myClip." Second, one Flash class is called Object (notice the capital O). If you use *object*, you can sometimes get confused between Object and *object*, especially when starting out in ActionScript. You're much less likely to be confused if you use Object and *instance*.

You create an instance via a special method called a *constructor function*, and you can call this constructor through the keyword new. To create a new instance, you need to tell the constructor at least the name of the instance you want to create. This name is called the *instance name*.

For example, if you wanted to create a new Aircraft instance with the instance name airforce1, you would do something like this:

```
var airforce1 = new Aircraft();
```

The process of creating an object via a class constructor function is known as *instantiation*.

Often, it's useful to keep track of the class used to create an object. You can do this by assigning *type*. Type simply tells you to which class an object belongs. For example, airforce1 is an Aircraft, so you could say, "airforce1 is an object of type Aircraft."

Type is usually assigned at instantiation. If you wanted to define type as you created airforce1, you would modify the line to read as follows:

```
var airforce1:Aircraft = new Aircraft();
```

The first Aircraft is assigning type, and the second one is telling you which class (or more correctly, which constructor function) you want to use to create airforce1. The way you end up stating the class name twice in the instantiation process can be confusing to beginners, especially because type is often the same as the class name. It's worth noting that they can be different in advanced ActionScript.

In Flash, it's customary to stick to a naming system whereby classes always start with a capital letter and instance names always start with a lowercase letter. Thus, good class names would include Aircraft, MovieClip, and Number, and good instance names would include aircraft6, blueInvader, and numberOfToys.

Using lowercase for instance names is fine until you want to use multiple words as a variable name, such as *number of toys*. Variable names can't contain spaces, and *numberoftoys* isn't very legible. Flash developers tend to capitalize the start of each word, so that gives you numberOfToys as the variable—it doesn't have spaces, but it remains legible. This type of capitalization is sometimes referred to as camelCase because of the "humps" created by the capital letters.

Type is an example of an ActionScript concept that becomes much easier to understand once you know about classes and objects. As you have just seen, type is simply something that tells you what class was used to create each object. If you didn't know what a class was, you would have to use a much more cumbersome definition of type that used terms such as *data* and *datatypes*. This would make the discussion much more complex. So remember, although the concept of classes and objects may seem a bit difficult at the moment, it's the only tough concept you have to learn to understand most of ActionScript quickly and easily. Once you understand classes, a lot of other seemingly difficult concepts suddenly become easy!

Introducing Methods

A class defines what something is, and it can also specify how that something will work via its *methods*.

A method is simply a piece of code that allows you to make the class perform some task. The Aircraft method fly() would specify the aerodynamics of each Aircraft instance and would be able to tell you how far and how high an Aircraft instance would be able to fly.

Introducing Properties

An F-16 looks different from a paper airplane, and both look different from a helicopter. However, all three come from the same class—machines that fly, or Aircraft. The reason all three can be different yet be from the same class is because of *properties*.

Properties are values associated with an instance. These values specify quantities and attributes associated with each instance.

The Aircraft class will most likely specify a property called wings, but other properties will also be associated with the wings per instance. For example, numberOfWings might be a property that specifies how many wings the object has (two for the F-16 and paper airplane and zero for a helicopter). Other properties might relate to wing color, size, thickness, drag, lift, and so on. Obviously, a paper airplane will fly differently than an F-16. By feeding the properties (and other values) of these two aircraft into the methods, you can use the physical differences specified by the properties to also modify the values that are returned from the methods. For instance, you can do the following:

- The method for calculating maximum speed would come out high for the F-16, because it has properties specifying a higher power, thrust, and size.

- The paper airplane would have a zero thrust property, and the methods relating to its flight would pick this up in their calculations, resulting in an `Aircraft` instance that *glides*.

- The methods used for calculating whether the `Aircraft` instance would be able to down an enemy warplane would return a low value for the paper airplane because its properties (no armament and very little in the way of dog-fighting ability) suggest it would not be great in a fast-turning, supersonic duel.

Properties can themselves be instances of other classes. For example, the `Aircraft` property `numberOfWings` would be a number, but Flash doesn't know what a number is unless a corresponding Number class exists, which, luckily, it does.

Phew! That was a lot of information to take in, so the following list is a recap of what you have learned so far:

- An object is a useful element you want the computer to know about. Most elements you want a computer to know about relate to information needed to solve a task rather than to real and physical entities. In Flash, objects include items such as Movie Clips and buttons. Flash uses the term *instance*, which is the same as *object*.

- A class (as in *classify*) is a template that allows you to create objects. A class tells Flash what each object should have and look like (properties) and what it can do (methods).

- The process of creating an instance is called *instantiation* and is performed via a special method called the *constructor function* that is invoked through the new keyword.

- Flash can remember the relationship between a class and instance after instantiation via *type*. Type tells you what class was used to create the object.

You'll now see how classes, objects, properties, and methods work in Flash.

Using Flash's Built-in Classes

The easiest classes to use in Flash are the built-in classes (also called *native classes* or *default classes*). To use them, you don't have to know how to create the associated class because Macromedia has already done that for you; you just have to know how to create and use instances.

> Flash also allows you to create your own classes, but for the purposes of this chapter, you'll stick to using the built-in classes.

Using Properties

You already know all about Movie Clip symbols, but Flash also has a MovieClip built-in class. Looking at the MovieClip class is useful because the results of method calls and property changes affect the visual appearance of the instance.

To use MovieClip properties to control a Movie Clip:

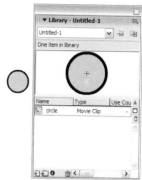

1. Select the Oval tool from the Toolbox. Select Object Drawing mode by selecting the appropriate icon in the Toolbox's Options section. Draw a circle with color and fill colors of your choice.

2. Select the circle by clicking it. Change it into a Movie Clip by pressing F8 or selecting Modify → Convert to Symbol. Name the Movie Clip symbol **circle** (see Figure 11.1). Note that *circle* is the symbol name and not the instance name.

3. Test the movie. You'll see the circle just sitting where you drew it on the Stage.

   A Movie Clip without an instance name is like a person in a busy office whose name you don't know—you'll find it difficult to ask this person to do anything. Before you can tell them to do anything efficiently, you need to be able to *address* them, and you do this via a name. As you have probably guessed, in Flash, this name is the instance name. You'll now give the Movie Clip an instance name so you can start ordering it to perform tasks.

4. Exit the movie. Open the Properties tab of the Property Inspector, and click in the field currently containing `<instance name>`. Inside this field, enter the text **myClip** (see Figure 11.2).

5. Before adding code to control the Movie Clip, you can better understand the concept by doing it manually via the Debugger, a feature of Flash that allows you to debug your SWFs at runtime. Select Control → Debug Movie. You'll see the Debugger appear (see Figure 11.3). Click the Continue icon (toward the top-right edge of the Debugger). This starts the debug session. Next, select the Movie Clip called `_level0.myClip` in the top-left pane. This pane is the Display list. It shows all Movie Clips currently being displayed on the Stage. Finally, select the Properties tab in the pane directly below the Display list (the Debug pane).

Figure 11.1

Change the circle symbol to a Movie Clip, and give it a name.

Figure 11.2

Add the instance name using the Property Inspector.

> You'll also use the Display list in the next chapter, when you look at the relationship between multiple Timelines.

The Debugger is now showing all the properties of your Movie Clip. The Debug pane allows you to change these directly, thus allowing you to see how the properties of `myClip` relate to the `myClip` instance.

6. The first property listed in the Debug pane is `_alpha`. Change this property's value from 100 to 25 by double-clicking the current value 100, entering **25**, and then clicking outside the field for the value to be accepted. (You can't simply press Enter for

the value to be accepted in the Windows version of Flash.) You'll see the alpha of the Movie Clip change from 100 to 25 percent; the clip is now partially transparent (see Figure 11.4).

7. Further down the Debug pane you'll see the _y property. Change the value of this property by adding 20 to the current value. You'll see the Movie Clip move down by 20 pixels.

Leave your FLA open. You'll use it again in the next section.

The grayed-out properties in the Debugger are ones you can't change (they are read-only). Also, some properties begin with an underscore. This is for purely historic reasons (in earlier versions of Flash all properties began with an underscore), and the underscore has no special significance.

Figure 11.3

You can use the Debugger to view your code.

The Properties tab of the Debug pane

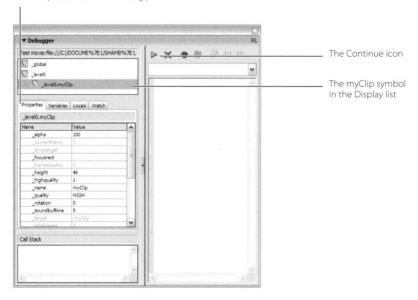

The Continue icon

The myClip symbol in the Display list

Figure 11.4

The circle to the left shows the original clip. The one to the right shows the effect of changing the _alpha property to 25.

Although the changes look pretty underwhelming, you have actually seen an important concept—that changing properties of a Movie Clip changes the appearance and position of the Movie Clip. For example:

- If you wrote code that changed the _alpha value by one per frame, you would end up with a fade effect.
- If wrote code that changed the _y value by one pixel every frame, you would see movement and animation.

You can perform the same task with tweens, but the effects of performing the same tasks with code are numerous:

- With code you can change the animation at runtime. This is how a space invader controlled by ActionScript can change its animation in a video game so that it appears to respond to your inputs.
- Code-driven animation is usually easier to change than tweens.
- Code is more bandwidth friendly than tweening, especially when you have a lot of separate animations.
- With code you can animate hundreds of Movie Clips, allowing you to create a large number of animated effects that are just not possible through tweening.

As you'll see, it's easy to change a property every frame. For now, though, experiment with the other available properties in the Debug pane to see what each one does. Learning what each property does in this way is good because you'll see what happens firsthand.

Although this "changing properties changes the appearance of the Movie Clip" deal seems obvious for the MovieClip class, it can be less obvious for other classes (such as XML and XMLNode, two classes concerned with sending, receiving, and reading XML documents). This is because most Flash classes have no graphic appearance (in fact, only a few classes have a graphic appearance, the most obvious being MovieClip, Button, and TextField). In classes with no visual appearance, the class is designed to control *data*, and changing properties changes the following:

- The data held in the instance
- What the data held in the instance represents
- How the data will be handled

This isn't to say that MovieClip, Button, and TextField are special cases in some way. All three classes are identical to all other classes in that they are designed to handle only data. However, Flash represents this data graphically for these three classes.

Knowing what each of the MovieClip class's properties do to a Movie Clip instance is important when mastering Flash because they are key to learning scripted animation. If you want to look at the Flash documentation to see exactly what each property does as you play with the Debug pane, you can do so via the following:

- Press F1 to open the Help panel, and then select Language Reference (ActionScript & Components) from the drop-down list at the top-left corner of the panel.

- Open the ActionScript 2.0 Language Reference book (you'll see this on the left of the Help panel), and then open the ActionScript Classes book. Scroll down to MovieClip, and open that book by clicking it.

- On the right of the Help panel, you'll see the help page for the MovieClip class. Scroll down until you see the Property Summary table. This table gives you brief information about each MovieClip property (see Figure 11.5). For example, the entry for _alpha tells you this property contains the alpha value of a Movie Clip instance.

You can get more information about the _alpha property by either clicking the page icon labeled _alpha (the MovieClip._alpha property) or clicking the link in the Property column of the Property Summary table (see Figure 11.6).

Either way, you'll end up at the help page for the _alpha property.

It's instructive to spend some time looking at each of the properties of the MovieClip class and using the Debugger to manually change each property and see the effect.

Properties that can be either true or false (such as the _visible property) can't be set in the Debugger by entering the obvious values, true/false. Instead, enter **0** for false and **1** for true.

Changing properties through code is simple; you use dot notation. As well as allowing you to access properties, dot notation allows you to start using methods as well.

Figure 11.5

You can view the property summary for the MovieClip class via the Help panel.

Modifiers	Property	Description
	_alpha:Number	The alpha transparency value of the movie clip.
	blendMode:Object	The blend mode for this movie clip.
	cacheAsBitmap:Boolean	If set to true, Flash Player caches an internal bitmap representation of the movie clip.
	_currentframe:Number [read-only]	Returns the number of the frame in which the playhead is located in the movie clip's timeline.
	_droptarget:String [read-only]	Returns the absolute path in slash-syntax notation of the movie clip instance on which this movie clip was dropped.

Figure 11.6

Click the link in the Property Summary table to get more information about a property.

Property summary

Modifiers	Property	Description
	_alpha:Number	The alpha transparency value of the movie clip.
	blendMode:Object	The blend mode for this movie clip.

Accessing Methods/Properties with Dot Notation

So far you know the general relationship between classes, objects (instances), methods, and properties, but you don't know how to reflect that structure in ActionScript. In ActionScript (and in fact, in most modern computer languages), the structure is represented as a *path*.

Consider the file system on your computer hard drive. Let's say you have a Windows XP computer, and the folder that contains the Flash program is the Flash 8 folder. This folder is defined by the folder pathname `C:\Program Files\Macromedia\Flash 8`. The pathname is simply a set of directions to the Flash 8 folder: "In the C: hard drive, open the folder Program Files, then open the folder Macromedia, and finally open the folder Flash 8." The Windows file explorer shows the same path graphically as a *tree*, as shown in Figure 11.7. The tree shows you that the Flash 8 folder is inside the Macromedia folder, and the Macromedia folder is inside the Program Files folder. Finally, the Program Files folder is on the C drive.

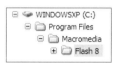

Figure 11.7

Windows shows a folder's path graphically as a tree diagram.

Dot notation is similar to a file path in that it too defines a path. Instead of a backward slash (\) to delimit the different parts of the path, a dot path (unsurprisingly) uses a dot (.). The path to the Movie Clip `myClip` is simply as follows:

```
myClip._alpha
```

To assign this property a value, simply use the assignment operator (=):

```
myClip._alpha = 50;
```

To add this line to the FLA so far:

1. In your FLA, add a new layer called **actions**, placing it above the current layer (see Figure 11.8).

2. Select frame 1 of the actions layer, and press F9 / Opt+F9 to open the Actions panel. In it, add the following line of code, and then test the movie in debug mode (see Figure 11.9):

   ```
   myClip._alpha = 50;
   ```

Figure 11.8

Add the actions layer above the current layer.

3. As soon as you click the Continue icon in the Debugger, you'll see the Movie Clip alpha value. If you look at the `_alpha` property in the Debugger, you'll see it's now 50.

4. You can also access methods in the same way. Back in the FLA, change the line of code as follows:

   ```
   myClip.startDrag();
   ```

   The `startDrag()` method makes the Movie Clip instance draggable.

5. Test the movie. As you move the mouse, you'll see that `myClip` changes position to keep up with it.

   You can see how `startDrag()` performs this animation by debugging the movie.

Figure 11.9

Use the Actions panel to add the line of code.

6. Test the movie in debug mode. Click the Continue icon, and look at the _x and _y properties of myClip. You'll see that as the Movie Clip moves, these properties also change.

The startDrag() method changes the _x and _y properties of myClip. By using startDrag() instead of varying the _x and _y properties, you save considerable time, and that is why methods are so useful—they are predefined functions that address common requirements, such as making Movie Clips draggable.

> You can learn more about the methods and events used in this example by searching for them in the Help panel (in much the same way as you found information about the _alpha property).

This has a problem, though—the startDrag() method currently runs when you call it, but you would prefer it to run as soon as the user clicks myClip. Special methods called *events* allow you to do this. *Event handlers* are functions that don't run when you call them but when a predefined event (such as "someone just clicked me") occurs. The event you need is called onPress.

7. Change the code as follows, and then test the movie:

```
myClip.onPress = function() {
        myClip.startDrag();
};
```

The Movie Clip myClip is now clickable. (You can tell this is so because the mouse cursor turns into a hand when you roll over it.) If you click myClip, the function block associated with myClip.onPress (that is, the lines of code between {and}) will execute, thus starting the drag.

If you wanted to stop dragging when the user releases the mouse, you would use the onRelease and onReleaseOutside event handlers.

8. Change the code as follows, and then test the movie:

```
myClip.onPress = function() {
        myClip.startDrag();
};
myClip.onRelease = function() {
  myClip.stopDrag();
};
myClip.onReleaseOutside = function() {
  myClip.stopDrag();
};
```

So now you have some simple drag-and-drop functionality. Cooler still, you didn't actually have to write the drag-and-drop code! You didn't have to look at the mouse states or work out whether the mouse is over the Movie Clip, and you didn't have to write the animation code that makes the Movie Clip change position to keep up with the mouse. All you did was use some predefined methods.

Handling Data with Built-in Classes

The MovieClip class is cool because its methods and properties cause changes that are immediately obvious on-screen. Other classes are concerned with something that is invisible and works behind the scenes: data. Although they may seem less interesting, the classes concerned with data are as important (if not more so) because they allow your ActionScript to perform *really* cool tasks such as the following:

- Structure your data so that you can solve complex problems
- Provide a large number of methods that you can use instead of having to write your own code

Flash has a large number of data classes. The three most common types of data you'll use in Flash are numbers, strings, and arrays (lists).

You can use the Number and String classes to create instances that contain numerical and string (textual) values. You can use the Array class to hold lists.

Number (and Math)

To create (instantiate) a Number instance called `myNumber` (and using typing), you would use the following:

```
var myNumber:Number = new Number();
```

To assign the number with an initial value of 10 at the same time as creating it, you can use either of the following lines:

```
var myNumber:Number = new Number(10);
var myNumber:Number = 10;
```

Rather paradoxically, you'll get more robust code if you use the shorter version of the two lines. Only the second version checks that the value you're assigning (10) is actually a number.

Although the Number class has a few properties, you're unlikely ever to need them. You're more likely to use another class, Math, to work with numbers. The `Math` class contains a large number of useful mathematical functions. The Math class has no constructor, so you can't create new instances of the Math class. Instead, you reference the Math class directly.

A class that has no constructor is called a *static* class. You typically create static classes when you need only one instance, and this "instance" is the class itself. Other good examples of static classes are Mouse and Stage. Because you have only one mouse and one Stage in Flash, both these classes are static.

One method of the Math class that is often used with numbers is `Math.random()`. It returns a random number value from 0 to 1. Random values are useful because they allow you to make the animations run in a nonlinear way.

To make Flash generate a random number, open a new FLA, and attach the following lines of code to the first frame of the root Timeline:

```
var randomNumber:Number = Math.random();
trace(randomNumber);
```

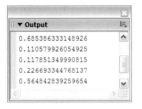

Figure 11.10

You can generate random numbers; check out the results in the Output panel.

Test this movie several times by pressing Ctrl+Enter. Each time you do this, you'll see a random number appear in the Output panel (see Figure 11.10).

Numbers from 0 to 1 aren't normally useful, and you'll typically need larger and/or integer values. The following code will generate a number from 0 to 5:

```
var randomNumber:Number = Math.random()*5;
trace(randomNumber);
```

The following code will generate a number from –5 to 5:

```
var randomNumber:Number = Math.random()*10-5;
trace(randomNumber);
```

You can, of course, also use random numbers to control the position of a Movie Clip (you'll see this in action in the next chapter).

Random numbers are often used in advanced scripted animation. For example, in a Flash space invaders game, you would use random numbers to vary where (and when) each space invader moves. Doing this makes each game different (even if the player performs the same actions), and this tends to make the game more challenging.

Some methods require arguments. Arguments are simply values that the method uses as part of its execution. For example, if you need a whole integer only, you can use Math.round(), Math.ceil(), or Math.floor(). These three methods take a number as their argument and round it to the nearest, next-highest, and next-lowest number, respectively.

The following code will round the number 3.75 to the nearest integer number (4):

```
var roundedNumber:Number = Math.round(3.75);
trace(roundedNumber);
```

The following code will give a random integer from 1 to 6 (and would therefore be useful when building a Flash game that needs to simulate dice rolls):

```
var randomNumber:Number = Math.ceil(Math.random()*6);
trace(randomNumber);
```

You can find the math_examples.fla file, which contains all the previous Number and Math examples, on this book's CD.

String

To create a string instance called myString, use the following line of code:

```
var myString:String = new String();
```

Just as with the Number class, you can also define your string's value at the same time as instantiation:

```
var myString:String = "some text";
```

You can add strings to other strings, a process called *concatenation*. For example:

```
var myString1:String = "Hello";
var myString2:String = " there!";
trace(myString1+myString2);
```

This will output "Hello there!" to the Output panel.

For anything more complex than concatenation, you need to use the methods of the String class. For example, to turn a string to uppercase or lowercase, use the `String.toUpperCase()` and `String.toLowerCase()` methods. The following code will turn a string into lowercase:

```
var upperCase:String = "CHANGE ME TO LOWERCASE!";
var lowerCase:String = upperCase.toLowerCase();
trace(lowerCase);
```

Figure 11.11 shows the output of this code.

To change all but the first letter, you would have to use the `String.slice()` method to cut the string into two parts: "C" and "HANGE ME TO LOWERCASE!" Then you would change only the second part to lowercase. `String.slice` has two arguments:

```
String.slice(a, b);
```

The method cuts out a portion of text from the string, starting at (and including) character position *a* and ending at (but not including) character position *b* (NB—the first character is taken to be at position 0). If *b* is omitted, the last character position in the string is assumed for *b*.

Thus, the *C* is character 0, so you would get it with `upperCase.slice(0, 1)`, and the remainder of the string is `upperCase.slice(1)`.

The following code will give you the string output you want (see Figure 11.12):

```
var upperCase:String = "CHANGE ME TO LOWERCASE!";
var lowerCase:String = upperCase.slice(0,
1)+upperCase.slice(1).toLowerCase();
trace(lowerCase);
```

You can find the `string_examples.fla` file, which contains all the previous String examples, on this book's CD.

Typing

As soon as you start using a number of different data classes together in the same code, a big problem can arise. You can't see data classes, so it's possible to mix them up. In fact, this mixing up is actually much easier than it may seem.

Figure 11.11
The `String .toLowerCase()` method turns the string to lowercase.

Figure 11.12
The `String .slice()` method gives you the output you want.

For example, consider what would happen if you entered the following code:

```
var aNumber = new Number();
aNumber = "five";
trace(aNumber+1);
```

If you were to run this code, you would get the result "five1." Why?

Line 1 creates a new number, but line 2 assigns a string to it. You know "five" can be converted to the number 5, but Flash doesn't know that because it doesn't understand the English language—it simply assumes strings are sequences of characters, and Flash can't assign any meaning to them. Consequently, five is taken to be a string.

Flash has done nothing wrong here, but line 3 assumes aNumber is still holding a numeric value (because you are trying to add 1 to aNumber). Flash does the best it can under these conditions, but since computers tend to lack much in the way of good sense, it comes up with the rather nonsensical result "five1."

> Although nonsensical, the result is actually logical. Because aNumber is holding a string, Flash converts the 1 into the string value 1 and then uses string concatenation. This concatenation splices five and 1 together to give you "five1."

If the code was expecting a numerical result (such as "6"), you would have a serious bug, made all the more dangerous because Flash doesn't see it as a bug and raises no errors.

Typing overcomes this issue by specifying the type of data the instances can hold, therefore limiting the data you can assign to an instance to that type only. If you change line 1 to the following, the variable becomes typed:

```
var aNumber:Number = new Number();
```

When you do this, Flash raises an error (as shown in Figure 11.13) at line 2 because the type of the data you are trying to assign (String) is mismatched to the instance type you are trying to assign it to (Number).

Unless you *always* type all your instances at instantiation, Flash will not warn you about type errors.

You may be thinking, "Hey, what's so good about adding more code so that Flash can raise *more* errors?" Well, programming can be a tricky process at times (that is, when your code doesn't work, and when you don't know why it doesn't work), and the more help you get in these situations, the better! Getting Flash to check as much of your code as it can is always good. Also, it's worth noting that a script that runs without errors but has bugs is harder to fix than a script that refuses to run but forces Flash to tell you why it doesn't run!

Figure 11.13

Flash raises a type mismatch error with this code.

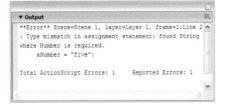

Although typing can seem like something that isn't necessary or useful, it becomes important as the size and complexity of your scripts increase. We strongly recommend you always
use typing. Typing is, of course, relevant to all classes, not just to strings and numbers.

Array

A String or Number instance can hold only one value. Often, you'll want to hold
several related values together in a list, and the class that allows this is called Array.

An *array* is simply a numbered list of elements (values). To create a new
Array instance, you use the new constructor as before:

```
var myArray:Array = new Array()
```

To define values for an array during instantiation, use a comma-delimited list
of values, enclosed by [ ] brackets:

```
var beatles:Array = ["John", "Paul", "George", "Ringo"];
```

To access any value in the array, you use an *index*, with zero as the first entry. Thus, 'John'
is entry 0 and 'Ringo' is entry 3. To access the first and third Beatle in the list (John and
George), you would use the following:

```
trace(beatles[0]);
trace(beatles[2]);
```

Although tracing arrays is useful, it can become confusing when you have
arrays with lots of data in them. A better alternative is to use the Debugger.
Assuming you've entered the previous code, attaching it to frame 1 of a new
FLA, your Debug pane would look like Figure 11.14. This view clearly matches
the indexes (that is, the numbers 0, 1, 2, 3, and 4 in the left column) with the
element values. Clicking the plus/minus signs next to the array name (left column)
allows you to open/close the array. (The Mac version uses triangles instead of
plus/minus signs.)

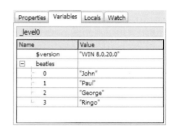

Figure 11.14

**View your Array
instance in the
Debugger.**

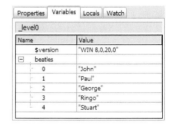

Figure 11.15

**You can add a
new element with**
`Array.push()`.

If you ever get confused by arrays, use the Debugger. We can't overstate its usefulness in
debugging incorrect indexes or incorrectly structured arrays!

Once you've created an array, you can add, delete, or sort elements within the array. To
add a fifth Beatle to the list, you can use the `Array.push()` method (see Figure 11.15):

```
beatles.push("Stuart");
```

To remove the last or first entry, you would use the `Array.pop()` or `Array.shift()`
method.

Arrays are especially useful when you want to apply the same action to many values. For example, suppose you were having a sale and wanted to reduce everything in your store by 50 percent. One way to do this would be to multiply each price by 0.5:

```
var price1:Number = 56.50;
var price2:Number = 22.82;
var reduction:Number = 0.5;
price1 = price1*reduction;
price2 = price2*reduction;
trace(price1);
trace(price2);
```

This is cool if you have a store that sells only two items, but what if you had ten items? The code would become repetitive and wasteful!

Using an array of prices and looping through each element in the array is the answer:

```
var prices:Array =
[56.52, 22.82, 6.26, 25.68, 99.56, 220.58, 430.98, 560.12, 0.52, 21.02];
var reducedPrices:Array = [];
var reduction:Number = 0.5;
trace(prices);
for (var i = 0; i<prices.length; i++) {
  reducedPrices[i] = prices[i]*reduction;
}
trace(reducedPrices);
```

Line 1 defines the ten original prices, placing them in the array prices. Line 2 defines a second array, reducedPrices, that you'll use to hold the reduced prices.

By equating reducedPrices to square brackets with nothing in them, you're defining it as an empty array.

These three lines form a loop that runs once for each array element in prices:

```
for (var i = 0; i<prices.length; i++) {
  reducedPrices[i] = prices[i]*reduction;
}
```

The Array.length property defines the length (number of elements), and you use the prices.length value in the loop to define how many times the loop will execute. The loop variable i will start at zero and increase by one on every loop iteration so that on subsequent iterations, the line within the loop becomes the following:

```
reducedPrices[0] = prices[0]*reduction;
reducedPrices[1] = prices[1]*reduction;
reducedPrices[2] = prices[2]*reduction;
```

This continues all the way to the last iteration, which will be as follows:

```
reducedPrices[9] = prices[9]*reduction;
```

You can find the two files, `array_example1.fla` and `array_example2.fla`, containing the previous Array examples on this book's CD.

Arrays are also a good way of sorting values. The `Array.sort()` method is a quick way of doing this, and adding the following lines would sort the reduced prices in ascending numeric order (see Figure 11.16):

```
reducedPrices.sort(Array.NUMERIC);
```

Once sorted numerically, you can pick out the highest and lowest reduced price by looking at the first and last element in the array:

```
trace("Lowest price: "+reducedPrices[0]);
trace("highest price: "+reducedPrices[reducedPrices.length-1]);
```

You can find the `array_example3.fla` file, which contains this example, on the book's CD.

Note that you use the value `reducedPrices.length-1` (which works out as $10 - 9 = 9$) to determine the index of the last element, rather than just sticking in the value 9.

Using the `Array.length` property is much more useful than assuming a literal value in your code (such as 9), because as the array grows and shrinks, the element with index length – 1 is *always* the last element.

Another use of arrays is as lookup tables. For example, the Date class allows you to get the date and time (as specified by your computer's internal clock).

To create and view the date and time, open a new FLA, and attach the following script on frame 1 of the root Timeline:

```
var aDate:Date = new Date();
trace(aDate);
```

As of this writing, this code results in the output "Tue Nov 22 22:26:22 GMT+0000 2005." The day and month are abbreviated to Tue and Nov, but what if you needed to show the full version of the date Tuesday, November 22, 2005?

Dates are usually shown in one of two formats. In the United States mm/dd/yyyy is used, whereas in the United Kingdom dd/mm/yyyy is used. When you're designing sites for a global audience, it therefore makes sense to show dates in full.

You can get the current day, date, and month by using the `Date.getDay()`, `Date.getDate()`, `Date.getMonth()`, and `Date.getFullYear()` methods of the Date class.

Figure 11.16

This is the reduced-Prices **array follow-ing a numeric sort.**

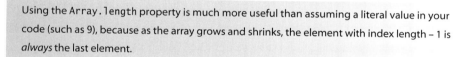

reducedPrices	
0	0.26
1	3.13
2	10.51
3	11.41
4	12.84
5	28.26
6	49.78
7	110.29
8	215.49
9	280.06

You can, of course, see the full details of these methods by looking up the Date class in the Help panel.

You can use these four methods to get the raw day, date, month, and year via the following listing:

```
var aDate:Date = new Date();
var day:Number = aDate.getDay();
var date:Number = aDate.getDate();
var month:Number = aDate.getMonth();
var year:Number = aDate.getFullYear();
trace(day);
trace(date);
trace(month);
trace(year);
```

Figure 11.17 shows the expected output.

The output certainly doesn't constitute a very readable date! The day value given is 2, the date is 22, the month is 10, and the year is 2005. Only the date and year look right for the expected date (Tuesday, 22nd November, 2005).

The Date.getDay() method returns a number from 0 to 6, with 0 = Sunday and 6 = Saturday, so Tuesday = 2. The Date.getMonth() method returns a number from 0 to 11, with January = 0 and December = 11, so the month at the time of this writing, November, is 11.

You can convert the numbers you see into what you actually want to see by using the numbers as indexes into a lookup table.

You'll look at the code first, and then I'll explain it:

Figure 11.17

You can get the raw date values using the Date.getDay(), Date.getDate(), Date.getMonth(), and Date.getFullYear() methods.

```
var months:Array =
["January", "February", "March", "April", "May",
"June", "July", "August", "September", "October",
"November", "December"];
var days:Array = ["Sunday", "Monday", "Tuesday",
"Wednesday", "Thursday", "Friday", "Saturday"];
var dates:Array = ["st", "nd", "rd", "th", "th", "th",
"th", "th", "th", "th", "th", "th", "th", "th", "th",
"th", "th", "th", "th", "th", "st", "nd", "rd", "th",
"th", "th", "th", "th", "th", "th", "st"];
var aDate:Date = new Date();
var day:Number = aDate.getDay();
var month:Number = aDate.getMonth();
var date:Number = aDate.getDate();
var year:Number = aDate.getFullYear();
var fullDate:String = days[day]+", "+months[month]+
" "+date+dates[date-1]+", "+year+".";
trace(fullDate);
```

For those who don't want to type in the above code, the date_example.fla file on this book's CD contains the example.

You define three Array instances at the top of the code: months, days, and dates. If you look at the 11th element of months, you see November. Similarly, you can convert the 2 you see from Date.getDay() into Tuesday by looking at days[2], which equals Tuesday. The dates array allows you to work out the letters that appear after the date, as in 1**st**, 2**nd**, 3**rd**, 4**th**, and so on.

Using the three arrays allows you to convert the numbers into a meaningful string, in this case, "Tuesday, November 22nd, 2005." Better still, this example uses everything you've learned so far in this chapter—you use strings (for the concatenation), numbers (for the indexes), and arrays (for the lookup tables), plus you're using your knowledge of how classes, instances, methods, and properties work to use a class you previously knew nothing about (Date)!

Once you know about classes, objects, methods, and properties and use them for one class, you'll find no real surprises if you try to learn another class, because the underlying structure is the same. This is why learning about classes is an important part of learning ActionScript.

Learning about classes is also more important for Flash 8 than in previous versions of Flash, because the Help panel's entries are sorted by class. Once you know about classes and about how methods and properties are structured underneath them, reading the help pages becomes much easier, because you know how (and why) they are arranged the way they are.

In the next chapter, you'll look at some of the other pieces of the ActionScript puzzle when you look further into dot notation and a related concept called *scope*.

CHAPTER 12

Scripting for MovieClip Objects and Multiple Timelines

Almost everything you build in Flash will consist of multiple Timelines. Knowing the best way to use ActionScript to manage multiple and nested Timelines is one of the defining features of a competent ActionScript-savvy designer. In this chapter, you'll examine what nested Movie Clips look like to ActionScript and the different ways you can access and control nested Timelines.

- ■ **Nesting Movie Clips**

- ■ **Working with multiple Timelines**

- ■ **Duplicating and attaching Timelines**

- ■ **Dynamically loading Timelines**

- ■ **Detecting collisions and simulating different types of motion**

Using Nested Movie Clips

When creating tweened animation in Flash, using nested Movie Clips is a common technique. Using nested clips allows you to create *nested animation*. For example, you could have an animation of a car moving from left to right. Nested inside the car clip would be other Movie Clips containing animated spinning wheels. The wheels would move with the car as they spin, because they're nested inside the car.

ActionScript-based sites also use nested Movie Clips for animation—and for much more besides. Common applications of nested Movie Clips include the following:

Using Movie Clips as "pages" It's often desirable to build sites using Movie Clips that act as content holders or pages. Each such Movie Clip will typically contain nested Movie Clips that make up the actual page content. This type of nesting is useful because it allows you to build different types of navigation—running the Timeline that the page clips are on allows you to navigate between pages, whereas running the Timeline of a page Movie Clip allows you to navigate within an individual page's content.

Building and targeting content hierarchies Many ActionScript classes control Timelines rather than everything on the Stage. For example, you can use the Color class to control the color of all the content on a Timeline. By separating your content into Timelines that contain the content you *do* and *don't* want to be affected by color changes, you can decide exactly which content is affected.

Using components Components are an advanced form of Movie Clip that allow you to create "off-the-shelf" versions of commonly used elements, such as scroll bars, drop-down menus, alert boxes, and radio buttons. Knowing about nested Movie Clips is also often helpful when you're using components (because you often have to build complex user interfaces using many nested, simpler components).

In all these cases, you need to know how to make your ActionScript control Movie Clips on Timelines other than the one the ActionScript is on. To do this effectively, you need to know three key issues, which we will discuss in this chapter:

- Understanding the hierarchy of nested Movie Clips (the *parent*, *this*, and *child* Timelines) and how to view the hierarchy graphically via the Debugger.

- Understanding how to access and control (or *target*) nested Timelines through ActionScript.

- Understanding the relative path terms `_parent` and `this`

Also, a subtler reason exists for needing to know how to control nested Movie Clips through ActionScript. Most commercial site designs that use ActionScript not only use nested Timelines but *require* them. You need at least a basic understanding of how to target Timelines to control the Flash environment through scripting. Using nested Timelines becomes even more important if you want to build more advanced scripted content such as Flash applications, advanced interfaces, or interactive Flash games.

Viewing Nested Timelines

The first step in understanding nested Timelines is to view them:

1. Open a new Flash document by selecting File → New.

2. On the Stage, use the Oval and Rectangle tools to draw a circle and square (see Figure 12.1). You can make your oval a circle and your rectangle a square by holding down the Shift key as you drag the shapes.

3. Select each of the two shapes in turn (you'll have to double-click the stroke on each shape if you didn't use Object Drawing mode; otherwise, you can just click once anywhere on the shape to select it). Press F8 to turn each into a Movie Clip symbol, naming the circle **circle** and the square **square**.

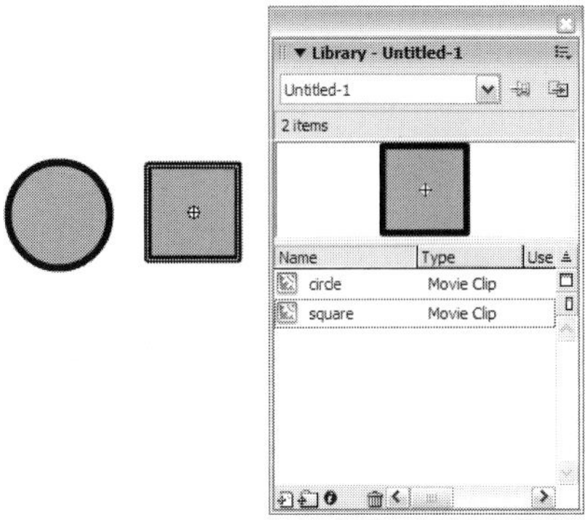

4. Select the `circle` symbol on the Stage. Using the Property Inspector, give the circle an instance name of **circleClip**. Do the same for the square, giving it a name of **square-Clip** (see Figure 12.2).

5. Test the movie in debug mode by pressing Ctrl+Shift+Enter / Cmd+Shift+Enter (or by selecting Control → Debug Movie). Once in debug mode, click the Continue icon (the green, right-pointing arrow toward the top right of the Debug panel).

> You used the Debugger in Chapter 11, so feel free to refer to that chapter if you have difficulty in using the Debugger.

6. Look at the top-left panel of the Debugger. This is the *Display list,* and it shows all the Movie Clips that are currently viewable on the Stage (see Figure 12.3).

   Each Timeline appears in the Display list with a labeled Movie Clip icon. The first Timeline is called `_global`, and below that is a second Timeline called `_level0`. The Timeline `_level0` is synonymous with the root Timeline of the SWF you're testing.

> Mac users may see the Timelines displayed in a different order. The order isn't crucial, so don't worry if you see the Timelines in a different order than described in this chapter.

On the `_level0` Timeline, you see the two Movie Clips you added to the Stage, `circleClip` and `squareClip`.

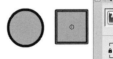

Figure 12.1

On the Stage, create a `circle` **Movie Clip and a** `square` **Movie Clip.**

Figure 12.2

Give an instance name of `square-Clip` **to the** `square` **Movie Clip.**

Figure 12.3

The Display list shows all the Movie Clips currently viewable on the Stage.

The _global "Timeline" isn't really a Timeline. It is a *scope*. You can safely ignore it for this chapter.

The important feature of the Display list to note is that it is a *tree diagram*. Tree diagrams are traditionally used to illustrate hierarchies, and that is just what the Timelines in a Flash movie are doing.

In this tree, circleClip and squareClip are children of the _level0 Timeline. In elementary terms, this means the two Movie Clips are inside (or "on") the _level0 Timeline. The tree is also displayed in terms of *dot paths*, something you started to look at in Chapter 11.

The labels for the four Timelines you see in the Display list are as follows:

- _global

- _level0

- _level0.squareClip

- _level0.circleClip

The dot path to squareClip and circleClip tells you that squareClip and circleClip are in the _root Timeline. If you have difficulty with this concept, it's worth considering the same sort of tree structure on your computer. In this case, the paths might be as follows:

- C:\

- C:\folder1

- C:\folder2

This tells you that both folders are in location C:\, or the root drive (assuming a typical Windows-based machine).

Let's continue with the exercise:

7. Close the Debug panel, and exit the Debugger.

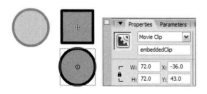

Figure 12.4

Embed the circle clip inside the square **symbol.**

8. Double-click the square Movie Clip on the Stage. This takes you into Edit in Place mode for the square Movie Clip symbol. Drag an instance of the circle Movie Clip onto the Timeline, placing it below the square (see Figure 12.4). Select the circle, and give it an instance name of **embeddedClip**.

9. Debug the movie by pressing Ctrl+Shift+Enter / Cmd+Shift+Enter.

10. Once you've started the Debugger (clicked the continue icon), you'll see the Display list (see Figure 12.5).

This time, an additional branch appears in the tree, showing an instance called embeddedClip inside squareClip. In Flash, another way of saying this is "squareClip is the *parent* of embeddedClip."

Figure 12.5

The updated Display list shows your new Movie Clips.

> Windows users can open and close branches in the Display list tree by clicking the plus (+) and minus (–) icons next to the Movie Clip icons. Mac users can perform the same task by clicking the triangles that appear.

11. Close the Debug panel, and exit the Debugger.

12. Back on the main Stage, enter Edit in Place mode by double-clicking the square Movie Clip on the Stage (if you're not already in Edit in Place mode).

13. Select frame 2 of the Timeline. Press F6 to add a new keyframe. Select the new keyframe. On the Stage, delete the circle. You should now have a circle instance on frame 1 but no circle on frame 2 (see Figure 12.6).

Figure 12.6

This is the square symbol's Timeline.

> If you're susceptible to quickly flashing graphics (or if you simply want to see the result of the next step occurring slowly so you can see it better), lower the frame rate before continuing with the next step. You can access the document properties (which contain the frame rate setting) by double-clicking the frame rate value at the bottom of the Timeline or by selecting Modify → Timeline.

14. Debug the movie again. When you start the Debugger, you'll see embeddedClip blink as it disappears and appears on the Stage. At the same time, you'll see the branch containing embeddedClip blink as it's added/removed from the Timeline of the square symbol.

15. Remove the keyframe you added in step 13 by selecting the keyframe and then selecting Edit → Timeline → Remove Frames. (Don't close the file just yet; you'll continue working with it in the next section.)

Although the Debugger is useful in seeing the nested Timelines within your movie, its use can be problematic at times, because it can become confusing if lots of Timelines are being added/removed. The Display list is, however, an important tool in seeing how your Movie Clips are arranged within your SWF, because you need to be aware of this structure before you can start to control it with ActionScript.

Targeting Timelines

You now have some insight into how Timelines are arranged in a tree, with _level0 at the tree's root (which is hence the reason why this Timeline is more commonly referred to as _root or as "the _root of the current SWF under test") and nested branches that represent the nested Movie Clips that exist on the Timeline.

You now need to start using this tree hierarchy so that your code can access/control (or target) individual Movie Clips within the tree. To be able to do this, you need to know about two types of dot path: absolute paths and relative paths.

Say you're giving a friend directions to an out-of-town store. If this person is your neighbor and asks you for directions before setting off, you'd give full directions for the complete journey, starting from their home. If your friend met you partway through their journey and wasn't sure of the directions for the rest of the journey, you'd give them directions starting from their current location. It's easier to give directions starting from the friend's current location if you can, because the directions would then be shorter, but if the friend called you and you didn't know where he was, the best option would be to give directions starting from home because they're the most complete set of directions you could give.

In Flash, "home" is the root Timeline, so an absolute path to a Movie Clip is one that starts from the root Timeline, and a relative path is one that starts from where your code is currently attached (or, more correctly, scoped).

Using Absolute Dot Paths

An absolute dot path is a path that starts at the root Timeline. If you refer to Figures 12.3 and 12.5, you'll see that the Debugger lists the absolute paths, because the dot paths next to the Movie Clips all start with the root Timeline (_level0 in this case).

To access a Movie Clip using dot paths, you can do one of the following:

- Work out what the dot path will be by looking at the Timelines your Movie Clip is on.
- Read the path from the Debugger's Display list.
- Let Flash work out the target path for you with the Insert Target Path icon.

Suppose you wanted to change the alpha property of embeddedClip to 25 percent. You can see from Figure 12.5 that the path to this Movie Clip is _level0.squareClip.embedded-Clip, so you could remember this and type it in your code. Unfortunately, as you can see, absolute dot paths tend not to be particularly memorable, and Flash never raises any errors if you get them wrong in your code.

It is, therefore, always a good idea to use the Insert Target Path icon:

1. Continuing with the file from the previous section, add a new layer in the main Timeline. Call this layer **actions**.

Insert Target Path icon

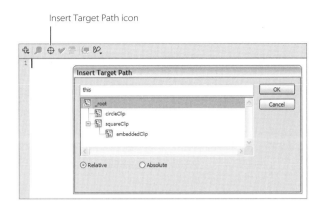

Figure 12.7

The Insert Target Path dialog box shows a tree of your Timelines for the current frame.

2. In the Actions panel, click the Insert Target Path icon. You'll see the Insert Target Path dialog box appear (see Figure 12.7).

   In the Insert Target Path dialog box, you'll see a tree view similar to the tree you saw in the Debugger. This tree represents the Timelines available to your ActionScript for the current frame.

3. Select `embeddedClip` (you may have to click the + next to `squareClip` to see `embedded-Clip`), then select the Absolute radio button at the bottom of the Insert Target Path window, and finally click OK.

   Flash will put the following code in the Actions panel:

   ```
   _root.squareClip.embeddedClip
   ```

4. To finish this line, add to the path as shown (don't forget the period in front of `_alpha`!).

   ```
   _root.squareClip.embeddedClip._alpha = 25;
   ```

5. Test the movie. You'll see that `embeddedClip` is now semitransparent, because you've set its alpha property to 25 percent (see Figure 12.8).

   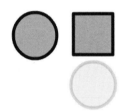

   Figure 12.8

   You changed the alpha of `embeddedClip`.

   It's worth stopping for a moment to recap what you've done here. The code is on the root Timeline, but through the use of a dot path, you've given the code "directions" on how to navigate through the Display list tree to find `embeddedClip`. The cool feature of this is that your code doesn't have to be attached to the Movie Clip it controls.

   Another cool feature scripted nested clips share with tweened nested clips is that nested clips do whatever their parent Movie Clip does. Recall the example given at the start of the chapter of a car Movie Clip with spinning wheel Movie Clips nested inside it. If you move the car clip, the wheels move. The same thing happens with nested ActionScript.

6. Add the following new line of code, as shown in Figure 12.9, and test the movie:

   ```
   _root.squareClip.embeddedClip._alpha = 25;
   _root._alpha = 25;
   ```

Figure 12.9

You now change the alpha of `_root`.

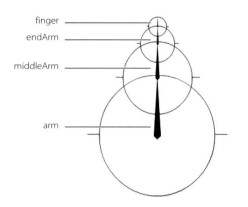

finger

endArm

middleArm

arm

Figure 12.10

**This is the arm's
four parts.**

7. The new line changes the alpha property of the _root Movie Clip to 25 percent. (Yes, the main Timeline is also a Movie Clip, and you can change its properties just like any other Movie Clip!) Unsurprisingly, all the Movie Clips on the root Timeline also reduce their alpha values, but notice that embeddedClip appears to have a lower alpha value than the others. Logically, it would have an alpha value of 25 percent × 25 percent, or 6.25 percent. If you retest in debug mode and check the _alpha property of embeddedClip (you learned how to do this in Chapter 11), you'll see that this Movie Clip has an alpha value of 25 percent, and the Movie Clips on the root Timeline have alpha values of 100 percent...yet they're semitransparent on the Stage!

8. Save your FLA; you'll be using it yet again later in the chapter.

Why does this happen? As an analogy, consider a Movie Clip representing a supersonic passenger aircraft cruising at, say, 450 miles per hour. If you were inside this aircraft and saw the drinks trolley wheeling toward you, the trolley would appear to be traveling much slower than 450 miles per hour. This is because you're on the same aircraft as the trolley, and you'll sense only the _relative_ motion. When the aircraft comes in to land, an observer would see the aircraft, you, and the drinks trolley all traveling at the speed of the aircraft.

In the same way, a Movie Clip doesn't "see" the alpha changes applied to its parent (that is, its alpha values won't change), although it will reflect the parent's alpha changes visually, because the Movie Clip is part of the parent.

For an example of nested ActionScript control, refer to arm1.fla on the book's CD. This shows how you can animate nested Movie Clips through ActionScript to produce effects that are just not possible any other way.

When you open the FLA, you'll see the "arm," which consists of four sections: arm, middleArm, endArm, and finger (see Figure 12.10).

The ActionScript that controls the arm is on layer actions on the main Timeline. The important lines to look at are the last four in this script:

```
_root.arm.onEnterFrame = armMover;
_root.arm.middleArm.onEnterFrame = armMover;
_root.arm.middleArm.endArm.onEnterFrame = armMover;
_root.arm.middleArm.endArm.finger.onEnterFrame = armMover;
```

As implied by this script, the following is true:

- finger is inside endArm.

- endArm is inside middleArm.

- middleArm is inside arm.

- arm is on _root.

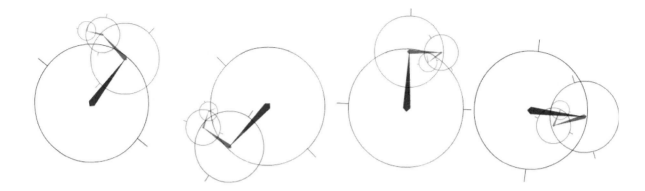

Figure 12.11
The arm motion is like a robot arm.

You have a function called armMover, and this is attached to each of the arm segment's onEnterFrame event. The function armMover simply rotates the arm segment it's attached to, changing the direction and speed of rotation randomly.

> The armMover function uses the this scope, something we haven't covered yet (but something we'll cover in the "Understanding scope and Timelines" section). Don't worry if you don't understand armMover just yet—you will by the end of this chapter!

If you test arm1.fla, you'll see that the arm segments move rather like an industrial robot arm (see Figure 12.11).

When you rotate arm, you also rotate middleArm, endArm, and finger. When you rotate middleArm, you also rotate endArm and finger; when you rotate endArm, you also rotate finger.

Another interesting fact about this script is that it will perform the same action wherever you put it. For example, refer to arm2.fla on the book's CD. This time, the script is attached to the Timeline of finger (the quickest way to get to the Timeline of finger is to double-click the finger symbol in the Library). Notice that no changes are made to the script at all—the script simply works from any Timeline!

This is a big advantage of using absolute paths—the script can run from anywhere. This is because all the paths start from _root, and the place where the script actually is doesn't matter.

Using Relative Paths

A *relative path* is one that starts from where the script is attached. To create a relative path (and assuming your code isn't an event handler—more about this later in the "Using the *this* path" section), you simply create a path starting from the Timeline your script is on.

Load the FLA you created earlier (the one with circle and square clips), and continue with these steps:

1. Select frame 1 of layer `actions` (the main Timeline). Remove the script currently attached by opening the Actions panel and deleting all the lines you see there.

2. Suppose you want to change the alpha of all `circle` Movie Clips to 25 percent. Still in the Actions panel (and with frame 1 of layer `actions` selected), click the Insert Target Path icon. Select `circleClip`, and leave the Relative radio button selected. Click OK. You'll see the following code at line 1:

   ```
   this.circleClip
   ```

3. Flash adds the `this` part of the path whenever you select a relative path, but it is required only if you're writing code inside an event handler (more about this later in the "Using the *this* path" section). So in this case, you can delete it. Change the line so it reads as follows:

   ```
   circleClip._alpha = 25;
   ```

4. Place the cursor at the start of the next line, and click the Insert Target Path icon a second time. This time, select `embeddedClip` (it's inside `squareClip`, so you'll have to press the + next to `squareClip` to see it). Leave the Relative radio button selected, and click OK.

5. Delete the `this` as before, and modify the line so you have the following code:

   ```
   circleClip._alpha = 25;
   squareClip.embeddedClip._alpha = 25;
   ```

Both the circles should be set to 25 percent alpha when you test the movie.

You can achieve the same result in an easier way:

1. Delete the code you just added.

2. Double-click the `circle` Movie Clip in the Library (double-click the icon, not the text) to edit this symbol.

3. Add a new layer called **actions**. Add the following code to frame 1 of this new layer, and test the movie:

   ```
   _alpha = 25;
   ```

You'll see the same result as before—both circle instances change alpha values. You've specified no path in front of `_alpha`, so Flash assumes the target is the current Timeline, which works out as all the `circle` Movie Clips.

Notice that this line of code affects *all* circle instances irrespective of where they are.

> The fact that your code affects all the instances can be a blessing because it leaves less work for you to do. Some Flash developers follow best practice rules that specify code should never be added to symbols in the Library. This is because you won't be sure what code you're introducing to the Stage when you drag a symbol from the Library.

Relative paths are usually better than absolute paths because they're more general. As an example of this, refer to arm3.fla on the book's CD.

This time, the code is in the arm symbol. You can see the code by double-clicking any of the instances on the Stage and looking at the code attached to the actions layer. The last four lines of this code are as follows:

```
onEnterFrame = armMover;
middleArm.onEnterFrame = armMover;
middleArm.endArm.onEnterFrame = armMover;
middleArm.endArm.finger.onEnterFrame = armMover;
```

These lines include relative paths, so the path starts from the current arm symbol. Thus, the armMover event handler is attached to all the arm segments in each arm. Since this code is in every instance, this will occur for every instance of the arm Movie Clip.

On the Stage of arm3.fla, no fewer than six instances of the arm Movie Clip appear, and if you test this FLA, you'll see that they *all* animate (see Figure 12.12). Urgh…it looks like a table full of still-twitching spider legs! The stuff of nightmares….

The reason this works is the same as the _alpha = 25 line you added to the circle clips earlier—the symbol contains this code, so every instance of the symbol is controlled by it.

Also, note that in arm3.fla each arm instance doesn't have an instance name—the code already knows which instance it needs to control—the one to which it's attached.

Understanding Parent-Child Timelines

So far, you've seen how to move forward (away from the root Timeline) through the Timeline hierarchy using relative paths. You don't know how to move back (toward the root Timeline). The way to do this is via the special path _parent.

A Movie Clip's parent Timeline is simply the Timeline it's inside.

Figure 12.12

The multiple arm motion is creepy!

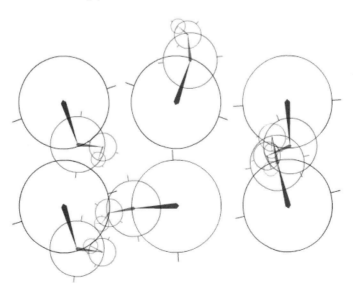

As an example of this, refer to `arm4.fla` on the book's CD. This FLA contains the same robot arm/detached-but-still-twitching-spider-leg effect, but the lines of code containing the paths (look in the finger Movie Clip to see the code) now look as follows:

```
onEnterFrame = armMover;
_parent.onEnterFrame = armMover;
_parent._parent.onEnterFrame = armMover;
_parent._parent._parent.onEnterFrame = armMover;
```

The first line attaches the event handler `armMover` to `finger`. The second line attaches the same event to `finger`'s parent, and the third line attaches it to `finger`'s parent's parent, and the fourth line…I guess you get the picture.

Cool, but does this have an advantage? Well, if you look at any of the arm segments on the Stage, you'll see that none of them has an instance name.

Although this may seem to be a small point, it has a major implication: you can access Movie Clips even if you don't know their instance names! Since any given Movie Clip has only one parent ever, Flash doesn't have to know the instance name (and the parent Movie Clip doesn't even have to have one!), making your code extremely general—it will work with *any* Movie Clip!

To access a Movie Clip without knowing its name:

1. Open a new Flash document.

2. Select Insert → New Symbol, and create a new Movie Clip symbol called **rotator**.

3. You'll now be in Edit symbol mode for `rotator`. Change the name of layer 1 to **actions**, and attach the following ActionScript to frame 1 of this layer:

```
_parent.onEnterFrame = function() {
  _parent._rotation += 10;
};
```

This code attaches an event handler to the parent Movie Clip of `rotator`, and this event handler will rotate the parent by adding 10 to its rotation property per frame.

So, what is the parent of rotator? *Any Movie Clip you put it inside!*

4. Return to the main Stage, and draw some shapes—they can be anything. Turn each shape into a Movie Clip (select the shape, and press F8). You can name each symbol anything you want.

5. Double-click each of the Movie Clips you've created (either on the Stage or in the Library). On frame 1 of each Movie Clip, drag an instance of `rotator` from the Library. The `rotator` clip has no appearance (it contains only code), and Flash's way of showing an empty clip is via a hollow circle. Note that you don't have to set any instance names during this process.

Actually, the hollow circle is the center point of rotator, and all Movie Clips have such a center point—it's just that for an empty clip, the center point is all you see! Since empty clips are hard to find unless you have them selected, you should put empty clips on their own layers. To select the empty clip, you can then lock all other layers and press Ctrl+A / Cmd+A.

6. Test the movie. You'll see all Movie Clips that you dropped rotator into will do just that—rotate! Exit, and test the movie.

7. As a grand finale, drop an instance of rotator onto the main Timeline. See if you can guess what happens before testing it…. You guessed it. Not only do the various Movie Clips rotate, but the whole SWF rotates!

8. Delete the instance of rotator on the main Timeline.

9. In the same way you created rotator, create a new empty Movie Clip called **fade in**, and in it attach the following script:

```
_parent._alpha = 0;
_parent.onEnterFrame = function() {
  _parent._alpha += 5;
  if (_parent._alpha>100) {
    _parent._alpha = 100;
    delete _parent.onEnterFrame;
  }
};
```

This script will set the alpha property of its parent to 0 (totally transparent) and then increase it to 100 (fully opaque) over time. The result is a fade-in transition—just the thing for the start of a website or every time a new page appears!

10. To fade in the movie, simply place an instance of fade in on the main Timeline.

That's a cool trick—small pieces of code can work on *any* Movie Clip via a simple drag and drop!

Using *targetPath()*

The targetPath() function returns the absolute path of an instance. To find out the path of a given instance myInstance, use this:

```
targetPath(myInstance);
```

The arm5.fla file on the book's CD is the same as arm1.fla, except that the following code has been added to each of the arm segment Movie Clips:

```
var myName:String = this._name;
var myLocation:String = targetPath(this);
trace("I am called "+myName+" and my path is "+myLocation);
```

When you test this FLA, you'll see the following in the Output panel:

I am called arm and my path is _level0.arm

I am called middleArm and my path is _level0.arm.middleArm

I am called endArm and my path is _level0.arm.middleArm.endArm

I am called finger and my path is _level0.arm.middleArm.endArm.finger

> Notice the order the added code executes in—from the arm toward the finger. In general, code attached to nested Movie Clips executes in the order least nested to most nested.

The `targetPath()` function seems pretty useful to know, until you realize its one big failing—to use it on a Movie Clip, you have to know where that Movie Clip is, so your code already knows the target path!

The `targetPath()` function is most useful when you're debugging code that doesn't seem to work. It's also useful when you want to know how Movie Clips are nested but can't see this in the Display list of the Debugger (because, for example, the Movie Clips don't stay on the Timeline long enough for you to use the Debugger).

You have one more topic to learn about before you move on from multiple Timelines—*scope.*

Understanding Scope and Timelines

Scope is perhaps one of the most feared concepts for nonprogrammers. They know it's important (because professional ActionScripters seem to say it almost as often as they breathe), but it isn't something many designers understand fully.

Most designers also know scope ties in to the `this` keyword, but that's even more unfathomable! Well, not to worry—we intend to explain both scope and `this` as simply and directly as possible.

Flash has three kinds of scope—Timeline scope, the `this` scope, and function scope. We'll tackle the first two in this chapter. We cover function scope in Chapters 7 and 9.

Understanding Timeline Scope

Timeline scope is simply "the Timeline you have to look in to find me." If you have a Movie Clip on the main Timeline, then the scope of that Movie Clip is the main Timeline. If a Movie Clip is in `_root.apple.pip`, then the scope of that Movie Clip is `_root.apple.pip`. This has two issues, though:

- You can have two Movie Clips with the same name but in different places.

- Once the Timeline that anything is scoped to is removed, that "anything" also gets removed.

Most e-mails we get from readers dabbling in ActionScript stem from these two issues. By this alone, Timeline scope is probably something you should spend time learning, because it will stop a lot of head scratching in the future.

To see Timeline scope in use:

1. Open a new Flash document. On the Stage, draw a small filled circle approximately 50 pixels in diameter.

2. Select the circle, make it a Movie Clip symbol, and call it **circle**.

3. Repeat the operation, creating a square this time, and call it **square**.

4. Create a new layer on the main Timeline, calling it **actions**. Your Stage and Timeline should now look like Figure 12.13.

5. In the Property Inspector, give the circle an instance name of **circleClip**, and give the square an instance name of **squareClip**.

6. Select frame 1 of the actions layer, and attach the following script to it:

```
speed = 5;
squareClip.speed = 1;
circleClip.speed = 3;
```

Figure 12.13

The Stage and Timeline looks like this after completing step 4.

This creates three variables:

• The first one is on the main Timeline and has a value of 5.

• The second is in squareClip and has a value of 1.

• The third one is in circleClip and has a value of 3.

We haven't used either typing or var to create these variables to keep this example simple and quick.

The twist is that all three variables have the same name, speed. Variables can be named the same as long as they're on different Timelines. You can see the variables by looking at them via the Debug panel.

7. Debug the movie by pressing Ctrl+Shift+Enter / Cmd+Shift+Enter (or by selecting Control → Debug Movie). Click the Continue icon on the Debugger to start debugging.

8. Below the Display list in the Debugger, you'll see four tabs. Select the Variables tab. Using the Display list, select _level0 (which, as you'll recall, is the main Timeline), circleClip, and squareClip in turn. Each time, you'll see the variables on each Timeline. In this case, you'll see the three variables, all with the name speed, and each with a different value (see Figure 12.14).

Figure 12.14

The Debugger shows the three speed variables.

The scope of each version of variable speed is the Timeline (Movie Clip) you have to select in the Display list to see it. If that Movie Clip disappears from the Display list, it's because the Movie Clip isn't there, and thus, neither is the associated variable.

9. Modify the listing by adding new lines as follows:

```
squareClip.onEnterFrame = function() {
  squareClip._y += squareClip.speed;
};
circleClip.onEnterFrame = function() {
  circleClip._y += circleClip.speed;
};
//
speed = 5;
squareClip.speed = 1;
circleClip.speed = 3;
```

This creates an onEnterFrame handler for each of the two Movie Clips. Each event handler animates its Movie Clip in a downward direction by varying the MovieClip._y property and adding an amount held by the version of speed contained within the respective Movie Clips. Thus, the circle Movie Clip moves quicker because it has the faster speed variable (3 pixels per frame as opposed to 1 pixel per frame of the square clip).

10. By changing the version of speed the two event handlers access, you can change the speed of the two Movie Clips. Change the two event handlers as follows:

```
squareClip.onEnterFrame = function() {
  squareClip._y += speed;
};
circleClip.onEnterFrame = function() {
  circleClip._y += speed;
};
```

Leave your FLA open; you will be looking at it in the next section when you look at the this path.

This time, you're accessing (or to use the proper term, *scoping*) the version of speed that is on the main Timeline, and both Movie Clips will now move at a speed of 5 pixels per frame.

You know that the code will access the version of speed that is on the main Timeline because if you add no dot path in front of speed, Flash will assume a scope of the current Timeline, and that equates to the Timeline the code is on: the main Timeline.

You may be thinking that using the same names for all your speed variables makes it easier to confuse the different versions of speed. Why not just have three variables on the main Timeline called (say) speed, squareSpeed, and circleSpeed? The answer is because you can then pick up the appropriate value per Timeline by using the this path.

Using the *this* Path

The this path is a special path that simply means the Timeline to which the code is currently attached. In most cases, this refers to the Timeline to which your code is attached. For example, if you wanted to create a variable called apple on the main Timeline and your code was on the main Timeline, you could use any of the following lines:

```
apple = 3;
_root.apple = 3;
this.apple = 3;
```

The first one is the most convenient (it's quicker to type and looks the least scary) and is usually the one to use. Thus, in most cases, you can simply ignore this, because it is optional—Flash assumes it if you don't add it.

The only time this becomes important is when you're writing lines of code in an event handler. In these cases, this equals the same Movie Clip (scope) as the one the event to which the event handler is attached. This may sound tricky, but it becomes easy (and obvious) if you try it.

Continuing with the FLA from the previous section, change the event handlers as shown:

```
squareClip.onEnterFrame = function() {
  this._y += this.speed;
};
circleClip.onEnterFrame = function() {
  this._y += this.speed;
};
```

Whoa! What does this all mean? Easy. In each event handler, this equals the Timeline to which event handler is attached. The first event handler is attached to squareClip, so the following:

```
this._y+= this.speed;
```

becomes this:

```
squareClip._y+=squareClip.speed
```

This is the same for circleClip.

So what? Well, this means both event handlers are essentially the same, and you can replace the whole script now with this one:

```
function moveDown() {
  this._y += this.speed;
}
```

```
//
speed = 5;
squareClip.speed = 1;
squareClip.onEnterFrame = moveDown;
circleClip.speed = 3;
circleClip.onEnterFrame = moveDown;
```

Both Movie Clips now use the same function (moveDown) as their onEnterFrame event handler. Even though both Movie Clips use the same code, the two Movie Clips actually move in different ways, because both have different speed values.

The this path is the key to creating advanced animations in Flash. For example, you could write a set of routines in a Flash space invaders game that makes each invader fly in formation or dive at the player. Each type of alien would need to behave in a different way: the Blue Meanie alien might be more aggressive (and fetch a higher score when you shoot one) than the Mellow Yellow alien, and so on.

You could write this game using *exactly* the same code for the Blue Meanie and the Mellow Yellow. The only part you'd need to change is the variables on each alien clip's Timeline.

- The Blue Meanie alien might have a skill variable set to 5 (very skillful) and a killScore variable of 500 (a good score).

- The Yellow Mellow alien might have its skill variable set to 1 (not very skillful) and a killScore of 50 (hardly worth hitting).

Each set of values would be picked up by using the this path: for each alien, the code would pick up the variables on the current alien's Timeline. Thus, although the code would be the same for all aliens, the different alien types would act differently.

Using Movie Clips and Nested Timelines

Several of Flash's features require a good understanding of Movie Clips and how you control them through ActionScript. Such features also require an understanding of how nested Timelines are accessed.

Now that you have both these perquisites, you can start looking at detecting collisions and attaching and duplicating Movie Clips.

Detecting Collisions

The MovieClip.hitTest() method detects collisions between the following:

- Two Movie Clip bounding boxes. A *bounding box* is the rectangular outline you see during author time when selecting a symbol on the Stage.

- A point and the pixels within a Movie Clip. The pixels within a Movie Clip are collectively called the Movie Clip *shape*.

Notice that you can't perform shape collision detection between two Movie Clips. This is the most accurate kind of collision detection, and it's also the one most designers would choose if it were available. As you'll see in the "Performing advanced collision" section, it's entirely possible to create accurate, pixel-perfect collision detection using your own custom collision code.

Detecting Bounding Box Collisions

When detecting collisions between two Movie Clip bounding boxes, a collision takes place whenever the bounding boxes of the clips overlap. Although this collision detection route is fast, it has one big disadvantage (see Figure 12.15). The two circles on the left are obviously in collision, but the two circles on the right are also in collision because they have overlapping bounding boxes—yet they certainly don't look like they're touching because the two circle shapes aren't overlapping.

Figure 12.15

Overlapping bounding boxes can result in collisions.

If your Movie Clips are rectangular, bounding box collision detection is all you need. For example, if you wanted to create draggable file icons, you'd create rectangular icons so that bounding box collision would be sufficient.

Early video games could perform bounding box collision detection only, and many early video game graphics are rectangular for this reason…and if the early video game developers could get away with using rectangular collisions without anyone noticing, then so can you!

Another trick to hide bounding box collisions is to simply make your animations fast. If everything is moving quickly, the user will never notice the approximations being made in the collision detection.

The syntax for detecting a collision between two Movie Clips, `instance1` and `instance2`, is as follows:

```
instance1.hitTest(instance2);
```

If you test the `collision01.fla` file on the book's CD, you'll see that both circles are draggable. If you drag one circle near the other, you'll see the word *Collision* appear when a bounding box collision occurs. Notice that this collision doesn't look authentic (in other words, it's obvious that the circles aren't touching) if you drag slowly. If you drag quickly, it's difficult to see that the collision is a bounding box collision.

The important section of code (layer `actions`, frame 1) is as follows:

```
if (this.hitTest(target)) {
  messageTxt.text = "Collision";
} else {
  messageTxt.text = "";
}
```

The first line in this section checks for a collision between `this` (that is, the circle currently being dragged and the Movie Clip `target` (that is, the circle that's stationary).

hitTest returns a Boolean value depending on whether a collision was detected (true) or not (false). The if statement uses this Boolean value to either show the word *Collision* or show a blank text field.

> It's also worth spending some time looking at the drag-and-drop code in this FLA. The code produces a much smoother drag animation than the previous example in this chapter because it uses an onMouseMove event with updateAfterEvent(). Using these two pieces of code forces Flash to redraw the dragged Movie Clip every time the mouse moves, and the resulting frame rate is significantly faster than using an onEnterFrame for the same animation.

Detecting Point Collisions

The next most accurate form of collision is the point collision. This checks for collisions between an (x, y) point and a Movie Clip's shape.

To test for a collision between the point (x, y) and the shape of the Movie Clip instance1, use the following:

```
instance1.hitTest(x, y, true);
```

Figure 12.16

Examples of Flash collision detection.

The last parameter, called the *shape flag*, is set to true to force the method to check for a shape collision rather than a bounding box collision. Although you can force bounding box collisions by setting the shape flag to false, developers rarely use this form of collision detection because there are few practical situations where it is necessary.

In Figure 12.16, the leftmost point isn't in shape collision with the circle, although it is in bounding box collision. The other point is in collision with the circle when either collision type is tested.

If you test the collision02.fla movie on the book's CD, you'll see that the text *Collision* appears whenever you mouse over the black pixels that make up a Movie Clip (see Figure 12.17).

Figure 12.17

An example of point collision in action

Collision

The entire code for this effect is as follows:

```
function collide(target:MovieClip):Void {
  this.onEnterFrame = function() {
    if (target.hitTest(this._xmouse, this._ymouse, true)) {
      messageTxt.text = "Collision";
    } else {
      messageTxt.text = "";
    }
  };
}
//
//
collide(clip);
```

The if statement again uses a hit test to decide whether to show the *Collision* text.

Performing Advanced Collision Detection

When writing games or other interactive content, bounding box and shape collision detection isn't usually enough to give the impression of pixel-perfect collisions. Instead, think of MovieClip.hitTest as the raw building block with which to build your own collision routines.

As an example of a common collision detection problem, refer to collision03.fla on the book's CD. If you test this file, you'll see a spaceship that you have to navigate through a cavern (see Figure 12.18). Use the up and down keys to move the ship, avoiding the cavern edges.

If you hit the cavern, you'll see that not only is the collision near pixel perfect, but Flash also knows which part of the ship was involved in the collision. When a collision occurs, the Output panel will output one of the following:

hit from front!

hit from top!

hit from bottom!

The collision detection makes three separate collision checks. It checks for a collision between the cavern and three points on the ship. These three points are at the front, top, and bottom of the ship.

Figure 12.18

Try flying the ship through the cavern.

Note that you don't make a collision check between the cavern and the back of the ship. You don't need to because the ship is unlikely to hit the cavern from that direction as the ship is moving forward. As in all motion graphics, it's just as important to know which checks you don't need to make as to know which ones you do have to make. Doing so makes your code more efficient and your animations smoother.

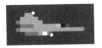

Figure 12.19

The ship symbol has two empty Movie Clips.

Inside the ship symbol, you'll see two empty Movie Clips (shown as hollow circles in Figure 12.19) called topHit and bottomHit. The third detection point is the registration point of the ship Movie Clip itself, and this is at the nose of the spaceship.

The coordinates of the ship Movie Clip and the two empty clips form the three individual points that make the three collision detections:

```
if (cave.hitTest(this._x, this._y, true)) {
    trace("hit from front!");
    hit = true;
} else if (cave.hitTest(this._x+this.topHit._x,
    this._y+this.topHit._y, true)) {
    trace("hit from top!");
    hit = true;
} else if (cave.hitTest(this._x+this.bottomHit._x,
    this._y+this.bottomHit._y, true)) {
    trace("hit from bottom!");
    hit = true;
}
if (hit) {
    delete this.onEnterFrame;
    delete cave.onEnterFrame;
}
```

The if…else if…else if makes the three shape collision tests, using the (x, y) positions of the ship, topHit, and bottomHit Movie Clips. A variable, hit, tracks whether a collision has been detected. If it has, then the two onEnterFrames that drive the animation are deleted via the if statement at the end of the code.

Making separate collision checks on several points around a Movie Clip's edge is thus the way to fake true pixel-based collision detection in Flash.

Another common problem is making collision detections between several Movie Clips. For example, if you have the ship in the last example move through a meteor storm rather than a cavern, you might have to make the same three collision detections against every meteor (see Figure 12.20). This would slow your game down considerably.

Figure 12.20

The ship moves through a meteor storm.

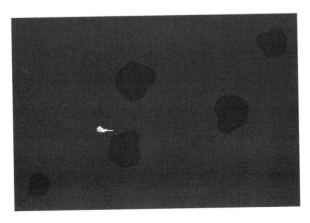

The file `collision04.fla` on the book's CD illustrates one way to overcome this. If you test the movie, you'll see the cavern is now replaced by several meteors, each of which moves at a separate speed.

The way the SWF gets around making three collision detections per meteor is by placing all the meteors into a single Movie Clip (called `meteors`) and then making collision detections against that one Movie Clip. Since all the separate meteors are part of the `meteors` clip, they're all automatically included in the collision detection. This nesting of Movie Clips appears in the Display list pane of the Debugger (see Figure 12.21).

Figure 12.21

The Display list displays the nesting.

Attaching and Duplicating Movie Clips

So far, you've placed content onto the Stage via keyframes. By placing symbols and graphics onto the Stage at author time, you arrange how the content will appear at runtime. Flash also allows you to attach Movie Clips to the Stage at runtime.

Runtime attaching has a number of advantages:

- It allows greater levels of interactivity. Rather than the designer placing content onto the Stage at author time, it's possible to allow code to attach content at runtime. The code will typically look at user interaction to decide when and where content appears on the Stage, resulting in a much more interactive Flash site or application.

- It allows the creation of complex effects that can't be achieved in any other way. Where an effect requires large numbers of Movie Clips (think thousands!), placing each Movie Clip onto the Stage manually would be time-consuming. Using code makes the job far quicker. Using code in this way also leads to smaller SWF sizes because the position of each Movie Clip is calculated at runtime rather than held within the SWF.

- It allows greater flexibility. Well-written code is easier to change than graphics, and this allows you to change your FLA much more quickly. In particular, attaching content at runtime rather than relying on keyframes allows you to shorten your Timelines significantly.

- It's a required skill for Flash applications. Complex user interfaces and applications have a greater number of states than the simple four- to six-page site with which most beginners start. This makes more complex applications impossible to create using Timeline-based navigation, especially where the navigation is based on rules. Instead, pages are attached directly to the Stage using code.

We build interfaces for e-learning, online examinations, and teacher reporting (so that a teacher can review pupil progress). Such applications typically consist of a Timeline one keyframe long—all content is attached dynamically and is driven by a set of logic rules that form the navigation. The same applies for other content such as Flash games that typically consist of short Timelines and lots of attached content. You simply can't attempt these types of content with keyframe-only designs!

Duplicating Movie Clips

The `MovieClip.duplicateMovieClip()` method allows you to copy any Movie Clip instance that is already on the Stage. To copy the Movie Clip `original` as a new instance called `copied`, use the following:

```
original.duplicateMovieClip(copied, depth);
```

The `depth` parameter refers to the stacking order used in Flash Timelines. Depth is a numerical value from 0 to 1048575. Each depth can contain one Movie Clip, and if you try to add a Movie Clip at a depth that already contains a Movie Clip, the existing Movie Clip will be deleted by the new one. Movie Clips with higher depth values will appear in front of Movie Clips that have lower depth values.

It's important to make sure your depth value per Movie Clip is unique.

The `duplicateMovieClip()` method also returns a reference to the Movie Clip it just created. You'll see this in action in the following example. The great thing about using `duplicateMovieClip` is that once you have an effect that works for one Movie Clip, you can easily create other instances of the same Movie Clip.

 If you test the `bouncer01.fla` movie on the book's CD, you'll see a ball that bounces around within a rectangular container. Looking at the images for this effect won't do justice to this effect—the graphics are fairly basic, but it's the way everything moves that gives this effect its charm.

As usual, the code is on frame 1 of layer actions. The code looks like this:

```
function initialize(clip:MovieClip):Void {
  clip._x = 275;
  clip._y = 15;
  clip.xSpeed = Math.random()*20-10;
  clip.ySpeed = Math.random()*20-10;
  clip.cacheAsBitmap = true;
  clip.onEnterFrame = mover;
}
function mover():Void {
  this.xSpeed = this.xSpeed*FRICTION;
  this.ySpeed = (this.ySpeed*FRICTION)+GRAVITY;
  this._x += this.xSpeed;
  this._y += this.ySpeed;
  if (this._x<20) {
    this.xSpeed = -this.xSpeed;
    this._x = 20;
  } else if (this._x>530) {
    this.xSpeed = -this.xSpeed;
    this._x = 530;
  }
  if (this._y>380) {
    if (this.ySpeed>1.5) {
```

```
      this.ySpeed = -this.ySpeed;
    } else {
      delete this.onEnterFrame;
    }
    this._y = 380;
  }
}
var GRAVITY:Number = 0.5;
var FRICTION:Number = 0.99;
initialize(ball);
```

Nothing much is new in this code. The call to function `initialize()` (the last line in the listing) initializes the `ball` clip's starting speed values and sets up `mover()` as the `onEnterFrame`.

The code sets two constants, `GRAVITY` and `FRICTION`, and these are used within function `mover()` to simulate the effects of gravity and friction on the bouncing ball.

Mathematically minded readers might notice that the equations of motion for the ball (the first two lines of `mover()`) are simpler than the physics equations used in the real world—the equations look linear whereas the real world equations typically include terms that imply acceleration. The equations are iterative in that they calculate the ball's path for the *current frame* only, so there is no time-based part (the frame rate provides the time-based portion of the motion). Because iterative equations have no time-based term, they become much simpler than real-world (time-based) equations of motion.

If you press Ctrl+Enter / Cmd+Return a few times quickly, you might start thinking that this would look better with lots more elements moving at the same time.

Because the code is split into general functions (that is, an `initialize()` function that initializes the general Movie Clip `clip` and an `onEnterFrame` that is written to control any Movie Clip, `this`), it's possible to generate thousands of animated graphics with just a few more lines of code.

The file `bouncer02.fla` on the book's CD changes the main code as follows:

```
var GRAVITY:Number = 0.5;
var FRICTION:Number = 0.99;
var thisBall:MovieClip = new MovieClip();
initialize(ball);
for (var i = 0; i<100; i++) {
  thisBall = ball.duplicateMovieClip("ball"+i, i);
  initialize(thisBall);
}
```

After initializing `ball`, you duplicate it 100 times to create 100 copies called from `ball0` to `ball99`; these are initialized in the same way as `ball`, and all will act in the same way. As you can see in Figure 12.22, you change the simple animation into one that looks much more involved…numerous balls are now bouncing, all following the same physics equations.

 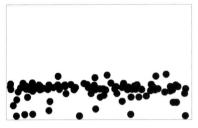 

Figure 12.22

**You can see
the many balls
bouncing.**

You should notice three important concepts here. First, each instance you create has to have a unique instance name and depth. You can do this easily via the loop variable, i. Each time the loop runs, i increments (and is therefore unique). You can thus simply call the instances ball+i, giving you ball0, ball1, ball2, ball3…ball97, ball98, ball99.

Second, you define a variable of type MovieClip called thisBall. This isn't the same as other variables you've created (such as strings, numbers, and arrays). thisBall is a *reference*. If you equate a Movie Clip to it, thisBall will hold a reference to that Movie Clip. The reference isn't a true Movie Clip but a pointer to one.

> Think of a reference as a pointer or signpost. A signpost to New York tells us where New York is, but the signpost isn't New York. If you somehow removed New York, the signpost would still point to New York, but since New York no longer exists, the signpost would now be invalid (or undefined, because it points to nothing). If you removed the signpost, New York would still exist, but if you had no other way of finding your way to it, New York might as well have disappeared as far as you're concerned, because you'd have no way of finding it again!

If you equate any variable to something other than a string or number, you'll create a reference rather than a copy. References are useful when you're generating new instances, because you have a general way of referring to the last generated instance, and this is what you do in the for loop:

```
thisBall = ball.duplicateMovieClip("ball"+i, i);
initialize(thisBall);
```

Rather than call each ball by its instance name, you make thisBall point to it (because you equate the ball clip just created to thisBall). Thus, rather than having to run these lines:

```
initialize(ball0)
initialize(ball1)
…
…
initialize(ball98)
initialize(ball99)
```

you can just run the following line immediately after creating each ball instance:

```
initialize (thisBall);
```

Third, you have to treat the original Movie Clip (ball) slightly differently than the duplicated balls. It's the only Movie Clip that is on the Stage when the code starts, so you don't have to duplicate it. Although this may seem like a minor point, it's actually a major failing of the MovieClip.duplicateMovieClip() method—*you have to treat the original Movie Clip as a special case.* As you do more work with duplicated Movie Clips, you'll soon see that this special case causes your code to become longer than it needs to be because you have to cater to two cases, not one. As you'll see next, the original Movie Clip is a special case in other ways, and we don't mean in good ways!

Suppose you wanted to remove the balls once they stopped bouncing, because they tend to clutter the place up a bit. The method to do this is MovieClip.removeMovieClip(). To remove a Movie Clip called instance1, simply use this:

```
instance1.removeMovieClip();
```

You can add this method within the last if statement in mover(). Each ball stops moving when you delete the onEnterFrame. Replace the line that does this with the one shown here:

```
if (this._y>380) {
  if (this.ySpeed>1.5) {
    this.ySpeed = -this.ySpeed;
  } else {
    this.removeMovieClip();
  }
  this._y = 380;
}
```

You can see this change in bouncer03.fla on the book's CD.

You'll see that Movie Clip removal works for all ball Movie Clips except one. The remaining one is the original Movie Clip ball—you can't delete it!

The MovieClip.removeMovieClip() method has a caveat in its operation—you can delete Movie Clips at runtime only if they were created at runtime. This means you can use MovieClip.removeMovieClip()only on Movie Clips that were created using runtime Movie Clip creation methods such as MovieClip.duplicateMovieClip().

MovieClip.duplicateMovieClip() has another disadvantage. The copied Movie Clip will be on the same Timeline as the original. This isn't desirable for many applications. As you've already seen, the Timeline hierarchy is important in Flash, and not being able to attach a Movie Clip exactly where you want reduces flexibility.

Attaching Movie Clips

Rather than duplicate Movie Clips already on the Stage, you can also attach Movie Clips to the Stage from the Library. Attaching Movie Clips has none of the disadvantages of duplicating Movie Clips and is the preferred method for dynamically attaching content to the Stage. As with all good things, attaching Movie Clips has one disadvantage over duplicating Movie Clips—it's a little harder.

You need to be aware of three issues when attaching movies:

- ActionScript uses instance names to control instances, but these names exist only for Movie Clips already on the Stage. The Flash development team could have instead allowed ActionScript to use the symbol names (that is, the titles that appear next to each symbol name in the Library). Symbol names aren't suitable because they don't get exported to the final SWF. Instead, you have to define a *linkage identifier* for each Movie Clip symbol you want to attach to the Stage.

> As well as symbol names, layers aren't exported to the final SWF. Instead, Flash converts the layer order into depth values.

- A second issue concerns what does (and doesn't) get exported into the SWF when you compile a FLA. Flash keeps track of the order each symbol is used in the movie and places symbols in that order in the final SWF. Thus, Flash makes sure the first symbol used in a Timeline is the first one to stream in when the SWF is viewed across the Web. If Flash doesn't find any instance of a Movie Clip on any Timeline, it assumes that the Movie Clip isn't used and doesn't export it into the final SWF at all. If you have a Movie Clip you want to attach to the Stage at *runtime only*, Flash won't see any instance of the Movie Clip being used during compilation, and your Movie Clip won't get exported.

- Even if you forced Flash to export the Movie Clip as per the previous item, Flash still doesn't know which keyframe the Movie Clip has to be available by (and, depending on your code, you might not know either!). Flash has a way around this—you can force Flash to export Movie Clips with a linkage identifier to frame 1 of the compiled SWF. This ensures that any Movie Clip that may be attached at runtime is always available.

Let's see this in practice. If you get stuck with the following exercise, the finished file is included on the book's CD as bouncer04.fla.

Starting with the file bouncer03.fla, follow these steps:

1. Delete the ball instance on the Stage.

2. Open the Library panel. Select the ball symbol so that it is highlighted (it will be the only symbol in the Library).

3. Open the Linkage Properties dialog box by opening the Library panel's menu (click the icon at the top-right corner of the Library), and select Linkage. If you're using Windows, you can also right-click the ball Movie Clip and select Linkage from the menu that appears.

4. Check Export for ActionScript. The Identifier field will now display the text *ball*. Flash assumes a default linkage identifier of the symbol name. Leave the default. You'll also

see the Export in First Frame check box become selected. Leave it selected.

Your Linkage Properties dialog box should now look like Figure 12.23.

5. Click OK to close the Linkage Properties dialog box.

The linkage identifier will now appear to the right of the `ball` symbol in the Library. You may have to widen the Library panel to see it (see Figure 12.24).

You're now ready to add the method used to attach Movie Clips, `MovieClip.attachMovie()`. To attach a Movie Clip with the linkage identifier `linkage` with the instance name `instance1` to the Timeline `instance2` at a depth of `depth`, you use this:

```
instance2.attachMovie(linkage, instance1, depth);
```

6. To change the code so that it attaches rather than duplicates Movie Clips, change the main code (at the bottom of the listing) so that it now reads as follows:

```
var GRAVITY:Number = 0.5;
var FRICTION:Number = 0.99;
for (var i = 0; i<100; i++) {
  thisBall = ball.duplicateMovieClip("ball"+i, i);

  initialize(thisBall);
}
```

If you now test the movie, you'll see that all the Movie Clips eventually disappear. All the balls are attached at runtime, so now all of them can be successfully removed.

With `MovieClip.attachMovie()` on the book's CD, you can create more complex effects. For example, refer to `bouncer05.fla`. This time, you aren't simulating a bouncing ball but one that breaks every time it hits the floor. Every time a ball hits the ground, it shatters into several pieces. These pieces also act the same way—they will also break every time they hit the floor (see Figure 12.25).

Figure 12.23

Verify that your Linkage Properties dialog box looks like this.

Figure 12.24

The Library panel shows the linkage columns.

Figure 12.25

See the breaking bouncing ball effect in action.

This code uses the `MovieClip.getNextHighestDepth()` method to find the next available free depth. This method is useful when you're not keeping track of depth yourself.

> The `MovieClip.getNextHighestDepth()` method won't work properly if you use it with v2 components (that is, the ones that ship with Flash 7 and 8). This is because the v2 components place a Movie Clip at the highest available depth so that certain component elements that always need to be in front of everything else (such as drop-down menus) can be.

Loading External Content

You've seen how you can use Flash to place content on the Stage from the Library via `MovieClip.attachMovie()`. Flash can also load external SWFs or images (JPEG, GIF, or PNG files) at runtime.

> Runtime support for GIF and PNG files is new for Flash 8 and isn't backward compatible with Flash 7 or earlier.

You can load external SWFs onto the Stage as levels or into Movie Clips (also known as *targets*).

Loading Levels

Levels are simpler when you see them in operation, so let's look at an example straight-away; we'll cover the theory after the example.

Load the file `menu.fla`. Before you can test it, you need to make sure the following files are in the same folder as `menu.fla`: `option1.swf`, `option2.swf`, and `option3.swf`.

The file `menu.fla` consists of three buttons with instance names of `option1`, `option2`, and `option3`. Notice that nothing else appears in this FLA—it has no symbols apart from the ones you see and no other scenes.

The script attached to frame 1 of layer actions looks like this:

```
option1.onRelease = function(){
  loadMovieNum("option1.swf", 1);
}
option2.onRelease = function(){
  loadMovieNum("option2.swf", 1);
}
option3.onRelease = function(){
  loadMovieNum("option3.swf", 1);
}
```

When you click the first button, the following line will run, and the same is true for the other two buttons:

```
loadMovieNum("option1.swf", 1);
```

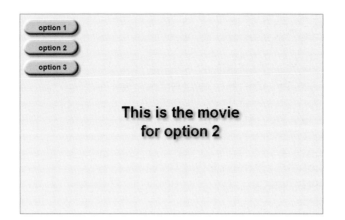

Figure 12.26

Test the `menu.fla`
file to see the simple
text animation.

Test the movie. When you click any button, a corresponding simple text animation will appear (see Figure 12.26). These animations are `option1.swf`, `option2.swf`,
and `option3.swf`.

You'll get a better impression of what is going on if you debug `menu.fla`. Press
Ctrl+Shift+Enter / Cmd+Shift+Enter (or select Control → Debug Movie).

Figure 12.27

This is the Display
list at this point.

The Display list on the Debugger initially looks like Figure 12.27. The instances shown
here aren't the buttons (buttons don't appear in the Display list) but are instead Movie Clips
created by the filters applied to the buttons (each button has a bevel and a drop shadow).

If you click the first option button, the Display list looks like Figure 12.28.

OK, now for the theory. A level in Flash is simply a SWF file within the Flash
Player. So far in the book, you've used only single SWFs. The first SWF loaded
always goes into the first level, level zero, or `_level0`. The SWF in this level defines
the Stage color and frame rate.

Figure 12.28

This is what the Dis-
play list looks like
after a button click.

Subsequent levels are loaded into a specified level. If you load a SWF into level 0,
you replace the entire movie with the newly loaded SWF. If you load into another
level, such as `_level1`, the new SWF will appear over `_level0`.

Load levels are useful when you want to load content that is bandwidth heavy and
capable of streaming, such as video or complex animations. By separating your content
into a lightweight user interface (such as `menu.fla`) and separate content files (`option1.swf`,
`option2.swf`, and `option3.swf`), you ensure that the content files are only downloaded as
required.

The loaded SWFs are no different from a standard SWF, and you can open the associated FLAs if you want (`option1.fla`, `option2.fla`, and `option3.fla`).

Refer to the code again. It's now probably obvious what's going on here—to load a
SWF as a new level, you use `loadMovieNum()`. To load a SWF with the URL `mySwf` into level
n, use the following:

```
loadMovieNum( mySwf, n);
```

You can also load image files using `loadMovieNum()`. You can use any level number from 0 to 1048575. You don't have to use levels sequentially, so, for example, you can load content into levels 9, 345, and 7890 with no ill effect (apart from anyone reading your code wondering what your logic for choosing those levels is!).

Each SWF that is loaded in a level above `_level0` will appear with a transparent Stage and the same frame rate as `_level0`. Each loaded level will stream in much like the main Timeline of a standard single SWF movie.

When you click any button in `menu.fla`, the code loads the new SWF into `_level1`, overwriting the previously loaded SWF. This doesn't mean the SWF will have to be reloaded if the user requests a previously loaded SWF, because the browser saves all loaded content into its own cache.

You can see the effect of loading multiple levels by changing the code as follows:

```
option1.onRelease = function(){
    loadMovieNum("option1.swf", 1);
}
option2.onRelease = function(){
    loadMovieNum("option2.swf", 2);
}
option3.onRelease = function(){
    loadMovieNum("option3.swf", 3);
}
```

This time, you load each SWF into a unique level. If you click all three options, you'll see all three SWFs (see Figure 12.29). Yeah, it looks like a mess, but sometimes you might want to overlay stuff in this way. For example, if your site consists of a TV showing an animation, you could load the animation at `_level1` and the TV (with a space cut out where the screen should be) at `_level2`.

Figure 12.29

This shows all the SWFs together.

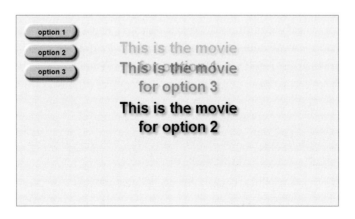

A final change to look at is changing one of the levels to _level0. Change the last event handler as follows:

```
option3.onRelease = function(){
    loadMovieNum("option3.swf", 0);
}
```

When you click the option3 button, you overwrite _level0 with option3.swf. More important, loading anything into _level0 also resets the Flash Player—all other levels are cleared, and the frame rate, Stage dimensions, and Stage background color reset to those of the SWF loaded into _level0.

To clear a level, use unloadMovieNum(level). To make the option3 button clear all other levels, change the code in the last event handler to the following:

```
option3.onRelease = function(){
    unloadMovieNum(1);
    unloadMovieNum(2);
}
```

If you now click the three option buttons in the order 1-2-3, you'll see that the first two buttons load SWFs into levels 1 and 2, and clicking the third button clears them.

> It's a bad idea to clear _level0 unless you actually *want* to leave the user with a blank Stage for no apparent reason!

To access a particular level, you add the level number as part of the dot path. For example, to access a Movie Clip called myClip on the main Timeline of _level3, you use the path _level3.myClip.

The big advantage of load levels is that you can separate your content into modules at both author time (each SWF is created by a different FLA) and runtime (you can selectively load the separate SWFs, thus avoiding loading everything in one go).

Load levels were used extensively in the days of Flash 3. Nowadays, load levels are used much less often because content has become more complex (especially in their use of ActionScript, which isn't always compatible with streaming). Further, ActionScript has much less control over load levels than other multiple-SWF schemes, and this has also reduced the use of load levels in recent years.

Loading Targets

When you load targets into Flash, you load content into a Movie Clip (this Movie Clip is called the *target*):

- You can control the position of the loaded content by controlling the target, and you can do this even before the content has loaded.

- You have a large number of events that are generated during the loading. Using these events, you can easily manage the loading process. You can also use the events to drive graphics that show the loading progress (preloaders).

- A load target doesn't play until the content has fully loaded. This is an important feature if your content contains ActionScript.

You can load targets in Flash in two ways—using `MovieClip.loadMovie()` and using the `MovieClipLoader()` class. We'll cover the former because it's the easiest to use (as well as being the most backward compatible).

> You can find a site template that contains general code that uses the `MovieClipLoader()` class at `http://weblog.motion-graphics.org/archives/2005/09/previews_of_stu_1.html`. Using `MovieClipLoader()` to load external content is much more flexible for intermediate and advanced ActionScript users, especially because it allows you to generate events for all stages of the load process. This event handling also makes your code much more efficient.

Loading Targets with *MovieClip.loadMovie()*

Once again, we'll start with an example. Load `imageLoader01.fla` from the book's CD. You need to run this FLA from a folder containing the three images, `face.jpg`, `burst.jpg`, and `swimmer.jpg`.

Looking at the strip at the top of the Stage, you'll see three numbered buttons. These three buttons have the instance names `btn01`, `btn02`, and `btn03`. You may have to lock all other layers to select these buttons.

If you now look near the bottom-left corner of the black strip, you'll see an empty Movie Clip (denoted by a hollow circle). This empty Movie Clip will be the target—all the content will load into it. Again, you may have to lock all layers except `holder` to be able to select this empty Movie Clip.

On frame 1 of layer `actions`, you'll see the following script:

```
btn01.onRelease = function() {
  holder.loadMovie("face.jpg");
};
btn02.onRelease = function() {
  holder.loadMovie("burst.jpg");
};
btn03.onRelease = function() {
  holder.loadMovie("swimmer.jpg");
};
```

The script is fairly trivial, consisting of three event handlers for the three buttons. Each script runs a `MovieClip.loadMovie()` method. From this, you can see that the general syntax to load some external content located at the URL `url` into a Movie Clip `target` is as follows:

```
target.loadMovie(url);
```

If you test `imageLoader01.fla`, you'll see that three images are loaded depending on which button you click (see Figure 12.30).

If you don't see the menu when you test the movie, you can't see all the Stage because the Stage is taller than the standard Flash Stage. You can fix this by closing any panels you have above or below the Stage.

This movie has a problem, though, and you can see it if you test the movie with bandwidth limiting on:

1. Press Ctrl+Enter to test the movie.

2. Press Ctrl+B / Cmd+B to see the bandwidth profiler (if it isn't already there).

3. Select View → Download Settings, and select the 56k option.

4. Press Ctrl+Enter to test with the movie as a 56k user would see it.

When you click any of the buttons, you'll now see a long delay.

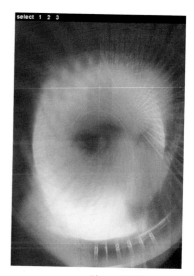

Figure 12.30

This is the image loader.

The SWF in this example is very tall, and you may need to close the Bandwidth Profiler and/or any panels docked at the bottom of the screen to see the buttons.

This occurs because the images are 20–30KB each, and they will take a few seconds to appear. Unfortunately, the user doesn't know when an image will appear, what Flash is doing, or even if the images will appear at all!

You need to add something that shows the loading progress to the user. Refer to the version of the image loader that does this, `imageLoader02.fla` on the book's CD.

The Library now has some additional symbols, all of which are contained within the preloader assets folder (see Figure 12.31).

The preloader bar is simply a bar whose length is controlled by the loading progress—the more fully loaded the image is, the closer to its full length the bar becomes. You control the width of the bar simply by varying the `_xscale` property of the bar. By calculating the percentage of the image that is loaded per frame and then equating the bar's `_xscale` property, you have a good visual progress indicating the loading process.

The new code looks like this:

```
function preloaderDriver(target:MovieClip) {
  preloader.bar._xscale = 0;
  preloader._visible = true;
  preloader.bar.onEnterFrame = function() {
    var percentCompleted:Number = 100*
target.getBytesLoaded()/
target.getBytesTotal();
    this._xscale = percentCompleted;
    if (percentCompleted == 100) {
      preloader._visible = false;
```

Figure 12.31

This is the preloader assets folder.

```
        delete this.onEnterFrame;
      }
    };
  }
  btn01.onRelease = function() {
    holder.loadMovie("face.jpg");
    preloaderDriver(holder);
  };
  btn02.onRelease = function() {
    holder.loadMovie("burst.jpg");
    preloaderDriver(holder);
  };
  btn03.onRelease = function() {
    holder.loadMovie("swimmer.jpg");
    preloaderDriver(holder);
  };
  preloader._visible = false;
```

Each button event now has a call to `preloaderDriver()` in it. Thus, each time a new load is started, `preloaderDriver()` is also called. The first two lines of this function set the preloader to display 0 (the bar is zero length) and to be visible.

The code then sets up an `onEnterFrame` that constantly calculates the percentage loaded. The `MovieClip.getBytesLoaded()` and `MovieClip.getBytesTotal()` methods return the bytes currently loaded and the total bytes in total. Dividing the former by the latter and multiplying by 100 gives you a percent loaded value. You use this value, `percentCompleted`, to drive the bar's `_xscale` property, giving you a bar that increases in size as the loading progresses.

If `percentCompleted` is equal to 100, then you've finished the current load and can make the preloader invisible and stop the preloader animation. You do this all via the `if` statement at the end of `preloaderDriver()`.

The preloader code is general, which means you can easily take the `preloaderDriver()` function and the preloader assets in the Library and use them in your own designs. You can also use the preloader with load levels if you add a `stop()` on frame 1 of the loaded level and restart the level with a `play()` when the level is loaded (that is, `percentCompleted = 100`).

This has solved the problem of the user not knowing what is happening when Flash is loading content, but the FLA still looks a little unfinished. You could fix this by just adding a better user interface, but a few simple transitions in code will also help immensely (and unlike the graphics, will take only a few minutes!).

The final file is `imageLoader03.fla`. This FLA adds a nice fade transition to the proceedings, fading the preloader in and out and also fading in each loaded image. It also centers the loaded image on the Stage once the image is loaded, something that leads to a neater layout. Now all *you* have to do is tidy up that interface!

In this chapter, you looked at what nested Movie Clips look like to ActionScript and the different ways to access and control nested Timelines. Nested Timelines aren't special cases in Flash but are instead the norm. Almost everything you build in Flash will consist of multiple Timelines. Knowing the best way to make ActionScript manage multiple and nested Timelines is one of the defining features of a competent ActionScript-savvy designer.

Media

Part III begins *one of the most interesting, important, and powerful aspects of working with Flash—media assets. Gone are the days when Flash movies and applications look and sound like they were created in Flash. The application has matured from its status as "everyone's favorite vector animator" to a fully featured, digital-authoring application capable of delivering rich audio and video content on a variety of platforms.*

Flash has responded to the growth of broadband media distribution in ways that allow content creators and media artists to disseminate their work in greater variety of formats and with better fidelity than ever before. Projects such as creating custom music players and video conferencing systems are now within the grasp of every Flash user. We don't want to create a false impression—it's not always easy! However, with determination and the right ActionScript know-how, Flash will enable you to use audio and video in ways that were formerly the sole domain of software companies and professional media developers. If your project requires audio and video assets to make it a success, this part of the book will help get you started.

CHAPTER 13

Flash Audio Basics

Audio elements such as music, sound effects, and narration can add greatly to the depth and interest of your Flash productions. Sound provides extra impact for scenes that are funny or scary, gives your characters voices, and allows your audience to take a break from reading and to listen to your story or presentation. It is also an invaluable means of providing user feedback for interfaces. You can make button clicks, error messages, scrolling behavior, and so on, more responsive by using sound. As a unique, nonvisual medium, sound can push your animations and interactive movies to a new level of creativity, expression, and fun.

As do most other interactive authoring applications, Flash has its own set of rules governing the way it handles audio. These rules are what you are about to learn. When approaching them, however, try not to think of them as rules, because the term *rules* carries a bad connotation. When you think of rules, it's too easy to focus on the limitations, or what *cannot* be done. Think of this chapter's topic as a set of techniques that you must implement to work with audio in Flash.

More specifically, the rules are a set of techniques that you can master. And when you are completely comfortable with them, your potential is limited only by your ability to use the techniques creatively to achieve your goals. Not only can Flash be a tool for dynamic animations and interactivity, but you can use it to deliver great audio as well.

This chapter covers the following topics:

- ▪ **Preparing sounds for an interactive media application**
- ▪ **Bringing sounds into the Flash environment and implementing them in your movies**
- ▪ **Attaching sounds to buttons**
- ▪ **Controlling sound playback**
- ▪ **Understanding sound export options and audio compression**

Preparing Sound Files for Flash

Sound and music can add another dimension to your Flash movies. They can add the finishing touches to your animations and graphics by communicating tone. With the right sound components, a scene can be truly funny, dramatic, scary—whatever you like. Selecting or producing the right sound can make a huge difference in the success of a Flash production.

You are probably excited about getting some sounds into your movie so that you can see how all this works. However, it's important to be sure your sounds are ready to be a part of a Flash movie before they hit the vector stage. First, no matter where or how you acquire your sound files, it's important to edit them and make sure they are ready for the Flash environment. This can accomplish several things. Because sound files demand a fair amount of storage space and add to the final size of a Flash production, it's important to make sure you trim any unneeded material from the sound file. Also, you want to ensure that the file is free of clicks, pops, and other strange noises that might have made their way into your recording.

Second, if you can't hear a sound file, it is virtually useless unless you are going for an effect that requires an especially low sound volume. Before you bring any sounds into a Flash movie, you want to make sure the volume level is as high as possible without causing distortion in the sound. This gives you a sound file that will be easy to optimize in Flash later. Once a sound is in Flash, you can always turn it down, but you can never turn it up.

The next two sections cover the most important and essential audio-editing techniques for preparing a sound for a career in your Flash movie, trimming and normalizing. Although you might want to perform many other tasks to ready a sound, these techniques are the most important; you should perform them on every sound file before implementing it in a Flash movie.

Trimming and Cutting Sound Files

The name of this editing technique says it all, but why is it so important to trim your sound files? Well, an extra second of CD-quality, mono sound can add from 80kb to 90kb to your final movie before it is published. If you have lots of sound files with lots of extra space in them, this figure will really start to add up. The difference in file size between a three-second drumbeat and three seconds of silence is…nothing. It takes the same amount of space to store silence as it does a full symphony orchestra, so make your files count!

Anytime you open a recorded sound file or music file, you are bound to have some dead space at the beginning and end of the sound. Your task is to make sure you eliminate this empty space. Not only does this help keep your movie file size down, but also it helps the file play more quickly. If a sound has a quarter-second pause before anything is heard, it will always sound as though it is starting late—not because Flash is running slowly but because it has to play through the silence or other junk before it gets to what is important.

Trimming sound files takes away the unnecessary parts and helps optimize their performance in a movie.

To trim a sound file:

1. Open the sound in your audio editor of choice. In a Windows environment, Sony Sound Forge or Adobe Audition are great choices. If you use a Mac, Soundtrack Pro, GarageBand, or Bias Peak should do the trick.

> Looking for a good audio editor? We recommend Audacity. It works with mono, stereo, and multitrack audio files. And best of all, it's free! You can download a copy at `http://audacity` `.sourceforge.net`. See the SourceForge website for information about Audacity and the features it offers.

2. Navigate to the beginning of the sound file. Depending on the instrument or object that makes the sound, the wave will look different. Play the sound, and watch the playback head as you listen. You should be able to see and hear the point in the wave where the significant part of the sound begins (Figure 13.1). You might need to do this several times to pinpoint the spot.

3. Once you have found the "real" beginning of the sound, click that spot, and drag a selection to the beginning of the sound file. You should see something like Figure 13.2.

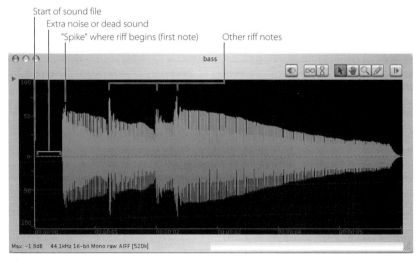

Figure 13.1

This sound file of a bass riff has unnecessary information at the beginning. Of course, listening is the key, but here you can tell where the musical information begins by the "spike" in the waveform. The wave is most active (tallest) where notes and other sounds are heard in the recording.

Figure 13.2

To trim a sound file, you start by selecting the unneeded material at the beginning of the file.

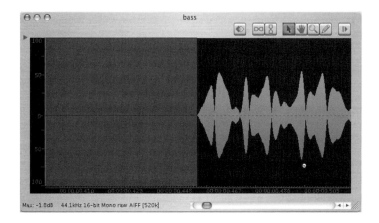

4. Play back the selection, and listen. Do you hear anything important to the sound? You shouldn't. Remember, you are trimming the *unwanted* material out of the file. When you play back the selection, you should be listening to all the dead space that you want to trim from the file. If your audio editor supports this function, play back the unselected portion of the sound file. In this case, playing the unselected portion should allow you to hear exactly what you want with no extra space or silence.

5. If your selection is correct and all the extra material is selected, clear the unwanted material by either pressing Delete or selecting Edit → Delete in your audio editor. If your selection is not quite right, you can always delete the unwanted material and take another pass to get the remaining portion of the wave. Or choose Edit → Undo, and start the process again.

   Remember that a sound file has two parts, a head and a tail. You just learned how to trim the head. To trim the tail, the steps are the same. The only exception, of course, is that you will make changes to the end of the file rather than to the beginning.

You need to consider a few other factors when trimming files. You should try as much as possible to trim files at points where the wave crosses the zero-amplitude center axis. A single sound file has many crossings, because a wave is constantly in flux between negative and positive amplitudes. By trimming at an axis point, you eliminate the possibility of a pop or click when the file plays back, because the wave is starting at a point of silence (see Figure 13.3). Alternately, after making your edit, you can fade out a tiny portion (a few samples or milliseconds) at the beginning of the sound to bring the wave down to zero amplitude.

It can also be helpful to use fade-outs when trimming files, especially if you have a sound that sustains. If you select the beginning or end portion of a waveform and apply the fade-out effect, your audio editor will gradually decrease the sound's current volume to silence over the portion of the wave you selected (see Figure 13.4). A fade-out allows you to shorten the length of a sound that decays over a long time, such as that of a gong or cymbal crash.

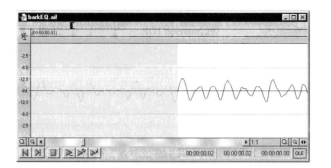

Figure 13.3

When the selection is deleted, the wave will be trimmed at a zero point (shown here in Sound Forge as infinity) to ensure a smooth start.

Normalizing Audio Files

Volume is one of the most important aspects of sound. If a file doesn't have a strong volume, you will be unable to hear it. In general, it's better to have to turn something down because it's too loud than to crank it up because it's not loud enough. As the chief audio engineer for your Flash movie, you have the responsibility of ensuring that all your sounds are heard, and heard at the correct volume.

While assembling your audio, it can be difficult (if not impossible) to tell how loud a sound should be because it's out of context. The good news is that with Flash, you can bring all your sounds into the program and then tweak the volume as you create your movie. This provides a great deal of flexibility and takes much of the pressure and guesswork out of the audio production.

Because Flash allows you to manipulate volume from within your movie, you want to be sure that all your sounds come into the movie at the strongest possible volume. Your audio editor can help you do this through *normalizing*. Normalizing looks at an entire waveform and boosts it proportionally within a volume range that you specify without clipping or distorting the sound. Basically, it ensures that a sound is as loud as it can be without going over its limit.

Before fade-out

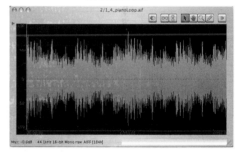

After fade-out

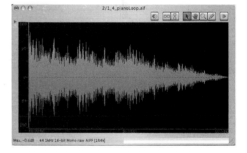

Figure 13.4

Here you can see the difference in a sound file before and after applying a fade-out effect.

Clipping and/or distortion are what happen when a sound's level is set too high and pushed beyond the capabilities of the digital recording or playback device. Although in some analog applications distortion is an interesting effect, digital audio distortion is especially harsh.

To normalize audio for your Flash movie:

1. Using your audio editor of choice, open the sound file you want to normalize. Then choose Edit → Select All.

2. Depending on which editor you use, the Normalize command could be in a variety of locations. Generally, it's on a menu named something like Effects or Process. Choose Normalize from the menu where you find it.

3. A dialog box should open, asking what settings you want to use for normalizing. For most multimedia work, a good rule of thumb is to normalize from 96 percent to 98 percent. This boosts the entire file proportionately from 96 percent to 98 percent of its maximum volume. If your audio application measures normalize levels in decibels (dB), normalize from –1dB to –0.04dB. After you have executed the normalization, save the sound file.

You can see the difference between files that have been normalized and those that have not. In Figure 13.5, note the difference in the amplitudes of the various waveforms.

One potential pitfall when normalizing a file is that the process will increase the volume of everything in the sound file. If your file is "noisy" because of background hiss, static, or other artifacts of recording, these qualities will be even more apparent in the normalized version. As much as possible, try to work with sounds that have been professionally recorded so that what you hear is as "clean" as possible. If using a noisy file is unavoidable, try the noise reduction features of your audio application to remove the unwanted hiss, scratch, hum, and so on.

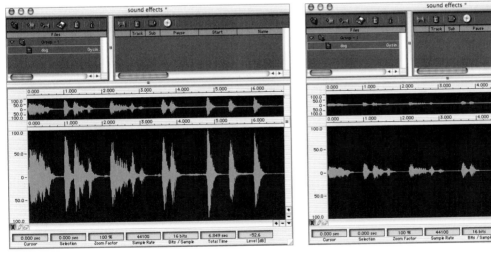

Figure 13.5

The sound on the left has been normalized, while the sound on the right has not.

Working with Sound Files

Flash is capable of handling most of the contemporary sound file formats that you will encounter. Each file format has its own particular idiosyncrasies. However, once the sound has been *imported* into the Flash environment, it's available for use in your movie in a variety of ways.

Exploring Sound File Types

The following are the kinds of digital sound files you can use with Flash:

Audio Interchange File Format (AIFF) This format is for Macintosh import only, although most Windows-based computers should be able to read and play `.aif` files with the help of QuickTime 4 or higher.

Windows Audio File (WAV) This format is primarily for Windows, although Macintosh computers can import .wav files into Flash if QuickTime 4 or higher is present.

MPEG Layer 3 (MP3) This format can be imported on both the Macintosh and Windows platforms. This is the only compressed audio format that can be imported into Flash. However, it's important to note that Flash cannot import variable bit rate (VBR) MP3 files. If you use iTunes or a similar application to compress MP3 files, be sure you are using a fixed bit rate. Higher bit rates mean larger file sizes, which create longer download times for your users. As such, 112kbps is the highest bit rate recommended for MP3 compression in a Flash project. Given most users' computer speaker setup, it's unlikely anyone would notice a difference higher than this setting.

Device sounds Device sounds are unique in that they can neither be imported into nor played by a Flash application. They are platform-specific audio files used by mobile devices while running a Flash application. Types include Musical Instrument Digital Interface (MIDI, `.mid`), Melody Format for i-mode (MFi, `.mld`), and Synthetic Mobile Application Format (SMAF, `.mmf`). To learn more about developing with sound for the Pocket PC, see Chapter 20.

The following sound types require QuickTime 4 or higher:

Sound Designer II Although Digidesign no longer manufactures the software, the Sound Designer II format (Macintosh only) is still used with Pro Tools audio-editing and audio-mixing software.

QuickTime movies (sound only) QuickTime movies don't have to contain video information. These videoless files are called *sound-only* movies and can be used in Flash on either the Windows or Macintosh platform.

Sun AU This format is used primarily with Sun or Unix computers and can be used in Flash on either the Windows or Macintosh platform. Files have an .au extension.

System 7 Sound This is a Macintosh-only sound format that is used for the general system sounds of the Macintosh operating system.

In most cases, the best files to import are raw, uncompressed WAVs and AIFFs. Flash provides excellent, internal audio compression codecs and an interface that allows you to test and hear the effect of compression on each sound file. To learn more about these compression options, see "Selecting a Compression Option" later in this chapter.

Importing Sound Files

To begin using audio in the Flash environment, you must first get the audio files into your movie Library. You do this by importing sounds. Your computer's operating system determines what kinds of sounds you can import. In general, Flash can import WAV files with Windows, AIFF files with Macintosh, and MP3 files with both platforms.

To import sound files in Flash:

1. Select File → Import → Import to Library. The Import dialog box opens.

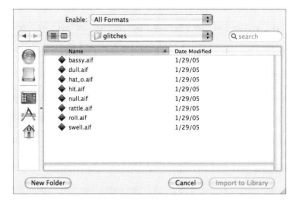

2. From the Show drop-down menu, choose the All Sound Formats option. This causes the Import dialog box to render anything that is not a sound file unavailable. This can make it easier to find the files you need. Locate the folder containing the file you want to import. If you need to select multiple files, use Ctrl+click / Shift+click.

You can import sounds as a group (as discussed here) or individually, depending on your needs and work flow.

3. When you're finished selecting all your sound files, click Import to Library. All the selected files will be imported into your movie's Library. You can confirm this by checking the contents of the Library. Select Window → Library (F11) to display the Library panel. All the sounds you just imported should appear with the speaker icon beside the filenames (see Figure 13.6). When a sound is selected in the Library, its waveform appears in the top of the Library window. You can audition the sound by pressing the Play button in the upper-right corner of the panel.

4. Once the sound files are in your movie's Library, they will be available for unlimited use within your movie. Sounds can also be part of Shared Libraries, which are shared among several movies. To read more about Shared Libraries, see Chapter 4.

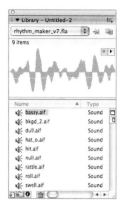

Figure 13.6

The Library panel displays sound files with a speaker icon beside the filenames.

Adding Sound to a Movie

Importing sounds is the first part of adding sound to your movie. Once you have sounds in your Library, you must then place them in the movie Timeline so that they become part of a movie's playback. To add sounds to a Timeline, you use the Properties Inspector (see Figure 13.7). This multifaceted interface element is your window to many of the parameters affecting sound behavior in your movie.

To add a sound to your movie:

1. Create a new layer, and name it something like **sound**. This isn't an essential step, but it can help keep individual sounds on separate layers in your movie. Each layer's name can be a title that describes the sound it contains (`introRiff`, for example). And it's easier to position sounds when they are independent of other movie elements.

> The Flash 8 Player can now support up to 32 tracks of audio. This means you can use Flash to play 32 sounds simultaneously! Additionally, Flash has virtually no limit to the number of sound layers you can have in a movie. On a *very* basic level, these features make Flash behave like a multitrack audio application, where you can stack many sounds on top of one another.

2. Click the frame where you would like the sound to start playing, and then select Insert → Timeline → Keyframe to insert a new keyframe.

3. Select Window → Properties → Properties (Ctrl/Cmd+F3) to display the Property Inspector.

    At this point, you should already have imported sounds into your movie. If you haven't, see the preceding section to learn how to do this.

Figure 13.7

The Property Inspector serves as the interface for sound control in your movie.

4. Choose a sound from the Sound drop-down menu. Once a sound is selected, the Property Inspector will display the attributes of the file you select: its sample rate, bit depth, length in seconds, and file size. The sound you select will be the sound that is cued when Flash plays the currently selected keyframe.

5. To add a default pan effect, select an option from the Effect drop-down menu. Or, click the Edit button to create a custom volume or pan envelope.

6. Select an option from the Sync drop-down menu:

   • In general, use Event for shorter sounds that you want to be played in time with a visual event in your movie, for example, a "thud" sound of a cartoon character falling down. Event sounds will play in their entirety until they are stopped or the sound ends.

   • Use the Stream sync if you want Flash to force the movie animation to lock playback with a sound file. To learn more about the various sync modes in Flash, see Chapter 14.

Unlike event sounds, stream sounds will play only through the number of frames they occupy in the Timeline. You must add frames to accommodate the length of a stream sound. Also, if you plan to use an MP3 file as a stream sound, you must recompress the file within Flash before publishing your movie. To learn more about this, see the section "Exporting and Compressing Audio Files" later in this chapter.

7. Select one of the following repeat options for the sound:

   • Select Repeat, and enter **1** in the adjacent field (or leave the field blank). This will play the sound only once.

   • Select Repeat, and enter a number between 0 and 65,535 in the adjacent field. The sound will repeat the number of times that you specify.

   • Select Loop. The sound will repeat continuously until it is stopped at a different keyframe or silenced via ActionScript.

   When you are finished, you should have something that looks like Figure 13.8.

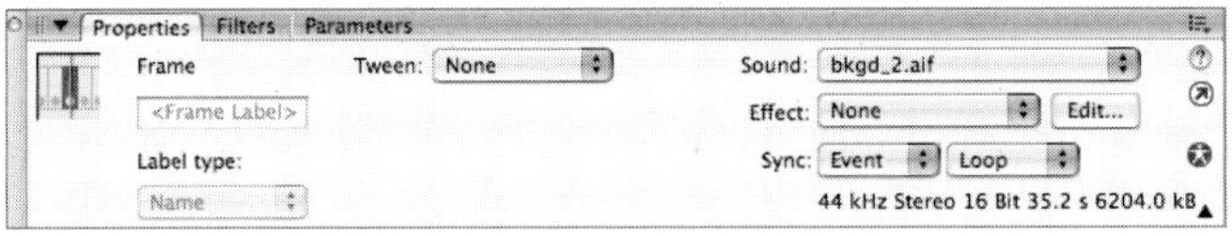

Figure 13.8

Here the sound bkgd_2.aif is cued as an event sound that will be looped continuously.

Stopping Sounds

Once a sound starts playing in Flash, few actions can interrupt it. In most cases, a sound will continue to play until it runs out of frames (if it is a stream sound), it finishes, or it runs out of loops. These events depend largely on the length of the sound file and the parameters you assign the sound when it first plays in your movie. Sometimes, though, it might be necessary for you to intervene and stop a sound or series of sounds explicitly.

To stop a specific sound from playing:

1. Click the frame in the sound layer where you would like to stop the sound.

2. Select Insert → Timeline → Keyframe to insert a new keyframe.

3. Select Window → Properties to display the Property Inspector if it is not already visible.

4. In the Sound drop-down menu, select the name of the sound file you want to stop playing. Choose the Stop option from the Sync drop-down menu. When the new keyframe is reached, the specified sound will stop playing.

To stop all sounds from playing:

1. Choose the frame where you want to stop the playback of every sound in your movie. It is also common to provide a button that can be used to stop your movie's sounds.

2. Open the Actions panel, and enter the following statement:

```
stopAllSounds();
```

If you want to use a button to stop the sounds in your movie, write the following function:

```
sound_ctrl.onRelease=function(){
   stopAllSounds();
}
```

This function is specific to the button instance `sound_ctrl`. You can replace that name with a button or Movie Clip instance name in your own projects.

3. Depending on where you attach this function, when the frame is played, or when the button clicked, every sound that is currently playing in your movie will stop. Playback cannot resume until you explicitly start each sound once again.

This technique of stopping all sounds is particularly useful if you need to stop several sound files simultaneously to sync with an animation or to create a "sound off" button for your movie. To learn additional (and more precise) means of stopping sounds, see Chapter 15.

Attaching Sound to a Button

It is common to use sounds in conjunction with a button. In the same way that the various button states offer visual indications of interaction, sounds can help add to the interactive experience by offering audible feedback. For example, if you wanted to create a button that looked and sounded like the door to a haunted house, you could add the sound of a low "creeeeak!" to the button's Over state. Then you could use the sound of a rusty latch or doorknob for the Down state. Ultimately, both of these sounds would make the door button much more interesting (and scary) in the context of your movie.

Adding a sound to a button is a simple and effective way to add some audio interest to your Flash production:

1. Import into your movie any sounds you need for the button. To learn how to do this, see the section "Importing Sound Files" earlier in this chapter.

2. Select the button on the Stage where you would like to attach the sound, and choose Edit → Edit Symbols. Flash jumps into Symbol Editing mode for the button you selected. In this mode, you should be able to see the button's Timeline with the Up, Over, Down, and Hit keyframe states. To learn more about the various states of a button, see Chapter 8.

3. Insert a new layer in the button Timeline, and name it **sounds**.

4. Click the Over state frame in the new layer, and then select Insert → Timeline → Keyframe to insert a new keyframe.

5. Select Window → Properties → Properties to display the Property Inspector if it isn't already visible. In the same way you added a sound to the main Timeline, you will add a sound to the button's Timeline (see Figure 13.9). Select a sound file from the panel's Sound drop-down menu. Assign any effect you want to use, and set the sync to Start. To learn more about Start sync and the other sound sync options, see Chapter 16.

6. Select Edit → Edit Document to return to the main Timeline, and select Control → Test Movie. Roll your mouse cursor over the button to hear the sound you just attached.

In the same way you attached a sound to the Over state of a button, you can attach a sound to the Down state. This helps create a more realistic "click" effect. Simply follow the steps outlined in this section. Create a new keyframe for the Down state, and attach the sound you want to use. Because the two keyframes represent different button events, they will be cued separately—one when the cursor rolls over the button and another when the button is clicked.

Figure 13.9

This button Timeline has a sound attached to the Over state keyframe.

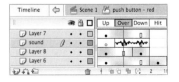

If you remember the discussion of symbols from Chapter 4, you should know that if you use this technique to associate a sound with a button, *every instance* of that button symbol will have the sound. If your projects require more flexibility, see the sound-related ActionScript techniques discussed in Chapter 15.

> When working with button sounds, it is important to trim the waveform so that no dead space appears at the start of the audio file. If your sound has dead space, a lag will exist between when the sound is cued and when you actually hear it.

Exporting and Compressing Audio Files

When you finish creating a Flash movie, you must go through the process of *publishing* your movie, or finalizing it for presentation to your audience. When you publish a Flash movie, all the audio content used in the project is bundled with the final movie. When a sound is bundled with an SWF or other published file, it is often changed from its original format to something that is more manageable in a bandwidth-sensitive environment. Because audio can greatly add to the size of a movie file, the process of bundling sounds generally involves *compression.*

Compression comes in many forms and is used to shrink, or *compress,* the final size of a sound file. Compression takes the original file and squeezes it down to a more portable, compact file that is easier to use in situations where file size is a crucial part of development. Sound great? Not always. Compression can have an adverse affect on sound files. In general, file size and sound quality are directly related. As you add more compression, the file size drops but so does the sound quality.

As you compress a sound file, you remove certain parts of the sound (usually those deemed least important by the compression codec). Although this works to create a more compact sound, it also takes away certain elements of the original. The more you compress a file, the fewer original elements remain, which can leave you with a sound of marginal quality. Don't be too discouraged, though. Flash offers several compression and resampling options that allow you to strike a happy balance between file size and sound quality.

Adjusting Individual Export Settings

You have a great deal of control when it comes to exporting sounds in Flash. In general, it is best to use individual settings for each sound in your movie. First, all sounds are different. Some sounds might sound fine at a low quality level or under high levels of compression. Second, sounds that are short or not as important in your movie can be squeezed down even further with high-compression, minimum-quality settings.

To set the export settings for a sound in your movie:

1. Select Window → Library to display the Library panel.

2. Highlight the sound name in the Library, and then select Properties from the Options drop-down menu in the Library panel. Alternatively, you can double-click the sound's speaker icon. The Sound Properties dialog box opens.

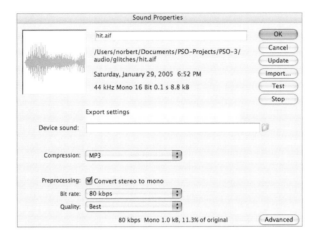

3. If the sound has been changed outside Flash since it was imported, click the Update button. This retrieves the most recent version of the file.

4. Choose an option from the Compression drop-down menu, and select the settings you want to use. To learn more about your options, see the next section of this chapter.

5. Click the Test button to audition the sound and readjust the compression settings as needed. When you are finished, click OK to return to your movie. Each sound you adjust in this fashion will be exported with the settings you specify.

Selecting a Compression Option

Flash offers several compression choices that are suited to different applications depending on your needs. When you select one of these from the Compression drop-down menu, its options (sample rate, bit depth, and so on) appear at the bottom of the Sound Properties dialog box. Note that as you change these options, the dialog box updates information about the size of the compressed sound.

Default Compression

To use the default compression options, leave the menu selection as Default. This will apply whatever options are set in the Publish Settings dialog box to the sound. To check the publish settings for your movie, select File → Publish Settings (see Figure 13.10). Here you can set the compression options for both stream and event sounds in your movie.

To learn more about the export settings in the Publish Settings dialog box, see the following sections.

If the Override Sound Settings box is checked, Flash will export all sounds, regardless of their settings in the Library, with the parameters defined in the Publish Settings dialog box.

ADPCM Compression

ADPCM, which stands for *adaptive differential pulse-code modulation*, is best for short sounds that can work well at lower quality settings. In particular, ADPCM is good for sounds with a metallic or buzzy quality and for some percussive sounds. It can also work well on short sound effects where quality isn't vital.

To use ADPCM compression:

1. Select ADPCM from the Compression drop-down menu.

2. Check the Convert Stereo to Mono box if you want to mix your stereo sounds into a single channel.

3. Select a sample rate from 44kHz to 5kHz. In general, the higher the sample rate, the better the sound quality you can expect. Every sound is different. Some may sound great at 5kHz, while others are unacceptable at 44kHz. Let your ears be the judge when testing compression settings.

4. Select ADPCM bits from 5 to 2. Again, a higher number of bits equals better quality. Test each setting to see whether what you hear is acceptable in terms of fidelity and size.

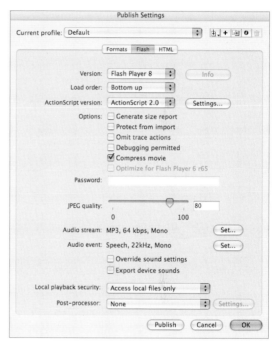

Figure 13.10

The Publish Settings dialog box enables you to define the default sound compression parameters for sounds in your movie.

MP3 Compression

MP3 compression is popular for distributing CD-quality or near-CD-quality audio in a compact digital format. MP3 compression is usually the best choice for music, some dialogue, long or detailed sound effects, and most kinds of stream sync sound in your movie. It yields great results in terms of both final file size and sound quality and is the most common setting used by Flash designers.

To export with MP3 compression:

1. Select MP3 from the Compression drop-down menu.

2. Choose a bit rate from 160Kbps to 8Kbps. You should get good results with MP3 settings at just about any quality; however, the general rule that higher settings equal better quality still applies. When in doubt, produce multiple versions, and weigh the aesthetics of exported sound quality versus file size. Your ears should be the final judge. A setting of 56Kbps yields a happy medium between acceptable quality and manageable size; use 112Kbps or higher to achieve near-CD-quality sound.

3. If you select a bit rate of 20 or higher, you have the option to mix stereo channels to a single mono channel by checking the Convert Stereo to Mono box. As expected, this will decrease file size by half.

4. Select a Quality setting:

   - Fast compresses files quickly but has the poorest quality. This option is not recommended for sounds that are predominant or significant in your movie.

   - Medium takes longer to compress but renders the files at a better quality than Fast.

   - Best is your best choice for music or files where quality is important. Although it takes longer to compress the files, it renders the highest-quality MP3s for your movie.

   These settings also effect the final size of a compressed MP3 file. Best can render smaller files than Medium or Fast, so it may be worth the extra time spent compressing when you consider the bandwidth savings.

Raw Compression

The Raw option translates to no compression. Instead of being compressed, the sound is either mixed to a single channel and/or sampled down to a lower sampling rate.

To use the Raw setting:

1. Select Raw from the Compression drop-down menu.

2. Check Convert Stereo to Mono if you want to mix your stereo sounds into a single channel.

3. Select a sample rate from 44kHz to 5kHz. In general, the higher the sample rate, the better the sound quality you can expect.

Use Raw when you specifically don't want to compress sounds. For a specific example of one such scenario, see "Audio Compression on a Deadline" later in this chapter.

Speech Compression

The Speech compression option is designed specifically for spoken sounds. When used on narration and dialogue, it produces decent-sounding results while maintaining a small file size.

To use the Speech option:

1. Select Speech from the Compression drop-down menu.

2. Select a sample rate from 44kHz to 5kHz. In general, the higher the sample rate, the better the sound quality you can expect. Be sure to test each sound before settling on a compression setting.

Speech compression doesn't support stereo sounds. All sounds are automatically converted to mono.

QuickTime Compression Options

Flash allows you to publish your movie as a QuickTime Flash movie rather than as Shockwave Flash. With this publish option, additional sound options affect the quality of sound in the QuickTime movie. Note that the compression options presented here are available *only* if you plan to publish your movie as a QuickTime Flash movie.

QuickTime compression settings apply only to the *streaming* sounds of a Flash movie published in QuickTime format. Event sounds will not be published with the QuickTime settings. If you are using event sounds in your movie, use the Property Inspector to change their sync to Stream before publishing the final movie file.

When working with Flash movies that will be published as QuickTime, you have a good deal of flexibility in terms of what you can do with audio. Flash has no limit to the number of tracks, so feel free to use as much audio as you deem necessary. And, because QuickTime files are linear, all the sounds will be mixed to a single audio track (or a pair of tracks if you use stereo sounds).

To implement QuickTime compression settings:

1. Select File → Publish Settings. In the Formats tab, check the QuickTime box. A QuickTime tab is displayed; select it.

2. For the Streaming Sound option, check the Use QuickTime Compression box. This activates the Settings button.

3. Click the Settings button, and the Sound Settings dialog box opens. (Several dialog boxes carry the name *Sound Settings*. In this step, the Sound Settings dialog box will affect QuickTime streaming sounds.)

Here you can choose from a variety of QuickTime sound settings, each of which has its own individual options. See Table 13.1 for a complete list. Because some compression schemes are better suited to certain tasks than others, try to find a codec that fits your specific needs. It might help to experiment with several different options and test them back to back on several systems before making a final compression decision.

Table 13.1

Compression
Options

COMPRESSION CODEC	DESCRIPTION/APPLICATION
24-bit integer, 32-bit integer	Increases bit depth (sample size) to 24 and 32.
32-bit floating point, 64-bit floating point	Increases bit depth (sample size) to 32 and 64. Most computers are incapable of playing sounds at this high bit depth and will convert back to 8- or 16-bit.
ALaw 2:1	Poor-quality compression. Not recommended.
IMA 4:1	Decent compression ratios. Must be 16-bit. Fine for CD delivery.
MACE 3:1, MACE 6:1	Dated codecs. Not worth the trouble.
Q Design Music 2	Superb compression ratios. Great for streaming music.
Qualcomm PureVoice	Superb compression ratios. Preferred format for streamed dialogue and narration.
uLaw 2:1	Old codec. Not worth the trouble.

4. After you have selected the right compression options, click OK in the Sound Settings dialog box, and then select the Flash tab in the Publish Settings dialog box.

5. It's necessary to disable the Stream and Event sound options in the Flash tab when exporting a QuickTime Flash movie; otherwise, sounds are doubled in the final QuickTime file. Click the Set button next to the Audio Stream label. The Sound Settings dialog box opens again, this time for Flash streaming sounds.

6. Choose Disable from the Compression drop-down menu. This prevents extra streaming sound instances from getting into your final movie. Click OK.

7. Repeat this process with the Set button beside the Audio Event label. This disables event sound compression in your Flash movie. Click OK in the Publish Settings dialog box when you have finished. Even though the compression options in the Flash tab have been disabled, your movie's stream sounds will be published with the settings you specified in the QuickTime tab.

Audio Compression on a Deadline

Some of the compression options in Flash (MP3 in particular) work slowly to compress the sounds in your movie. Publishing a movie with lots of sounds can take a *really* long time. This is fine for the final round of publishing, but when you're testing your movie, it can bring your development process to a screeching halt. One way to work around this is to *not* compress sounds while testing your movie. This way, no extra time is involved, and the sounds are added to the temporary SWF file as is.

To avoid compression-related delays when testing movies:

1. In the Publish Settings dialog box, check the Override Sound Settings box.

2. Set the compression options for event and stream sounds (as appropriate in your project) to Raw.

3. Deselect Convert Stereo to Mono, and set Sample Rate to match the sample rate of the sounds you imported. The sounds will still be added to your movie but with no compression.

This process is great during developmental stages. Because Flash is *not* taking the time to compress sounds, the process of testing your movie will go much faster. However, be sure to compress when you publish your final version. Uncheck the Override Sound Settings box, and you're ready to publish a final file using the settings you specified for each sound in the Library.

Equalizing Audio Files for Flash MP3 Compression

An *equalizer* is a tool you can use to alter the frequency balance of a sound file. *Equalization* (EQ) adjusts the frequencies of a sound by either boosting or cutting them. For example, cutting the low frequencies of a sound will take out the "boominess" or "muddy" quality of a sound. Boosting the high range will make a sound "brighter"; too much of this can make a sound shrill or tinny.

Generally, an equalizer makes a sound clearer. As with most effects, your ears are the best judges. Work with the equalizer until the file sounds the way you think it should. And as always, monitor the levels of a sound so that you don't *clip*, or distort, the file. Too much EQ can send a sound flying off the meters!

To apply EQ to a sound file or sample:

1. Select the portion of the file you want to equalize. This is usually the entire sound file.

2. Choose Equalizer from one of the application's menus (usually Process or Effects). An Equalizer dialog box opens.

3. Using the equalizer's slider controls (this is typical in most interfaces), set values for the various frequencies of a sound.

4. Some equalizers allow you to preview the new settings. Click Preview to audition the sound. When you have the sound where it sounds best, click OK to finalize the edit.

If you have exported sounds with Flash's internal MP3 compression, you have surely noticed a drop in sound quality of the exported files. Every sound responds to compression differently. For some, the changes rendered by the compression are minimal, while other sounds show a definite difference in their overall character and quality. In general, the lower you set the bit rate, the lower the quality your sound file will be and the more drastically a sound will be changed.

These changes in sound quality, however, don't have to be a permanent part of your movie. You can correct the effects of compression by using EQ to bring a sound to a point of equilibrium. By attenuating the frequencies that compression boosts and boosting the frequencies that compression dampens, you will be able to retain more of a sound's original character after your movie is published.

You should apply these changes to the original sound file (or copy of the original file) *before* importing it into Flash. By doing this, you will compensate ahead of time for the adverse effects MP3 compression has on the sound file. Ideally, when the Flash movie is published, all sounds will return to their original character. A sound will probably never be exactly the same, but it will be a definite improvement over the unequalized alternative.

Use Figure 13.11 as a starting point for your EQ. This EQ setting boosts the low end, cuts the low-to-mid range, and slightly boosts the high-mids and the highs. All EQ settings affect different sounds in different ways, however, but with a little tweaking and experimentation you should be able to bring your compressed Flash sound files closer to the original.

Figure 13.11

Use this as a starting point for your EQ.

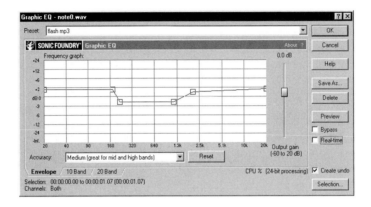

CHAPTER 14

Synchronizing Audio with Animations

When you think about animation, it is hard not to be reminded of the classic Warner Bros. cartoons starring Bugs Bunny, Daffy Duck, the Road Runner, Wile E. Coyote, Elmer Fudd, and Marvin the Martian. And, when you think about these animated cartoons, it's impossible not to remember all the crazy sounds that were so much a part of the show: anvils clanking on heads, zips, swooshes, and nimble violin strings plucking out the sound of a character's tiptoe entrance onto the screen. All these sounds were crucial to the success of the animation; they communicated the actions left unsaid by the visual track.

As you know by now, Flash is much more than an animation program. You can use it to create interactive menu systems, games, websites, and more. Are these animations? No, not really, but in the Flash environment, you have to think about everything as if it were an animation. Flash's Timeline structure applies to just about every element of the program, including buttons, Movie Clips, and scenes; even graphics are affected by this structure because they're *used* in Timelines. Whatever your design goals might be, try to think of every project as a kind of animation.

As in the classic Warner Bros. cartoons, you'll get more from your Flash movies by creatively using sound, and one of the keys to this is *synchronization*. When what you hear matches what you see on the screen, the effect is powerful. An animation will appear more lively and realistic, or an interface will seem more responsive. This chapter discusses how Flash deals with sound in the context of animations and how you can get the best results by synchronizing audio and visual events.

- Using the Flash synchronization options: Event, Stream, Start, and Stop
- Synchronizing for Flash Lite 1.1 applications
- Lip-syncing and forcing the animation frame rate
- Creating complex animation and button sound events
- Syncing audio with Movie Clips

Exploring Synchronization Options in Flash

Any time you attach a sound to a frame in the Timeline, you must set the Sync option (short for *synchronization*) in the Property Inspector (see Figure 14.1). This option—Event, Stream, Start, or Stop—tells Flash how to treat a sound when it is encountered in

your movie. Synchronization determines the relationship between the sound (music, sound effects, dialogue, and so on) and the animated components of your movie.

Figure 14.1

You can use the Property Inspector's Sync drop-down menu to assign the type of sync you want to use for each sound. Here the option is set to Event.

In Flash, you can make a sound play and loop independently of the animation in the Timeline, resulting in loose synchronization. Or you can have the sound lock the movie's frame rate to keep tight sync between the audio and visual tracks. Flash also considers the act of stopping a sound to be a kind of sync and will allow you to halt playback to match a visual event. Learning how these choices affect your movie is an important part of fine-tuning an animation and getting the most from your movie's sounds.

Using Event Sync

Event sync is one of the most commonly used means of audio synchronization in Flash. Its name is fairly self-explanatory; this option creates a sound event by responding to an animation event in your movie. When Flash plays a frame that contains an event-synced sound, that sound is cued to play in its entirety, independently of the Timeline. If the Timeline stops playing frames, an event sound will continue to play until it has finished or has run out of loops. Think of an event sound as a kind of cue that you can attach to a Timeline frame.

Event sounds offer a lot of flexibility with your movie because all you have to do is set them in motion and let the sound take it from there. Because event sounds play independently of your animation, you don't have to worry about having enough frames to accommodate the length of the sound. These characteristics make event sounds ideally suited to the following uses in a Flash movie:

Buttons Button sounds are usually attached to the Over and Down states of a button animation. When the mouse cursor is moved over a button, a sound is played; when the button is clicked, another sound is played. Because these button events (Over and Down) can happen quickly, it is important to use a sync option that will respond quickly. If a button is moused over or clicked more than once, Event sync will cue the sound each time and will mix multiple instances of the sound together. Consequently, this allows you to create interesting layered sound or musical effects with multiple button sounds. To learn more about the specifics of this technique, see the section "Working with Event Sound Effects and Music" later in this chapter.

If you're adding sound to a button and you specifically *don't* want sounds to layer and overlap, see the "Using Start Sync" section.

Sound effects If your movie calls for sound effects, the Event setting is definitely the one to use. It allows you to perfectly sync an animation event; for example, you could sync a basketball going through the hoop with the sound *swish!!* Create a new keyframe with an event sound on one of your movie's sound layers. The frame should line up with the correct moment in the animation. When your movie plays back, you'll see the ball go through the hoop and hear a gratifying *swish!!* to make the animation complete. To learn more about the specifics of this technique, see "Working with Event Sound Effects and Music" later in this chapter.

Stingers In film scoring, sudden musical stabs that add dramatic punch are called *stingers*. For instance, a woman is peacefully sleeping in her bed when the French doors to her chamber mysteriously open…you hear nothing. Then suddenly, as the vampire's face appears, you hear a high violin tremolo, and the hairs on the back of your neck stand up straight! This device has been used for years to enhance the dramatic tension of cinematic and cartoon scenes. In the same way that you add sound effects, you can use the Event option to cue dramatic musical stingers in your movie.

To take full advantage of this sync functionality, a sound that uses Event sync must be fully loaded into the Flash player before it is played. In most cases this is accomplished when your movie is initially loaded. If your projects require specific control over how assets are loaded, see Chapter 12.

Using Stream Sync

Stream sync is quite a bit different from the other sync techniques available to you in Flash. Stream sync locks the movie's frame rate to the playback of the sound and will skip (or *drop*) frames if the animation cannot keep the pace. This option makes Flash more like a video-editing application, where the audio and video tracks are locked together to preserve their synchronization. The opposite of event sounds, stream sounds will play only if they have enough frames to accommodate their length. In many cases, you'll have to add frames to enable long sounds to play completely. Figure 14.2 illustrates this concept.

Because of the nature of the Stream option, we recommend you avoid looping stream sounds if possible. You cannot reuse audio data as efficiently when sounds are set to the Stream option. Flash will add unnecessary information to your final movie and create a larger SWF file. The Stream option does, however, have some excellent uses:

Scored music If you have long sections of music that are supposed to sync precisely with an animation, the Stream option is your best bet. The stream audio will force Flash to maintain a consistent frame rate and keep tight synchronization between audio and animation events.

Figure 14.2

The top sound (Layer 2) does not have enough frames to play the entire file. You can tell because the waveform is cut off at the last frame. Notice that the bottom sound (Layer 1) does have enough frames. The waveform ends as a straight, horizontal line similar to what you'd see in a digital audio editor.

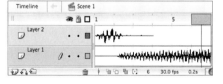

Lip sync To create tightly synchronized talking or singing animations, use the Stream option. It allows Flash to maintain a consistent pace and keep the dialogue or music in sync with the mouth animation. To learn more about the specifics of this technique, see the section "Creating Lip Sync Animations" later in this chapter.

Multitrack audio All sync options in Flash allow you to play up to 32 different sounds simultaneously. If you place each sound on its own layer, you can create a multitrack sound movie. Using the Stream option, it is possible to do this in a way that keeps all the tracks (individual sound layers) synchronized perfectly.

Stream sounds can start playing before they have fully loaded, which makes them particularly useful in situations such as these where you require long sound files that are played once.

Using Start Sync

Start sync is similar to Event sync. When the sound's frame is played, Start sync cues the sound and plays it in its entirety. The only difference is that if another instance of the sound is already playing, the new instance will not be heard. You can use Start sync as a kind of filter to prevent too many occurrences of a single sound.

Start sync is the best choice for buttons in situations where you do not want a button's sound to play more than once. For example, if you attach a sound to the button's Over state frame and use event sync, the sound will be heard each time your mouse moves over the button. If the mouse crosses over the button frequently, this can cause too many simultaneous instances of the sound. Start sync prevents this because only one instance of the sound is allowed to play at a time.

For an example of Event sync versus Start sync with buttons, open the file `buttonSync.swf` on the CD. Quickly move your mouse over the Event button several times. You'll hear the sound repeated each time your mouse crosses over the button. The more you do this, the more confusing things can start to sound. Next, do the same with the Start button. This time, no matter how often your mouse crosses over the button, you'll hear only one instance of the sound. Start sync helps to keep your button sounds tidy.

Syncing Sounds to Stop

The final sync option Flash offers is Stop, and as you probably guessed, this is what you use to silence a sound's playback. Stop sync silences sounds that were cued via Event or Start sync. To sync the end of a sound:

1. Insert a new keyframe where you'd like the sound to end. The keyframe should be positioned so that the sound will stop in sync with an animation event.

2. Select Window → Properties→ Properties (Ctrl+F3 / Cmd+F3) to display the Property Inspector. From the Sound drop-down menu, choose the name of the sound you want to stop. From the Sync drop-down menu, select the Stop option. When the Timeline reaches this frame, the sound you have specified will stop.

Figure 14.3

In this Timeline, the stream sound that starts at frame 1 is stopped to sync with an event in the animation at frame 20.

The Stop option works for event and start sounds, but you must handle stream sounds differently. You must make the last frame of the stream sound match the animation event. To stop a stream sound:

1. Find the animation event in the Timeline you want to sync with the end of a stream sound. The event is usually represented by a keyframe. Remember the frame number where the event takes place.

2. Stream sounds will play only through the number of frames they occupy, so to stop a stream sound, you must determine the number of extra frames and clear them from the Timeline. Find the last frame of the stream sound you want to stop.

3. Click the last frame of the stream sound, then Shift+click to extend your selection backward to the frame *immediately following* the frame that contains the event where you want to stop the sound. For example, if you wanted to sync the sound to stop at keyframe 20, you'd extend the selection to frame 21. Press Shift+F5, and the range of selected frames will disappear from the Timeline. The frames that remain should end at the same frame number as the event to which you synced the sound. The results in the Timeline should look something like Figure 14.3.

4. After you clear the unnecessary frames, select Control → Test Movie to see and hear how the sync works. You can add or subtract frames to the sound if the sync needs some tweaking.

Setting Up Sound Sync for Mobile Device Applications

Flash Professional 8 now allows you to create applications for mobile devices that support Flash Lite 1.1. This new feature is especially helpful if your application requires sound synchronization. With Flash Lite 1.1 you can use uncompressed WAV files and compressed MP3 files. Rather than link to an external device sound, you can add these files to the FLA file just as you would when creating a Flash application for the Web or a desktop computer. Additionally, these "native" sounds can sync to animation on the Timeline.

With Flash Lite 1.1 you can use both Event and Stream sync methods. The good news is that no extra limitations exist—event and stream sounds will behave as described earlier in this chapter. Event sounds play when their containing frame is reached and will stop when finished or when told to do so via ActionScript. Stream sounds are bound in lockstep with the Timeline and will set the pace for an animation.

For specifics on sound and synchronization in Flash Lite 1.0 and 1.1 applications, choose Help → Flash Help (F1), and see the article "Working with Sound" in the "Developing Flash Lite Applications" section.

Exploring Flash Synchronization Techniques

Now that you know how Flash handles animation/sound synchronization, you're ready to dig deeper into the subject and see how these techniques work in the context of your movie. As with many things in Flash, the techniques are simple; the real magic comes from your ability to use them creatively and move beyond the basic capabilities of the software. The examples presented in the following sections are merely points of departure for your own wild and creative uses of sound synchronization.

Creating Lip Sync Animations

Many options are available to you for creating lip sync animations. Depending on the kind of animation you want to create, Flash allows you to animate either with loose, stylish synchronization, with lifelike accuracy, or with anything in between. A good lip sync sequence can make animated characters come to life in your movie.

This technique uses the Stream option to force the animation to keep pace with the audio track. Another advantage of this option is that with stream sounds, you can *scrub* the audio track. In other words, you click the playback head and drag it across the timeline to hear what part is synchronized with a particular frame. Scrubbing allows you to test certain sections manually to see how the audio and animation line up.

To create a lip sync animation, first draw a character, record some dialogue, and import it into your movie. The only quirk to this technique is that your character's mouth has to be on its own layer. The reason is that when you animate a lip sync, you don't use just one mouth graphic. Rather, you use several mouth graphics that have different shapes representing the different mouth positions for the various words and letters in your character's language. The various mouth positions occupy their own keyframes on their own layers and change to match the character's speech. The character's face and body can be left unchanged.

In this lesson, all the media files have been created for you. Open the `lipSync.fla` file on the CD, and save it to your hard drive. If you'd like to see what you're getting yourself into, open `lipSync_final.swf` to see and hear the finished file, or open `lipSync_final.fla` to inspect the finished authoring file.

To create a lip sync animation:

1. Using the `lipSync.fla` file, insert two new layers above the existing **paws** layer; name one **dialog** and the other **mouth**.

2. Insert a new keyframe (press F6 or select Insert → Timeline → Keyframe) in the second frame of the dialog layer. Select Window → Properties → Properties and choose `woofwoofbark.aif` from

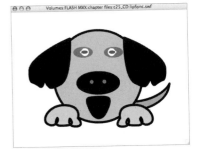

the Sound drop-down menu. Set the Sync option to Stream. You want to use Stream sync so that the animation will be forced to keep pace with the audio and maintain a tight synchronization.

3. You're now ready to create the animation for the phrase *woof woof, bark*. Notice that the waveform looks chunky in some places and flat in others. The dense, chunky areas are where the sound is the loudest (see Figure 14.4). If you click the playback head and drag it across the Timeline (scrubbing the sound), you'll hear the audio track play back slowly. This should give you an idea of what "words" fall on which frames in the Timeline.

4. Select keyframe 1 of the mouth layer. Drag the closed graphic symbol from the Library to the Stage, and place it where the mouth should be. This will start the mouth animation in a closed position. Use the Info panel (Ctrl+Alt+I / Cmd+Opt+I) to help position the various mouth graphics. This helps ensure that the mouth can be placed in the same position (X = 275, Y = 300) and that it doesn't shift unnaturally on the face. Click the middle square marker in the Info panel's symbol position option. This tells Flash to determine a symbol's X and Y coordinates from the vertical and horizontal center of the symbol.

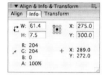

5. Create a blank keyframe (press F7) in frame 2 of the mouth layer, and drag the W Graphic symbol to the Stage, placing it where the mouth should be (again, X = 275, Y = 300). To be sure your alignment is consistent, use either the Align panel or the Info panel. The W Graphic symbol creates a mouth position to say the letter *w* and starts the first part of your animation.

6. Create another blank keyframe in frame 3 of the mouth layer, and drag the F Graphic symbol to the Stage. Add another blank keyframe to frame 4, and drag the closed Graphic symbol to the Stage. This completes the first word, *woof*.

7. Continue adding blank keyframes and placing symbols on the Stage until the entire phrase is paired with mouth position graphics. It can be fun to experiment with this on your own, but if it becomes frustrating, you can refer to Table 14.1 to see which symbols go in which frames.

8. When you have finished, select Control → Test Movie to hear and see what the dog has to say! This dialogue is short, so the synchronization is not a great issue here. However, when you select the Stream option, you can start to work with longer lines of dialogue, and the animation will keep the sync.

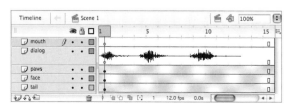

Figure 14.4

The peaks of the audio waveform show you which places are the loudest, and the valleys represent the quiet sections.

	FRAME	GRAPHIC SYMBOL (MOUTH POSITION)
Table 14.1	1	Closed
Frame and	2	W
Graphic Symbol	3	F
Combinations for		
the lipSync.fla	4	Closed
Movie	5	W
	6	F
	7, 8	Closed
	9	B
	10	A
	11	K
	12	Closed

Lip sync animation is a topic that can grow extremely complex. Although this simple example offers just a glimpse of the big picture, it addresses all the important concepts. You can practice the following additional tips to become more proficient with this technique:

- Keep a hand mirror with you when you work so that you can speak the words and watch the position of your mouth as you speak.

- Don't lose sight of the entire phrase. Some letters and words don't always match with the mouth shapes you think they should.

- Use temporary gotoAndPlay() statements to isolate and loop specific parts where you need to focus on a word or words.

- Drawing good mouth shapes (or *phonemes*, as they're known in the animation business) is critical! You can read about the art of drawing animation in any of the following books:

    - *The Animator's Workbook* by Tony White (Watson-Guptill Publications, 1988)

    - *The Animation Book: A Complete Guide to Animated Filmmaking—From Flip-Books to Sound Cartoons to 3-D Animation* by Kit Laybourne (Three Rivers Press, 1998)

    - *Cartooning: Animation 1 with Preston Blair* by Preston Blair (Walter Foster Publishing, 1986)

- See the following article at the Gamasutra website to learn about animation from artistic and scientific perspectives: http://www.gamasutra.com/features/20000406/lander_01.htm. Gamasutra articles are for subscribed members only, but the membership is free and it's well worth the effort to sign up.

Working with Event Sound Effects and Music

Event sounds offer you the greatest amount of freedom and flexibility when cueing your sounds. As a result, it is also the loosest of all the sync options in Flash. This is not necessarily bad. Even though "loose sync" might sound negative, sometimes it is especially useful.

Event sync is appropriately named because you pair the sound (music, effect, and so on) with an *event* in your movie or animation. When the visual event occurs, the sound is triggered. This is, of course, a tight kind of sync, where both a visual event and a sound happen at the same moment. However, after the initial sound cue, the sync becomes much less clear. Event sounds will play independently of the Timeline and continue to be heard until the entire sound has finished playing or has been stopped explicitly. For example, if you wanted to use the sound of a cymbal crash for a "falling down" animation, the cymbal would continue to ring long after the character's rear end hit the pavement.

Because event sounds will continue to sustain depending on their specific length, you can achieve all sorts of interesting layering effects with multiple sounds in your movie. For example, if a waiter drops a tray full of dishes and glasses, you'd hear not one *crash!* but a flurry of cracks, shatters, and smashes! Depending on how the scene is animated, you can pair a specific sound effect to each event where a bowl, plate, or glass hits the floor. All you need to do is create a separate sound layer for each effect you want to use. Then, insert a new keyframe that lines up with the animated event you want to sync, and attach a sound with the Event option. As the Timeline plays through the series of animated events, each sound will be cued at the appropriate time. See Figure 14.5 for an example of this in a movie Timeline. Because each sound is left to play independently, each will continue to ring until the sound ends, creating a great, layered sound effect to enhance your animation. The advantage of this technique is that rather than having to create a long sound effect and guess when each element falls into place, you can build the entire effect in Flash and get much better synchronized results.

Keep the following tips in mind when working with event sound effects:

- Event sounds are a little bit like Movie Clip symbols, they can be used over and over and over again. A sound cued with Event sync only needs to load once. After it's in memory, the sound will be available to play as often as your project demands with no additional load time.

- Event sounds are heard when they're first encountered in the Timeline. To prevent latency, be sure that the sound is trimmed and has no dead space or silence at the start of the sound file. To learn more about trimming audio files, see Chapter 13.

- If you're layering several loud sounds, you might need to adjust their envelopes so that the sounds aren't distorted when played in your movie. In the Property Inspector, click the Edit button to open the Edit Envelope dialog box (see Figure 14.6). Drag the handles of the edit envelope down in order to lower the volume for the left and right channel of a sound.

Figure 14.5

This Timeline shows how you can pair event sounds with animation keyframes to create a layered sound effect.

Figure 14.6

You can use the Edit Envelope dialog box to change the volume of individual sounds. This is the easiest way to achieve a good balance when several sounds play simultaneously.

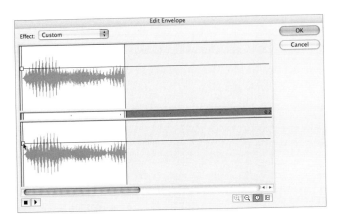

- Flash 8 can play 32 sounds simultaneously. However, older versions could only handle eight. If your project must be compatible with older Flash Player versions, you will be much more limited in the amount of audio you can employ. Look at your Timeline to see whether any spots exist where more than eight different audio layers have active sounds at the same time. If you encounter this in your Timeline, try some readjustments to prevent too many overlaps.

- In the same way that this technique works for sound effects, it can also work for music, particularly sweeping flourishes, melismatic vocal cues, horn and guitar riffs, and so on. Experiment with this technique to see what kinds of interesting musical effects you can create with event sounds.

Syncing Audio with Movie Clips

Movie Clips are one of the most important elements in any Flash movie. They can perform their own independent animations, apart from the activity taking place on the main Timeline. Consequently, Movie Clips can be great assets to the synchronization of sound in your movies. In Chapter 4, you learned about the autonomy of Movie Clips. This is especially relevant when it comes to the playback control and synchronization of sound files. You can create Movie Clips that contain sound files attached to their various frames. Then, by targeting a clip, you're able to control the sound or sounds it holds in its frames. This technique takes you one step beyond playing sounds from your main Timeline and offers a great deal of audio playback control.

In this example, you'll learn how to use Movie Clips to control sound playback. You can take a look at the finished files, `audioMC.fla` and `audioMC.swf`, on the CD. To use Movie Clips to sync sounds, you must perform two steps: create the sound Movie Clip, and set up a means of controlling the clip.

To create a Movie Clip that can sync sounds:

1. If you have not done so already, import a sound into your movie. Then select Insert → New Symbol, assign the name **audio**, and check the Movie Clip radio button.

2. Click frame 2 of the audio Timeline, and press F6 to insert a new keyframe; then press F5 to insert an additional frame in frame 3.

3. Create another new keyframe at frame 4, and add one new frame after it. Finally, add one last keyframe at frame 6. The finished frame construction should look like Figure 14.7.

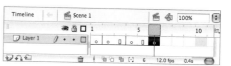

Figure 14.7

The frame structure for the sound Movie Clip has keyframes at frames 1, 2, 4, and 6.

4. Now that the clip has its basic structure, you can start to fill in its elements. Attach the following statement to keyframe 1:

   ```
   stop();
   ```

   This stops the clip from playing any further in the Timeline; it is ready and waiting at frame 1.

5. Enter another ActionScript statement in keyframe 2:

   ```
   stopAllSounds();
   ```

   This will silence all sounds in the movie when this Timeline reaches frame 2.

6. Attach your sound to keyframe 4, and set the Start sync option in the Property inspector. Enter the number of repeats, or set the sound to loop. Here you use the Start option so that if the sound is already playing, it will not be interrupted or overlapped.

7. Attach the following ActionScript statement to keyframe 6:

   ```
   stop();
   ```

   This line is an important part of the Movie Clip because it completes the "cycle" of statements contained in the clip. The clip cues the sound at frame 4; then, as it continues through the Timeline, it reaches the stop() statement at frame 6. The clip's playback halts, but the sound continues. Because the sound was cued with Start sync, it will play independently of any Timeline until it has either finished playing or exhausted its repetitions. If the sound was set to loop continuously, it will play until it is explicitly stopped.

Now that you have completed the Movie Clip, you can create a means to control it in your movie. You can do this in many ways. Here you'll learn both how to make the controls part of the clip itself and how to control the clip from the main Timeline.

To put controls in the clip itself:

1. If you aren't already in Symbol Editing mode, select the audio Movie Clip from the Edit Symbols menu , or double-click the clip's icon in the Library.

2. Insert a new layer in the clip, and drag a button onto its Stage and assign the instance name **play_btn** in the Property Inspector. (If your movie's Library has no buttons, you'll need to create some.) Drag a second button to the Movie Clip's Stage and assign the instance name **stop_btn**. These will serve as your Play and Stop buttons.

3. Select the keyframe in frame 1 and add the following statements after the stop() function you typed earlier:

```
play_btn.onRelease=function(){
    gotoAndPlay(4);
}

stop_btn.onRelease=function(){
    gotoAndStop(2);
}
```

These statements should make perfect sense: because the sound file is cued at frame 4, you have to send the Movie Clip to play at frame 4 to start the sound. To silence the sound, the Movie Clip jumps back to frame 2. When it gets there, it will encounter the stopAllSounds() function. This will halt the clip's playback at frame 2 and stop any currently active sounds in the movie.

Let's recap what is happening in the clip. When you first load the clip into the movie, the clip stops at frame 1, and no sound is heard (remember, the sound is at frame 4). When the clip receives a message to go to frame 4, the sound is cued, and the clip is told to stop at frame 6. The sound continues to play independently of the Timeline. Then, when you want to stop the sound, the Stop button sends the clip to halt at frame 2, where it encounters the stopAllSounds() function. This quiets the clip and prevents it from playing any further.

4. These statements complete the controls for your Movie Clip. Exit Symbol Editing mode, and return to the main Timeline. Drag an instance of the audio Movie Clip to the Stage of the main Timeline. Select Control ➔ Test Movie, and experiment with switching the sound on and off.

It's great to be able to toggle the sounds on and off from the clip itself, but it's equally important to be able to control the clip from the main Timeline. To do this, you'll need to target the clip specifically so that you can send it to play at the correct frames:

1. Give your audio Movie Clip the instance name **soundMC** in the Property Inspector.

2. Then, drag two buttons to the Stage of the main Timeline, one to play the sound and one to stop it. Use the Property Inspector to assign the instance names **play_btn** and **stop_btn** as appropriate.

3. Create a new layer and give it the name **code**.

4. Select the first frame of the **code** layer, open the Actions panel (Alt+F9 / Opt+F9) and enter the following statements:

```
play_btn.onRelease=function(){
    soundMC.gotoAndPlay(4);
}

stop_btn.onRelease=function(){
    soundMC.gotoAndStop(2);
}
```

Both sets of statements target the soundMC instance with an absolute target path and send it to a frame to play or stop the sound as necessary.

5. Select Control → Test Movie. You should now be able to toggle the sound with both sets of buttons—those in the Movie Clip and those on the main Timeline.

When you control a clip from the main Timeline, it's not necessary to have buttons built into the clip itself. If you want, take the buttons from the clip, and leave them in your movie as sound-only Movie Clips. A Movie Clip does not have to have graphics to work, only frames. In this case, the clip's frames are filled with nothing but actions, keyframes, and a sound cue.

The demo file for this exercise has a few additional features. Refer to audioMC.fla on the CD. Here, the Movie Clip Timeline has frame labels. The ActionScript that controls the audio playback uses the frame labels rather than frame numbers. This technique can be helpful if you have a hard time remembering what happens at each frame number.

CHAPTER 15

Controlling Audio with ActionScript

Up to this point, your exposure to audio in the Flash environment has consisted mainly of sounds that are attached to your movie's Timeline and cued when their host frames are played. This technique works well for cueing music, sound effects, and dialogue in such a way that they're synced with an animation. The only disadvantage to this approach is that all sounds are bound to frames, within either a Movie Clip or your main Timeline. As a result, if a Timeline has sounds you need but isn't currently available, sound playback may not be possible. Luckily, you can change this with ActionScript. By making sounds accessible via code, you have the flexibility to cue audio files at any time and in any situation.

When Flash evolved to version 5, it introduced the Sound object. The Sound object is an element of ActionScript that allows you to have complete control over every sound in your movie, whether the sound is in a Timeline or not. Flash MX (a.k.a. version 6) continued the tradition by allowing you to load external sounds, manage sound playback, and track sound-related events. The Sound object opens the possibilities for interactive audio in Flash and allows you to change every sound parameter dynamically through scripting rather than with keyframes and sync options. Now, with 32 channels of audio, Flash 8 offers more flexibility with sound than ever before.

- **Creating Sound objects**
- **Playing and stopping sounds with ActionScript commands**
- **Setting and dynamically changing a sound's volume**
- **Setting and dynamically changing a sound's pan position**
- **Applying stereo effects to sounds**
- **Using interactive controls to manipulate sound in your movies**
- **Loading and streaming external MP3 sound files into a movie**

Working with the Sound Object

The Sound object is one of ActionScript's predefined objects. You use it to control the playback parameters of sounds in your movie. The Sound object allows you to play and stop sounds, set their volume level, and change their position and volume in the left and right speakers. The Sound object also makes it possible for you to monitor the volume, panning, and effects applied to a particular sound. To use this object, it's important to understand what it is and how it works as part of the ActionScript language.

Understanding the Sound Object

As do all objects in ActionScript, the Sound object holds information about various components of your movie. Just as the MovieClip object holds information about the properties of a particular clip and the Math object stores specifics of arithmetic, the Sound object stores information about a movie's sounds and their properties. More specifically, it stores information about whether a sound is currently playing and, if so, how loud, in what speaker(s), and so on. To monitor or control a sound via ActionScript, you must create a new Sound object. Once a sound has an object associated with it, the object allows you to pass information to and from the sound.

Objects can encapsulate the specific attributes of an element in your movie and allow you to control them. They also serve as a medium of exchange. In the exchange, you must have currency—something common that can be understood and used by both your movie and its objects. ActionScript refers to this kind of currency as *methods*. You can use methods to send and retrieve information between your movie and its objects. Every object has a particular set of methods that it implements. The Sound object has methods that check and set volume and panning and that play (start) and stop active sounds in your movie. When you need to communicate with an object, you must use its methods.

Using the Sound Object

The first step toward working with the Sound object is creating a Sound instance. Without it, you'll have no means of communicating with a particular sound. When you create a new Sound object, you can use it to control the following:

- All sound files exported in your movie's Library
- Any sound file you load during runtime
- All sound files attached to a particular Timeline
- All sound files attached to the object

Depending on how you create the Sound object, you'll be able to use it for any of these applications. The generic constructor for a Sound object is as follows:

```
soundObjectName=new Sound("targetInstance");
```

Here, *soundObjectName* is a placeholder for whatever you want to call the object. *targetInstance* is an optional argument (enclosed in quotes) for the function. If you plan to control the sounds in a particular Movie Clip, you must target the clip specifically using the *targetInstance* argument.

To create an object for every movie currently available in the Flash Player, no target argument is necessary. Use this constructor:

```
globalMovieSound=new Sound();
```

Here, *globalMovieSound* is the name of a new object to control the sounds on all Timelines.

To create an object for all sounds in a Movie Clip or on a specific Timeline, you must create the object and specify a target argument as a string (in quotes):

```
monkeyClipSound=new Sound("bananas");
loadedSound=new Sound("_level1");
```

The first example creates an object named monkeyClipSound to control the attributes of sounds in the Movie Clip named bananas. The second statement creates an object named loadedSound for all sounds on the Timeline of the movie loaded at _level1. It's important to know that this technique (specifying a target instance) is the preferred means of creating a Sound object. Not using a target (as in new Sound()) forces you to manage all sounds simultaneously and severely limits your flexibility.

When a Sound object targets a sound in another Timeline, the object can control only the volume and panning of the sound. Playing and stopping via ActionScript don't work because the sound is bound to the frames of the Timeline where it resides. To leverage control over specific sounds using ActionScript, Sound objects control individual sounds that reside in a movie's Library. To facilitate this, you must attach the sound directly to the object. To learn how to do this, see the section "Attaching Sounds with Linkage Identifiers" later in this chapter.

Controlling Sound Playback

Creating a Sound object is an essential step to controlling your sounds dynamically with ActionScript. Without the object, you have no means of issuing commands to the sound. After you construct an object for a specific sound, you're free to invoke the methods of the Sound object to control the playback.

Controlling a sound via ActionScript offers several advantages over the conventional frame-based sound cues. First, if you want to cue only a particular sound, you don't have to target a Movie Clip or Timeline to play a specific frame. In many cases, the Sound object allows you to refer to a sound specifically, and you can cue it without having to play the frame where it resides in your movie. ActionScript has provisions for you to stop all sounds in your movie. In addition to providing this same stop feature, the Sound object allows you to start all the sounds in your movie with a single set of script commands.

Second, controlling a sound through ActionScript offers greater flexibility. Any element of your movie that uses scripting represents an opportunity to control sound playback. As graphic elements of your movie are dynamically manipulated or moved, you can reflect these changes in your sound scripting. You can represent all button clicks, menu transitions, progress bars, and network connections with sound.

Here are some Sound object methods used to control sound playback:

start(*secondsOffset*,*loops*) Cues sounds. `start()` can take two optional arguments. The *secondsOffset* argument starts a sound from any point within the sound file. To start a 10-second sound at its halfway point, you'd specify an offset of 5. The *loops* argument establishes the number of times a sound will play. If no loop is specified, the sound will play once (the default). To play it twice, enter a value of 2; enter 3 to play it three times, and so on.

> To cue a sound using the `start()` method of the Sound object, you must first export the sound from the Library using the Linkage option. To learn more about this, see the section "Attaching Sounds with Linkage Identifiers" later in this chapter.

stop("*soundID*") Stops sounds. `stop()` will silence all sounds in the object that it is used to control. The optional argument *soundID* stops sounds that were attached to the Sound object directly with symbol linkage.

To see specific examples using these methods, see the section "Playing and Stopping Sounds" later in this chapter.

Setting Volume and Pan Parameters Dynamically

Without the help of ActionScript and the Sound object, you must set parameters that affect a sound's volume and panning in the Edit Envelope dialog box (see Figure 15.1). Although this technique gives you a convenient graphical representation of the changes affecting a sound's envelope, the changes are noninteractive, are permanent, and cannot be altered after the movie is published.

ActionScript expands the possibilities tremendously by providing four methods for setting and monitoring the volume and pan parameters of a sound. And because you do this via scripting, you have the potential to dynamically change volume and pan information at any time and from any location in your movie.

setVolume(*volume*) Controls the volume of a sound's playback. Specify the argument *volume* from 0 (muted) to 100 (full volume). The default volume setting is 100. You're able to boost the volume to levels beyond 100, but do this with caution! It can produce unpleasant distortion and possibly damage speakers or headphones.

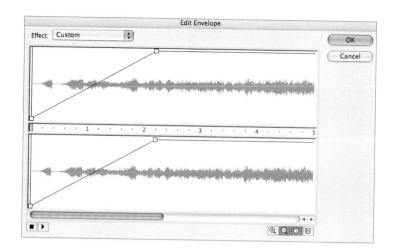

Figure 15.1

**Use the Edit Enve-
lope dialog box to
set volume and
panning. Once set,
the level is fixed and
can only be changed
by re-editing the
envelope and
re-publishing
your movie.**

getVolume() Monitors the volume of a Sound object. This method returns a value from 0 to 100, representing the current volume of the object.

setPan(pan) Sets the pan position for a Sound object. The argument *pan* determines where the sound is positioned. A value of 100 indicates that the sound is panned hard right (panned completely to the right speaker), –100 indicates that the sound is panned hard left (panned completely to the left speaker), and 0 indicates that the sound is centered (the default pan position). Once an object's panning has been set, it will remain in that position until it's changed.

getPan() Monitors the pan position of a Sound object. This method returns values ranging from –100 (hard left) to 100 (hard right), which represent the pan position of the object. The value 0 (the default) means a sound is shared equally between the two speakers.

To see specific examples using these methods, see the section "Setting Volume and Pan Levels" later in this chapter.

It's important to understand that Sound objects are subject to the same hierarchy as graphic objects in Flash. For example, a Movie Clip with an _alpha value of 50 will be semitransparent *along with all other Movie Clips nested within it*. Sound objects are affected in a similar fashion. For example, global Sound object A that has its volume set to 50. Inside the Timeline where A was created, the nested Sound object B has a volume of 80. In this scenario, since 50 is half of 100, the total audible volume of sound B will be 40 (half of 80). A contains B, and its parameters directly affect the clips within it. You can use these hierarchical characteristics to control sounds on a group basis and leverage control in a broader fashion.

Creating Special Stereo Effects

ActionScript provides a special Sound object method that allows you to create unique effects with stereo sounds in your movie; it's called `setTransform()`. Although the effects it creates are similar to those accomplished with panning, this method offers a bit more functionality. For instance, a barbershop quartet might have the bass and lead voices mixed more heavily in the left channel, while the baritone and tenor voices are mixed more to the right. If you were to listen to only one channel of a stereo mix, you'd hear an incomplete rendition of the overall sound because it would be missing about half of its components.

The `setTransform()` method doesn't affect sounds directly. To use it, you must create a generic object that applies the transform information to the Sound object you want to alter. The generic object (call it `transformer`) allows you control each channel of a stereo mix and assign output values for each as percentages. For each channel of stereo sound, the `transformer` object has two properties, one that controls a channel's left output and one for the right. This gives you four properties that can alter the stereo composition of a sound. See Table 15.1 for a rundown of the generic object (`transformer`) properties.

Confused? We'll now provide two examples of property settings to show how they'd work in context. The following properties play a stereo sound as true stereo; all the left information is played in the left speaker, and all the right information is played in the right speaker:

```
ll = 100
lr = 0
rr = 100
rl = 0
```

The next property settings swap the left and right channel information to create a reverse stereo effect; all left information is played right, and all right information is played left:

```
ll = 0
lr = 100
rr = 0
rl = 100
```

Of course, by changing the values assigned to each property, you can create many kinds of interesting stereo effects.

Table 15.1	PROPERTY	VALUE	DESCRIPTION
Properties for the `transformer` **Object Used with** `setTransform()`	ll	0–100	Percentage of left channel sound to play in the left speaker
	lr	0–100	Percentage of right channel sound to play in the left speaker
	rr	0–100	Percentage of right channel sound to play in the right speaker
	rl	0–100	Percentage of left channel sound to play in the right speaker

Once you've stored the properties in the generic `transformer` object, you pass the `transformer` object to the Sound object via the `setTransform()` method. Here's a breakdown of the method's syntax:

`setTransform(transformer)` Applies the properties stored in the `transformer` object to a Sound object.

`getTransform()` Retrieves the properties applied to a Sound object in the last `setTransform` command.

For an example of using the `setTransform()` method and creating a generic `transformer` object, see `setTransformer.fla` in the Chapter 15 folder of this book's companionon the CD.

Cueing Sounds with the Sound Object

The Sound object provides you with a great deal of flexibility in controlling sound playback. You'll find that it offers substantial advantages over conventional frame-based sound cues because you can cue sounds at any time and manipulate their attributes dynamically. Now that you know what the Sound object is and how it works, you're ready to put it to use in the context of your Flash projects. The following sections show you how to use the Sound object to export and attach a sound from your movie's Library and then cue it in your movie.

Attaching Sounds with Linkage Identifiers

One of the most useful functions of the Sound object is that it allows you to play sounds that aren't directly inserted in a Timeline keyframe. However, before you can do this, you must attach the sound to the object you're using to cue the sound and control it. By attaching a sound, you're adding it to your movie while it's running. In some ways, this is the ActionScript equivalent of cueing a sound from a frame. The main difference is that when you attach a sound, you do it with ActionScript. Consequently, you can pair it with button clicks, keystrokes, and other types of user interaction.

To attach a sound to a Sound object, you must first export the sound from your movie's Library:

1. In your movie's Library, highlight the name of the sound you want to export.

2. In the Options pop-up menu, select Linkage. You can also right-click / Ctrl+click the file in the Library and select Linkage from the context menu. The Linkage Properties dialog box opens (see Figure 15.2).

Figure 15.2

Use the Linkage Properties dialog box to export a sound from the Library so that you can attach it to a Sound object.

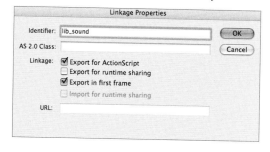

3. Check the Export for ActionScript box, and give it a unique name in the Identifier box. The identifier is the name you'll use to attach the sound to a Sound object. In Figure 15.2, the exported sound will be attached to an object as `lib_sound`.

   Notice that the Export in First Frame option is checked by default, and for now, leave it as is. This means the sound will be added to the first frame of your movie when it's loaded into the Flash Player. If you're using large audio files, this puts a heavy burden on the first frame, because the sounds and other elements in frame 1 must be loaded before any other content. Ultimately, this can result in a long initial download that must take place *before* a preloader is encountered. To learn an alternate technique that overcomes this issue, see "Preloading Files with Linkage Identifiers" later in this chapter.

4. Click OK when you're finished. The sound is now ready to be attached to a Sound object.

> You can also use the Linkage Properties dialog box to include sounds as a Shared Library asset. Shared Libraries allow you to exchange common files between several Flash movies. To learn more about creating and working with Shared Libraries, see Chapter 4.

After you export the sound from the Library, you're able to attach it to a Sound object. This step officially associates the sound with an object, which in turn can be used to control the various parameters of the sound's playback. An object can have only one sound attached at a time. Attaching a new sound to an object will replace any sounds the object previously contained. To attach a sound, you use the `attachSound` method, which has this generic syntax:

```
sndObj.attachSound("idName")
```

Here, *sndObj* is a placeholder for the name of the object to which you'll attach the sound. The argument *idName* (a string, entered in quotes) declares the name of the identifier associated with the exported sound you want to attach.

The following example creates a new global Sound object called `movAudio` and attaches the sound exported from the Library with the linkage identifier `libSound`:

```
movAudio=new Sound();
movAudio.attachSound("libSound");
```

After completing these steps, any methods applied to the `movAudio` object will affect the playback of the sound file exported as `libSound`.

Preloading Files with Linkage Identifiers

As discussed, when the Export in First Frame box is checked, the sounds are added to frame 1 of your movie and loaded into the Flash Player along with everything else in frame 1. This doesn't add to the download time of a movie, but it prevents your users from seeing anything in frame 1 until all the sounds have loaded. If you use a lot of sounds, the wait can be considerable before your audience sees or hears something. When this happens, it looks as if your movie doesn't work.

One way to overcome this delay is to deselect the Export in First Frame option. However, when you do this, the sounds will not be loaded into your movie at all. You have to incorporate the sounds manually so that they're available when you need them.

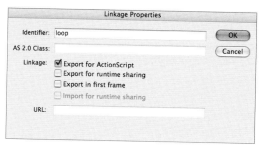

To prepare your linkage ID files for loading:

1. While in the main Timeline, press Ctrl+F8 / Cmd+F8 to create a new symbol. Give it the name **linkage_sounds**, select Movie Clip as its Behavior, and click OK.

2. Flash jumps into Symbol Editing mode. Add new layers to the Timeline of the linkage_sounds Movie Clip so that one layer exists for every sound that has a linkage ID. Name the top layer **code**. Name the remaining layers **sound 1**, **sound 2**, and so on.

3. Click frame 2 of the sound 1 layer, and then Shift+click frame 2 of the last sound layer. Press F7 to convert these frames to blank keyframes. The Timeline should look like Figure 15.3.

Figure 15.3

This linkage_ sounds Movie Clip Timeline has five layers. Layers sound1–sound4 require two keyframes.

4. Select the first keyframe of the code layer. Enter the following statement in the Actions panel:

    ```
    stop();
    ```

5. Select the second keyframe of the sound 1 layer. Use the Property Inspector to attach the first sound to this keyframe. Do the same for the remaining keyframes.

6. For each sound, use the Property Inspector to set the Sync option to Event. This step is important! Stream and Start sync sounds aren't available via ActionScript.

7. Press Ctrl+E / Cmd+E to return to the main Timeline. Drag an instance of the linkage_sounds Movie Clip to an empty keyframe in frame 1 of the main Timeline.

So, what does this clip do? It's important to remember that the sounds in the Library were marked to *not* export in the first frame. Because they will not be automatically added to your movie, they have to be included through another means. This Movie Clip does that. The first keyframe has a stop() function, so frame 2 (the frame that holds the sounds) is never reached. However, because frame 2 is part of a Movie Clip Timeline and that clip has been placed on the Stage, the sounds will be loaded into the Flash Player as part of the `linkage_sounds` Movie Clip. This accomplishes the same task as exporting the sounds in the first frame; it's just done in a different order, which allows the elements in frame 1 to load more quickly.

Playing and Stopping Sounds

Two of the most important methods of the Sound object are those used to play and silence sounds. After all, a sound has to be cued (or stopped and re-cued) before you can make any audible changes to its panning, volume, or stereo composition. To cue a sound from scratch:

1. Go through the steps of exporting the sound from the Library and assigning it a linkage identifier. To learn more about this, see the preceding section.

2. Once you've exported the sound, you can add the following script statements to the script of a button, frame, or other movie element:

```
mySound=new Sound(this);
mySound.attachSound("bkgdLoop");
mySound.start(0,999);
```

This script example performs three tasks:

- It creates a new Sound object named `mySound` and scopes it to the current Timeline.
- It attaches the sound exported as `bkgdLoop` to the object.
- It cues the sound from its beginning and loops it 999 times.

Assume for the moment that this object controls a sound that is four seconds long. To loop the sound 999 times from its halfway point, you'd enter this:

```
mySound.start(2,999);
```

This statement uses the `secondsOffset` argument to start the four-second sound two seconds (or halfway) into the file. This becomes the new "beginning" of the audio file. Each new loop will start from this point.

Another variation on this would be to use a variable to set the number of loops for a particular sound. For example:

```
var loop=4;
mySound.start(0,loop);
```

In this example, the variable `loop` is initialized to 4 and will cause the `mySound` object to loop four times. However, because `loop` is a variable, you're able to manipulate its value with ActionScript in other portions of your movie. You can create some sort of interactive controller (slider, button, keystroke, and so on) that will increase or decrease the number of times a sound will loop when it's cued.

When playing sounds via the Sound object, you'll find that you can also exert a fair amount of control when stopping sounds. Consider the following statements when attached to frame 1 of the main Timeline:

```
addASound=new Sound();
```

```
addASound.attachSound("ambient");
addASound.start();
```

This script example performs the following tasks:

- It creates a new global Sound object named addASound.
- It attaches the linked sound ambient to the object.
- It cues the sound.

To silence the sound, you could add this line to a later frame in the same Timeline:

```
addASound.stop();
```

This statement actually stops all sounds in the movie (because the object is global). If the addASound object were targeted to a specific level or Movie Clip, this final statement would stop the sounds in that target clip only.

The stop() method will also accept an argument in its parentheses; this argument is known as soundID. The argument is available so that you can silence a specific sound by referring to its symbol identifier. Consider the following examples:

These statements are on the main Timeline:

```
sound1=new Sound();
sound1.attachSound("ambient");
sound1.start();
sound1.stop("ambient");
```

These statements are attached to a Movie Clip called effect_mc:

```
onClipEvent (load){
    sound2 = new Sound(this);
    sound2.attachSound("effect");
    sound2.start();
}
```

Here you see the same set of commands as before. The main difference is that the stop() method uses an argument in its parentheses. In this case, even though sound1 is a global Sound object, the only sound that will be stopped is ambient. Because ambient is an attached sound, and because it is stopped explicitly, it will cease to play. Other sounds, such as effect (attached to sound2), will continue playing. If the line read

```
sound1.stop()
```

then all sounds would cease playing. If the line read

```
effect_mc.sound2.stop()
```

then effect would cease, but others would continue. This is because sound2 was created on the effect_mc Movie Clip Timeline. Its sounds belong to (or are *scoped*) to that Timeline because the Sound object was created using this.

Controlling Volume and Panning via Scripting

At this point, you've learned about the Sound object, how it's used, and how to cue sounds in your movie using ActionScript and the Sound object methods. The Sound object allows you to control all parameters of sound playback through scripting; this includes Action-Script techniques that can dynamically set the volume level and pan position of a sound in your movie.

The following sections present several key concepts that show you how to set volume and pan levels using ActionScript. You'll also learn techniques for creating audio fades and stereo effects. Like many of the examples presented in this book, these are *germ* ideas. The intention is that you grasp the basic concepts here and then use them in interesting ways for projects of your own. With the precise audio control that ActionScript adds to your movies, you'll discover an entirely new level of sound possibilities in Flash.

The techniques presented in the following section require little ActionScript. If you need to control sound but don't like doing a lot of script-related work, this is the section for you.

Setting Volume and Pan Levels

Volume and panning are two of the most important considerations when it comes to putting together an audio mix. By assigning each sound its proper level, you're able to create an ideal balance among all audio components of a movie: sound effects, music, dialogue, and narration. Positioning a sound in the stereo field helps create an audio environment where each element has its own niche in the overall sound composition of your movie. With the help of ActionScript, you can do all this using a few simple lines of code that set the audio changes in motion.

When you manipulate volume and pan data in Flash, it's assumed that the sound you want to affect is already playing. If a particular sound associated with the Sound object has not yet been cued, Flash can set pan and volume values, but you won't hear the effects. However, once a sound *is* playing, your volume and pan settings will be heard and can be further changed in real time.

To set the volume level of a sound, you must use the `setVolume()` method. This method uses the dot operator to apply the volume information to the Sound object instance that you specify in your script. For example, to set the level of a sound to full volume (the default), enter the following statement:

```
myObject.setVolume(100);
```

In this example, `myObject` is the name of the Sound object you'll affect. This script example is often preceded by statements that create the Sound object `myObject` and attach a sound from the Library. Of course, these elements don't have to appear in the same script window as the `setVolume()` call, but they must be executed in the movie before you can manipulate the sound's volume. Taking this another step further, it's recommended that you set an initial volume level before cueing a sound, as in the following example:

```
myObject.setVolume(40);
myObject.start();
```

Though only a fraction of a second passes between these lines of code when they're executed, the default volume of 100 is significantly higher than 40. If you heard a noticeable delay when executing these statements, then the initial burst at full volume would be jarring. Set the volume before cueing sounds to avoid these kinds of disruptions.

You can use the `setVolume()` method to control a frame-based sound in your movie once it has started playing. Sounds attached to the frames of Movie Clips or to loaded SWF files can have their volume manipulated by the Sound object as well. Consider the following example:

```
loaded=new Sound("_level1");
loaded.setVolume(50);
```

In this script, a new Sound object named `loaded` is created for the sound(s) of the SWF file playing on level 1. The `setVolume()` method lowers the level of these sounds to 50 percent of their total volume. Using this same syntax, the method can also target the volume of sounds in Movie Clip instances:

```
sound3=new Sound("_root.intro.part2");
sound3.setVolume(80);
```

When you create a Sound object and enter the target path to a specific Movie Clip, the object can manipulate the volume (and pan) of any sounds that belong to its Timeline.

Controlling panning with ActionScript is similar. The main difference is that the `setPan()` method takes both positive and negative numbers as arguments: use −100 to pan hard left and 100 to pan hard right. Consider the following script:

```
bass=new Sound("bass_mc");
bass.attachSound("fenderjazz");
guitar = new Sound("guitar_mc");
guitar.attachSound ("strat");
bass.start(0,100);
bass.setPan(-75);
guitar.start(0,50);
guitar.setPan(75);
```

This example cues two sounds after creating objects for each and attaching sound files from the Library. After each cue, the `setPan()` method is invoked to position each sound in an individual location: `bass` is panned mostly to the left, and `guitar` is panned mostly to the right. We say *mostly* because each statement pans 75 percent of the sound to one speaker but leaves the remaining 25 percent in the opposite speaker. This pan configuration creates a fair amount of stereo separation for the sounds but still allows them to mingle and blend a bit.

> You can also use setPan() to manipulate the panning of sounds in a Movie Clip or loaded SWF file. Simply enter a target argument in the parentheses when you create the Sound object. Any methods that manipulate that Sound object will apply to the targeted Timeline.

When setting the pan position of sounds, you don't have any "golden rule" to follow. Your best bet is to work with mono files so that the full effect of the pan is audible. Flash allows you to pan stereo sounds, but since two channels already exist in the sound file, the pan effect is rather weak. As always, use your ears, and develop a scheme that sounds good and fits your sound design goals. Remember, to correctly hear the panned sound, you must have a two-speaker stereo setup for your computer. If you don't have access to a set of speakers, headphones are always a good way to hear the subtle details of an audio mix.

Scripting Volume Controls

Once you've mastered the basics of manipulating volume settings, it's possible to combine that knowledge with what you already know about ActionScript and create controls for changing the volume of various sounds in a movie. In previous chapters of this book, you used ActionScript to control several parameters of graphic elements in your movie. The only difference here is that rather than use ActionScript to change the visual properties of Movie Clips, you'll use it with the Sound object methods to change the properties of audio playback.

You already know that the setVolume() method is the part of ActionScript used to create changes in audio level. In this section, you'll incorporate that technique with a few basic statements inside a Movie Clip to create a simple, yet flexible and powerful, volume controller.

To get an idea of what you'll be creating, open the volumePanner.swf file on the CD. Although this example doesn't cover the specifics of creating this movie's graphic component, you can refer to the finished Timeline in the volumePanner.fla file to get an idea of how it was constructed.

To create a set of volume control buttons:

1. Prepare a couple of items before you begin working on this exercise:

    • First, you need a sound to control. Import a sound to your movie's Library, and export the sound symbol using the Linkage Properties dialog box. To learn more about linking sounds, see the section "Attaching Sounds and Symbol Linkage" earlier in this chapter.

- You also need at least one button to serve as part of your volume controller. One is sufficient because you can use it several times in the same Timeline. However, if you want to create two buttons, you can. To learn more about creating buttons, see Chapter 8.

2. After you've set up your sound and button, begin by selecting Insert → New Symbol. Name the symbol **volume**, and select Movie Clip as its behavior. Click OK, and Flash jumps into Symbol Editing mode.

3. Rename the first layer **code**, and press F7 six times to create six empty keyframes in the layer.

4. Click the first keyframe, and press F9 to open the Actions panel. Enter the following statements:

```
cue=new Sound();
cue.attachSound("yourLinkedSound");
cue.start(0,100);
```

In this example, the reference yourLinkedSound is a placeholder based on whatever name you assigned to the sound you exported using the linkage properties. Also, the name of the Sound object cue is arbitrary and can be changed if you want; just be sure to use the new name consistently throughout your scripts.

5. Click the second keyframe to display the Actions panel once again. Enter these statements:

```
cue.setVolume(100);
stop();
```

These statements set the initial volume and stop the playback head at frame 2.

6. In the remaining five keyframes, you'll enter similar lines of ActionScript. See Table 15.2 for the scripts and keyframes they go in. When you've finished entering all the statements in their various frames, close the Actions panel, and return to the volume Movie Clip Timeline. We'll explain the role of these statements in a moment.

KEYFRAME	ACTIONSCRIPT	Table 15.2
3	cue.setVolume(80);	**Keyframe statements for the volume movie clip**
4	cue.setVolume(60);	
5	cue.setVolume(40);	
6	cue.setVolume(20);	
7	cue.setVolume(0);	

7. Insert a new layer, and name it **buttons**. The frames in this layer should span all seven frames of the code layer. Grab a button from your movie's Library, and drag it to the Stage of the volume Movie Clip. Drag another button to the Stage, and position it near

the first button. If you use different buttons, you don't need to change them once they're on the Stage. The buttons used in `volumePanner.fla` are identical, but one has been rotated 180° to help show which one raises the volume and which one lowers it.

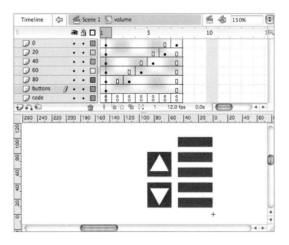

8. Click the button you want to use as the Lower Volume button, and open the Actions panel. Enter the following statements:

```
on(release){
    if(_currentframe<7){
        nextFrame();
    }
}
```

When this button is clicked, the script checks to see the position of the playback head in the Movie Clip. If it's at a frame number less than 7, the clip is told to advance a frame using the `nextFrame()` function. Your `volume` Movie Clip has seven frames. Once the clip is in frame 7, it doesn't advance if the button is clicked. Also, because the script uses `nextFrame()`, it advances the Timeline only one frame at a time. In the Timeline, each frame contains a statement that sets a new volume level. With each new frame, the clip stops and updates the volume level of the Sound object.

9. Click the button you want to use as the Raise Volume button, and open the Actions panel. Enter the following statements:

```
on(release){
    if(_currentframe>2){
        prevFrame();
    }
}
```

This button works similarly to the Lower Volume button. Each time the button is clicked, the script checks the current frame where the clip is stopped. If the frame is greater than 2, the playback head moves to the preceding frame number or to the left across the Timeline. Because the `setVolume()` statements increase in value from right to left, the Sound object volume gradually raises as the head moves closer to frame 2.

10. Close the Actions panel, and return to your movie's main Timeline. Grab an instance of the `volume` Movie Clip, and drag it from the Library to the Stage. At this point, you don't need to assign an instance name to the clip. Select Control → Test Movie to give this controller a spin. As you click the Lower Volume button, you should hear the sound level drop; conversely, the Raise Volume button should increase the volume of the sound.

Creating Audio Fade-in and Fade-out Effects

What exactly are *fade-ins* and *fade-outs*? They're audio effects that gradually raise or lower the volume of a sound to either ease it up to full volume or taper it off to silence. As you've probably already guessed, fade-ins and fade-outs require you to manipulate the volume of a sound as you did to create a volume controller. This is true, but with one exception: fades are gradual effects. Once they're set in motion, they happen slowly over time. To create a fade, you must design a Movie Clip structure that can gradually take a sound from one volume extreme to another in a single step, rather than with the individual mouse clicks you used to create volume controls.

Open the `fadeInOut.swf` or `fadeInOut.fla` file on the CD. Play around with the fade-in and fade-out buttons to see and hear exactly what happens with a fade controller. The process of creating a fade is simple; based on what you already know about volume controls, you should easily grasp the concepts behind a fade controller.

To create controls that fade a sound in and out:

1. Prepare a couple of items before you begin working on this exercise:

   • Here again, you need a sound to control. Import a sound to your movie's Library, and export the sound symbol using the Linkage Properties dialog box. To learn more about linking sounds, see the section "Attaching Sounds with Linkage Identifiers" earlier in this chapter.

   • You need at least one button to serve as part of your fade controller. One is sufficient because you can use it several times in the same Timeline. However, if you want to create two buttons, you can. To learn more about creating buttons, see Chapter 8.

2. Begin by selecting Insert → New Symbol. Name the symbol **fader**, and select Movie Clip as its behavior. Click OK, and Flash jumps into Symbol Editing mode.

3. Rename the first layer to **code**, and enter 13 empty keyframes in the layer. (You should have a total of 14 in the entire clip.) Click the first keyframe, and press F9 to display the Actions panel. Enter the following statements:

```
cue=new Sound();
cue.attachSound("yourLinkedSound");
cue.start(0,100);
cue.setVolume(100);
```

In this example, the reference yourLinkedSound is a placeholder based on whatever name you assigned to the sound you exported using the linkage properties. Also, the name of the Sound object cue is arbitrary and can be changed if you want; just be sure to use the new name consistently throughout your scripts.

4. Click the keyframe at frame 2, and enter a stop() function in the Actions panel. The remaining 12 keyframes will need fairly repetitive and similar statements. See Table 15.3 for a listing of each keyframe and its corresponding script.

This step completes your work for the fader Movie Clip. If you looked at the fadeInOut.fla file on the CD, you'll notice some graphic enhancements to the clip. These are optional and won't influence the functionality of the Movie Clip in your movie.

5. Close the Actions panel, and switch to Movie Editing mode and your main Timeline.

6. Drag the fader Movie Clip to your Stage, and assign it the instance name fade in the Property Inspector.

	KEYFRAME	ACTIONSCRIPT
Table 15.3	3	cue.setVolume(80);
Keyframe Statements for the Fader Movie Clip	4	cue.setVolume(60);
	5	cue.setVolume(40);
	6	cue.setVolume(20);
	7	cue.setVolume(0);
	8	stop();
	9	cue.setVolume(10);
	10	cue.setVolume(20);
	11	cue.setVolume(40);
	12	cue.setVolume(60);
	13	cue.setVolume(80);
	14	cue.setVolume(100);gotoAndStop(2);

As it appears on the CD, `fadeInOut.swf` has a simple graphic element that represents a light-emitting diode (LED) volume meter. Add this option if you want. If you followed the preceding step, the clip won't have any sort of significant graphical representation—only a hollow circle to serve as a placeholder for the clip. The `fade` instance (as described in this lesson) is what you call a *sound-only Movie Clip,* meaning that the clip has sound(s), frame(s), and, in most cases, some ActionScript. Sound-only clips are ideal for holding and controlling audio. They can be targeted just as any other clip can; the only difference is that they don't have any kind of visual animated components.

7. Create a new layer in the main Timeline, and name it **buttons**. Drag two buttons to this layer of the Stage to serve as your fade-in and fade-out controls. If necessary, change one of the two buttons graphically so that it is distinguishable from the other. It should be clear which one will perform the fade-in and which one will perform the fade-out.

8. Select the fade-out button, and open the Actions panel. Enter the following statements:

```
on(release){
    _root.fade.gotoAndPlay(3);
}
```

This script targets the clip instance `fade` when the button is clicked and sends it to play at frame 3. The clip is sent to frame 3 because this is the button used to fade out a sound. Frame 3 is the frame where the volume begins to decrease. Notice, however, that no `stop()` function exists until the clip reaches frame 8. Between frames 3 and 8, the `setVolume()` method gradually decreases the volume of the sound. Then, once it has been set to a level of 0, the clip is stopped.

9. Select the fade-in button, and open the Actions panel. Enter the following statements:

```
on(release){
    _root.fade.gotoAndPlay(9);
}
```

This script targets the clip instance `fade` when the button is clicked and sends it to play at frame 9. The reason should be clear. At frame 9, the volume is set to a level of 10; at frame 10, it's set to a level of 20; and so on. When the volume finally reaches a level of 100 at frame 14, the clip is sent to frame 2 and told to stop. It will sit there until another button click executes a script that runs it through the fade-in or fade-out animation once again.

10. Select Control → Test Movie to give your fade controller a try.

After testing this Movie Clip, you might find that the fade is either too short or too long for your purposes. You can fix this easily because the following are a couple of strategies for tweaking the length of a fade.

If your fade is too short, do one of the following:

- Create a longer animation. If you put a greater distance between the keyframes that set volume levels, it will take Flash longer to execute the animation.

- Adjust your volume levels in smaller increments. In this exercise, you adjusted the sound in increments of 20 percent. Adjusting the volume in chunks of 5 percent or 2 percent will create a longer, more gradual fade effect.

- Lower the frame rate of your movie. The more slowly a movie's frames are played, the slower the individual setVolume() scripts execute. Realize, however, that this will affect the speed of animated elements in your movie.

If you want to *shorten* a fade (that is, decrease its length), simply reverse either of the techniques for lengthening the fade.

> To learn another technique for creating fade-ins and fade-outs using only ActionScript, see the "Scripting Dynamic Volume Transitions" section of this chapter.

Scripting Pan Controls

Another important element of audio control is *panning*. By placing sounds in the stereo field, you can create a sense of space in the "world" of your movie. Panning assigns a source location to ambient sound effects and allows you to balance the positioning of multiple music tracks. And with the help of some additional ActionScript, you can use the Sound object to create controllers that dynamically adjust the pan position of a particular sound.

The finished file described in this exercise is the same that you used if you worked with the volume control buttons. If you haven't yet seen and heard this movie, open the volumePanner.swf or volumePanner.fla file on the CD. In addition to the volume button controls, a slider, when moved left or right, adjusts the panning of the movie's sound accordingly. This exercise assumes you're already familiar with the basics of creating drag-and-drop functionality. If you'd like to learn more about this topic, see Chapter 8.

To create a stereo pan controller:

1. Prepare a couple of items before you begin working on this exercise:

   - You need a sound to control; for this exercise, either a mono or a stereo sound will do. However, because you'll be manipulating the pan position, a mono sound really makes the most sense. Import a sound to your movie's Library, and export the sound symbol using the Linkage Properties dialog box. To learn more about linking sounds, see the section "Attaching Sounds with Linkage Identifiers" earlier in this chapter.

   - You'll need one button to serve as the knob of your slider.

2. You can begin with the sound elements of this movie. You'll create a new Movie Clip that is a sound-only clip. It will have one purpose: to cue a sound to play in this movie.

3. Select Insert → New Symbol. Give the symbol a name, and set its behavior to Movie Clip.

4. In this new Movie Clip, insert one empty keyframe in the first layer. In frame 1, enter the following statements:

```
cue=new Sound();
cue.attachSound("yourLinkedSound");
cue.start(0, 100);
```

In the volumePanner.fla file on the CD, the Sound object is created in the Movie Clip labeled volume, which has the instance name audio.

Again, yourLinkedSound is a placeholder for the sound you exported from your movie's Library.

5. In the second keyframe, attach a stop() function. This series of ActionScript commands creates a Sound object, attaches a sound from the Library, and plays the sound (all in frame 1). When the clip finishes executing these statements and moves to frame 2, the Movie Clip will stop, but the sound will continue to play.

6. Return to Movie Editing mode, and drag the clip to the Stage of the main Timeline.

7. Press Ctrl+F3 / Cmd+F3 to open the Property Inspector, and assign the instance name **audio** for the clip. This will allow you to target the clip so that you can control the panning of the Sound object you created in frame 1.

8. With a Sound object in place, you can create the pan controller. Select Insert → New Symbol. Name the symbol **slider**, and select Movie Clip as its behavior. Click OK, and Flash jumps into Symbol Editing mode.

9. Drag the button to the Stage of the slider Movie Clip, and use the Align panel to position it in the exact middle of the Stage. Click the button to be sure it's selected. Use the Property Inspector to give it the instance name **pan_button**.

10. Return to the Movie Clip's Timeline, and rename the layer that contains the button controller. Then, add a new layer to the Timeline, and name it **code**.

11. Select the first empty keyframe of the code layer, and press F9 to open the Actions panel. Enter the following statements:

```
L=pan_button._x-50;
T=pan_button._y;
R=pan_button._x+50;
B=pan_button._y;
mid=pan_button._x;
```

These statements help define the bounds of the slider. With these variables in place, you can complete the code for the pan controller:

```
pan_button.onPress=function(){
    startDrag(this,false,L,T,R,B);
    dragging=true;
}
pan_button.onRelease=function(){
    stopDrag();
    dragging=false;
}
pan_button.onReleaseOutside=function(){
    stopDrag();
    dragging=false;
}
this.onMouseMove=function(){
    if (dragging){
        _root.audio.cue.setPan((pan_button._x-mid)*2);
        updateAfterEvent();
    }
}
```

These statements are similar to those used in Chapter 8 to create the recycle bin. The main difference is the addition of the variables *mid* and *dragging*. *dragging* simply tracks when the slider is moving (*true*) and when it isn't (*false*). If the clip is being dragged and *dragging* is *true*, it executes the following statement:

```
_root.audio.cue.setPan((pan_button._x-mid)*2);
```

This pans the sound in your movie. This line targets the sound using an absolute path from the main Timeline and uses the setPan method to control the sound's left or right speaker position. The expression ((pan_button._x-mid)*2) returns a value from –100 to 100 based on pan_button's current horizontal position. It subtracts the starting position (mid) from the current position (_x) and multiplies that by 2. Because the value for _x lies between –50 and 50, the expression always returns from –100 to 100.

12. Now you're ready to assemble the final component of the slider controller. Create a new layer in the Timeline, and name it **track**. Position this layer *below* the controller layer in the Movie Clip's Timeline.

13. Draw a horizontal line 100 pixels long on the track layer. (You can use the Property Inspector to confirm the length.) This guideline is the other graphic component of the slider. Position it so that it's directly behind the button (pan_button), making sure the two elements have their centers aligned (see Figure 15.4). Pan information in Flash can have a maximum value of 100 and a minimum of –100. By using a line graphic that is 100 pixels long, it will always appear that the slider button is "locked"

to the line because pan_button starts in the middle of the line and can move 50 pixels left or right. When the values in this range are multiplied by 2, the pan values are updated accurately.

14. Return to Movie Editing mode, and drag the slider Movie Clip onto the Stage of the main Timeline.

The pan slider is now complete! Select Control → Test Movie to give it a try. As the sound plays, you should be able to drag the slider left and right, manipulating the position of the sound in your stereo speakers or headphones.

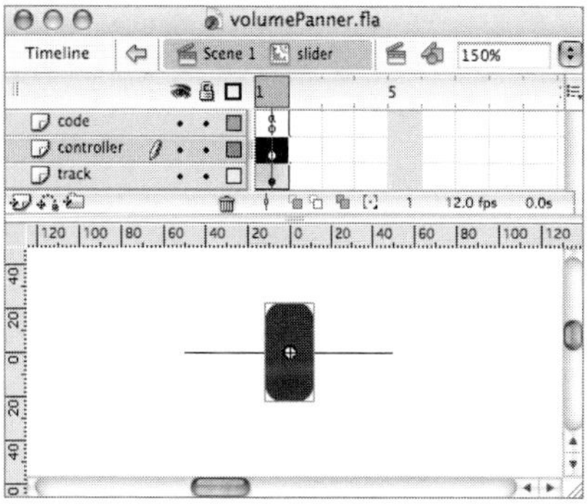

Figure 15.4

The pan slider button (inside the slider Movie Clip) should have its guideline positioned behind it with the centers aligned.

Scripting Advanced Audio Functionality

When it comes to audio, ActionScript can be addicting. The powerful parameters of the language enable a great variety of control over the sound effects, voice-over, and music that make up your Flash productions. If you're up for the challenge, we've included a few additional "goodies" to push your scripting abilities further and add new layers of sonic possibility to your movies and applications.

Loading External Sounds with ActionScript

One of the most compelling audio-related features of Flash is its ability to load external MP3 sound files. Rather than include a sound or group of sounds in your movie, you can now leave them outside your movie and call them as needed.

This approach presents several advantages. First, sounds always add to the size of your final SWF file. So, keeping sounds outside the final movie allows it to be smaller and might help it load more quickly. Additionally, because using external files cuts down significantly on a movie's file size, you'll be able to use an array of sounds from which your audience can pick and choose. If they want to browse your movie while listening to classical music, reggae, western swing, or whatever, you can give them a host of files to choose from and then load the appropriate soundtrack for each visitor. External sounds can be loaded into a Flash movie from any location on the Internet. This means it's also possible to use Flash to create a forum for MP3 playback. Your users can share the uniform resource locators (URLs) of sounds they want you and others to hear, making your movie a sort of MP3 jukebox.

The list of other possibilities goes on and on. As always, Flash is limited only by your time, budget, and creativity. The capability to load external MP3 files was originally introduced with Flash MX, so your movie must be published for Flash Player 6 or higher to take advantage of it. The required ActionScript terms are as follows:

Sound.loadSound("*url*",*stream*) Loads external MP3s into the specified Sound object. loadSound() takes two arguments. Enter the external MP3's URL as a string, and enter a Boolean value for *stream*. A setting of false means that the sound is treated as if it used

Event sync in the Timeline—it must load entirely before it can begin playback. A setting of true makes the sound a streaming sound, and it will begin to play once a sufficient amount has been downloaded.

Sound.getBytesLoaded() Monitors the number of bytes that have been loaded from an external sound into the specified Sound object.

Sound.getBytesTotal() Returns the total number of bytes for the specified Sound object. You can use the methods getBytesLoaded() and getBytesTotal() to create preloaders for external sound files.

Now that you're familiar with the Sound object terms for loading external sounds, you can get down to business. To make the following procedure as simple as possible, we've prepared the loadMP3.fla starter file for you on the CD. Copy this file to your computer's desktop. We've complete several additional steps so that you can focus on the most important aspects of this technique.

To load an external sound:

1. First, you must have a remote MP3 file to load. We recommend you start with a small file so that while you're testing this procedure, you don't waste time waiting for a large file to load. Upload an MP3 file to your web server, and write down the file's URL.

> If you don't have a web server or an MP3 file to use, we've provided one for you. Use the following URL to link to the file savvySound.mp3: http://www.vonflashenstein.com/resources/savvySound.mp3.

2. In the loadMP3.fla file, select the first (and only) keyframe of layer 1. Press F9 to open the Actions panel. You'll see something that resembles Figure 15.5.

Figure 15.5

The ActionScript for the first keyframe of the loadMP3.fla file. You'll enter the URL for your external sound within the quotes of the loadSound statement.

```
loaded = new Sound();
loaded.loadSound("enterYourURLHere", false);




function checkLoad() {
    if (loaded.getBytesTotal()>0 && loaded.getBytesLoaded()==loaded.getBytesTotal()){
        clearInterval(checker);
    } else {
        var loadBytes = Math.round(_root.loaded.getBytesLoaded()/1024);
        var loadTotal = Math.round(_root.loaded.getBytesTotal()/1024);
        var percent = Math.round((loadBytes/loadTotal)*100);
        status.bytes_txt.text = loadBytes+" / "+loadTotal+" = "+percent+"%";
    }
}
checker = setInterval(checkLoad, 100);
```

3. In line 2, notice the phrase `enterYourURLHere`. Replace that phrase with the absolute URL of the MP3 file you want to load into your movie. An absolute URL is written as `http://www.`*`myDomain.com`*`/`*`file.mp3`*, where *`myDomain.com`* is the name of your domain and *`file.mp3`* is the name of your MP3 file.

   Line 1 creates the Sound object `loaded`. Line 2 uses the `loadSound()` method to load the external file that you just specified. `false`, an argument to `loadSound()`, determines that the loaded sound will behave like an event sound and must be completely loaded into memory before it can begin its playback.

4. You'll notice that lines 3–6 are blank. This is where you write a function that cues the sound once it has loaded. Enter the following statements starting at line 3:

   ```
   loaded.onLoad=function(){
       loaded.start(0, 100);
       status.gotoAndStop(7);
   }
   ```

   When the Sound object `loaded` has completely loaded into the Flash player, its `onLoad` event occurs. This event executes the statements within the function: the sound is cued using `start()`, and a Movie Clip named `status` is skipped to frame 7 of its Timeline. If you look at the Timeline of the status clip (see Figure 15.6), you can see that in frames 1–6, it plays through an animation loop. This animation loops while the external MP3 is loading. Once the sound has loaded, it's sent to frame 7, where the animation stops.

   Figure 15.6

   The Timeline of the status Movie Clip instance has an animation loop that plays while the MP3 is loading.

5. There is a good deal of ActionScript in frame 1 that you don't have to write. Let's examine this script line by line:

   Line 7 This creates a custom function named `checkLoad()`.

   Line 8 This conditional statement checks the status of the sound while it's loading. It tests two things: whether the total byte count of the sound is greater than 0 and whether the bytes that have been loaded are equal to the total number of bytes. Only when both these statements are `true` (when the file has completely loaded) will the script execute line 9. Otherwise, when `false`, it skips ahead to lines 11–14.

It's good to check whether Sound.getBytesTotal() is greater than 0. This helps prevent a sound that's slow to load from jumping the gun. If the sound hasn't loaded at all, it contains 0 bytes. Because it has loaded 0 bytes and contains 0 bytes, the statement 0==0 will obviously return true, and Flash will think that the sound has loaded completely.

Lines 11–14 If the sound hasn't loaded completely into `loader`, a series of alternative statements will execute to show the load progress:

- `loadBytes` is a variable storing the number of loaded bytes.
- `loadTotal` is a variable storing the number of total bytes.
- `percent` stores the percentage of the sound that has loaded.
- `bytes_txt` is a text field in the `status` clip instance. Its contents are set to an expression that shows the number of loaded bytes over the number of total bytes and what percentage of the total sound this represents. This information is concatenated as a string and plugged into the text field.

Lines 11 and 12 use the `Math.round()` method to round the byte count to the nearest integer. Values are divided by 1,024 to give the kilobyte count.

Line 17 This line is probably the most important in the entire script sequence because it's responsible for calling the `checkLoad()` function. It creates the interval `checker` using the `setInterval()` function. This interval calls the `checkLoad()` function every 100 milliseconds. This means that, every one-tenth of a second, `checkLoad()` monitors the download progress of the MP3 and updates the movie accordingly.

Line 9 This statement falls within the block of code that executes when the MP3 has loaded completely. It uses the `clearInterval()` function to cancel the `checker` interval and stop monitoring the download progress of the MP3.

6. Select Control → Test Movie to try the loaded sound. As the sound is loading, the gold crescent spins, and the text field prints a numeric display of the loading sound's progress. Once the sound has finished loading, the spinning graphic stops, and the text in the Movie Clip changes to read "Welcome to the site."

If your movie doesn't work properly right away, here are a few things to check:

- Be sure you're connected to the Internet.
- Check the speed of your connection. A busy network will slow the loading process.
- Be certain your URL to the external sound is correct.

 You have now seen a glimpse of the possibilities offered by external sounds. To learn about additional ActionScript terms that can enhance your movies and their ability to work with external sounds, see the "Sound Object" section of the ActionScript Reference on the CD.

Adding Multiple Sounds to Buttons

When using an interface, you usually expect to encounter feedback. By *feedback*, we mean the kinds of things that confirm "you chose this option" or "you're currently loading this information." This kind of communication is useful because it allows the interactive system to tell you what it is doing and/or what it thinks you're doing. Sound is one of the best ways to provide this kind of feedback, and in many cases this feedback is tied to buttons.

This short lesson will show you how to attach multiple sounds to a button instance. In contrast to the example provided in the previous chapter, this technique keeps the sounds separate from the Button symbol. You can use these steps to create multiple button instances that each has its own unique sounds.

To start this lesson, open the file button_clicker_demo.fla in the Chapter 15 folder on the CD. For a completed version of this lesson, see button_clicker_demo.fla.

To attach multiple sounds to a button instance:

1. Click the red button in the middle of the Stage.

2. Use the Property Inspector (Ctrl+F3 / Cmd+F3) to give the button the instance name **red_btn**.

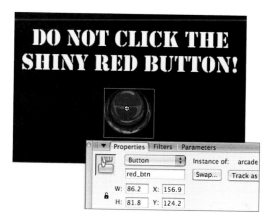

3. Open the Library (Ctrl+L / Cmd+L), and assign linkage identifiers to each of the two sounds. Give click-down.aif the name **down**, and give click-up.aif the name **up**.

4. Select the empty keyframe in the code layer of the main Timeline. Open the Actions panel (Alt+F9 / Opt+F9), and enter the following statements:

```
clk = new Sound(this);
red_btn.onPress=function(){
    clk.attachSound("down");
    clk.start();
}
red_btn.onRelease=function(){
    clk.attachSound("up");
    clk.start();
}
```

If you've been following along in this chapter, these statements should be clear. The Sound object instance for this button is called clk; it's scoped to the Timeline that contains the button. When the mouse clicks the button, the down sound is attached to the object and cued. When released, the up sound is treated in the same fashion. This quick interchange of sound files allows the button to have slightly different sounds for both press and release.

5. Choose Control → Test Movie to preview the SWF file and hear what the button sounds like.

You can extend this technique to support additional buttons. To do this, just make the following additions:

- Give each new button instance a unique instance name.

- For every new button, import an up and down sound to the Library and assign a unique linkage ID.

- Each new button needs its own Sound object to cue the sounds associated with it.

You may also want to consider writing a function that manages all buttons in your movie. To learn more about writing custom functions, see Chapter 10.

Scripting Dynamic Volume Transitions

Earlier in this chapter you learned how to use a combination of frame-based ActionScript and Timeline controls to create fade-in and fade-out effects. Although these techniques are reliable, they do not reflect the most current and efficient means of creating volume transitions. This lesson presents a somewhat complex script that can accomplish identical effects but with more power and flexibility than found in the earlier example.

 Although the steps involved in doing this are simple, the script isn't. For this reason, we'll present the script line by line and explain how each step creates the fade functionality. To see and hear the finished file, open script_volume.fla on the CD.

Figure 15.7 shows the entire script that creates the fade-in and fade-out effect. Refer to this image to check line numbers and see how the script is structured overall.

The fade-in and fade-out script works as follows:

Lines 1–3 These statements aren't doing anything you haven't learned so far. A Sound object instance is created, a sound is attached, and it's told to loop 100 times.

Lines 4–6 These lines take a small departure from examples mentioned earlier. Rather than set the volume value directly, this script creates the vol variable and uses it to assign the initial volume. This technique will be used later in the script to rapidly change the volume in the course of a fade-in or fade-out. Another variable called out is created here. This tracks the state of a fade and will test true when a fade is possible and false when it isn't. Since the loop is playing at full volume when this movie begins, a fade-out is possible, and the variable is set to true.

Line 7 This statement assigns a function to the release event for out_btn, the fade-out control. Within this block of code are the statements that produce the fade-out.

Line 8 This line checks the status of out to see whether a fade-out is possible.

Lines 9–12 This block calls a function on every onEnterFrame of the Movie Clip instance vol_mc. This example runs at 12fps, so the function is called in rapid succession. Each time it is called, lines 10–12 work through the process of fading: vol is reduced by 5, the value of vol is assigned to the cue sound instance, and the new volume is printed to a text field.

Lines 13–15 This block is used for clean-up. Eventually, vol will be reduced to 0, and the sound will be silent. At this point the fade is complete, and the script can stop calling the onEnterFrame function, which is precisely what happens here. delete removes the function associated with vol_mc because it's no longer needed and because its removal will free resources elsewhere. And, since the sound is completely faded out, it's impossible to fade any further, and out is updated to false.

Lines 16–19 These lines are significant in that they balance the script. For every opening curly brace ({) there must be a closing counterpart (}). If you want to re-create this script by hand, don't forget these important elements.

Lines 20–32 Everything that goes down must come up… The statements in these lines simply reverse the process described in lines 7–19. A fade-out isn't possible, so when you click in_btn, a new function is created to raise vol by 2 on every onEnterFrame. Once it reaches the maximum volume of 100, the function is deleted, and related variables are updated to reflect the new status of cue.

This example provides an efficient means of fading sounds in and out without the restriction of frame-based ActionScript in the Timeline. Additionally, it's a scalable technique that can accommodate the simultaneous fading of multiple sounds. Experiment with this code to see what kind of changes you can make to suit your particular needs.

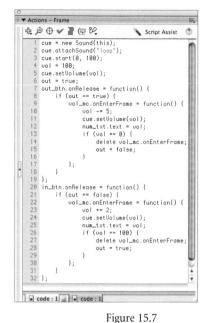

Figure 15.7

The Actions panel contains the code to create fade-in and fade-out effects using only ActionScript.

CHAPTER 16

Flash and Video

It's standard practice now to develop software applications that are *versatile*. Not only do you expect applications to perform their particular job, but you also expect them to work cooperatively with other applications. This increases their effectiveness as well as your creative possibilities. It's this kind of versatility that puts the *multi* in multimedia.

Flash is no exception to this standard. In fact, because of its popularity as well as the SWF file format's wide applicability, Flash, as an authoring tool, is one of the most versatile programs available today. Not only can Flash incorporate many kinds of media into an animation or interactive movie, but it can also create and work with files that are usable in a variety of non-Flash applications – such as digital video.

This chapter explores the possibilities of Flash in a different kind of setting: video. You can export Flash movies as video. Conversely, you can import videos into the Flash environment and control them interactively like any other part of a Flash production. Video and Flash are fundamentally different. Video has no vectors, no tweening, no painting tools, and, above all else, no interactivity. However, video has its own advantages. Whereas Flash is great at displaying stylized, cartoonlike images or sharp, vector based user interfaces, video can show your audience images that are lifelike and realistic. This chapter discusses the many ways you can combine video with Flash.

- ▪ **Importing video into Flash**

- ▪ **Understanding the Sorenson Spark codec**

- ▪ **Exporting FLV video**

- ▪ **Using the Video Import Wizard**

- ▪ **Using ActionScript to control video playback**

- ▪ **Preparing the elements of a Flash animation for video or digital video tape**

- ▪ **Working with Flash video and audio tracks**

- ▪ **Exporting Flash animations for use in video applications**

Understanding Video in the Flash Environment

One of the most sweeping changes originally introduced in Flash MX was the addition of support for digital video. When using previous releases of Flash, developers had to simulate video. They usually did this by putting still-image sequences inside a Movie Clip to create a sort of digital flipbook. From a functional standpoint, this technique worked fairly well, but it tended to increase the size of the final movie appreciably because there was no way to compress the "video."

Luckily for us, this has long since changed. Flash MX started the trend, and Flash 8 continues its significant support for video, which represents an important step forward for both the application and its community of users. What was once the best means of delivering animated content on the Web is now also one of the best means of distributing video content. Anyone whose browser is equipped with the Flash plug-in (version 6 or greater) is now able to see both traditional Flash movies *and* Flash movies that contain real video footage.

Introducing Flash's Video Codecs

The "wizards behind the curtain" that are responsible for video compression/decompression in Flash 8 are two codecs: Sorenson Spark and On2 VP6. While Sorenson Spark has been dealing with video compression/decompression in Flash since Flash MX, the On2 VP6 codec is a new addition in Flash 8. You can still use the Sorenson Spark codec when you export a Flash movie for Flash Player 7, but you'll be using the On2 VP6 codec when you're publishing a movie for Flash Player 8. The On2 VP6 codec allows for far higher video quality than the Sorenson Spark codec; it also supports alpha channels for video compositing. The kicker is that the On2 VP6 codec takes more time to encode and requires more processor power to decode than the Sorenson Spark codec. As a result, you need to be sure whether your audience can cope with the added technical requirements for viewing Flash video content compressed and decompressed with the On2 VP6 codec. If you anticipate that most of your audience is using older computers that don't necessarily meet the optimum requirements of the On2 VP6 codec, you should probably export for Flash Player 7 and use the Sorenson Spark codec.

When you bring video into Flash, you're automatically compressing it in Macromedia Flash Video (FLV) format. If you're using Flash 8 Professional, you can export video files in FLV format from video-editing applications such as Adobe Premiere and Final Cut Pro. This feature can significantly increase your work flow because you no longer need to wait for a video to be compressed upon importing it into Flash.

When imported, the codec applies *temporal* compression to your video. This type of compression looks at areas of change in a video file and encodes each frame based on the amount of change from one frame to the next. If a frame doesn't exhibit a significant change, its information is simply copied from the preceding frame. This kind of encoding is also known as *interframe*. When the change between video frames *is* significant, however, the import codec automatically inserts a video *keyframe* into the video file. A keyframe is a complete picture of a frame, and like a keyframe in your Flash Timeline, it marks a significant change in content.

Exporting FLV Video Files from Other Applications

Users of Flash 8 Professional can take advantage of the FLV QuickTime Export plug-in. With the help of QuickTime 6.1.1, the FLV QuickTime Export plug-in allows you to compress videos and save them from the native application as FLV files. In turn, you can import FLV files directly into Flash or access them remotely over the Web using the FLV-Playback component (if you're using Flash Player 8) or the MediaPlayback component (if you're working with Flash Player 7). This can be a huge time-saver for designers and developers working with a large amount of video content in their Flash projects.

The FLV QuickTime Export plug-in isn't directly integrated with Flash 8 Professional. Instead, it requires a separate installer that you can find on your Flash 8 installation CD.

> The QuickTime Export plug-in is separate from the main program for the sake of computing resources. Video based operations can take a long time, so separating this feature from the main application allows video work to be carried out as a background task

Once you've installed the FLV QuickTime Export plug-in, you'll be able to use it with many video-editing applications for both Macintosh and Windows. For a list of supported applications, see Table 16.1.

Exporting video with the FLV QuickTime Export plug-in is a simple but long process timewise. It will leave you with a file that is immediately ready to be used in a Flash movie.

To export an FLV video file:

1. Open the video you want to export in a video-editing application that supports QuickTime 6.1.1. (See Table 16.1 for a list of possible applications.) Choose File → Export → QuickTime.

2. A dialog box opens. For exporting, select Macromedia Flash Video (FLV), and click the Options button. The FLV QuickTime Exporter dialog box displays. Here you'll select options that affect how your video is compressed.

3. Select an option from the Encoding Method drop-down list:
   - Select Baseline (1 Pass) for rough drafts of videos or for simple video files such as talking heads and other clips with little motion.

WINDOWS	MACINTOSH
Adobe After Effects	Adobe After Effects
Avid Xpress DV	Avid Express DV
Apple QuickTime Pro	Apple QuickTime Pro
	Apple Final Cut Pro

Table 16.1

Video-Editing Applications That Support the FLV QuickTime Export Plug-In

- Select Better (1 Pass VBR) for producing a final FLV clip. This option takes longer to compress, but it dynamically applies compression frame by frame. Each frame is considered and encoded with as little data as possible to yield smaller overall file sizes.

- Select Screen Recording Codec for clips with a limited color palette, such as video captured from a computer screen. This option is perfect for compressing the video used in interactive tutorials that demonstrate how to use a piece of software.

4. Set the frames per second. You can obtain the best results by keeping the video's original frame rate. If you have to reduce the frame rate, cut it by half, a third, or a quarter of the original. For video shot at 30fps, you can drop the frame rate to 15, 10, or 7.5fps.

5. Data rate determines the rate (in bits per second) at which video information is transmitted. You can set a maximum data rate that allows the video to play within the limits of your audience's network connection speed. For the Limit Data Rate option, do one of the following:

   - Choose Low, Medium, or High. The exporter determines a generic setting based on your video's resolution and frame rate.

   - Choose a preset value from 5kbps to 500kbps.

   - Enter a value in the field to set a custom data rate. To cope with network congestion, you need to set a data rate that is less than the speed of your audience's connection. For 56kbps modems, set a data rate from 36kbps to 40kbps; for a CD, set a data rate of 250kbps. For a higher bandwidth connection such as cable modem, you can set the data rate to about 500kbps, which is closer to the device's actual bandwidth in a world of busy network connections.

   - For a list of maximum bandwidth you can expect over a variety of connections, see this article at the Indiana University Knowledge Base: `http://kb.indiana.edu/data/aijg.html?cust=199853.98885.131`.

6. For the Keyframes option, select Auto to let the exporter choose the number of keyframes, or select Custom to enter a keyframe value in the field. Remember, a keyframe is a complete picture of a frame. The more complete (uncompressed) frames you have, the more you can expect quality and file size to increase. To keep file size small, set large keyframe intervals between frames to reduce the number of total keyframes in the compressed clip.

7. For the Motion Estimation option, select Best for slower encoding and better quality or Faster for quicker encoding and lower quality.

8. Check the Audio box to export your video with sound. Choose a setting for bit rate and number of channels. Higher bit rates will yield better-sounding results at the cost of larger file size, while lower bit rates decrease file size and quality.

9. Use the options in the Other section to change the size of the video:

   • Select a preset size from the Resize To menu.

   • Enter a pixel value or percentage for the Width and Height options.

   • Check Lock Aspect Ratio to preserve the clip's original dimensions.

10. Choose an option for the Deinterlacing setting. If a clip was originally produced for television, it might have an interlaced signal. The Deinterlacing option will clean up the noise and jagged edges produced by interlacing and offers these choices:

   • Select None if the video isn't interlaced.

   • Lower deinterlaces video produced for television in the United States (NTSC format).

   • Upper deinterlaces video produced for television in Europe (PAL format).

11. Click OK. Then choose a destination for the compressed video, and click Save. The video will be compressed in FLV format and placed in the specified location.

Depending upon the length of the video you compress, the time it takes to complete the process will vary. Video clips with large dimensions and clips of long duration take longer to compress than smaller, shorter clips. Getting a video to compress correctly is a process of trial and error. Every video will compress differently based on the scene or event it portrays. Ultimately, you strive to strike a delicate balance between file size, acceptable quality, and smooth playback. Experiment with different settings and test the final FLV files side by side to compare the quality. You can now import your final, compressed FLV file into Flash.

> Sometimes, it's a good idea to compress a small sample clip before doing the whole thing. That way, you don't have to wait a while before realizing that the chosen parameters result in unacceptable quality/bandwidth.

Importing and Encoding Video

To get video into the Flash authoring environment, you must first import it—just as you do sounds, bitmap images, and other media. Flash supports a wide variety of digital video formats. If you have QuickTime 7 for Macintosh, QuickTime 6.5 for Windows, or DirectX 9.0 for Windows, you'll be able to import most kinds of video into Flash 8.

Table 16.2 summarizes the video import file formats supported by Flash 8.

If Flash 8 is unable to import a particular video format, it will display a message alerting you to this fact. In some situations, you might be able to import the video but not the audio. In that case, you'll have the option to import the video without sound.

	FILE TYPE	PLATFORMS
Table 16.2	Audio Video Interleaved (`.avi`)*	Macintosh, Windows
Video File Formats	Digital Video (`.dv`)	Macintosh, Windows
Supported	Moving Picture Experts Group (`.mpg`, `.mpeg`)*	Macintosh, Windows
for Importing	QuickTime Movie (`.mov`)	Macintosh, Windows
into Flash 8	Windows Media File (`.wmv`, `.asf`)*	Windows
	Macromedia Flash Video (`.flv`)**	Macintosh, Windows

These formats are supported in Windows only if DirectX 7 (or greater) is installed.

** *Macromedia Flash Video (`.flv`) files can be imported directly into Flash 8 without the help of QuickTime or DirectX, but they must be compressed using the FLV Exporter plug-in or Sorenson Squeeze.*

Even with On2 VP6 and the other great advances in video compression technology, you should still ensure that you've made your video as "compression friendly" as possible. This means optimizing video and audio content and targeting the video to the bandwidth requirements of your audience.

When you import video into Flash 8, you have several choices as to how you plan on deploying it once it has been imported and the movie is published as a SWF:

- The Progressive Download from a Web Server option requires that your user has Flash Player 7 or greater. Essentially, the Progressive Download from a Web Server option streams an FLV file from a server using the FLVPlayback component (if you're planning on publishing for Flash Player 8) or the MediaPlayback component (if you're planning on publishing for Flash Player 7). The one issue regarding the Progressive Download from a Web Server option is that Flash doesn't actually upload the video file to the intended server—you have to do that manually. Instead, it places the necessary component on the Stage and encodes the selected video clip according to your choices during the import process (and saves it to a designated location on your machine).

- The Stream from Video Streaming Service deployment option requires that the user has Flash Player 7 or greater. This option allows you to upload the video file to a Flash Communication Server that is hosted by a service provider with which you have an account. This option converts the imported video into an FLV file and places and configures the necessary playback component (the FLVPlayback component if you're publishing for Flash Player 8 or the MediaPlayback component if you're publishing for Flash Player 7).

For more information on the Flash Video Streaming Service, go to `http://www.macromedia.com/software/flashcom/fvss`. You should note, however, that this service is not cheap and therefore should not be considered if you want to server one or two videos.

- The Stream from Flash Communication Server option, which requires Flash Player 7 or greater, lets you upload the video file to a Flash Communication Server that you host. Much like the Stream from Video Streaming Service option, this option converts the imported video into an FLV file and places and configures the necessary playback component (the FLVPlayback component if you're publishing for Flash Player 8 or the MediaPlayback component if you're publishing for Flash Player 7).

> For more information on the Flash Communication Server (or its predecessor, the Flash Media Server 2), go to `http://www.macromedia.com/software/flashcom`.

- The Embed Video in SWF and Play in Timeline option embeds the video in the Timeline without the help of one of the playback components. While this option allows you to sync video with other elements on the Stage far more accurately than you'd be able to if you were using one of the aforementioned deployment methods, you may encounter some audio synchronization problems. As a result, this option is recommended for short video clips with no audio track.

> The process by which you embed video in the actual SWF file and play it in the Timeline will be covered separately later in this section.

- The Linked QuickTime Video for Publishing to QuickTime option works only when you're publishing for Flash Player 3–5. This deployment option lets you publish your Flash content as a QuickTime 4 movie.

The powerful, versatile Import Video Wizard facilitates importing any of these types of video. The wizard acts as *the* tool, regardless of the deployment method. Except in the case of the Embed Video in SWF and Play in Timeline option, most, if not all, of the steps required to import video are identical for all the deployment methods:

1. You have three options for beginning the import process:
   - Choose File → Import → Import to Stage (which places the playback component on the Stage).
   - Choose File → Import → Import to Library (which places the playback component in the Library).
   - Choose File → Import → Import Video (which places the playback component both in the Library and on the Stage).
2. When the Import dialog box appears, select the video clip you want to import.
3. When the Import Video dialog box appears, select the location of your video file (see Figure 16.1). If it's located on your computer, select the On Your Computer option, click the Browse button, and find the video file. If the video file isn't located on your computer, select the second option, and enter the location in the URL field.

Figure 16.1

Select the location of your video file in the Select Video portion of the Import Video dialog box.

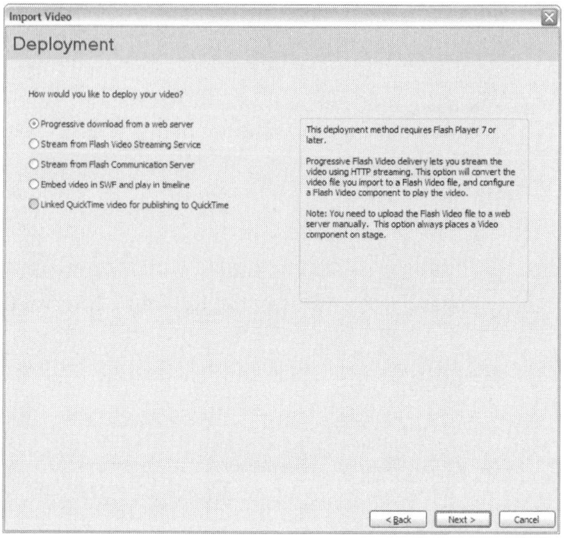

Figure 16.2

Select the method of deployment in the Deployment section of the Import Video dialog box.

4. Click the Next button. When you move to the Deployment screen, select the method of deployment for the imported video file (see Figure 16.2).

5. Click the Next button. When you move to the Encoding section of the Import Video dialog box, select a video-encoding profile from the drop-down menu (see Figure 16.3). These options will allow you to select the target Flash Player (7 or 8) as well as the quality of the video after it has been converted to FLV format. Notice that the specifics of the chosen profile (video codec, data rate, audio codec, and so on) appear below the drop-down menu.

> The target player you choose also determines which playback component is used (the FLV-Playback component for Flash Player 8 or the MediaPlayback component for Flash Player 7).

6. If you want extra control over how the video is encoded, click the Show Advanced Settings button [Show Advanced Settings] to access the advanced encoding tools (see Figure 16.4).

7. On the Encode tab, select the codec you'd like to use to encode your video. Remember, if you're targeting Flash Player 6 or 7 or users with low end computers, select Sorenson Spark. If you're targeting Flash Player 8, select the On2 VP6 codec.

8. Select a frame rate from the Framerate drop-down menu. By default, Flash matches the frame rate of the source video when it encodes the video file. However, if you want to change the frame rate, you can.

If you're planning on embedding the video file in your SWF file, you need to make sure the video's frame rate is the same as the SWF's frame rate. This is where manually setting a frame rate can come in handy.

9. Select the keyframe placement for your video. When you select Automatic, Flash places a keyframe every two seconds of playback. So, if you have a frame rate of 20fps, a keyframe will get added every 40th frame. Alternatively, you can select the Custom option and add a value in the Keyframe Interval field.

In video, a *keyframe* is a frame that contains complete data for the current frame. For the frames between the keyframes, Flash stores only the data that has changed from the preceding frame. The bottom line is that the more keyframes you put in your encoded video, the larger the file will be.

10. Select the quality at which you want your video encoded from the Quality drop-down menu. The maximum kilobits per second rate for each of the presets (Low, Medium, High) is displayed in the Max Data Rate field just under the drop-down menu. If you want to manually set the maximum kilobits per second rate, select Custom from the drop-down menu, and then enter a value in the Max Date Rate field.

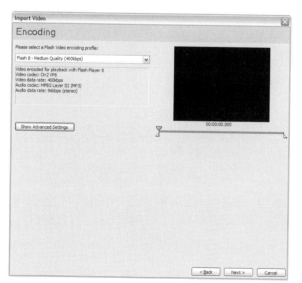

Figure 16.3

Select an encoding profile from the drop-down menu in the Encoding section of the Import Video dialog box.

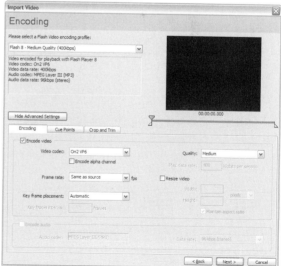

Figure 16.4

You can set advanced encoding options in the Encoding section of the Import Video dialog box.

11. If you want to resize the imported video, click the Resize Video check box, and enter a value in the Width and Height fields (in either pixels or percent). If you want to maintain the video's aspect ratio (a good idea if you don't want it to become distorted), click the Maintain Aspect Ratio check box. If you want a little more control over the size of the video, click the Crop and Trim tab, and adjust the four sliders (each representing one side of the video), as shown in Figure 16.5.

12. Additionally, you can trim the length of the imported video by dragging the In Point marker or the Out Point marker.

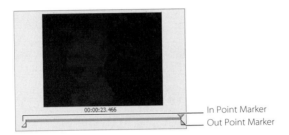

In Point Marker
Out Point Marker

13. Click the Next button to move to the Skinning section of the Import Video dialog box (see Figure 16.6). Select the specific skin you want for the video playback component (the preview of which will be displayed above the Skin drop-down menu). If you don't want to skin the video, choose None from the drop-down menu. You can also specify a custom skin by selecting Custom from the drop-down menu and entering a URL for the custom skin's SWF file in the URL field.

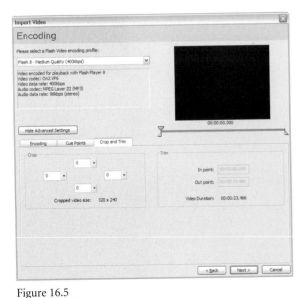

Figure 16.5

Adjust the sliders on the Crop and Trim tab to gain more control over the size of the video.

Figure 16.6

Select the skin you want in the Skinning section of the Import Video dialog box.

14. Click the Next button to move to the Finish Video Import section of the Video Import dialog box (see Figure 16.7). This section of the dialog box gives you some additional specific information about the video and the encoding process: where the video file will be located after it has been imported and encoded, and so on.

15. When you're ready to encode, click the Finish button. If you haven't already, Flash will prompt you to save the FLA file in which you're working. From there, Flash will encode the video and display the progress in the Flash Video Encoding Progress dialog box along with some additional information, such as the audio codec used, the video codec used, the name and location of the output file, and so on (see Figure 16.8).

Figure 16.7

This screen gives you information about the video and encoding process.

Adding Cue Points to an Encoded Video

Although the process by which you add cue points to your video is wrapped up in the encoding process (covered in the previous section), it's important enough to deserve its own section. You can add two kinds of cue points when you're encoding your video. The first, called an Event cue point, triggers an ActionScript method of some sort that affects other elements in your Flash movie. For instance, you could embed a cue point in your movie that, when triggered, will call and play a Movie Clip somewhere else on the Stage. The second kind of cue point, a Navigation cue point (sometimes also referred to as a Seek cue point), provides a bookmark of sorts within the video itself that, with the help of some navigational element (a button, for example), allows the user to jump around in the encoded video. For example, you could be working with a large video with multiple "chapters." You could create a cue point at the beginning of each of these chapters and then create buttons that jump to each of the cue points.

Figure 16.8

The Flash Video Encoding Progress dialog box displays the progress of the encoding.

To insert a cue point:

1. Follow the steps outlined in the previous section to get to the Encoding section of the Import Video dialog box. Click the Show Advanced Settings button , and then click the Cue Points tab (see Figure 16.9).

2. Drag the playback head to the location in the video where you want to insert a cue point. For finer control, you can also click the playback head (it will turn yellow) and use the right and left arrows to advance the Timeline in smaller increments.

Figure 16.9

Open the Cue Points tab of the Encoding section of the Import Video dialog box to insert a cue point.

3. When the playback head is positioned at the desired location, click the Add Cue Point button ⊞. A cue point will be embedded in the video, and Flash will populate the cue point list with a placeholder of the cue point.

4. Give your cue point a unique name, and select its type (Event or Navigation) from the drop-down menu that appears.

5. Repeats steps 2–4 to add more cue points.

6. If you want to pass a parameter to the cue point event handler, select the specific cue point, and click the Add Parameter button to add a parameter to the cue point. Then, you can give the parameter a name and value.

> You would send parameters if you were using the same event handler for many cue points and wanted the handler to be able to differentiate between cues.

7. From here, you need to add the appropriate ActionScript to your movie that can do something with the cue point. For more information on this, refer to the "Working with Cue Points" or "Adding Seek Functionality with Cue Points" topics in Flash help (Help → Flash Help).

Importing a Video and Embedding it in the Timeline

The Embed Video in SWF and Play in Timeline option embeds the video in the Timeline without the help of one of the playback components. Although this option allows you to sync video with other elements on the Stage far more accurately than you'd be able to if you were using one of the other deployment methods, you may encounter some audio synchronization problems. As a result, this option is recommended for short video clips with no audio track. The upside to importing video and embedding in your Timeline is that because no playback component is involved, you don't need to depend on the user having Flash Player 7 or Flash Player 8. Additionally, you can edit video (to a limited degree) if you're importing it and embedding it in the Timeline.

1. You have three options for beginning the import process:

   - Select File → Import → Import to Stage (which places the playback component on the Stage).

   - Select File → Import → Import to Library (which places the playback component in the Library).

   - Select File → Import → Import Video (which imports it to the library).

2. When the Import Video dialog box appears, select the location of your video file. If it's located on your computer, select the On Your Computer option, click the Browse button, and locate the video file. If the video file isn't located on your computer, select the second option, and enter the location in the URL field.

3. Click the Next button to move to the Deployment section of the Import Video dialog box. Select the Embed Video in SWF and Play in Timeline option, and click Next.

4. In the Embedding section of the Import Video dialog box, select the symbol type with which to embed the video from the Symbol Type drop-down menu (see Figure 16.10).

   - The Embed in Timeline option is the most common. It integrates the video directly into your Timeline as an embedded video.

   - The Embed as Movie Clip option places the video inside a Movie Clip. This is an excellent option if you want to offer some sort of user control over the video's playback (with the help of ActionScript) and don't want to use a playback component.

   - The Embed as a Graphic Symbol option sticks the video in a Graphic symbol. In this case, unlike when you embed it as a Movie Clip, you can't control the video with AcionScript.

5. If your video has audio, select one of the options from the Audio Track drop-down menu.

6. Select the Place Instance on Stage option if you want Flash to place an instance of the symbol in which the video has been embedded on the Stage.

7. Choose the Expand Timeline If Needed option if you want Flash to add enough frames to the main Timeline to accommodate the playback length of the video.

Figure 16.10

Select the symbol type in the Embedding section of the Import Video dialog box.

8. If you want to continue with the import, click the Embed the Entire Video radio button, and click the Next button. However, if you want to edit the video before importing it (a process we'll discuss in the next section), click the Edit the Video First radio button, and then click the Next button.

9. From here, you're confronted with an Encoding screen—whose options are the same as with the other deployment methods (except you can't place cue points in an imported video that has been embedded in the Timeline).

10. After you've set the encoding, click the Next button to go to the Finish Video Import screen, where you'll be given some final information about the encoding process. When you're ready to encode, click the Finish button.

Editing Video Clips before They're Encoded

One of the handy features of importing video and embedding it in the Timeline (a process discussed in the previous section) is that you can actually perform some basic edits on the video before importing it.

Editing a video is a fairly simple process. You set an *in point,* the location where you want the edit to begin, and an *out point,* the spot where you want the edit to end. The clip between the in and out points has been *edited,* or separated from the original. You can treat it as a single clip or combine it with other edited clips to create a new clip sequence.

If you don't have a video of your own, you can use one we've provided. If you want to use a QuickTime video, you can use `video.mov` on the CD. If you want to try using an FLV video, use `video.flv`.

To edit your video before it's been encoded:

1. Select the Embed Video in SWF and Play in Timeline option in Deployment, and then import your video. When you get to the Embedding section of the Import Video dialog box, click the Edit the Video First radio button, and then click Next. The Split Video section of the Import Video dialog box appears (see Figure 16.11).

2. Begin by viewing the clip. Click Play to play the clip from its current position; click Stop to halt the video. To scan through the clip quickly, click and drag the playback head from left to right. To advance one frame at a time, click the Step Back or Step Forward button.

3. Once you've isolated the section you want to edit, you can set in and out points. Move the playback head to the position where you want to start your edit, and click Set In Point to Current Position. The in point triangle snaps to that location on the playback Timeline. To set an out point, move the playback head to the position where you want to end your edit, and click Set Out Point to Current Position. You can also drag the in and out point triangles along the Timeline. Click Preview Clip to see the edited clip from start to finish.

4. After setting the in and out points, click Create New Clip on the List button 🞧 . This creates a new, edited clip starting at your in point and ending at your out point. The clip appears in the Clip pane at the side of the dialog box. Enter a name for the newly created clip. To create additional clips, repeat the process outlined in steps 2 and 3.

5. To re-edit a clip, select it in the Clip pane. Set new in and out points for the clip, and click Update Clip.

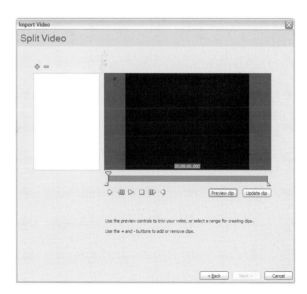

Figure 16.11

Open the Split Video section of the Import Video dialog box to edit your video.

6. One of the best features of the wizard is that it allows you to combine all your edited clips into a single, longer, composite sequence. This is great because you can take an edited segment that was originally at the end of a video and put it at the beginning, or vice versa. Another good feature is that it allows you to trim unwanted sections of video from your final piece.

> By default, if you have more than one clip in the Clip pane, Flash imports them as separate videos.

7. When you've finished editing the clip, click Next to continue the import process.

Using ActionScript to Control Video Playback

If you've imported the video and embedded it in the Timeline (as a Movie Clip), the best way to control the video itself is with ActionScript.

To write ActionScript that controls a video:

1. Drag an instance of your video Movie Clip to the Stage, and use the Property Inspector to assign it the instance name **trailer** (or something different if you prefer). This lesson uses `trailer` throughout.

2. Now that your clip has a unique name, you can add buttons that will allow you to interactively control the playback of the Movie Clip. Drag two buttons from your Library to the Stage: one for Play and one for Stop. Select the Play button, open the Actions panel, and enter the following statements:

   ```
   on(press){
       trailer.play();
   }
   ```

   The function of this script should be fairly self-explanatory. When clicked, the button plays the `trailer` clip from its current location.

3. Select the Stop button, open the Actions panel (if it's not open already), and enter the following statements:

   ```
   on(press){
       trailer.gotoAndStop(1);
   }
   ```

   Again, this is a straightforward script. When clicked, this button sends the clip instance back to frame 1 of its Timeline and stops it there.

4. Select Control → Test Movie to try these buttons. You'll notice that the Play button sets the clip in motion, and the Stop button both halts it and sends it back to frame 1.

Additionally, you can add all sorts of controls to manipulate video playback. Here are just a few samples:

Pause Attaches the following to a button to pause the video:

```
on(press){
   trailer.stop();
}
```

Fast-Forward This example involves a few more elements. Attached to a Fast-Forward button, you have two handlers that toggle the variable ffwd on and off:

```
on(press){
   ffwd = true;
}
on(release){
   ffwd = false;
}
```

Then, to respond to the change in variable value, you can assign a function for the video Movie Clip instance trailer. This script is attached to frame 1 of the main Timeline. When ffwd is "on," it sends the clip ahead by four frames. You can increase or decrease this number to change the speed of the fast-forward:

```
ffwd = false;
trailer.onEnterFrame = function(){
   if(ffwd == true){
       frame = trailer._currentframe;
       trailer.gotoAndPlay(frame+4);
   }
}
```

For this and other video-scripting solutions, check out the files named video2.fla and video2.swf on the CD. They'll show you this and other examples in the context of an actual movie.

Managing Video Files in Your Movie

Several techniques can be helpful for managing your video media inside and outside a Flash document. After you edit or change an embedded video file outside Flash, you can update the file rather than reimport it.

To update an embedded video clip:

1. Select the video clip in the Library.

2. Right-click / Ctrl+click the video in the Library, and choose Properties from the context menu.

3. Click Update in the Update Video Properties dialog box. The embedded clip is updated with the edited file.

This only works if you will still be using the same codec in the updated file. If you want to change the codec, you are best off deleting the current video and reimporting a new version.

Alternatively, you can replace the selected clip with an entirely different video clip. Click Import, and choose a different clip in the Import dialog box. That clip will replace the embedded clip in your Library.

You might also want to replace the embedded video clip that is used for an embedded video instance or change the clip's properties. To perform either of these tasks:

1. Select the clip on the Stage you want to change.

2. Open the Property Inspector (Ctrl+F3 / Cmd+F3) to display the instance information for the selected clip.

3. Depending upon your needs, do any of the following:

   - Click Swap, and choose the clip you want to exchange for the clip on the Stage. Click OK, and the clip instance is updated accordingly.

   - Enter values for W and H to change the width and height of a clip. Realize that increasing the size of the video can produce an ugly, "blocky" appearance. If a video needs to be larger, the best approach is to return to the source and re-export the video at a larger size.

   - Enter values for X and Y to set the Stage position of the video instance's upper-left corner.

When publishing a Flash movie as an SWF file, the soundtrack of any embedded video clips will be exported using the Stream sound settings. (These are the settings for Stream in the Flash tab of the Publish Settings dialog box.) Be sure these options are set at the appropriate rate for your target audience.

PART IV

Delivery

So, you've spent hours creating your Flash masterpiece. You've created cool images, crafted groovy animation, and added amazing interactivity with ActionScript. What's next? Well, after a bit of a breather and a good pat on the back, it's time to start thinking about what to do with this amazing piece of brain sweat. Yeah, that's right—it isn't finished yet. The whole point of creating interactive media of any kind is so that other people can enjoy, experience, and explore your creative vision.

CHAPTER 17

Publishing and Exporting Movies

You've spent hours creating beautiful graphics, prodding your animation, and tweaking your ActionScript, so what's next? Well, all your hard work is for naught if others can't experience your beautiful creation.

The process of converting an FLA file (the native type of Flash) to a format that can be distributed over the Web or via another medium is called *publishing*. Although publishing your movie is pretty straightforward, you need to make sure the FLA file's settings maximize your movie for its intended audience. As a result, familiarity with the available export options is therefore crucial.

- Testing your movie
- Manipulating Flash publishing settings
- Manipulating individual publish format settings
- Setting up publishing profiles
- Previewing and publishing your Flash movie
- Outputting printable Flash movies
- Publishing accessible movies for the visually impaired

Testing Your Flash Movie

Before you even start thinking about the format you'll publish your grand Flash creation in, you need to make sure everything is functioning as it should be and see how it will look in the Flash Player in SWF.

> When you're working in Flash, the vast majority of the work you'll publish will be in SWF. This is why, when you want to test your movie (before you actually set any of the publishing properties), you do so in the Flash Player as a SWF file. If your movie will ultimately be published in a different format, you can also test it from within the Flash environment; however, you first need to set the file's publishing settings. (See the section "Working with Flash Publishing Settings" later in this chapter.)

To test your movie, you have a few options:

- Choose Control → Test Movie to view the entire movie in SWF with the Flash Player.
- Choose Control → Test Scene to view the current scene in SWF with the Flash Player.
- If you're working in Flash 8 Professional and want to test the project you're currently working on, select Control → Test Project.

When you perform any of these procedures, Flash opens the movie within the workspace using the Flash Player. When you're finished testing the movie, choose File → Close, and you'll be returned to your original movie.

> It's important to note that the player used to preview in the authoring environment may not correspond with the version of the user's Flash player.

Testing Download Performance

Given that the vast majority of Flash movies are destined to be delivered over the Web in SWF, Macromedia has included a way for you to simulate the download process over an Internet connection—as opposed to the almost instantaneous performance you get from running the movie directly from your hard drive.

To test your movie's download performance:

1. Choose Control → Test Movie or Control → Test Scene.

2. When the movie opens in the Flash Player, choose View → Download Settings, and select the specific connection over which you want to simulate your movie's download. Your choices range from a 14.4kbps modem to a T1 dedicated connection.

3. If you want to view a graph displaying frame-by-frame download performance, choose View → Bandwidth Profiler from within the previewed SWF file.

The left side of the Bandwidth Profiler displays information about the movie (see Figure 17.1). The right side shows a graph in which each vertical bar represents a frame in the movie. The size of the bar corresponds to that frame's size in bytes. The red line beneath the Timeline header indicates whether a given frame streams in real time with the modem speed that you selected. If a bar extends above the red line, the document must wait for that frame to load. As the green bar along the top of the Bandwidth Profiler extends, it indicates when each individual frame is loaded.

The Bandwidth Profiler also gives you real-time feedback. For example, if the content in your movie results in a pause, you actually see the pause in playback during the simulation.

4. To turn the download simulation on or off, choose View → Simulate Download.

5. When you're finished viewing your movie over a simulated Internet connection, select File → Close, and you'll be returned to the original movie.

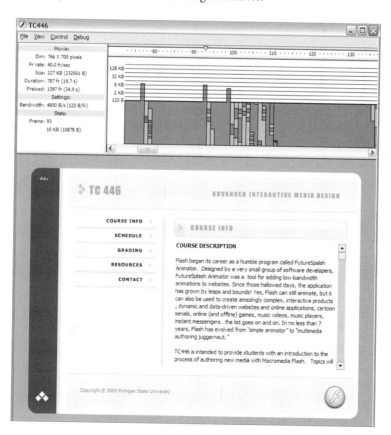

Figure 17.1

Use the Bandwidth Profiler to get all sorts of bandwidth information about your movie.

Working with Flash Publishing Settings

The majority of the time, you'll publish your movies as SWF files. However, Macromedia has provided a series of other file formats for publishing your movie. These formats enable you to tailor your Flash creation so you can reach the maximum number of people. And the cool part of publishing your movie is that you can do so in several formats simultaneously. For instance, if you created a series of noninteractive animated shorts, you could publish them as both SWF and QuickTime files to take advantage of those two formats' wide installation bases. As you might have guessed, all the file types have quite a few settings that allow you to further manipulate a movie's ultimate look and behavior.

In the following sections, you'll get an overview of the file types and then look at the individual publishing settings for each of them.

> Although the process of publishing your movie is relatively simple, it actually involves two tasks. We'll discuss the first task, inputting the publishing settings, after you've thoroughly explored all the file types to which you can output a Flash movie. We'll discuss the second task, telling Flash to publish your creation based on the settings, in the section "Publishing Your Flash Movie" later in this chapter.

Introducing the Publishing Formats

Flash offers several file types to which you can publish your creation. Each has its own strengths and weaknesses. You should learn about each one so that you know which to use.

Flash Most of the time, you'll publish your Flash movie as SWF files. The default publishing format, SWF, is viewable only if your intended audience has installed the Flash Player on their computers. It's definitely important to know that, of all the possible file types, SWF is the only one that fully supports all ActionScript and animation; other formats such as QuickTime don't fully support these features. So, if you want to leverage the full power of Flash, use SWF. It doesn't hurt that the Flash Player is one of, if not the, most prevalent plug-in on the web.

> If you plan to distribute your SWF movie over the Web (as opposed to creating a stand-alone SWF file that the Flash Player plays), you'll need to publish an HTML file as well—a process discussed in the section "Manipulating HTML Settings" later in this chapter.

HTML Playing an SWF movie in a web browser requires an HTML document in which the Flash movie is embedded. The HTML file serves to activate the movie, specify browser settings, and, to a certain degree, determine how the SWF file appears. As a result, if your SWF file is destined for distribution on the Web, you must publish it with an HTML file.

The Flash Player (placed on the user's computer when the user installs the Flash plug-in) can display SWF files without the help of an HTML file. As a result, if your movie isn't destined to be viewed in a web browser, you don't have to worrying about publishing an HTML file along with your movie.

GIF You can export a Flash movie as an animated GIF for distribution to users who don't have the Flash plug-in installed on their computers. A Flash movie published as an animated GIF is generally larger in size than if it had been published as an SWF file. In addition, you'll lose any interactivity in a Flash movie that's exported to an animated GIF. Generally speaking the only real reasons that you would export to GIF would be if you were creating banner ads or you were making a completely HTML version of your Flash site.

JPEG By default, Flash exports the first frame of a movie as a static JPEG. However, you can use a trick to force Flash to export an alternative frame (as opposed to the first one). We'll cover this in the section "Setting JPEG Publish Options" later in this chapter. In the case of exporting as a JPEG, you are going to get a higher quality image (especially when it comes to gradients or complex colors) than if you were exporting as a GIF. The downside to exporting as a JPEG is that, unlike a GIF, you can't create an animated JPEG.

PNG Much as in the case of JPEGs, Flash exports a single static PNG image. However, as in the case of a GIF, you can use a trick to set which frame is exported. PNGs provide lossless support as well as being a great format if you want to edit the exported image in an application like Fireworks or Photoshop.

Windows Projector A Windows Projector is a self-executing EXE file that doesn't need a browser or a plug-in to view it. This has some advantages over the other file types. First, you can distribute the Windows Projector without having to worry whether the intended audience has the necessary Flash plug-in, a compatible web browser, or even an Internet connection. Windows Projectors are self-contained little packages that are great for distributing media such as CDs or DVDs.

Macintosh Projector A Macintosh Projector is the Mac equivalent of a Windows Projector. A self-executing HQX file, a Macintosh Projector doesn't need the Flash plug-in or a browser to be viewed.

QuickTime Publishing your Flash movie to QuickTime creates a MOV file that plays in the QuickTime Player. This format retains the many, though certainly not all (especially when it comes to the latest version of Flash, of your movie's interactive features. However, users need to have the QuickTime plug-in installed to view Flash files published as MOV files. When rendered, your Flash creation occupies a single track in the QuickTime movie.

If you don't have QuickTime (version 4 or later) installed on your computer, you won't be able to publish your Flash movie in QuickTime format. The latest version of QuickTime can be downloaded at www.quicktime.com.

Manipulating Individual Publish Format Settings

Now that you've explored each of the various file formats you can publish your Flash movie in, you'll learn about the publishing settings of those file formats. All the work you'll do in the following sections takes place in the Publish Settings dialog box, which you access by choosing File → Publish Settings (see Figure 17.2).

As you select individual file types on the Formats tab of the Publish Settings dialog box, you'll notice that additional tabs (labeled with the specific file type) appear. By clicking any of these tabs, you can access that file type's settings. When you're finished manipulating the settings of all the file types you're publishing your Flash movie in, click OK.

By clicking the Use Default Names button [Use Default Names], your file is published with the same name you assigned to your FLA file. If you toggle the button off, you can name the file uniquely.

> Neither a Windows Projector nor a Macintosh Projector has any unique publishing settings, so we won't discuss those formats in the following sections. However, when you export a movie to Windows Projector or Macintosh Projector, its properties are set by the choices you make under the Flash tab.

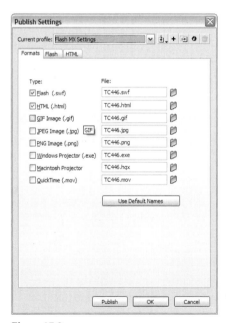

Figure 17.2

Use the Publish Settings dialog box to work with individual settings.

Figure 17.3

Use the Flash tab of the Publish Settings dialog box to work with Flash settings.

Working with Flash Settings

After you select Flash (.swf) in the Formats tab of the Publish Settings dialog box (see Figure 17.3), you can click the Flash tab to access those settings.

Version Specifies the version of Flash Player (1, 2, 3, 4, 5, 6, 7, 8, Flash Lite 1.0, or Flash Lite 1.1) with which your published movie will be compatible.

> Macromedia collectively refers to Flash Lite 1.0 and 1.1 as *Flash Lite 1.x*.

You'll have to be careful about which version you're publishing in if you've used newer Flash features not supported in older Flash Player versions. For the most part, when it comes to backward compatibility with older plug-ins, you need to be most concerned with the ActionScript you're using.

Load Order Sets the order in which the layers in each frame load (and are displayed). Your choice (either Bottom Up or Top Down) is particularly important if the Flash file is being loaded over a slow connection. In that case, you might want to set the load order to reflect the position of the larger elements (large graphics, audio, and so on) so that they load first. If, for instance, you set the load order to Top Down and the top layer in your movie is occupied by your ActionScript (which will load extremely quickly), you'll find that the script layer will load and run before some of the more bandwidth-intensive elements (that occupy lower layers in the movie) even get a chance to load.

If, on the other hand, the movie is being accessed over a fast connection, your choice really won't matter that much because the layers will load so fast that you won't see any perceivable difference between the options.

ActionScript Version Lets you set the specific version of ActionScript used in your published movie. For versions 1 through 5 (as well as Flash Lite 1.0 and 1.1), your only choice is ActionScript 1.0. However, if you're publishing for version 6, 7, or 8, you can choose either ActionScript 1.0 or ActionScript 2.0.

> If a script is incompatible with the player you've chosen, it will be highlighted in yellow in the ActionScript panel.

Generate Size Report Tells Flash to output a SimpleText (Mac) or TXT (Win) file that reports on the filesize of the movie's assets.

Protect from Import Prevents your published SWF file from being imported into Flash—a handy option for those conscious about their work being digitally plagiarized.

Omit Trace Actions Ignores any trace actions (which automatically opens the Output window) that you've added to your movie.

Debugging Permitted Allows the Debugger to work on the published file. In addition, when selected, this option also allows remote debugging via a browser using the Flash Debug Player plug-in or ActiveX control.

Compress Movie Compresses the movie to reduce its file size and download time. Beware, however, that movies that have been compressed using this option can be played only with the Flash 6 Player or later.

Optimize for Flash Player 6 r65 If you've selected Flash Player 6 in the Version drop-down menu, the Optimize for Flash Player 6 r65 option becomes available. This option allows you take advantage of a process called ActionScript Register Allocation, which improves performance. For this to work properly, users must have this version of the Flash Player (or later) installed.

Password Allows you to enter the password needed to either open the Debugger (remotely or locally) or import the movie into Flash. This option is enabled only if you selected either the Protect from Import option or the Debugging Permitted option.

JPEG Quality Lets you adjust the level of compression applied to all bitmaps in your Flash movie. Alternatively, you can also enter a value (from 0 to 100) in the field to the right of the slider. The lower the value you set, the more compression that will result. The kicker is that although lower quality means smaller image size, it also means the images will have a lower visual quality. The trick is finding the right balance between appearance and file size.

Generally speaking, if you want the best results, you should set image quality on a per-image basis, instead of setting the properties globally.

Audio Stream By clicking the Set button ⌈ Set... ⌋, you access the Sound Settings dialog box (see Figure 17.4). From here, you can manipulate the settings of your movie's audio. The Compression drop-down menu lets you set the type of compression used on your audio. Each of the options (MP3, ADPCM, RAW, Disable, and Speech) has unique settings that you can manipulate.

Audio Event By clicking the Set button ⌈ Set... ⌋, you open the Sound Settings dialog box (refer to Figure 17.4). From here, you can set the various compression properties of any event sounds in your movie.

Override Sound Settings Uses the settings you established in the Flash tab of the Publish Settings dialog box, automatically overriding any compression schemes set in the Library.

Figure 17.4

Use the Sound Settings dialog box to manipulate your movie's audio settings.

Export Device Sounds Select the Export Device Sounds option to export your audio in a format suitable for mobile devices.

Local Playback Security Allows you to control your Flash movie's network access. When you select Local Access Only, your published SWF file can interact with files and resources on the local system. If you select Access Network Only, your published SWF interacts with files and resources on the network but not on the local system. Ultimately, the Access Network Only option protects information on the user's computer from being accidentally uploaded to the network.

Post-processor If you've installed any post-processors, you can select them from the Post-processor drop-down menu. Post-processors are Windows DDLs or Macintosh bundles that perform a specific operation on a SWF file at the time it's created. It's important to realize that Flash 8 doesn't come bundled with any post-processors—and no post-processors are available at the time of writing.

Manipulating HTML Settings

If your Flash movie is destined for distribution over the Web, you need to embed it in an HTML file.

After you select HTML (.html) in the Formats tab of the Publish Settings dialog box, you'll be able to click the HTML tab to access the HTML-related settings (see Figure 17.5).

> If you don't have the Flash (.swf) option selected in the Formats tab of the Publish Settings dialog box, you don't have access to HTML as a file type. Likewise, if you select the HTML (.html) option from the Formats tab, the Flash (.swf) option is automatically selected.

Template Lets you choose from a set of predefined HTML templates that will be used to display the Flash movie.

Most of the time, you won't need to choose anything but the Flash Only template. However, some of the other templates are geared toward alternative file types, such as QuickTime, and will be useful in other situations. (For more information on each of the specific templates, see the Flash help.)

> To get information about a specific template, select it from the drop-down menu, and then click the Info button (to the right of the drop-down menu).

Detect Flash Version Configures your document to detect your users' Flash Player version. By selecting the Detect Flash Version option, users who access your Flash application are transparently directed to an HTML file that contains a SWF file designed to detect the version of their Flash Player. If they have the specified version (or later), the SWF file again redirects the user to your content HTML file, and your SWF file plays as designed. If users don't have the specified version, they're redirected to an alternative HTML file that Flash creates or that you've created.

By checking the Detect Flash Version box, you get access to the Minor Revision and Incremental Revision fields where you can specify the exact version of the Flash Player you set.

> Some versions of Flash are a little sneaky in that even if you set the SWF to export for previous versions of Flash (say, v6), the HTML will still look for the version 8 player unless you specifically state otherwise in the HTML.

Dimensions Controls the HTML document's WIDTH and HEIGHT values in the OBJECT and EMBED tags. It's important to understand that the value you enter in the Width and Height fields (just below the Dimensions drop-down menu) doesn't actually affect the size of your Flash movie, just the area of the web page through which your movie is viewed. The Scale setting (discussed later in this section) determines the way the movie fits in this area. These are the options in the Dimensions drop-down menu:

- Match Movie retains the same width and height of the actual movie.

- To enter a width and height value in pixels, choose Pixels from the drop-down menu, and then enter values in the Width and Height fields.

- By choosing Percent and entering values in the Width and Height fields, you set a percentage of the browser window that the movie fills.

Figure 17.5

Use the HTML tab of the Publish Settings dialog box to work with individual HTML settings.

Playback Controls how the Flash movie plays when it's downloaded:

- By choosing the Paused at Start option, your movie automatically stops at the first frame. A button with a play() action can restart the movie. In addition, selecting Play from the movie's right-click / Ctrl+click menu can restart the movie.

- When selected, the Loop option forces the movie to loop *ad infinitum.*

- The Display Menu option lets you determine whether the movie's right-click / Ctrl+click menu is active.

- When selected, the Device Font option, which applies to movies only when they're played on a Windows machine, replaces any font that the user doesn't have installed on their system with antialiased system fonts. This increases the legibility of small text and decreases the overall size of the movie.

Quality Determines the quality at which your movie is played. The options determine whether your movie sacrifices speed for quality, or vice versa:

- By turning off any antialiasing, Low sacrifices speed over visual quality.

- Auto Low starts the movie playing without antialiasing but bumps the quality up to High if the user's computer can cope with the improved quality while still maintaining quick playback.

- Auto High begins playback at High quality but shifts into Low mode if the user's computer can't cope with the increased visual quality and playback speed.

- By choosing Medium, your movie is partially antialiased with no bitmap smoothing. The option results in a higher visual quality than Low but a lower visual quality than High.

- When you select High, you force your movie to be antialiased. If the movie contains bitmaps that aren't animated, they're smoothed. On the other hand, if the bitmaps are animated in any way, they won't be smoothed.

- When you choose Best, you force your movie to play at the highest visual quality possible with little regard for playback speed.

Window Mode Sets options for movies played in Internet Explorer 4.0 (and later) with the Flash ActiveX control:

- By choosing Window, your movie is played in its own rectangular window on a web page. It's important to note that this option results in the fastest animation speed.

- The Opaque Windowless option pushes any Dynamic HTML elements (specifically, layers) behind so they don't appear over the Flash movie.

- The Transparent Windowless option displays the background of the HTML page on which the movie is embedded through all transparent areas of the movie.

> The Transparent Windowless option often results in slower playback.

HTML Alignment Positions your Flash movie within the web page. The default option centers the Flash movie horizontally and vertically within the web page. The other options align the Flash movie along the left, right, top, and bottom edges of the browser window.

Scale Works in conjunction with the option you set using the Dimensions drop-down menu:

- The Default (Show All) option expands the size of your movie (without distortion) to fit the entire specified area while still maintaining the movie's aspect ratio. As a result, even if you choose this option, you might have borders appear on both of the movie's two sides.

- By choosing No Border, your movie is expanded (without distortion) to fill the entire area defined by the Dimensions setting. As with the Default (Show All) option, the movie maintains its aspect ratio. However, the difference is that when you choose No Border, your movie might actually expand to be larger than the area defined by the Dimensions settings to maintain the movie's aspect ratio. As a result, the edges of your movie might appear as if they've been cut off.

- Exact Fit displays the entire movie in the specified area without reserving the original aspect ratio. As a result, your movie might be somewhat distorted.

Flash Alignment Determines the placement of the movie within the Dimensions area. You set it by choosing options from the Horizontal and Vertical drop-down menus.

Show Warning Messages Tells Flash to alert you to any conflicts created by your various publishing settings—there is almost never any reason to disable this.

Working with GIF Settings

By selecting the GIF Image (`.gif`) option from the Formats tab and then clicking the GIF tab, you can set GIF-specific options (see Figure 17.6).

Dimensions Allows you to set the dimensions of the static image or animated GIF that is published by entering values (in pixels) in the Width and Height fields. If you want the dimensions of the GIF to match those of the Flash movie, check the Match Movie box.

Playback If you want to export a single frame of the Flash movie, select the Static option. By default, Flash exports the first frame of your movie as the static GIF image. If you want to force Flash to export an alternative frame, attach a `#Static` frame label to the desired frame by using the Property Inspector.

If you want to export the Flash movie as a GIF animation, select the Animated option. If you want to avoid publishing the entire movie as an animated GIF, attach a `#First` label to the initial frame in the range you want to publish and a `#Last` frame label to the final frame in the range.

From there, you can select Loop Continuously (to have the animation play over and over again without stopping) or enter the number of repetitions for the animation in the Repeat *x* Times field.

Optimize Colors Tells Flash to remove any unused colors from the GIF's color table. This can reduce the final file size.

> If you've chosen Adaptive from the Palette drop-down menu, selecting the Optimize Colors option has no effect.

Interlace Publishes the movie as an interlaced GIF. An interlaced GIF is structured so that it comes into focus slowly as the browser loads the image.

Smooth Antialiases all the artwork in the movie when it's published to GIF. Be advised that this option results in a larger file size.

Dither Solids Applies dithering to both colors and gradients.

If you dither solids in an image that contains aliased text, the text will often look distorted.

Remove Gradients Converts all your gradients to solid colors. Because gradients don't translate well to GIF, leaving this option unchecked could result in some odd (and visually unappealing) results.

Transparent Determines the level at which the background of the movie is transparent, as well as how the Flash movie's alpha settings are converted:

- By choosing Opaque, the movie is published as a GIF with a solid background.
- By choosing Transparent, the movie is published as a GIF with a transparent background.

Choosing the Transparent option in conjunction with the Smooth option can result in semi-transparent halos around all objects.

- By choosing Alpha, you control the transparency of individual objects. By entering a Threshold value from 0 to 255, you make all colors less than the value completely transparent and colors greater than the threshold partially transparent. A value of 128 corresponds to 50 percent alpha.

Figure 17.6

Use the GIF tab of the Publish Settings dialog box to work with GIF settings.

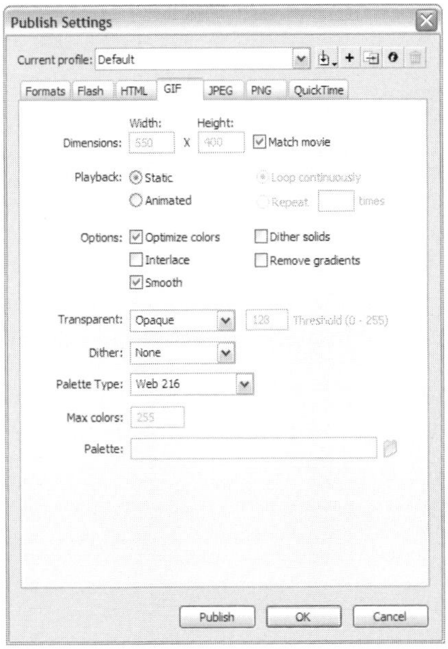

Dither Generates colors not in the current palette by combining pixels from a 256-color palette into patterns that approximate other colors. The options in the Dither drop-down menu let you set the method by which the pixels are combined when the movie is exported to GIF:

- By choosing None, dithering is turned off, and colors not in the basic color table are replaced with solid colors from the table that most closely approximate the specified color. Although not dithering can produce smaller files, it often results in strange colors.
- Choosing Ordered results in good-quality images with a relatively small file size.
- Choosing Diffusion results in the best-quality image. However, file size and load time increase.

Dithering is usually not recommended if the image has gradients, because it may break up the gradient.

Palette Type Lets you choose the type of palette that's used when the GIF is published:

- The Web 216 palette comprises 216 colors that are identical on both Windows and Macintosh computers.
- By choosing Adaptive, you set a custom palette of colors derived from the actual colors in the image. When you choose Adaptive, you can also limit the number of colors by entering a value (up to 256) in the Max Colors field.
- The Web Snap Adaptive palette is almost the same as the Adaptive palette. The only difference is that it converts similar colors to the Web 216 color palette.
- By selecting the Custom option, you can specify a custom-created palette by clicking the ellipsis (…) button just to the right of the Palette field and browsing for an ACT file.

Setting JPEG Publish Options

If you want to publish a single frame of your Flash movie as a JPEG file, select JPEG Image (.jpg) from the Formats tab, and click the JPEG tab to manipulate its publishing settings (see Figure 17.7). Much as in the case of a GIF file, you can force Flash to export a frame other than the first one by attaching a #Static frame label to the desired frame with the Property Inspector.

Because the Dimensions option on the JPEG tab is the same as on the GIF tab, we'll skip that option in this section. For a refresher, see the previous section.

Quality Adjusts the level of compression applied to the published JPEG. Alternatively, you can enter a value (from 0 to 100) in the field to the right of the slider. The lower the value you set, the greater compression that will result.

Progressive Creates a JPEG similar to an interlaced GIF.

Working with PNG Publishing Settings

If you want to publish a single frame of your Flash movie as a PNG file, select PNG Image (.png) from the Formats tab, and click the PNG tab to manipulate its publishing settings (see Figure 17.8). Much as in the case of GIFs and JPEGs, you can force Flash to export a frame other than the first one by attaching a #Static frame label to the desired frame with the Property Inspector.

Figure 17.7

Use the JPEG tab of the Publish Settings dialog box to work with JPEG settings.

Figure 17.8

Use the PNG tab of the Publish Settings dialog box to work with PNG settings.

Because the majority of options for publishing a PNG file are the same as those for publishing a GIF file, we won't cover them in this section. For a refresher, see the section "Working with GIF Settings" earlier in this chapter.

Bit Depth Determines the amount of colors in the published PNG image:

- Choosing the 8-bit option results in an image with a maximum of 256 colors.

- The 24-bit option results in an image that can display a maximum of 16.7 million colors. As one would expect, this produces larger file sizes but renders your Flash movie far more accurately.

- The 24-bit with Alpha option includes support for 16.7 million colors as well as an additional 8-bit channel for transparency support. When you choose this option, the unfilled areas in a PNG image turn transparent when the file is published.

Generally speaking, you would only use the 24-bit with Alpha option if you were planning on editing the image in another program (such as Fireworks or Photoshop) as it results in an image far too large in file size to be appropriate for the web.

Filter Options Determines the compression algorithm used on the PNG image:

- By choosing None, no compression algorithm is applied to the image. This results in a significantly larger image.

- The Sub option, which transmits the difference between each byte and the value of the corresponding byte of the prior pixel, works best on images that have repeating information (such as stripes or checks) along the horizontal axis.

- The Up option works in the opposite manner from the Sub option and is most effective on images that feature vertically repeating information.

- The Average option, which uses a pixel's two adjacent neighbors to predict its value, works best on images that have a mix of both horizontally repeating and vertically repeating information.

- The Path option generates a linear function of the pixels above, to the left, and to the upper left and then makes a prediction based on the neighboring pixel closest to the computed value.

Setting QuickTime Publish Options

If you want to publish your Flash creation as a QuickTime movie (MOV), select the Quick-Time (.mov) option from the Formats tab, and click the QuickTime tab (see Figure 17.9).

Dimensions Allows you to set the dimensions of the QuickTime movie that is published by entering values (in pixels) in the Width and Height fields. If you want the dimensions of the QuickTime movie to match those of the actual Flash movie, check the Match Movie box.

Alpha Lets you control the transparency of the Flash information in the QuickTime movie:

- By choosing Auto, the Flash movie becomes transparent if it's on top of any other tracks in the QuickTime movie (such as additional QuickTime video tracks), but it becomes opaque if it's at the bottom or the only track in the movie.

- The Alpha-Transparent option makes the Flash track transparent, displaying the contents of any additional lower tracks.

- When you choose the Copy option, the Flash track is rendered as completely opaque, blocking all lower tracks.

Layer Controls the position of your Flash content relative to any QuickTime content in the exported movie. Choose Top if you want the Flash content to occupy the top layer and Bottom if you want it to occupy the bottom layer. When you choose Auto, the Flash track is placed in front of other tracks in the QuickTime file if the Flash objects in the movie are in front of video objects. If they aren't, the Flash track is placed behind all other tracks in the QuickTime file.

Streaming Sound Forces Flash to export all the streaming audio in the movie to a QuickTime soundtrack. In the process, the audio recompresses using the standard QuickTime audio settings. To manipulate the default settings, click the Settings button Settings... to open the Sound Settings dialog box.

From here, you can set the compressor used, the bit rate, and the audio to mono or stereo.

Controller If you've ever viewed a QuickTime file, you probably noticed that it had an interactive controller at the bottom of the player. With it, you can perform such actions as pause, play, and adjust volume. The Controller drop-down menu lets you determine whether you want the standard controller to be displayed (by choosing Standard), no controller to be displayed (None), or the QuickTime VR controller to be displayed (QuickTime VR).

Loop Sets the QuickTime movie to loop indefinitely.

Paused at Start Sets the QuickTime movie to not automatically play. The user can begin playback by clicking the Play button in the controller.

Play Every Frame Overrides the frame rate and plays every frame without any of the skipping characteristics of QuickTime's attempt to maintain time. It's important to note that when this option is selected, the audio track is turned off.

Flatten (Make Self-contained) If this option is unselected, the Flash content won't be combined with the QuickTime movie. Instead, the file content is published as a separate file and referenced separately by QuickTime. If all the files aren't in the same place, the QuickTime movie can't display the Flash content. When you select the Flatten (Make Self-contained) option, all the content is combined into one file.

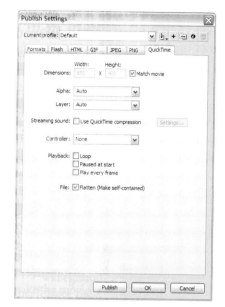

Figure 17.9

Use the QuickTime tab of the Publish Settings dialog box to work with Quick-Time settings.

Previewing Your Flash Movie

To preview your movie in any of the various file types you selected in the Formats section of the Publish Settings dialog box, select File → Publish Preview, and choose from the available list of file types.

You'll be able to access only those file types that were selected in the Formats section of the Publish Settings dialog box.

Flash automatically loads the selected file type.

Publishing Your Flash Movie

Now that you've manipulated the publishing settings of your various file types and previewed those files (and you've done any necessary tweaking), you can publish your Flash movie. All you have to do is choose File → Publish, and Flash does all the work. All the various file types you set in the Publish Settings dialog box will be published simultaneously to the folder on your hard drive where you saved the FLA file on which they're based.

Besides the Publish command, you'll also see an Export command in the File menu. Export is almost the same as Publish; the difference is that, by using Export, you bypass the Publish Settings dialog box and can use an Export Movie dialog box where you set the file type and export location. The drawback of exporting is that you don't have access to the file type's publishing settings.

Working with Publish Profiles

Publish profiles are a group of publish settings saved under one name. You can create publish profiles and then apply them to any of your projects, saving you from specifying all the publish settings manually. You can also export the profiles and use them across projects to publish consistently under different conditions.

> The real drawback to working with publish profiles is that once you create one, it isn't instantaneously available in another document. But don't worry—you can use a publish profile across multiple documents. You'll just need to export it from the document in which it was originally created and then import it into the document in which you want to use it.

Applying a publish profile is easy. Select the profile you want to use from the Current Profile drop-down menu at the top of the Publish Settings dialog box (File → Publish Settings), and click OK.

Creating a Publish Profile

To create a publish profile:

1. Choose File → Publish Settings.

2. When the Publish Settings dialog box opens, click the Create New Profile button ➕.

3. When the Create New Profile dialog box opens, enter the name for the profile in the Profile Name field, and click OK (see Figure 17.10).

4. From there, you'll need to set the properties of the publish profile (by following the steps outlined in the "Manipulating Individual Publish Formats" section earlier in this chapter). The properties automatically are saved under the profile you just created.

Importing and Exporting Publish Profiles

As already mentioned, a publish profile created in one document isn't instantaneously accessible in other documents. You must first export and then import your publish profile.

Figure 17.10

Enter a name for your profile in the Create New Profile dialog box.

Publish profiles are exported as XML files.

To export a publish profile:

1. Make sure the Publish Settings dialog box is open (File → Publish Settings).

2. Select the publish profile you want to export from the Profile Name drop-down menu at the top of the Publish Settings dialog box.

3. Click the Import/Export Profile button, and choose Export from the drop-down menu.

4. When the Export Profile dialog box opens, enter a name for the exported profile in the Name field, navigate to where you want the profile exported, and click Save.

Once you've exported a publish profile, you can then import and use it in another document entirely:

1. Make sure the Publish Settings dialog box is open (File → Publish Settings).

2. Click the Import/Export Profile button, and choose Import from the drop-down menu.

3. When the Import Profile dialog box opens, navigate to the publish profile you want to import, select it, and click OK.

Duplicating a Publish Profile

What happens if you want to create a new publish profile that is almost identical to an existing publish profile, but you don't want to go through the process of creating the new publish profile from scratch? Thankfully, you can duplicate an existing profile and then make any changes you want to the copy:

1. Make sure the Publish Settings dialog box is open (File → Publish Settings).

2. Select the publish profile you want to duplicate from the Current Profile drop-down menu.

3. Click the Duplicate Profile button.

4. When the Duplicate Profile dialog box opens, enter a name for the new profile in the Duplicate Name field (see Figure 17.11).

5. You'll notice that the duplicate profile now appears in the Current Profile drop-down menu. You can select it and make any changes you want. When you're finished, click OK.

Figure 17.11

Duplicate your profile with the Duplicate Profile dialog box.

Changing the Name of a Publish Profile

To change a publish profile's name:

1. Make sure the Publish Settings dialog box is open (File → Publish Settings).

2. Select the publish profile whose name you want to change from the Current Profile drop-down menu.

3. Click the Profile Properties button ❶ .

4. When the Profile Properties dialog box opens, enter a new name in the Profile Name field, and click OK (see Figure 17.12).

Figure 17.12

To rename a profile, use the Profile Properties dialog box.

Deleting a Publish Profile

At some point, you might want to delete a publish profile you've created:

1. Make sure the Publish Settings dialog box is open (File → Publish Settings).

2. Select the publish profile you want to delete from the Current Profile drop-down menu.

3. Click the Delete Profile button 🗑 .

4. When the alert appears, click OK to delete the profile.

Publishing Accessible Flash Movies

Although you can publish your movie in a myriad of file types—all of which extend the scope of your audience—you'll want to consider another way of making your movie available to a wider audience.

In recent years, a growing trend has been to make web content *accessible*, that is, usable for individuals with a variety of disabilities. One of the most pressing concerns is that, up until now, Flash movies couldn't be interpreted by a *screen reader*—a type of software the "reads" the contents of a computer screen and then "speaks" it to a visually impaired user. This problem occurs because visual information (as opposed to text) involves a subjective interpretation. In other words, one person's description of an image will probably differ from another's. As a result, simple screen readers are completely incapable of describing visual imagery. So, visually impaired individuals aren't only cut off from visual content, but they're often also cut off from navigation schemes, many of which depend heavily on graphical interface elements (buttons, menus, and so on).

So, where does this leave visually impaired individuals who want to access Flash content? In Flash 8, you can attach information to certain elements in your movie that can then be interpreted by screen readers—cool, huh? That way, *you* determine how your visual creation will be described.

Sometimes, however, you need to address some pretty heavy caveats. First, for an object to be accessible to screen readers, it must have an instance name. As a result, you can make a limited number of objects accessible to a screen reader: Dynamic Text, text input fields, buttons, Movie Clips, and entire movies.

> To make Static Text accessible, you must first convert it to Dynamic Text.

Second, and perhaps most important, users must be running a Windows operating system, complete with screen reader software and at least the Flash 7 Player to access accessible content.

To make your movie accessible so that you don't exclude a portion of your potential audience:

1. Select the object you want to make accessible to the screen reader.

2. Choose Window → Other Panels → Accessibility to open the Accessibility panel (see Figure 17.13).

> If the object you've selected can't be made accessible, you won't have access to any options in the Accessibility panel.

3. If you want to make the currently selected object accessible, check the Make Object Accessible box.

4. If the object you selected is a Movie Clip, you'll also see a Make Child Objects Accessible option. If you check this box, all the various elements within the Movie Clip will also become accessible.

5. Enter a name in the Name field. The name, which will be read and vocalized by the screen reader, is a fundamental aspect of making your object accessible.

> If you make some Dynamic Text accessible, you won't have access to its name. The actual Dynamic Text will be used automatically.

6. Enter a description for the selected element in the Description field.

7. If you want to add a keystroke to individual buttons, Movie Clips, or text input fields, enter a shortcut in the Shortcut field. However, you need to follow a few guidelines:

   • Spell out the abbreviations of key names; for example, enter **Control** for the Ctrl key.

Figure 17.13

Use the Accessibility panel to make objects accessible.

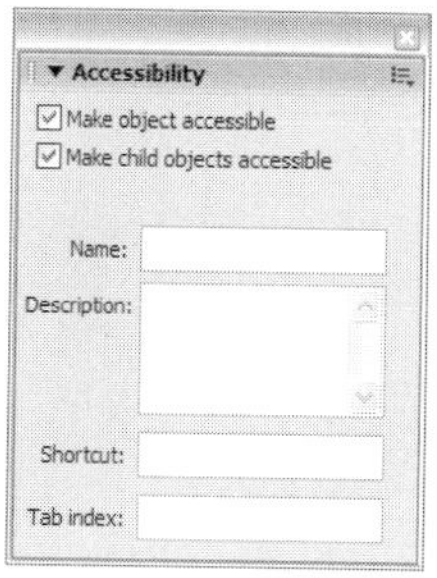

- Use capitals for letters of the alphabet.
- Use the plus (+) sign between key names; for example, use Alt+5, Ctrl+H, or Shift+9.

8. Enter a value in the Tab Index field. This determines the order in which the user's screen reader cycles through the accessible objects in your movie when the Tab key is pressed.

If you don't specify a tab order, the order that will be assumed is the order that the symbols were placed in.

9. When you've finished setting the accessibility options, simply close the Accessibility panel.

This process is helpful for making certain objects accessible to a screen reader (a process sometimes referred to as *exposing*), but what if you want to make the entire movie accessible?

1. Make sure you deselect all the elements on the Stage.

2. Choose Window → Accessibility (see Figure 17.14).

3. Check the Make Movie Accessible box.

4. If you want all the accessible objects within the movie to be exposed to screen readers, check the Make Child Objects Accessible box.

5. Enter a name for the movie in the Name field.

6. Enter a description for the movie in the Description field.

7. If you want, select the Auto Label option. By doing this, Flash will use text that's integrated into buttons or text input fields as the object's name.

8. When you're finished, close the Accessibility panel.

Creating Printable Movies

By this point, you're probably convinced that Flash content, because it's based on vectors, looks crisp and is scalable. What you might not have realized is that because Flash content is vector-based, it looks equally cool when it's printed. You can create all sorts of content that looks just as good on a screen as it does when printed.

The processes described in this section set your movie so that it's printed as vectors, maintaining its crisp, clean appearance. If you elect to skip this section, your movie can still be printed. However, it will print like any other 72dpi image—with very low quality.

You can use two methods to configure your movie so that it prints as vectors. First, you can designate specific frames in the Timeline that will print; all the frames that aren't designated as printable won't print. Second, you can designate certain areas within certain frames that will print; all the space outside the printable area won't print.

> The kicker about creating a printable movie is that you're controlling how your content is being printed only when the user is selecting the right-click context menu. Users can still print your movie using their browser's Print command—you have no control over that.

Before you learn how to configure your movie to be printable, you should be aware of a couple of important details:

- All elements must be fully loaded to be printed.
- For a Movie Clip to be printed, it must be either on the Stage or in the work area, and it must have an instance name.
- Flash Players earlier than 4.025 (Win) or 4.020 (Mac) don't support frame printing.

We'll now cover how you configure your Flash movie so that it's printable.

Designating Printable Frames

To designate specific frames as printable:

1. In the Timeline, select the specific frame you want to make printable.
2. If it isn't open already, open the Property Inspector.
3. Enter **#p** in the Frame Label field to set that frame as printable.
4. Repeats steps 1–3 on any additional frames that you want to make printable.

Specifying a Printable Area

To designate a specific area in a frame as printable:

1. Select the frame you want to designate as a printable area. The frame must not have already been designated as printable with the #p label.
2. Select the frame that contains the object you want to use to designate the frame as printable.
3. If it isn't open already, open the Property Inspector.
4. Enter **#b** in the Label field.

CHAPTER 18

Publishing Stand-Alone Movies and Applications

One of Flash's greatest strengths is its ability to deliver high-quality audio and animation in a single, compact file. This characteristic makes Flash ideally suited for the Internet and other environments in which bandwidth is a major concern. What is often forgotten, though, is that you can also distribute Flash in ways that aren't limited by download time or plug-in issues.

One of the best ways to distribute your Flash movies is to pass them to your audience on optical media (CD or DVD) as stand-alone or self-contained applications. In this format, Flash can either rely on the stand-alone Flash Player or be completely independent and run on both Windows and Macintosh platforms without additional software. Plus, with the capacity of optical media, you're able to deliver a greater amount of information without the concerns of bandwidth that you encounter on the Web.

While no single delivery method can do it all, you'll find that each has its particular advantages and allows you to distribute your movies in new ways that offer many new possibilities.

- Delivering Flash Player movies

- Delivering stand-alone Flash projectors for Windows and Macintosh

- Publishing movies for optical media delivery

- Using ActionScript FSCommands and the Stage object

- Designing and scripting interface elements for a Flash-based CD/DVD

Introducing Stand-Alone Flash Files

Although Flash most commonly appears on the Internet in the context of a website, don't forget that other options can help you reach your audience. Flash can produce two types of stand-alone movies that enable you to share your work without requiring that your audience go to the Web. The first is a standard SWF file. If your audience has the stand-alone Flash Player application, they will be able to see your movie without the aid of a web browser. The other type of stand-alone movie is a self-contained *Flash projector*. This is a self-running application that allows your movie to run on any computer, whether or not the Flash Player is installed.

One of the best advantages of both stand-alone options is that you can publish your movies so that they will run on all platforms. Regardless of the operating system that you use to run Flash, you'll be able to create final files that match the playback capabilities of your audience. This characteristic makes Flash one of the most portable multimedia applications currently available.

> Of the two formats, SWF and stand-alone Projector, the Projector format is usually your best option. It is the most flexible and allows you (the author) to have more control over playback and appearance. SWFs usually need a web browser to have full-functionality and aren't completely dependable as stand-alone files.

Distributing Movies with the Flash Player

SAFlashPlayer

The Flash Player application comes with Flash. It can play any SWF file without the assistance of a web browser (see Figure 18.1). The Flash Player offers several menu options with which you control the playback and appearance of a movie. You can find the application in the Players folder, inside the folder where Flash resides on your computer's hard drive. For Windows folks, the stand-alone player is named SAFlashPlayer.exe; for Macintosh users, it's called SAFlashPlayer.

Because the Flash Player will play any SWF file, it's easy to distribute your movies in a compact manner, over a variety of platforms, and with minimal fuss. The average computer user won't have this application, however. Thus, it isn't the best delivery option if you're trying to target a large number of people—unless you're sure they all have the Flash Player application installed (meaning they already own the Flash authoring application). To make your movie deliverable to the widest possible audience, use a self-contained Flash projector.

Delivering Movies as Self-Contained Flash Projectors

Self-contained Flash projectors are quite possibly the best way to distribute your movies outside the Web. A self-contained projector is an executable file—an autonomous application that will run your movie just as you created it on either a Windows or Macintosh platform. Anyone using Windows or a Mac (which is just about everybody) will be able to see your Flash masterpiece without the help of any additional software or web browser plug-in. Brilliant! Plus, by putting a self-contained projector on an optical media disc, you're able to distribute it to fans, clients, customers, students, and so on, in a format that is easily accessible on any computer with a optical drive. Figure 18.2 shows a Flash projector in context.

RORY STARKS COPYRIGHT 2004

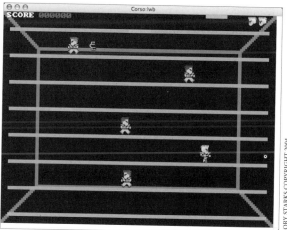

Figure 18.1

A movie can run on a local computer with the Flash Player application.

NORBERT HERBER AND YACOV SHARIR ©2005.

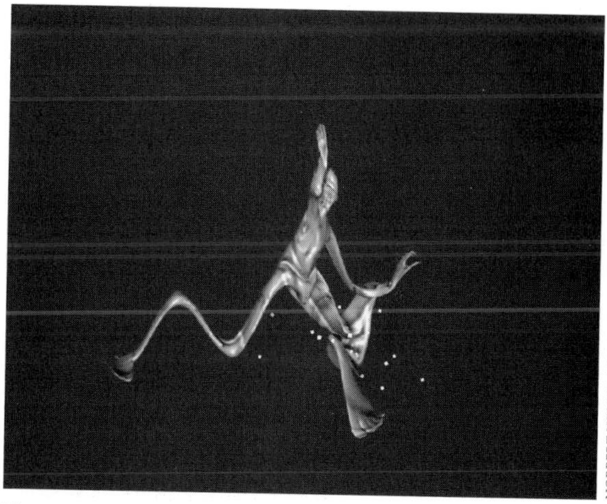

Figure 18.2

A self-contained projector can run in its own window or as a full screen (as shown here).

Creating Flash Projectors

Creating—or, more appropriately, *publishing*—a Flash projector is simple. And because Flash allows you to create both Windows and Macintosh projectors, you can take care of creating both files in a single step. One minor disadvantage is that the self-contained projector will be a few hundred kilobytes larger than the SWF version of the same movie. This is because the projector file must contain information necessary for playing your movie using the resources of the operating system on which the projector is running.

To publish a self-contained Flash projector:

1. When you've finished creating the movie, choose File → Save to save it with any final changes in place.
2. Choose File → Publish Settings. The Publish Settings dialog box opens (see Figure 18.3).
3. Check the box next to Windows Projector or Macintosh Projector depending on what kind of projector you need to create. Check both boxes if you want to create both varieties. You can give each version a name in the adjacent File field. Be sure to leave the `.exe` suffix on the name of your Windows projector.

Figure 18.3

The Publish Settings dialog box contains the options for creating self-contained projectors.

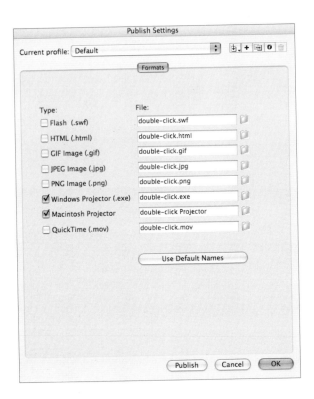

4. As an optional step, take advantage of two publishing-related features that will help improve your work flow:

- Click the Select Publish Destination button to save each published projector to a unique location. In this case, you could put one in a folder named Windows and the other in a folder named Mac.

- Use the Current Profile menu to create a "projectors only" profile. To learn how to create publishing profiles, see Chapter 18.

5. If you haven't done it already, set the Flash Player version you would like to use. Click the Flash tab and choose a player version from the version menu. This is another advantage of the stand-alone format. Whereas web-distributed Flash movies depend on the version your users have installed in their browser, a stand-alone file will be published and play in whatever version you specify.

6. To finally publish the projector, do one of the following:

- Click the Publish button. This will publish your projector immediately. This option is helpful if you need to publish several kinds of movies in one sitting.

- Click OK to accept the selections you've just made in the Publish Settings dialog box. Then select File → Publish (Shift+F12) to publish your projector(s).

The Publishing window opens, showing the progress of publishing your movie. When it's finished, your projector file(s) should be sitting in the same folder as the Flash file you're currently using.

7. Quit Flash (File → Quit/Exit). After being published, Flash stand-alone projectors are given a circular icon showing the Flash MX *f*. Double-click the projector's circular icon to launch the self-contained projector application. The file is now ready to be burned to an optical disc.

projectorDemo

> Windows users who publish projectors for Macintosh will notice slightly different results. The Macintosh file is published as a "stuffed" (compressed) file with the extension .hqx. To prepare this file for its end users you will need to decompress it. Copy the file onto a Macintosh computer and double-click to open it. The file will be un-stuffed and you will have access to the stand-alone Macintosh projector file.

Using Flash to Create CD/DVD Interfaces

Although publishing your self-contained projector is the final step of the process, you can perform many additional tasks with your movie to make it look and act more like a self-sufficient application. With the help of a few ActionScript commands, you can take your Flash movie and turn it into an independent multimedia production that is controlled in precisely the ways you define. Not only does this give your piece a more professional look and feel, but it allows you to set the stage for the ways in which your users choose to view your work.

Using FSCommands and the Stage Object

FSCommands are elements of ActionScript that allow Flash and the Flash Player to communicate with the application that is hosting your movie. In the context of this chapter, that application is the Windows or Mac operating system. By issuing FSCommands in your movie, you can set many parameters for the movie's presentation and the options available to the audience viewing it. The syntax for `fscommand()` is as follows:

```
fscommand("command","argument");
```

The following are the available commands for `fscommand()`:

`fullscreen` This command takes one of two arguments, `true` or `false`. When set to `true`, the projector fills the entire monitor window and displays no menu bar at the top of the screen. When set to `false`, the projector appears in a window whose size is set by the dimensions specified in the Movie Properties dialog box.

`allowscale` This command, when set to `true`, allows the movie to stretch to fit the size of the window (or monitor) playing it. When set to `false`, the window that contains the movie can be stretched as needed, but the movie itself isn't scaled.

`showmenu` When set to `true`, this command enables the options in the context menu (Ctrl+click / right-click) for a projector file. These options allow your users to play, stop, rewind, zoom, and change the display quality of the projector file. When set to `false`, all options are disabled or removed, with the exception of the Settings option and the About Macromedia Flash Player option.

`trapallkeys` This command, when set to `true`, disables the keyboard. When set to `false` (the default), the movie can accept input from the keyboard. Watch out—by setting `trapallkeys` to `true`, you're effectively cutting off the keyboard. If you do this to prevent nonscripted interaction with your movie, be sure to include a button or other element with the `fscommand("quit")` statement for shutting down the projector.

`quit` This command takes no arguments. When it's issued, your computer will close the projector file.

You enter all FSCommands (`quit`, `exec`, and so on) and their arguments as strings. For example:

```
fscommand ("fullscreen", "true");
```

This statement sets a projector to play in full-screen mode. The command `fullscreen` and its argument `true` are listed in quotation marks, making each a text string. If you don't enter the arguments as strings, Flash won't be able to communicate properly with the operating system and perform the actions you specify.

The best place for FSCommands is in a frame on the main Timeline. Put them in the first frame of the movie so that they're executed before any other scripts are called. If you place your FSCommands in your movie's first frame, they will require no handler and will be one of the first movie parameters loaded into memory.

The Stage object offers an alternative approach for achieving some of the same effects and functionality as `fscommand()`. Technically speaking, the Stage object is the preferred method for scaling the Stage and controlling the context menu when developing movies for Flash Player 6–8. However, the reality is that the Stage object and its related properties aren't able to do everything that `fscommand()` can accomplish. You don't have any Stage object counterparts to run a movie in full-screen mode, limit keyboard input, or exit/quit a projector.

To compare and contrast both techniques, see the file `projectorDemo.fla` on the CD. Read the code and comments in frame 1 of the main Timeline to learn how these terms are so closely related. Pragmatically speaking, when compared to the Stage object `fscommand()` is sufficient to manage the playback parameters of your movie and communicate with the host operating system.

Though it is out of the scope of this book it's worth mentioning a new Flash 8 feature related to this discussion of `fscommand()`. The ExternalInterface class is a part of Action-Script 2.0 that enables communications between your movie and its host application. To learn more about this class and related ActionScript 2.0 terms, choose Help → Flash Help (F1) and navigate to ActionScript 2.0/Learning ActionScript in 2.0 in Flash/Working with External Data/About the External API/ Creating interaction with the External API.

Using Letterbox Projectors and Interface Elements

Using FSCommands is the first step toward creating a truly unique interface for your Flash projector. This section introduces you to a few design-related techniques that you can employ to create a stylish and functional movie for cross-platform distribution.

The first technique involves creating a letterbox-style projector. *Letterbox* describes the appearance of a full-screen video image. When you go to a movie theater, you see films on a screen that is quite different from the monitor on your television or computer. Rather than the standard 4:3 aspect ratio, movie screens have a 16:9 aspect ratio. These screens are much wider than they are tall and accommodate a broader field of view. Consequently, when studio films are re-released on video and DVD for consumers' televisions and VCRs/DVD players, they're often modified to fit the 4:3 aspect ratio.

In some cases, though, this isn't done. To preserve the 16:9 cinematic aspect ratio, videos and DVDs can be released in letterbox (or *widescreen*) format. Roughly the top one-third and the bottom one-third of the screen are left black, and the image fills the entire width of the display. Ultimately, this format makes the image smaller than if it were in the 4:3 ratio but preserves the original proportions of the film. Although letterbox is used as a technical convention, it has a stylish look and can lend an interesting visual quality to Flash projector files.

Creating the letterbox effect is simple and involves only a few small modifications to your movie:

1. Select Modify → Document. The Document Properties dialog box opens. Set your movie dimensions so that they conform to the 16:9 aspect ratio (such as 320×180 or 640×360).

> Changing the movie dimensions of a finished animation often creates problems with the alignment and position of movie elements. It's best to adjust the dimensions *before* you create the Flash movie.

2. Set the background color of the movie to black, even if you want your movie to have a different background color. When you create a self-contained projector, the background color of the movie determines the color of the monitor when you play the movie in full-screen mode. Click OK to close the Document Properties dialog box.

3. Create a new layer in your movie and name it **letterbox**. Drag this layer so that it's at the bottom of all other layers in the Timeline. Select Insert → New Symbol, and create a new Graphic symbol. Make it a rectangle that's exactly the same size as your Stage.

Make the rectangle whatever color you want for your movie background. Drag the rectangle onto the `letterbox` layer, positioning it in the center of the Stage. Lock the layer once it's in position.

4. Create another new layer, and name it **code**. Insert a new keyframe in frame 1 of this layer, highlight it, and press F9 to display the Actions panel. Enter the following statements:

```
fscommand ("allowscale", "false");
fscommand ("fullscreen", "true");
```

The first statement in this script prohibits the movie from being scaled and preserves the dimensions set in the movie's properties. To scale the movie so that it fills the width of the screen, you can set `"allowscale"` to true. This allows the letterbox effect to be more pronounced; however, you'll get a larger matte when this is set to `false`. You can see an example of each in Figure 18.4. Depending on the nature of your project, one look may be more appropriate than the other.

The second statement in the script sets your projector so that it plays back full-screen— meaning that it fills the entire monitor, covering the computer's desktop and any applications that are running. The `"fullscreen"` statement is crucial to the success of the letterbox technique, because it uses the background color of your movie (black) to create the matte that surrounds the 16:9 area of your Stage.

5. Publish your movie as a self-contained projector, and see the letterbox effect in context.

By setting the movie dimensions to a 16:9 ratio, you established the initial effect. The black background color created the black mask. Then, by using a symbol as a colored backdrop for the movie, you created the impression that the Stage's color is something other than black. The size of the backdrop matches your Stage size, and the letterbox effect is complete.

Figure 18.4
Two letterbox projectors playing in full-screen mode. On the left, `"allowscale"` **is** `false`, **allowing for a larger matte around the Stage. On the right,** `"allowscale"` **is** `true`, **creating a more dramatic letterbox effect.**

This technique treats the rectangular symbol like background scenery in a theater production. In the same way that a stage crew might change props during a play, you can change the color or other attributes of the background symbol in your movie.

You can also create custom menus for your movie. Using the button techniques outlined in Chapter 8, you can create a series of buttons (a menu bar) to serve as navigational controls for your projector. Then, with some basic ActionScript, you can attach commands to the buttons that will start, stop, rewind, skip, and perform all the necessary behaviors you require for navigation and other kinds of interactivity. To learn more about Action-Script commands that allow your users to interactively navigate through your movie, see Chapter 14 or the ActionScript Reference on this book's CD.

Something interesting that you can do with a menu bar is allow your users to toggle it off and on—it's there when they want it and gone when they don't. This is especially useful for full-screen projectors, where you don't want a permanent menu or other navigational element cluttering your screen and distracting from your movie. You have many ways to toggle something off and on; consider the following example:

```
_root.menu._visible=false;
keyWatcher = new Object();
keyWatcher.onKeyDown=function(){
    if(Key.getCode()==Key.SPACE){
        _root.menu._visible=true;
    }
}
keyWatcher.onKeyUp=function(){
    if(Key.getCode()==Key.SPACE){
        _root.menu._visible=false;
    }
}
Key.addListener(keyWatcher);
```

This script creates a simple toggle behavior for a Movie Clip instance called menu. Any time a key is pressed, events are broadcast to the Listener object keyWatcher. When the events are either keyDown or keyUp, the script tests to see whether the key creating the event happens to be the spacebar. If it is, then menu is shown while the spacebar is down and hidden when it's up. Of course, while menu is visible, all the navigation buttons it contains are available. This allows your users to toggle the menu "on" with the spacebar and then click the buttons within the Movie Clip that make your movie do whatever it is that the users need to do: rewind, skip to another section, exit/quit, and so on. To work properly, menu must be invisible when the movie is first played. The first line of the script handles this.

To see both the letterbox projector technique and a spacebar menu toggle in a self-contained projector, see the file `projectorDemo.exe` (Windows) or `projectorDemo` (Macintosh) on the CD. To examine the source file and to witness these scripts in context, see `projectorDemo.fla` on the CD.

Writing to Optical Media

Burning a CD or DVD is faster and cheaper than ever. A task that might have once seemed expensive and somewhat mysterious is actually very doable, provided that you have the necessary resources. The following list provides a variety of tools and advice for all your optical media burning needs:

`www.roxio.com` Roxio is the manufacturer of Toast 7 Titanium, the premiere tool for burning DVDs and cross-platform (hybrid) CDs in a Macintosh environment.

`www.apple.com/powermac` If you have a new Apple computer, your machine is probably equipped with a SuperDrive. A SuperDrive is an all-in-one CD/DVD authoring device available in many Apple computers. This resource on the Apple website offers technical specifics about the 16× SuperDrive that ships with many Apple computers.

`ww2.nero.com` Nero 7 is the Windows-compatible CD-burning and DVD-burning tool for creating hybrid CDs in a Windows environment.

`www.microsoft.com/windowsxp/using/windowsmediaplayer/default.mspx` This resource on the Microsoft website fields a variety of issues concerning CD burning in a Windows XP environment. See this and related pages to learn more about CD-burning basics, troubleshooting tips, and a list of Windows XP-compatible devices.

CHAPTER 19

Creating Flash Content for Windows Mobile

As computers continue to become smaller, mobile, and more web enabled, Flash is right there in the forefront of the handheld device revolution. The Flash Player has begun delivering content to a wide variety of consumer gadgets and mobile devices. This content includes business applications, news services, games, educational applications, maps and geographical aids, event guides, entertainment, wireless applications, and so much more—the works!

In this chapter, you'll learn the basic techniques for creating Flash content for devices that run the Windows Mobile operating system.

- Introducing Flash and Windows Mobile

- Dealing with performance issues

- Creating your Windows Mobile Flash movie

- Using the Windows Mobile input methods

- Testing and previewing your Windows Mobile Flash movie

- Publishing your Windows Mobile movie

Introducing Flash and Windows Mobile

Flash isn't just for desktop computers anymore. Flash is pushing its way into broadcast media, WebTV, mobile phones (with the Flash Lite Player), game consoles, and, most important (at least in terms of this chapter), Windows Mobile handheld devices.

More than just simple organizers, Windows Mobile devices are increasingly powerful, easy-to-use, mobile platforms that can display all sorts of rich media content, including Flash movies. The great part is that handheld devices that run the Windows Mobile operating system (manufacturers include Dell, Toshiba, HP, and ViewSonic) all ship with the Flash Player. As a result, you can confidently develop Flash content and not worry about whether your intended audience can play it.

> The term *Windows Mobile* is a relatively new one. Previously, the operating system was referred to as *Pocket PC*. For more information about the Pocket PC operating system and Pocket PC handheld devices, refer to www.microsoft.com/windowsmobile/products/pocketpc.

Understanding the Base Specifications of Windows Media Devices

Although different devices have different specifications, the vast majority of handheld devices running the Windows Mobile operating system (at press time, the current edition is Windows Mobile 5.0) at the least share the following characteristics:

- Intel StrongARM processor
- 32–64MB of random access memory (RAM)
- 240×320, 64,000-color screen
- Built-in expansion slot(s) for CompactFlash, Secure Digital (SD), and Multimedia Card (MMC)

The powerful features in the Windows Mobile operating system, as well as the inherent mobility of devices, make them excellent platforms for creative, nontraditional Flash applications, such as conference guides, mobile accounting programs for traveling salespeople, or mobile patient record apps for doctors.

However, the marriage of Flash and Windows Mobile devices isn't all sunshine and roses. First, as you'll see shortly (in the next section "Handling Performance Issues"), Windows Mobile devices have nowhere near the level of power or memory you're accustomed to in your desktop computer. As a result, you need to consider special performance issues when you're creating a Flash movie destined for Windows Mobile devices. Second, by default, when you create Flash content for Windows Mobile devices, you display the content by placing the SWF file in an HTML page and using Pocket Internet Explorer (PIE) to view the page. The kicker is that using PIE has some frustrating limitations. As you'll learn in the section "Publishing Your Windows Mobile Flash Movie" later in this chapter, you can work around these limitations—but those workarounds often carry additional problems of their own.

Handling Performance Issues

Unfortunately, despite their ever-increasing sophistication, Windows Mobile devices still don't measure up to desktop or laptop computers in terms of speed and power. As a result, when you're creating Flash content specifically destined for a Windows Mobile device, you should be aware of certain issues so that your grand mobile Flash creation can perform at its best.

Setting the Device Speed and Frame Rate

The higher the frame rate, the higher the ultimate quality of your Flash movie. However, with increased frame rate comes increased file size (and an increased demand on the computer's processor). The problem compounds when developing Flash content for a Windows Mobile device. Realistically speaking, because of the hardware limitations of the Windows Mobile platform, you'll get an adequate level of playback only with a frame rate from 12fps to 15fps.

Although devices running the Windows Mobile operating system are nowhere near as powerful as desktop systems, new devices with faster processors that can handle higher frame rates are constantly being released. As a result, you need to remain aware of the optimum frame rate on the device for which you're developing your Flash content.

Optimizing ActionScript

ActionScript isn't often thought of as an element that might cause performance issues in your Flash movie. Well, it can. ActionScript, like any other kind of data, needs to be dealt with by the processor in the user's computer. The more ActionScript that exists, the more information the user's computer has to process. Now, when someone is viewing a Flash movie on a desktop or laptop, the ActionScript is the least of your concerns—in terms of the movie slowing down. However, when you're developing Flash content for Windows Mobile, given that mobile devices have far slower processors than desktops or laptops, you have to make sure your movie is as lean as possible. The more bloated your movie's ActionScript, the more likely your movie will suffer a slowdown.

To avoid this, here are some suggestions to optimize your ActionScript:

- Avoid any unnecessary characters.
- Keep your movie's variable, method, instance, and function names as short and as compact as possible.
- Use functions for menu and button events.
- Use functions for repetitive events in your movie.

Using Audio

Audio in a Flash movie consumes a great deal of your Windows Mobile device's system resources. As a result, you really need to think about whether your movie actually needs sound. Also, you need to realize that given the nature of the device, most people don't actually expect sound to be part of their experience. As a result, if you're conscious of the limitations imposed by slow processors and low memory (relatively speaking), you probably won't encounter the kind of high demand for audio in a Flash movie for a Windows Mobile device than you would in a Flash movie destined for viewing on a desktop or laptop.

However, if you do decide to include audio in your Windows Mobile Flash movie, you should follow these guidelines:

- Always include a built-in method for turning the audio off. This is especially important if your movie is full-screen.

> When a Flash movie is full-screen on a Windows Mobile device, the user doesn't have access to volume controls in the user interface.

- Make sure that when you publish the movie, the audio is at the lowest-possible quality (while still maintaining its intended sound).

Creating Content for Your Windows Mobile Flash Movie

When you create a Flash movie for distribution to a Windows Mobile device, you aren't using a different authoring environment than you'd use if you were creating Flash content for distribution to the Web. All the techniques covered in this book are applicable. The only difference is that you should be aware of some added issues and specialized techniques if you want your Windows Mobile Flash movie to be the best it can be.

In the following sections, you'll explore the full range of specialized issues and topics involved in creating a Flash movie destined for a Windows Mobile device.

Setting Screen Size

One of the most obvious design issues when you're creating Flash content for a Windows Mobile device is the screen size. Although not all Windows Mobile devices have the same screen size, the overwhelming majority of them have a screen size of 240×320. If you're creating a Flash movie that will play full-screen, you can use all this space. However, if you're using PIE (with the help of the Flash Player) to display your content, you'll have some additional size constraints.

Specifically, the Windows Mobile 5.0 user interface has two areas in which you absolutely can't place any content (see Figure 19.1).

Figure 19.1

When you're creating a Flash movie that will be viewed in PIE, no content can appear in either the caption bar or the menu bar.

Caption Bar ———

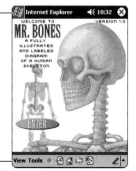

MenuBar ———

Each bar removes 26 pixels from the vertical resolution of your screen. Therefore, at the very least, if you design content for PIE that fits on one page, the page cannot exceed 240×268. In addition to these two areas, there are some additional nagging features that potentially take away from the amount of screen real-estate you have to work with:

- First, the user can also choose to turn off the address bar, as shown in Figure 19.1— a decision that might ultimately provides you with an extra 23 pixels of space in your design. However, because turning off the address bar is optional, you can't initially design your page to use that space.

- Second, PIE has a scroll bug that allows you to use only 263 pixels of the available height, not the real 268 pixels—bummer.

- Thirdly, after a page exceeds 263 vertical pixels, a vertical scroll bar appears. A vertical scroll bar, which takes up 11 pixels, means that your screen width gets reduced even further to 229 pixels. Likewise, if your movie requires a horizontal scroll bar, you'll lose an additional 11 pixels from the screen's height. So, if you want to maximize the amount of space you have for your Flash creation, you'll want to do your best to make the movie compact enough that it doesn't actually require a vertical or horizontal scroll bar.

The result of all of these screen real-estate issues is that you should probably design your Flash movie so that it fits into a space no larger than 229 pixels of vertical space and 229 pixels of horizontal space.

If you're planning to let your user enter information in your movie, you need to shave an additional 80 pixels off the height of your screen to accommodate the interface's Soft Input Panel (SIP)—(the area that pops up at the bottom of the Windows Mobile interface that has the keyboard and block recognizer).

Manually Setting Screen Size

To manually set the size of your movie to work within the constraints of Windows Mobile devices:

1. Choose File → New.

2. When the New Document dialog box opens, select the Flash Document option in the Type list box, and then click OK.

3. Choose Modify → Document.

4. When the Document Properties dialog box opens, enter **240** in the Width field and **260** in the Height field.

If you're creating a Flash movie that will play back in full-screen, enter **240** in the Width field and **320** in the Height field. Likewise, if you're creating a Flash movie for a Windows Mobile device that has a different screen size, enter the correct width and height.

Figure 19.2

The PDAs category in the Templates section of the New from Template dialog box lets you access several device templates.

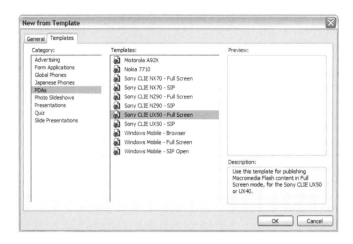

Using a Windows Mobile/PDA Template to Set Screen Size

One of the great features in Flash 8 is that you can use a series of starter templates with sizes geared toward Windows Mobile devices. So, if you're developing for a specific device and aren't entirely sure of the screen size, you can use one of the handy-dandy templates to set the size of your Stage.

To set the screen size of your movie with a Windows Mobile device starter template:

1. Choose File → New.

2. When the New Document dialog box appears, click the Template tab.

3. When the New from Template dialog box opens, click the Templates tab.

4. Choose PDAs from the Category list to display the available device templates (see Figure 19.2).

5. Select one of the templates from the Templates list. Notice that a preview of the document size appears in the Preview box.

> You have access not only to Windows Mobile templates but also to a series of other personal digital assistants (PDAs) that also support the Flash Player.

6. When you're finished, click OK.

Working with Type

When you're working with text in a Flash movie destined for display on a Windows Mobile device, you should be aware of some important issues. Because the screen size on Windows Mobile devices is so much smaller than on a regular desktop or laptop, your type will be relatively small. And in Flash, by default, all text is antialiased. Here's the problem: the vast majority of fonts aren't designed to be antialiased at a small size. They appear blurry and are difficult to read, such as the example shown here:

This is what happens to small text in Flash. This particular
text is Ariel, 10 point.

So, what happens when you need the text in your Windows Mobile Flash movie to be crisp and legible? As you'll see in the following two sections, you can either use pixel fonts or optimize the text using one of two font-rendering methods.

Using Pixel Fonts

Because they automatically display without any antialiasing, pixel fonts are specifically designed to be viewed at small point sizes and therefore are a great choice to use when you're creating a Flash movie for Windows Mobile devices. Here's an example:

This is a regular anti-aliased font at   ———— Regular Font
a small size (10 points)

This is an example of a   ———— Pixel Font
Pixel Font at 8 points.

Pixel fonts use the smallest unit of screen measure: the pixel. Because these fonts use pixels to create each character, they remain crisp and are easily read regardless of screen size and resolution. However, you should be aware of a few issues when using pixel fonts:

- Pixel fonts need to be used in increments of 8 points (8, 16, 24, and so on).
- Pixels fonts must be placed on whole X and Y coordinates (50, instead of 50.5). You can make sure they're sitting on whole X and Y coordinates by using the Info panel or the Property Inspector.
- If you're using Input Text or Dynamic Text, make sure you embed the fonts. Otherwise, your Flash movie will use the default Windows Media system fonts.

Pixel fonts aren't normally included in the collection of fonts that ship with a new computer. You need to purchase them separately. Here are some pixel font creators/vendors: www .miniml.com, www.fontsforflash.com, and www.atomicmedia.com.

Choosing a Font-Rendering Method

One of the best new features in Flash 8, especially when it comes to creating content for Windows Mobile devices, is the ability to increase the readability of small text in Flash by selecting an appropriate font-rendering method. The following two font-rendering methods are appropriate when you're developing content for Windows Mobile devices:

- The Bitmap Text (No Anti-Alias) option turns off antialiasing—thereby providing no text smoothing. The resulting SWF's file size increases because the font outlines are embedded in the file. While bitmap text looks sharp at the exported size, it tends to look bad when it's scaled.

- The Anti-Alias for Readability option, which takes advantage of Flash 8's new text-rendering engine, greatly improves the legibility of fonts—especially at small sizes. Because font outlines are embedded when you use the Anti-Alias for Readability option, the size of your SWF file increases.

The great part about using these two font-rendering methods is that, unlike when you're using pixel fonts, you don't have to place the text on whole X and Y coordinates. Also, you don't have to buy a specific font; the two font-rendering methods work with all the fonts installed on your machine. On the other hand, pixel fonts are custom-designed fonts that have their own artistic flair. As a result, you can pick the one that's best suited for your project.

Be aware of the following when using the two font-rendering methods covered in this section:

- If you're using a small font size (smaller than 8 points), the Bitmap Text (No Anti-Alias) option probably won't improve the readability of your text.

- In the case of some fonts, using bold or italics will actually reduce the readability of the text when you use either the Bitmap Text (No Anti-Alias) option or the Anti-Alias for Readability option.

- Sans-serif fonts (such as Arial or Helvetica) tend to look clearer with the Bitmap Text (No Anti-Alias) method than serif fonts (such as Times or Times New Roman) do.

To use either of these font-rendering methods to increase the readability of the fonts in your Windows Mobile Flash movie:

1. Select the block of small text you want to alias.

2. If it isn't open already, open the Property Inspector.

3. Select the appropriate option from the Font Rendering drop-down menu.

Opening External Files from within your Windows Mobile Flash Movie

When you create your Windows Mobile Flash movie, you might find you want to call external assets (such as an additional SWF or JPEG file) to display within the movie. You might also want to load an external file (such as a Microsoft Word or PDF document) that can't natively display within a Flash movie. In this case, you'd need to rely on the specific program (such as Acrobat Reader or Pocket Microsoft Word) installed on the user's Windows Mobile device that is associated with the external file you want to open.

Granted, in Flash 8, you have a host of options for integrating media (such as digital video and audio) into your Flash movie. However, no matter how well you can compress and optimize any embedded media when you bring it into Flash, you'll always increase the overall size of your movie—sometimes drastically so. And as you saw earlier in this chapter, given the slower processor and reduced memory of Windows Mobile devices, performance is a huge issue. As a result, you might decide to call an external media file instead of actually embedding it in your Flash movie. By doing this, you can reduce the overall size of your Flash movie. In addition, you can actually create a certain amount of modularity to your Flash movie by creating content that can be updated.

> If you're calling an external file to play or display within the Flash movie or be the Windows Mobile device's default application for that file, you have to make sure that when you publish, package, and distribute the movie, you include the file. Otherwise, the movie won't have anything to play or display when it runs on a user's device.

In either case, with the help of a little simple ActionScript, you can call external files from within your Flash movie. In the following sections, you'll explore how to call several types of external files from your Flash movie.

Opening Windows Media Player Files

Because the Windows Mobile operating system is a Microsoft product, it's no great surprise that its default media application is a stripped-down version of Windows Media Player. Given this, you know that everyone who is viewing your movie has a copy of the program and can therefore play Windows Media Video (WMV) files.

To play an external WMV file, you need to use the `getURL()` global function. Here's an example in which a WMV file (called `myvideofile.wmv`) will open in the Windows Media Player when a button is clicked:

```
on (press) {
getURL("myvideofile.wmv");
}
```

Notice that a relative path was used to target the video clip. If you want, you can easily use an absolute path instead.

> You can use Windows Media Player to play other media files such as Intel Indio video files, AIFF audio files, WAV audio files, MPEG files, MIDI files, AU audio files, and MP3 files.

Opening MP3 Files

The MP3 file format is a popular one for audio because it offers high quality within a relatively small file size. Although (as in the case of video) you can easily embed audio in your Windows Mobile Flash movie, sometimes you might want to call an external MP3 instead.

To do so, you'll use the getURL() global function. Here's an example in which an MP3 file (called music.mp3) will open in the user's default player when a button is clicked:

```
on (press) {
getURL("music.mp3");
}
```

In most cases, Windows Media Player is the default application that will open external MP3 files.

Opening HTML Files

Any external HTML file that you load (whether it's physically on the Windows Mobile device or on the Internet and being accessed through a wireless connection) will open in PIE.

As with many other external files, you can play external HTML files using the getURL() global function. Here's an example of an external HTML file (called pictures.html), which resides in the same directory as the actual Flash movie that is calling it, being opened when the user clicks a button:

```
on (press) {
getURL("pictures.html");
}
```

And here's an example of the ActionScript necessary to open a specific website:

```
on (press) {
getURL("http://www.captainprimate.com");
}
```

Remember, if your user isn't connected to the Internet (through either a physical connection or a wireless connection), the website won't open.

Opening JPEG and SWF Files

As you've probably figured out, you can use the getUrl() global function in many cases to load external files into a default player (usually PIE or Windows Media Player). However, you can load several kinds of files directly into your Flash movie without having to resort to an external application. That's where loadMovie() and loadMovieNum() (which are both global functions of the Movie Clip object) enter the picture. By using the `loadMovie()` and `loadMovieNum()` global functions, you can dynamically load JPEG images or external SWF files into a target Movie Clip (using `loadMovie()`) or a level within the main Timeline (using `loadMovieNum()`).

Here's an example of the ActionScript required to load an external JPEG file (or SWF file) when a user clicks a button:

```
on (press) {
loadMovie("someimage.jpeg", "somemovieclipinstance");
}
```

If the file is in the same directory as the Flash movie, you really have to enter only the image name. However, if it isn't located in the same directory, you'll have to enter the path (either as an absolute URL or as a relative URL) so that the Flash movie can locate it.

If you use `loadMovieNum()`, your script should look like this:

```
on (press) {
loadMovieNum("somemovie.swf", 2);
}
```

If the Movie Clip you're loading the JPEG or SWF file into isn't a direct child of the current Timeline, you'll need to enter the proper target path using dot syntax.

Although using `loadMovie()` or `loadMovieNum()` to dynamically load a JPEG or SWF file is pretty easy, you need to realize two facts. First, when it comes to using `loadMovie()`, the loaded file will replace all the contents of the target Movie Clip. Second, only one file can occupy a given level in the Flash movie. As a result, if you load a second file into `_level1`, the first one you loaded will be automatically replaced.

Older devices running the Pocket PC operating system run Flash Player 5. As a result, they can't dynamically load JPEGs and SWFs.

Using the Flash Windows Mobile Components for Interface Development

Under normal circumstances, because of the memory and processor speed limitations of Windows devices, interface components (such as radio buttons and check boxes) that would have no real effect on a normal Flash movie tend to have a harmful perform- ance effect when used in a Windows Mobile Flash movie. As a result, Macromedia has developed a series of user interface components specifically designed to run well in a Windows Mobile Flash movie:

- The CheckBox component adds a check box to your Flash movie.

- The RadioButton component adds a radio button to your Flash movie.

- The ListBox component adds a list box to your Flash movie.

- The DropDown component adds a drop-down menu to your Flash movie.

- The ScrollBar component adds a scroll bar to your Flash movie.

The great feature of all these components is that, except when it comes to the decreased level of stress they place on the device's system resources, they're identical to their counterparts found in the Flash user interface components.

The Windows Mobile user interface components don't ship with Flash 8. However, they're freely downloadable at www.macromedia.com/devnet/devices/pocket_pc.html.

To make the Windows Mobile components available for use in Flash, you have to manually place them in the First Run/Components subdirectory of the directory in which you installed Flash 8.

Testing Your Windows Mobile Flash Movie

As with a regular Flash movie, you need to test your Windows Mobile Flash movie to ensure that it doesn't have any problems and to ensure it functions exactly as it's supposed to before you publish it.

Unfortunately, Flash 8 doesn't ship with any Windows Mobile emulator that you can use to test your movie to see how it'll perform on its intended Windows Mobile device.

> An *emulator* is a piece of software that runs on a desktop and allows you to test applications in a virtual environment that reproduces the specific platform (in this case, Windows Mobile) for which you're developing.

Unfortunately, despite the increasing popularity of Windows Mobile devices, the only real emulator available comes packaged with Microsoft's Windows Mobile Software Development Kit (SDK), which can be downloaded at www.microsoft.com/windowsmobile/developers/default.mspx. However, because the emulator is designed to test full-fledged Windows Mobile applications developed in a programmed language such as eMbedded Visual C++, it's overkill (as well as amazingly complicated to use) for those wanting to test their humble Windows Mobile Flash movies.

Given these issues, you have only a couple of options for testing your movie on its target device:

- If you don't have one of the devices for which you're targeting your movie, buy one. However, this is a pretty unreasonable solution, especially if you want to test your movie on multiple devices.

- Post a request on a discussion group (such as the Macromedia Flash Handhelds Online Forum) asking for developers to test your movie on their devices. For the most part, other developers will be happy to test your movie and provide feedback about its content and performance.

Publishing Your Windows Mobile Flash Movie

After you've spent hours and hours developing your elegant Windows Mobile Flash movie, it's time to publish it. The way you publish your movie is not much different from publishing a regular Flash movie. In the following sections, you'll explore how to publish a Windows Mobile Flash movie that is intended to be viewed in PIE using the Flash Player. From there, you'll learn how to create a stand-alone, full-screen movie using a groovy third-party program called FlashPack.

Publishing a Windows Mobile Flash Movie for PIE

Remember, all Windows Mobile devices come with a version of the Flash Player. The kicker is that the standard Flash Player on all Windows Mobile devices can't display a

Flash movie in the same way that the Flash Player on a desktop or laptop can. Instead, it must use PIE to display the Flash movie. As a result, when you're publishing a movie destined for Windows Mobile devices, you also need to publish an HTML file.

To publish a Windows Mobile Flash movie for PIE:

1. With the movie open that you want to publish, choose File → Publish Settings.

2. When the Publish Settings dialog box opens, make sure the Flash and HTML file types are selected on the Formats tab.

3. From there, set all the publish properties of your SWF file.

> As of the time of this writing, Macromedia has yet to announce Flash Player 7 for Windows Mobile devices. As a result, you need to make sure you select Flash Player 6 (or below) for the correct version of your movie.

4. Set all the publish properties of the associated HTML file. Be sure to select Flash for Pocket PC 2003 from the Templates drop-down menu.

5. When you're finished, click Publish.

Creating a Stand-Alone Flash Projector with FlashPack

Easily one of the biggest drawbacks of creating a Windows Mobile Flash movie is that you can't create a stand-alone projector. This is a huge bummer, because a stand-alone projector would allow you to partially sidestep the screen size restrictions that come with displaying your Flash content from within PIE.

However, you have a couple of ways around this problem. The first is to use the Macromedia Flash Standalone Player (SAP). The SAP is a client-side player (meaning it installs on your machine) that allows you to create Flash projectors that run on Windows Mobile devices. Sounds good, right? Well, it will cost you $499 to license the SAP. We're talking about licensing here, not purchasing. And after one year, you need to renew your license—which will cost you another $499 (or whatever the price tag is at that time).

> To learn more about the SAP—though, honestly, there isn't much more to learn—refer to www.macromedia.com/software/flashplayer_pocketpc/productinfo/faq/#item-3.

The second way to bypass the inherent problems of the Windows Mobile Flash Player is to purchase a third-party program that allows you to convert your SWF file into a true, stand-alone executable file (.exe) that can play full-screen and doesn't actually require that any version of the Flash Player is installed on the user's device. Easily one of the best of these programs is FlashPack. Created by HandSmart (www.handsmart.com), FlashPack is a reasonable $89.95 (for the Standard edition)—which is a far cry from the whopping

$499 yearly licensing fee that you have to pay for the SAP. A drawback of using FlashPack is that, for your executable file to work properly, the Flash Player (not the SAP) must be installed on the target device. But given that all Windows Mobile devices have the Flash Player, this isn't such a big deal.

> A shareware version of FlashPack is available at www.handsmart.com/flashPackMain.asp. Any movie published with the shareware version will function for only 24 hours. Beyond that, this version is fully functional.

To create a stand-alone executable file (.exe) from your Flash movie:

1. Make sure you've already published your movie as a SWF file.

> Because you aren't using PIE to view your Flash movie, you don't need to publish an accompanying HTML file.

2. Open FlashPack.

3. Make sure you're working in the Source Movie section, which is accessible by clicking the Source Movie tab at the top of the interface (see Figure 19.3).

4. Click the Browse button [Browse...]. When the Select File dialog box opens, navigate to where your SWF file is located, select it, and click Open.

5. From here, select one of the options from the Dimensions drop-down menu, located in the Movie Appearance section. If you select either Custom Pixels or Custom Percent, you'll be able to enter your values in the Width and Height fields, just below the Dimensions drop-down menu.

6. From here, select one of the options from the Alignment drop-down menu to determine where on the Windows Mobile device's screen the movie will be aligned.

7. Select one of the options in the Scale drop-down menu to determine how your movie is cropped/scaled to fit within the dimensions you designated.

8. If you want your movie to pause at the start and wait for a command to play, check the Paused at Start box.

9. If you want your movie to loop continuously, check the Loop box.

10. If you want the movie to use the Windows Mobile device's system fonts (as opposed to those used in the movie), check the Device Font box.

11. If you want the full Flash right-click menu to be visible, check the Device Menu box.

12. Select an option from the Quality drop-down menu. Remember, the higher the quality, the larger the file and the more of a drain the movie will have on the device's system resources.

13. If you want to change the default background color of the movie, click the Background color swatch. When the Color Picker appears, select a new color.

14. To see how the changes you made affect the look of your movie, click the Reload Preview button Reload Preview .

15. Select the Publish tab to access the publish settings of the movie (see Figure 19.4).

16. Select one of the options in the FlashPack Window State drop-down menu (see Figure 19.5): Full Screen (No Close Button) or Windowed.

17. If you've chosen the Windowed option and you want your user to be able to toggle the Full Screen (No Close Option) option, check the Allow Fullscreen Toggle by User box. Then, from the FlashPack Window State drop-down menu, select the specific button on the device that you want to act as a toggle for full-screen mode.

18. Click the Publish Settings button Publish Settings... to access the FlashPack Preferences dialog box, where you'll manipulate some of the properties of the file (see Figure 19.6).

19. To set the location of FlashPack's output, click the Browse button to the right of the Output Directory field. When the dialog box opens, locate and select the directory into which you want the movie to be exported.

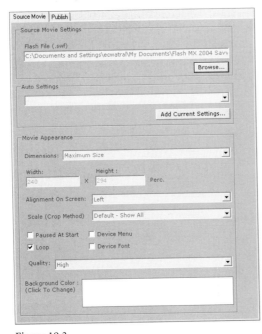

Figure 19.3

Use the Source Movie tab in FlashPack when creating a stand-alone EXE file.

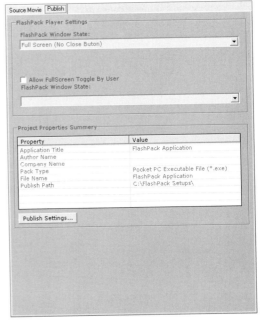

Figure 19.4

Use the Publish tab in FlashPack to set the publish settings of your movie.

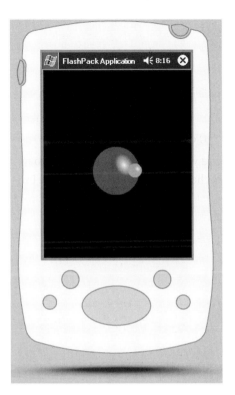 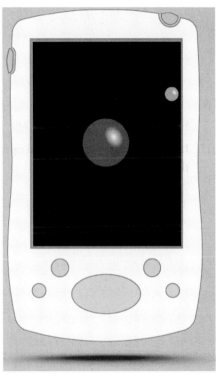

Figure 19.5
The left example illustrates the Full Screen (No Close Button) option, and the right example illustrates the Windowed option.

20. Enter the name of the exported file in the Setup File Name field.

21. Select an option for the type of exported file from the Pack Type drop-down menu.

22. Click the Setup Appearance tab (see Figure 19.7).

23. Enter a name in the Application Title (Shows During Setup) field. This name, as it says, will appear during the setup process.

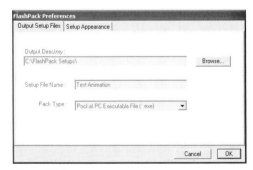 

Figure 19.6
Use the FlashPack Preferences dialog box to manipulate file properties.

Figure 19.7
Use the Setup Appearance tab in the FlashPack Preferences dialog box to tweak the movie's setup appearance.

24. If you want to include some information that appears after the setup process has finished, check the Show Setup Completion Info Page (Supports HTML) box, and then enter the text you want to show in the text field. This field, as it says, supports HTML.

25. When you're finished, click OK. You'll notice that the properties of your movie appear in the Project Properties Summary box.

26. When you're finished setting all the properties of the file, click the Publish button ⬚ Publish ⬚ , and your movie is published as an executable file to the location you set and with the properties you set.

Index

Note to the Reader: Throughout this index **boldfaced** page numbers indicate primary discussions of a topic. *Italicized* page numbers indicate illustrations.

B

E

W

X

Y

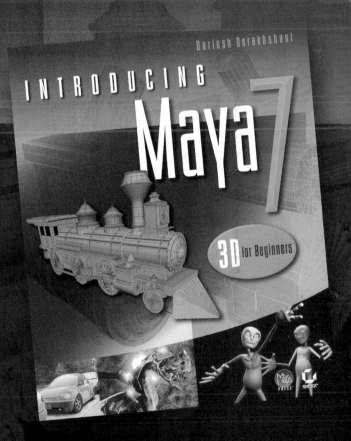

Your Complete AutoCAD® Solution from Sybex

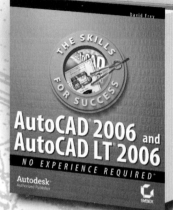

AutoCAD® 2006 and AutoCAD LT® 2006: No Experience Required®

by David Frey
ISBN: 0-7821-4414-4 • US $34.99

Updated for the 2006 releases of AutoCAD and AutoCAD LT, this best-selling introductory book gives you a solid grounding in the essentials. You'll get instant gratification by following the step-by-step instructions and hands-on projects that cover each phase of designing a summer cabin. You can progress sequentially through the book or begin at any chapter by downloading the drawing files from the Sybex website.

Mastering™ AutoCAD 2006 and AutoCAD LT 2006

by George Omura
ISBN: 0-7821-4424-1 • US $49.99

The world's best-selling, definitive guide to AutoCAD has been updated for the 2006 software! Acclaimed author George Omura delivers the most comprehensive coverage for AutoCAD and AutoCAD LT users, including discussion of all the new features. Throughout, Omura provides concise explanations, focused examples, step-by-step instructions, and hands-on projects. The CD offers six chapters of advanced material, files for all of the drawing exercises, plus general-purpose utilities for better productivity.

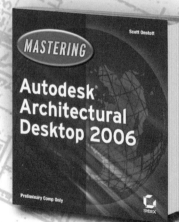

Mastering Autodesk® Architectural Desktop 2006

by Scott Onstott
0-7821-4429-2 • US $49.99

This book is the ultimate resource for beginning through advanced ADT users. In the tradition of Sybex's illustrious Mastering series, you'll get the most comprehensive coverage in a mix of tutorials and detailed reference. The companion DVD includes the Autodesk Architectural Desktop demo as well as sample files and useful utilities. This book also features a Foreword by Chris Yancharis, ADT Product Manager.

SYBEX®
www.sybex.com